The Soldiers' Revolution

1. Americanischer Scharffschütz oder Jäger, (Rifleman)
2. reguläire Infanterie von Pensylvanien.

Gregory T. Knouff

The Soldiers' Revolution

PENNSYLVANIANS IN ARMS
AND THE
FORGING OF EARLY AMERICAN IDENTITY

The Pennsylvania State University Press
University Park, Pennsylvania

Library of Congress Cataloging-in-Publication Data

Knouff, Gregory T., 1966–
　The soldiers' revolution : Pennsylvanians in arms
　and the forging of early American identity / Gregory T. Knouff
　　p.　　cm.
Includes bibliographical references (p.　) and index
ISBN 978-0-271-05849-8 (pbk : alk. paper)
1. Soldiers—Pennsylvania—History—18th century.
2. Pennsylvania—History—Revolution, 1775–1783—Influence.
3. United States—History—Revolution, 1775–1783—Influence.
4. Pennsylvania—History—1775–1865.
I. Title.

E263 .P4K57   2003
973.3'448—dc22
　　　　　　　　2003022422

Copyright © 2004 The Pennsylvania State University
All rights reserved
Printed in the United States of America
Published by The Pennsylvania State University Press,
University Park, PA 16802-1003

The Pennsylvania State University Press is a member of the
Association of American University Presses.

It is the policy of The Pennsylvania State University Press to
use acid-free paper. Publications on uncoated stock satisfy the
minimum requirements of American National Standard for
Information Sciences—Permanence of Paper for Printed Library
Material, ANSI Z39.48–1992.

Frontispiece: A Revolutionary-era German drawing of an American
rifleman and a Continental soldier from Pennsylvania.
The Historical Society of Pennsylvania (HSP), Stauffer Collection,
attributed to D. Chodwiecki.

CONTENTS

Acknowledgments   VII
Abbreviations   IX
Introduction   XI

1   Conflict and Community on the Eve of Revolution   1
2   Why They Fought   35
3   Identity and the Military Community   77
4   The Meaning of the War Against the British   119
5   Race and Violence on the Frontier   155
6   Civil War and the Contest for Community   195
7   The Memory of the American Revolution   233

Conclusion   273
Essay on Sources and Methodology   287
Index   297

ACKNOWLEDGMENTS

My greatest intellectual debt is to my graduate school mentor, Thomas P. Slaughter. His scholarly brilliance and enthusiasm for doing the work of professional history were inspiring. I thank him for the fine training I received under his guidance at Rutgers University. Tom and many other historians have provided useful critiques of parts, incarnations, and the whole of this monograph over the span of more years than I care to recall. Anything valuable in this study is due to their help; the problems that remain are my sole responsibility. Thanks to Stephen Aron, Wayne Bodle, Jean Boydston, John Chambers, Robert Churchill, Paul Clemens, Richard Dunn, John Frantz, Sara Gronim, Susan Klepp, Mark E. Lender, James McPherson, Jacqueline Miller, John Murrin, William Pencak, Elizabeth Perkins, Daniel Richter, Carroll Smith-Rosenberg, Jean Soderlund, and Marianne S. Wokeck. I must express, too, my special appreciation of Peter Messer's close friendship over the years and his incredibly helpful critical reading of the entire manuscript. Our conversations also provided much-needed comic relief when we both pondered how to remain sane in sometimes insane circumstances.

    I am deeply indebted to Peter Potter of The Pennsylvania State University Press for both his interest in my work and his consummate professionalism as a skilled editor. I thank Laura Reed-Morrisson for her superb copyediting of the manuscript. Thanks also to the readers for the Press, Ronald Schultz and Charles Neimeyer, for their close readings of the manuscript and very helpful suggestions.

    Various librarians and archivists facilitated my work. Foremost among them is my good friend David Fowler, the former director of the David Library of the American Revolution, who read and commented upon this project and introduced me to the library's fine holdings. Indeed, the David Library is the preeminent single repository for the study of the American Revolutionary era, and most of my research was conducted there. I would also like to acknowledge the assistance rendered me by the staffs of the Alexander Library at Rutgers University, the American Philosophical Society, the Darlington Memorial Library at the University of Pittsburgh, the Historical Society of Pennsylvania, the Historical Society of Western Pennsylvania, and the Library Company of Philadelphia.

Additionally, I would like to thank the David Library of the American Revolution, the McNeil (then Philadelphia) Center for Early American Studies, and the Rutgers Center for Historical Analysis for fellowships that allowed me to conduct vital research. They also furnished collegial forums for intellectual exchange. Keene State College provided me with a course release to work on writing the book.

It is my privilege to work with extraordinarily fine colleagues in the history department at Keene State. In particular, I would like to thank David Stowell and Matthew Crocker for commenting on parts of this book. David Price closely (and painfully) read the entire manuscript when it was a six-hundred-page monster and offered helpful suggestions. Curiously, his usual response—"burn it"—was not among them. I cannot overemphasize my appreciation for the close friendship and tireless support of the chair of my department, Andrew Wilson. I have never known a more gifted intellectual, able leader, or selfless friend.

Versions of Chapter 5 of this book appear in essay form in "Soldiers and Violence on the Pennsylvania Frontier," in *Beyond Philadelphia: The American Revolution in the Pennsylvania Hinterland*, ed. John Frantz and William Pencak (University Park, Pa., 1998), and "Constructing a Revolutionary Racial Frontier: Whiteness, Warfare, and Early American National Identity," in *Friends and Enemies in Penn's Woods*, ed. William A. Pencak and Daniel K. Richter (forthcoming from The Pennsylvania State University Press). In addition, my article "'An Arduous Service': The Pennsylvania Backcountry Soldiers' Revolution," *Pennsylvania History* 61 (January 1994): 45–74, contains early versions of some of my analysis in Chapters 2 and 5.

In the end, my greatest gratitude goes to my wife, Beth Staudt, who shared her life with me through it all. I thank her and our newborn son, Steffen Byron Knouff, for showing me the things in life that really matter.

ABBREVIATIONS

AO12   Records of the American Loyalist Claims Commission, 1776–1831, Public Records Office, Great Britain, Audit Office 12
AO13   American Loyalist Claims Commission Papers, 1780–1835, Public Records Office, Great Britain, Audit Office 13
DLAR   David Library of the American Revolution, Washington Crossing, Pennsylvania
DMC   Draper Manuscript Collection, State Historical Society of Wisconsin, Madison, Wisconsin
HSP   Historical Society of Pennsylvania, Philadelphia, Pennsylvania
LCP   Library Company of Philadelphia, Philadelphia, Pennsylvania
NYHS   New-York Historical Society, New York, New York
PA   Samuel Hazard et al., eds., *Pennsylvania Archives* (Philadelphia and Harrisburg, 1852–)
PCC   Papers of the Continental Congress, 1774–1789, National Archives, Washington, D.C.
PMHB *Pennsylvania Magazine of History and Biography*
PRG   Records of Pennsylvania's Revolutionary Governments, 1775–1790, Record Group 27, Pennsylvania Historical and Museum Commission, Harrisburg, Pennsylvania
RG-2   Auditor General, Revolutionary War Pension File, 1809–1893, Record Group 2, Pennsylvania State Archives, Harrisburg, Pennsylvania
RWPF   Revolutionary War Pension and Bounty-Land-Warrant Application Files (M804), National Archives, Washington, D.C.
WMQ   *William and Mary Quarterly*

INTRODUCTION

In the early nineteenth century, Jacob Stahley, a veteran of the American Revolutionary War, issued a statement in support of his erstwhile comrade, Peter Shindel, who was applying for a pension. Stahley stated that he remembered "the said Peter Shindel to have been actually engaged as a soldier in the cause of the people during the glorious struggle for independence."[1] It is a truism to say that the American Revolution was the crucible in which the United States was forged. But Stahley's brief statement raises a fundamental question: What exactly was the "cause of the people"? In the American popular imagination, colonists unified and inspired by egalitarian ideals fought a war for national independence and swept aside monarchy in favor of a republic. Such a perspective is shaped by histories of the nation's birth that focus on the so-called Founders. This somewhat imprecise term typically refers to various well-known political and military leaders, such as George Washington, Thomas Jefferson, and John Adams, about whose views on the Revolution historians know much. Many Americans also typically believe that the views of the Founders reflected those of most Revolutionaries. Such a presumption, however, is far from self-evident. As humble enlisted men, Stahley and Shindel were not famous, but they too were "founders" of a sort. Their understandings of the "cause" and of who constituted "the people" deserve to be addressed.[2]

1. Throughout this study, the spelling and punctuation of the primary sources have been modernized and abbreviations expanded to conform to modern usage. Revolutionary War Pension and Bounty-Land-Warrant Application Files (hereafter RWPF) (M804), National Archives, Washington, D.C., file S23911.
2. A few of the more eloquent popular works of history that view the Revolution primarily from the perspective of the Founders include Bernard Bailyn, *The Ideological Origins of the American Revolution* (Cambridge, Mass., 1967); Robert Middlekauff, *The Glorious Cause: The American Revolution, 1763–1789*

Soldiers—active participants in the War for Independence—affected the war's outcome and character. With a relative paucity of qualitative accounts left by poorer Americans (compared with those generated by literate elites), the task of piecing together how common people understood the Revolution is difficult. One possibility is that the lower and middling sorts adopted the ideologies of the upper sorts and framed the war in terms of a united struggle for independence against Britain. Such a formulation suggests that people were typically good Whigs who supported revolution or Tories who embraced the British empire. It is also plausible that poor people were forced to fight or that they took up arms in order to receive bounty money. Apathetic toward the politics of their day, they became involved primarily in return for a meager material reward. Either of these readings could grow out of analyses of ordinary people's behavior during the war and the commentaries of elites. Fortunately, though, many Americans who fought in the Revolution as common soldiers left records of their experiences (in the form of pension applications and loyalist claims, as well as letters and journals). Enlisted men were often poor, but payment for service was not their only goal. They had clearly defined ideas that affected the war and the nation. By recovering their voices, we will better understand America's Revolution and the development of the early United States. We will also discover that their perceptions, actions, and goals shaped American national identity in profound ways.[3]

(New York, 1982); Edmund S. Morgan, *The Birth of the Republic, 1763–1789* (Chicago, 1992); and Gordon S. Wood, *The Radicalism of the American Revolution* (New York, 1993).

3. Some social histories of the Revolutionary period that focus on ordinary people as actors and that have informed my own work include Eric Foner, *Tom Paine and Revolutionary America* (New York, 1976); Robert Gross, *The Minutemen and Their World* (New York, 1976); Woody Holton, *Forced Founders: Indians, Debtors, Slaves, and the Making of the American Revolution in Virginia* (Chapel Hill, N.C., 1999); Jesse Lemisch, "Jack Tar in the Streets: Merchant Seamen in the Politics of Revolutionary America," *William and Mary Quarterly* (hereafter *WMQ*), 3d ser., 25 (July 1968): 371–407; Gary B. Nash, *The Urban Crucible: The Northern Seaports and the Coming of the American Revolution* (Cambridge, Mass., 1986); and Alfred F. Young, *The Shoemaker and the Tea Party: Memory and the American Revolution* (Boston, 1999). I also build upon major works that examine the social and cultural aspects of Revolutionary War military service, including Mark E. Lender, "The Enlisted Line: The Continental Soldiers of New Jersey" (Ph.D. diss., Rutgers University, 1975); James Kirby Martin and Mark Lender, *A Respectable Army: The Military Origins of the Republic* (Arlington Heights, Ill., 1982); Charles Patrick Neimeyer, *America Goes to War: A Social History of the Continental Army* (New York, 1996); Edward Papenfuse and Gregory A. Stiverson, "General Smallwood's Recruits: The Peacetime Career of the Revolutionary War Private," *WMQ*, 3d ser., 30 (January 1973): 116–32; John Resch, *Suffering Soldiers: Revolutionary War Veterans, Moral Sentiment, and Political Culture in the Early Republic* (Amherst, Mass., 1999); Steven Rosswurm, *Arms, Country, and Class: The Philadelphia Militia and the "Lower Sort" During the American Revolution* (New Brunswick, N.J., 1987); Charles Royster, *A Revolutionary People at War: The Continental Army and American Character, 1775–1783* (New York, 1979); and John Shy,

This study is a cultural history of such soldiers. It analyzes the perceptions of ordinary Pennsylvanians who fought in the American Revolution. The primary focus is on the developing worldviews of poor "white" men who were rank-and-file Revolutionaries. These men held little, if any, property, and they are largely viewed by historians as "winners" in the American Revolution because their service led to enhanced political rights in the postwar era. Indeed, the participation of this group was vital to the success of the war and the viability of the republic. Military service provided these men, many of whom were formally disenfranchised during the colonial period, access to politics and participation in the public sphere as members of a Revolutionary army. Rather than being paid pawns of elites, they were active in shaping their own future—and that of the nation. Pennsylvanians who opposed or who were marginalized by the Revolutionaries are subjects as well, however. This book examines the experiences of Tories, African Americans, and Indian warriors for comparative purposes. Ultimately, I employ an analysis of soldiers (broadly defined as men who fought in the war) in order to provide a window onto how ordinary early Americans viewed and experienced the Revolution.[4]

The central premise of the book is that Revolutionary soldiers constructed what I call the "localist white male nation" before, during, and after the war. Localism, here defined as an outlook that purposefully emphasized the interests of an imagined community over those of nation, empire, or individuals, permeated the worldviews of enlisted men. Soldiers' understandings of what constituted their "community" were complex interstices of class, regional,

---

A People Numerous and Armed: Reflections on the Military Struggle for American Independence, rev. ed. (Ann Arbor, Mich., 1990). Lender, Martin, Neimeyer, Papenfuse, Stiverson, and Rosswurm have demonstrated the relatively lower social status of rank-and-file Revolutionary soldiers.

4. How radical the Revolution's enfranchisement of poor white men was is debated by Gordon S. Wood, "Equality and Social Conflict in the American Revolution," and Barbara Clark Smith, "The Adequate Revolution," both in *WMQ*, 3d ser., 51 (October 1994): 703–16 and 684–92, respectively. While I agree with Wood that the movement toward universal white manhood suffrage was radical in the context of the early modern world, I am less sanguine about the ultimately liberating consequences of this process and its concomitant order of competitive, liberal, individualistic capitalism. I agree with Clark Smith that such changes were inextricably bound up with the exclusion and oppression of those defined as Others in comparison to white men. On the concept of the "public sphere," see Jürgen Habermas, *The Structural Transformation of the Public Sphere: An Inquiry into a Category of Bourgeois Society*, trans. Thomas Burger with the assistance of Frederick Lawrence (Cambridge, Mass., 1999). Rather than relying on Habermas's notion of a public sphere of rational discourse created by the literate bourgeoisie, I draw upon Peter Thompson's use of the term "public space," in which different groups contend with and affect public discourse and politics. See Peter Thompson, *Rum Punch and Revolution: Taverngoing and Public Life in Eighteenth-Century Philadelphia* (Philadelphia, 1999), 17–19.

racial, ethnic, religious, and gender identities. These variables are the primary categories of analysis employed in this study, and no single factor can be understood in isolation from the others. For example, enlisted men's notions of masculinity were inextricably bound to their class status as members of the lower orders, their ethnic backgrounds, and their local situations. Perceptions of race differed by class and region. In other words, views of "locale" varied situationally. This study seeks to reconstruct what soldiers meant, exactly, when they referred to their "neighborhoods." In fact, much of the work of the Revolution was defining imagined communities, and soldiers were very active in this enterprise. Those who were marginalized by the Revolutionaries typically had ideas of community that were at odds with dominant ones in specific locales. Moreover, even the variances in ideas of what constituted a "patriot" order were myriad. Soldiers created what ostensibly appears to be a cacophony of competing and, at times, directly conflicting ideals of community. Cosmopolitan nationalists, especially many army officers, were often frustrated by enlisted men's localism. Ironically, though, soldiers' commitment to such a localist view was one of the bases of national identity in the early republic. Localism was the central strand of American nationalism for many citizens of the new republic. The perceived defense of diverse imagined communities was seen as a larger struggle to preserve local interests, one of the few underlying commonalities in various understandings of Revolutionary ideals. Contending views of community could then coexist under the rubric of valuing local difference. This *Weltanschauung* at once embraced and transcended regionalism and constituted what we may call popular nationalism. Without it, the Revolution could never have succeeded, and few ordinary people would have been willing to risk their lives.[5]

Obviously, such a formulation of a nation based on competing localisms could well be unstable. The potential for conflict was mitigated by the second

5. Thomas P. Slaughter, *The Whiskey Rebellion: Frontier Epilogue to the American Revolution* (New York, 1986), 223–28; Paul B. Moyer, "Wild Yankees: Settlement, Conflict, and Localism Along Pennsylvania's Northeast Frontier, 1760–1820" (Ph.D. diss., College of William and Mary, 1999); and Elizabeth A. Perkins, *Border Life: Experience and Memory in the Revolutionary Ohio Valley* (Chapel Hill, N.C., 1998), all make the case for the importance of localism in understanding early America. On communities and nations as "imagined" definitions of who is and is not a member, see Benedict Anderson, *Imagined Communities: Reflections on the Origins and Spread of Nationalism* (New York, 1991). On the American Revolution as a struggle for "local self-control," see Edward Countryman, "To Secure the Blessings of Liberty: Language, the Revolution, and American Capitalism," in *Beyond the American Revolution: Explorations in the History of American Radicalism*, ed. Alfred F. Young (DeKalb, Ill., 1993), 124–48. Royster, *Revolutionary People*, discusses the nationalism of Revolutionary officers. On regional views of America as vital to national identity in the early republic, see David Waldstreicher, *In the Midst of Perpetual Fetes: The Making of American Nationalism, 1776–1820* (Chapel Hill, N.C., 1997), 246–93.

major factor in the soldiers' outlook: the growing consensus over white male supremacy. The American Revolution helped consolidate a self-perception as "white" among ethnically diverse European Americans. Indeed, as being a "male white inhabitant" became the de facto definition for liability to militia service and oaths of allegiance in Pennsylvania during the war, the public sphere of military service became an important arena for defining who possibly could be an "American." The nineteenth-century shift in national identity from earlier economic and gender-based notions of citizenship (franchise based on male property-holding) to a purely biological definition predicated on white maleness was rooted in the American Revolution. Although "racial idioms" had long existed in Anglo-America, it was in the War for Independence that they were inextricably linked to political subjectivity in terms of U.S. citizenship. Soldiers, in their actions and their views of themselves compared to persons perceived as "non-white," took an active role in defining national identity. Perceived bodily categories of citizenship stabilized popular nationalism by providing another commonality beyond potentially divisive localism.[6]

What follows, then, is more than a study of the Revolutionary War and its armies. It is the story of a nation and its peoples. The book focuses most

6. Joyce E. Chaplin, *Subject Matter: Technology, the Body, and Science on the Anglo-American Frontier, 1500–1676* (Cambridge, Mass., 2001), explains the early origins of "racial idioms" based on the relations among customs, disease, and Native bodies in the minds of early English colonists. Also see Karen Ordahl Kupperman, *Indians and English: Facing Off in Early America* (Ithaca, N.Y., 2000). Works on the construction of the white male as the national political subject in the early republic include Dana D. Nelson, *National Manhood: Capitalist Citizenship and the Imagined Fraternity of White Men* (Durham, N.C., 1998); David Roediger, *The Wages of Whiteness: Race and the Making of the American Working Class* (New York, 1999); Alexander Saxton, *The Rise and Fall of the White Republic: Class Politics and Mass Culture in Nineteenth-Century America* (New York, 1990); and Carroll Smith-Rosenberg, "Dis-Covering the Subject of the 'Great Constitutional Discussion,' 1786–1789," *Journal of American History* 79 (December 1992): 841–73. On Pennsylvania's oath of allegiance law and the quotation from it, see its reproduction in *Pennsylvania Gazette*, June 4, 1777, Accessible Archives CD-ROM edition (Malvern, Pa., 1995).The militia law is also reproduced in *Pennsylvania Gazette*, March 26, 1777. The German Lutheran Henry Muhlenberg clearly mentions the wartime laws making all white men liable for test oaths and militia duty, regardless of their property holdings. See Theodore C. Tappert and John W. Doberstein, eds. and trans., *The Notebook of a Colonial Clergyman: Condensed from the Journals of Henry Melchior Muhlenberg* (Philadelphia, 1959), 171–73. Given such imprecise and historically evolving understandings of whiteness, it is no surprise that historians themselves have difficulty defining the term. For a critique of recent "whiteness studies scholarship" that takes its practitioners to task for definitional vagueness and elusive discussions of causality and power, see Eric Arnesen, "Whiteness and the Historians' Imagination," *International Labor and Working Class History Journal* 60 (Fall 2001): 3–32. In the same issue, Eric Foner's "Response to Eric Arnesen" (57–60) effectively acknowledges such limitations but defends the utility of the field. Also see the critical survey of the literature in Peter Kolchin, "Whiteness Studies: The New History of Race in America," *Journal of American History* 89 (June 2002): 154–73.

closely on the cultural construction of racial and gender identities that became linked with American identity and the effects of these processes on social conflict and the marginalization of outsiders. Additionally, the importance of localism to the soldiers' worldviews suggests that the war was, in many senses, a conflict over who would rule at home as well as a conflict with Britain. Conditions in America, specifically within states and regions, were as important as issues within the British empire (if not more so). The Revolution was not simply a two-sided affair as "patriots" rebelled against a "tyrannical" centralized government. While the war became one for independence from a colonial relationship, it was also a crucible for new self-definitions. Emerging "American" national identities—a sense of who was and was not fit to be a citizen—represented a radical departure from the colonial period and shaped politics and society into the nineteenth century and beyond. And as significant participants in the war and the military public sphere, soldiers were vitally important actors in these processes.[7]

I deliberately chose Pennsylvania as the subject of my work. This is not to imply that it was the most important state or that its wartime experience approximated that of all states. I do mean to suggest, however, that the state's many regional, social, and ethnic variables during the Revolution were emblematic of the conflict's diversity throughout North America. The Commonwealth was also one of the most culturally heterogeneous states in what would eventually be a very heterogeneous federal union. Pluralistic and conflict-prone, Pennsylvania was representative of the nation that emerged in the war; the ways in which alliances among groups in the state were negotiated during the war offer a model for understanding the Revolution. In short, my focus on a single state reflects the need to understand early America on a local scale in order to flesh out a complex larger picture. The plethora of competing communal interests and various definitions of "outsiders" in Pennsylvania

7. Examples of valuable recent scholarship on the construction of gender in early America include Kathleen M. Brown, *Good Wives, Nasty Wenches, and Anxious Patriarchs* (Chapel Hill, N.C., 1996); Mary Beth Norton, *Founding Mothers and Fathers: Gendered Power and the Forming of American Society* (New York, 1996); and Mark E. Kann, *A Republic of Men: The American Founders, Gendered Language, and Patriarchal Politics* (New York, 1998). On the cultural construction of racial ideologies, see Barbara Fields, "Slavery, Race, and Ideology in the United States," *New Left Review* 181 (May/June 1990): 95–118; Audrey Smedley, *Race in North America: Origin and Evolution of a Worldview* (Boulder, Colo., 1993); and Alden T. Vaughan, *The Roots of American Racism: Essays on the Colonial Experience* (New York, 1995). Consult Adam Hirsch, "The Collision of Military Cultures in Seventeenth-Century New England," *Journal of American History* 74 (March 1988): 1187–212, for an insightful account of the brutal warfare that emerged from Indian-European cultural misunderstanding. Richard White, *The Middle Ground: Indians, Empires, and Republics in the Great Lakes Region, 1650–1815* (New York, 1991), discusses how war on the Revolutionary frontier and racism mutually influenced each other.

specifically illustrates the emergence of a localist white male nation in very particular contexts. Thus, I seek to make connections between the microhistories of early American communities and a macrohistory of national identity.[8]

Pennsylvania's regional diversity facilitates a comparative framework involving urban, rural, and "frontier" soldiers as well. The state contained the major city of Philadelphia, a rural region that Anglo-Americans of the period would have called "settled" (that is, where colonists viewed Native Americans as largely subjugated), and a "frontier," where European Americans and independent Indian groups interacted. I use such categories to reflect the popular understanding of most Pennsylvanians in the Revolutionary era; by no means do I wish to posit that they reflected reality. Some Indians retained independence in areas that colonists viewed as "settled." And views of the trans-Appalachian west were clearly relative: though it was typically called a "backcountry" by Revolutionaries, Native peoples saw it as the forefront of European colonial expansion. I also do not wish to imply that Indians did not "settle" and practice agriculture on their lands. Nonetheless, this tripartite categorization of the state's political geography, rooted in the subjectivities of eighteenth-century European Americans, allows me to use evidence from Pennsylvania to suggest some basis for generalizations about how the Revolution played out differently among common people from cities, the European American dominated countryside, and frontiers where various groups struggled for control of the lands. Specifically, men considered to be urban soldiers are those who entered the service while residing in Philadelphia. "Rural" Revolutionary and Tory soldiers were from the regions of the state south and east of the Blue Mountain, which roughly cuts a diagonal swath across the southeastern third of Pennsylvania. This area included what during the Revolution were Bucks, Chester, and York Counties as well as parts of Berks, Cumberland, Lancaster, and Northampton Counties. Frontier troops and most Indian warriors came from the region north and west of Blue Mountain. This area comprised all of Bedford, Northumberland, Washington, and Westmoreland Counties. It also encompassed sections of Lancaster,

---

8. Wayne Bodle, "Themes and Directions in Middle Colonies Historiography, 1980–1994," *WMQ*, 3d ser., 51 (July 1994): 355–88; Wayne L. Bockelman and Owen S. Ireland, "The Internal Revolution in Pennsylvania: An Ethnic-Religious Interpretation," *Pennsylvania History* 41 (1974): 125–56; and Owen S. Ireland, *Religion, Ethnicity, and Politics: Ratifying the Constitution in Pennsylvania* (University Park, Pa., 1995), elucidate ethnic and religious heterogeneity in Pennsylvania. See the essays in (and introduction to) *Beyond Philadelphia: The American Revolution in the Pennsylvania Hinterland*, ed. John B. Frantz and William Pencak (University Park, Pa., 1998), on Pennsylvania's intensely localist and conflict-prone nature during the American Revolution.

Northampton, Cumberland, and Berks. These definitions are somewhat arbitrary, but again, they derive from eighteenth-century Pennsylvanians' views of the regions within the state. It would be a mistake, though, to assume that soldiers from a given region had uniform experiences. The greater Pennsylvania frontier, for example, was so vast that it included Connecticut farmers in the northeast, Anglo-American fur traders from the Pittsburgh vicinity, Delawares, Senecas, and Shawnees, just to name a few. Such differences within a region are vital to our understanding of soldiers' imagined communities.[9]

A few further specifics in regard to the parameters of the book are in order. First, the term "soldier" is broadly construed. Readers will soon see that the primary focus is on the perceptions of "white" (that is to say, European American) men who fought. Nonetheless, Indian warriors and runaway slaves and free blacks who served on both sides are subjects as well. Therefore, we will

9. The flowering of community and region studies in colonial American history in the past three decades demonstrates that scholars are taking locale into account as an important analytical tool. Slaughter makes a convincing case in *Whiskey Rebellion* for the significance of examining regions independent of state or colonial boundaries and integrating the study of class, ideology, and locale. Of course, many Pennsylvanians were not born in the area in which they enlisted. Internal migrants within the state as well as immigrants from Europe made communities dynamic. New arrivals to the locale, however, quickly acclimated themselves to the community's economy and culture. Deserters from the British army and enlistees from other states pose a more difficult problem. For the most part, they do not fit the definition of "Pennsylvania soldier" employed in this work, especially if they have no connection to the state before, during, or after the war. Of all the other states involved in the Revolutionary War, only New York had a large city, settled rural area, and expansive frontier like Pennsylvania's. While soldiers from these neighboring states undoubtedly had similar experiences, their political, cultural, and social institutions contained enough major differences to justify analysis on a state level. Compare, for example, Edward Countryman, *A People in Revolution: The American Revolution and Political Society in New York, 1760–1790* (Baltimore, 1981), with Robert L. Brunhouse, *The Counter-Revolution in Pennsylvania, 1776–1790* (New York, 1942). My definition of the frontier as an area where independent Native Americans and European Americans interacted and contested use rights to the land derives from that of Stephen Aron in "Lessons in Conquest: Towards a Greater Western History," *Pacific Historical Review* 63 (May 1994): 125–47. For analyses of Philadelphia's lower orders based primarily upon their behavior during the Revolution, see Foner, *Tom Paine*; Nash, *Urban Crucible*; Rosswurm, *Arms, Country, and Class*; and Richard Alan Ryerson, *The Revolution Is Now Begun: The Radical Committees of Philadelphia, 1765–1776* (Philadelphia, 1978). Two of the best monographs dealing with the Revolution in the "countryside" are Countryman, *People in Revolution*, and Gross, *Minutemen*. On the frontier, see, for example, seminal works such as Colin G. Calloway, *The American Revolution in Indian Country: Crisis and Diversity in Native American Communities* (New York, 1995); Andrew R. L. Cayton and Fredrika J. Teute, eds., *Contact Points: American Frontiers from the Mohawk Valley to the Mississippi, 1750–1830* (Chapel Hill, N.C., 1998); Gregory Evans Dowd, *A Spirited Resistance: The North American Indian Struggle for Unity, 1745–1815* (Baltimore, 1992); Michael N. McConnell, *A Country Between: The Upper Ohio Valley and Its Peoples, 1724–1774* (Lincoln, Neb., 1992); Perkins, *Border Life*; Daniel K. Richter, *Facing East from Indian Country: A Native History of Early America* (Cambridge, Mass., 2001); and White, *Middle Ground*. See Richter, *Facing East*, on the matter of perspective on the frontier and how Natives could plausibly see it as "frontcountry."

INTRODUCTION xix

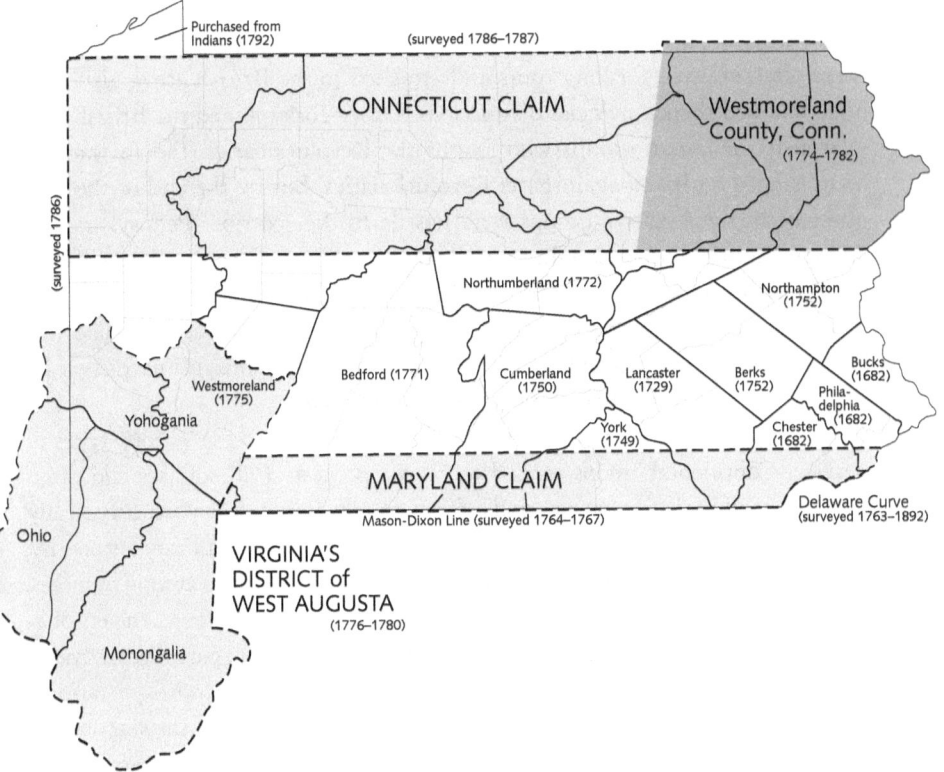

Early Pennsylvania. PSUP map modified from map in *The Atlas of Pennsylvania*, ed. David J. Cuff, William J. Young, Edward K. Muller, Wilbur Zelinsky, and Ronald F. Abler (Philadelphia, 1989), 81.

examine the experiences of members of the Continental army, the Revolutionary militia, informal frontier ranger units, Native war parties, and loyalist organizations. The Continental army was the Revolutionaries' regular army, raised under the auspices of the Continental Congress, with its soldiers serving relatively long tours. In contrast, the militia was under the authority of the states, concerned with local defense, and called into the field for short terms during times of emergency. In Pennsylvania, the militia was drawn from all white, able-bodied males in Pennsylvania between the ages of eighteen and fifty-three. Other units under state control included frontier rangers—usually volunteer troops serving slightly longer tours than the militia. The Flying Camp was a strategic reserve of militia troops for the Continental army drawn from the

Middle Atlantic states in 1776. These men were paid by the Continental Congress, although some remained under the jurisdiction of the state. Loyalist units were often enlisted for long tours and attached to the British army, although they retained their provincial distinctions. Other Tories joined the British regular army or Indian groups who fought the Revolutionaries. Indian warriors fought both with and against the Revolutionaries, but by the end of the war, most belligerent Native groups were hostile to the "patriot" Pennsylvanians. Like the militia, Indians fought typically on a local basis to protect their villages. Some nations split over whether to take sides—or which side to take. African Americans also served on both sides in combat and labor capacities. The vast majority of slaves who sought to free themselves in Pennsylvania did so by attempting to join the British forces.[10]

Obviously, there were major differences among these various types of service. Continental troops tended to be the poorest of all soldiers and often served out of state for long periods, for example; Indian war parties typically fought in coalition with their allies, but with a great deal of military autonomy. Among the Revolutionary forces, however, while dissimilarities among branches of the military are important and shall be noted when appropriate, the emphasis here is on the soldiers' common experiences. For the most part, Pennsylvania Revolutionary enlisted men shared motivations, outlooks, and expectations. Moreover, many served in different capacities over the course of the war and are difficult to categorize exclusively as Continentals, militiamen, rangers, Flying Camp troops, or even as Tories. John Davis, for example, served two times in the Bucks County militia as well as four years in the "standing army." George Leonard underwent four tours of duty with the Lancaster militia before joining the Continental army in 1780. Mathias Lockman, a regular in the Fifth Pennsylvania Regiment in 1777–80, also served in the militia and the Flying Camp. Daniel Doyley split his military career fighting in the East with the Third Pennsylvania Regiment of Continentals and then as a militiaman on the frontier. Joseph Fox served in the Revolutionary militia early in the war before switching

---

10. The best reference work that addresses the differences among Pennsylvania Continentals, militia, and Flying Camp troops is John B. B. Trussell, *The Pennsylvania Line: Regimental Organization and Operations, 1775–1783* (Harrisburg, Pa., 1993), iii–vii. On the militia, see Arthur J. Alexander, "Pennsylvania's Revolutionary Militia," *Pennsylvania Magazine of History and Biography* (hereafter *PMHB*) 69 (January 1945): 14–25. On Indian warriors, see Calloway, *American Revolution in Indian Country*, and White, *Middle Ground*. Sylvia Frey, *Water from the Rock: Black Resistance in a Revolutionary Age* (Princeton, N.J., 1991), and the still useful Benjamin Quarles, *The Negro in the American Revolution* (New York, 1961), both discuss African Americans in the military.

sides to fight with the British as a loyalist. In such a context, it is problematic to even try to categorize soldiers as being solely representative of a single branch of the military.[11]

Centering attention on these enlisted men, though, facilitates an analysis of "ordinary" men in the war. The early modern American military hierarchy was intended to mirror the social structure: military rank order was modeled on the class system. Soldiers and officers usually came from very distinct backgrounds. The overwhelming majority of the rank and file came from what we might call the lower and lower-middling orders of early American society. Most were young and relatively poor. Laborers, journeymen, servants, apprentices, and lesser craftsmen constituted the lowest social ranks entering the army. These men owned little or no property. Small farmers, artisans, and minor shopkeepers were among the middling classes serving as soldiers. Although these men owned a bit more than some of their comrades, they were far from well off. Even enlisted militiamen, while purportedly citizen-soldiers, were primarily lower-sort Pennsylvanians. More affluent men avoided militia service by paying fines or hiring substitutes. (Furthermore, the ranks of Tory forces—like the Revolutionary troops—were filled with common people.) Among the Revolutionaries, we will encounter men such as Richard Meggs, a wheelwright; Robert Peling, a basketmaker; and Henry Shantz, a carpenter. David Reamer, Thomas Rowe, and Joseph Roberts were all blacksmiths. Jacob Dowderman was a journeyman oak cooper. William Moore, John Harris, Adam Swager, and William Todd were laborers. Methuselah Davis was "by occupation a farmer," which was a common enough pursuit in the predominantly rural state. Robert Oldis identified himself as a poor farmer. Samuel Campbell candidly stated that he had "no occupation." Loyalist troops included William Dermont, a shopkeeper; John Laycock, a journeyman carpenter; George Peters, a free black miller; and Frederick Smith, a frontier farmer. Also among the Pennsylvanians who opposed the Revolutionaries were sizable numbers of slaves, such as Jacob Awl's "Negro man named Joe."[12]

11. The differences between Revolutionary regulars and militia is convincingly addressed in Lawrence Delbert Cress, *Citizens in Arms: The Army and Militia in American Society to 1812* (Chapel Hill, N.C., 1982); Martin and Lender, *Respectable Army*; Royster, *Revolutionary People*; and Shy, *People Numerous and Armed*. The examples of soldiers, in order of appearance in the text, derive from RWPF, files W4934, W8250, S40949; Auditor General, Revolutionary War Pension File, 1809–1893, Record Group 2 (hereafter RG-2), microfilm, Pennsylvania State Archives, Harrisburg, Pa., reel 155, frame 74; Records of the American Loyalist Claims Commission, 1776–1831, Public Records Office, Great Britain, Audit Office 12 (hereafter AO12)/100/230.

12. On the class composition of the Continental army rank and file, see Lender, "Enlisted Line," 110–39; Martin and Lender, *Respectable Army*, 90–91; Papenfuse and Stiverson, "General Smallwood's

In contrast, high-ranking officers came from the most prominent stations of early American society. Junior officers were more likely to come from the upper-middling and middling sort. Struggling professionals, fairly successful merchants, artisans, shopkeepers, and their sons sought to enhance their status by availing themselves of the prestige of officership. Continental officers, in particular, aspired to genteel status. Imitating their European counterparts, they believed that military distinctions should be reinforced by social ones. Even among the elected militia officers, the higher-ranking ones were drawn from the upper ranks of society and were fairly well known. Wealthy Tories usually became loyalist officers and often contributed money to the outfitting of their troops. These social and rank distinctions were, of course, not completely rigid. A few men of humble origins received commissions. Fewer still of the well-off served in the ranks. Still, the class distinctions inherent in military service—differences assumed by eighteenth-century Americans and quantified by recent historians—hold up well enough. The views and experiences of officers, contrasted with those of soldiers, facilitate class analysis.[13]

The chapters of this study are organized by interpretive themes rather than exclusively by chronology, but collectively, they do trace the development of soldiers' cosmologies before, during, and after the war. The first chapter explores colonial Pennsylvania on the eve of the Revolution. It elucidates the social conflicts that informed ideas about various communities before the war began and how those conflicts shaped soldiers' views of the constitutional crisis that had developed within the British Empire. The second chapter analyzes soldiers' motivations for fighting in the American Revolution. It addresses why Whigs, Tories, slaves, and Indians were moved to fight and how they viewed their communities. The third chapter takes up how soldiers developed identities within their respective military communities. It investigates how enlisted men refined their prewar views of self and how the worldviews of loyalists and Revolutionaries began to diverge. The next three chapters focus on the meaning

---

Recruits," 117–32; and Royster, *Revolutionary People*, 373. For a specific occupational analysis of the Pennsylvania regulars, see the sample in Trussell, *Pennsylvania Line*, 253–55. On the militia, see Rosswurm, *Arms, Country, and Class*, 49–77, and Alexander, "Pennsylvania's Revolutionary Militia," 25. See also RWPF, files S40151, S41052, W2701, W9621, W2862, S40358, W3399, S41882, S39657, S40387, S40583, S40880, S40221, W3072, and AO12/42/255, AO12/101/33, AO12/102/25, AO12/40/324. An advertisement referring to Joe's running away is in *Pennsylvania Packet*, January 14, 1778. Other than the *Pennsylvania Gazette*, newspapers cited in this text are on microfilm at the David Library of the American Revolution (hereafter DLAR), Washington Crossing, Pennsylvania.

13. On Continental officers, Royster, *Revolutionary People*, 86–87. On the militia, Alexander, "Pennsylvania's Revolutionary Militia," 21.

of wartime violence and the development of identities in terms of negative references to groups perceived as enemy Others. Chapter 4 explores the meaning of the war against the British regular army largely from the perspectives of Revolutionary soldiers. It probes the development of an Anglo-American military culture of supposedly "conventional" war and how it played out in the exigencies of military violence. In contrast, Chapter 5 explores the vehemence of war in the frontier region. It describes how the development of a common frontier military culture shared by Indians and European Americans abetted the construction of racial ideologies. The sixth chapter addresses the meaning of civil war among Pennsylvanians and how these conflicts shaped community definition. The final chapter explores both the memory and the meaning of the Revolution to veterans over time. It discusses what former soldiers remembered about the conflict—and why.[14]

Readers will quickly note that this story of the soldiers' Revolution is rife with ambiguity. While the construction of the localist white male nation proved beneficial to many soldiers, by definition, it excluded all deemed to be outsiders. Extreme localism limited the scope of communities that many could or would imagine. Enhanced freedom for some was predicated on racism, male dominance, and the obfuscation of class conflict. In addition to women, Indians, and African Americans, European American men who did not embrace dominant views of community were marginalized in the new nation. Even those poorer men who gained full political rights in the early republic via their military service did not find their material conditions much improved in the postwar order. Curiously, most American scholars of the Revolution, regardless of their politics, tend to assume that the conflict was ultimately "a good thing" (often for completely different reasons). I bring a far more critical perspective to bear and have no such presumptions. Nonetheless, I do not simply wish to designate Revolutionary soldiers as the "bad guys" in the nation's genesis. History—and human experience in general—is far too complex to create simply one-dimensional heroes and villains, no matter how comforting such a narrative may appear. While enlisted men sought to disenfranchise or conquer those deemed social outsiders, they also entered the army with understandable ambitions, such as expanding the definition of who could be a citizen and defending their ideals of

---

14. Those interested in an organizational and campaign history of Pennsylvania regulars should consult Trussell, *Pennsylvania Line*. Still one of the best syntheses of the entire Revolution is Middlekauff, *Glorious Cause*, which admirably incorporates the political and military history of the period into a highly readable narrative.

community. I approach my subjects with the intent of understanding them without endorsing or dismissing their cosmologies. I seek to reconstruct how common people viewed their world during a most uncommon time, to comprehend how their actions were limited by the cultures in which they lived, and to suggest the ways in which their participation in the Revolution influenced the culture of the United States well beyond their own lifetimes.

1

Conflict and Community on the Eve of Revolution

Many Americans imagine the coming of the American Revolution as a linear affair, one in which a singular colonial critique of British policy evolved that led to war and eventually resulted in national independence. Such a view tends to elide the very significant differences and bitter disputes among British colonists. The fact that roughly only half of Britain's American colonies rebelled and that significant civil war broke out among those that did most clearly suggests a plurality of perspectives. More subtly, the larger crisis over the constitution of the British Empire broadly politicized contentious provincial issues. This was certainly the case in Pennsylvania, one of the most culturally heterogeneous and conflict-prone colonies in an increasingly diverse empire. Long-standing internal disputes over which groups constituted viable communities became intertwined with imperial politics. To understand why various Pennsylvanians acted as they did in the American Revolution, it is necessary to comprehend colonial concepts of community on the eve of war and how these notions related to the growing rift with the mother country. Ultimately, the Revolution would prove to be a contest over "home rule"—and, quite literally, who would rule at home—as well as what "home" really was. American popular nationalism had its roots in the culture of late colonial British North America.[1]

Provincial British subjects in the 1760s and 1770s viewed their communities as combinations of physical spaces and perceived group memberships. A firm sense of place, the cornerstone of the localist outlook, was of paramount importance. Colonists necessarily attributed great significance not only to their home province but also, more particularly, to their towns, townships, and counties. As historians have demonstrated, late colonial Pennsylvania was a region characterized by high mobility, but even those who had lived in an area only a short time needed to acclimate themselves to the local culture in order to survive and prosper. People in a narrowly circumscribed vicinity depended on each other for goods, access to trade, services, and military defense. Moreover, the slowness of overland travel made sojourns to other regions arduous. A long hunter in the Ohio country, for example, might consider the provincial capital, Philadelphia, nearly as spatially and culturally distant as London. Colonial communities were not, however, utterly insular. Deeply embedded in an early modern British Atlantic world of goods, exchange, and ideas, early Americans saw their communities as important constitutive elements of a larger empire. Nevertheless, one's locale was the fundamental departure point for identifying one's place in the Anglo-American world.[2]

    1. Andrew Jackson O'Shaughnessy, *An Empire Divided: The American Revolution and the British Caribbean* (Philadelphia, 2000), focuses on the fundamental social, economic, and cultural differences between the West Indian and North American colonies and offers an important counterpoint to the somewhat presentist-minded bulk of "U.S.-centric" studies of the American Revolution. On the cultural, ethnic, and religious pluralism of colonial Pennsylvania, see Richard S. Dunn and Mary M. Dunn, *The World of William Penn* (Philadelphia, 1986), and Sally Schwartz, *"A Mixed Multitude": The Struggle for Religious Toleration in Colonial Pennsylvania* (New York, 1987).
    2. Robert V. Hine asserts in *Community and Frontier: Separate but Not Alone* (Norman, Okla., 1980) that understandings of community are contingent upon how one defines the term. I agree with him that "a sense of place is an ingredient common to almost all definitions of community. The group must exist in a definable space" (21). On migration and spatial mobility in early Pennsylvania, see David Hackett Fischer, *Albion's Seed: Four British Folkways in America* (New York, 1987); Mark Häberlein, "German Migrants in Colonial Pennsylvania: Resources, Opportunities, and Experience," *WMQ*, 3d ser., 50 (1993): 555–74; and Marianne S. Wokeck, *Trade in Strangers: The Beginnings of Mass Migration to North America* (University

Furthermore, localism was one of the political building blocks in both Britain and its empire. The popular, republican element of British constitutional monarchy was based upon the local representation of voters. This was true of the House of Commons and of colonial assemblies. Additionally, both Britain and British America shared a tradition of sovereignties divided into national and local levels. In everyday life, Britons were most likely to be in contact with county officials or institutions. Their local representatives to legislative bodies were their links to larger polities. Indeed, the empire itself was a complex amalgam of centralized and local authority; the American Revolution expressed a debate over the relative power of provincial local authorities within the larger context of the nation. This British politicization of localism further strengthened the tie between ordinary people and the communities in which they lived. Provincial Pennsylvanians looked at their locale not only as a center of social interaction but also as their point of contact with the county, colony, and empire. Not surprisingly, regional, town, and village concerns were the stuff of colonial politics.[3]

This abiding concern with local affairs was not the singular domain of colonists from the British Isles. German Pennsylvanians (the colony's largest non-British European ethnic group) came from diverse polities and also placed a premium on the culture of their particular villages. Issues regarding inheritance, law, liberty of conscience, and religious meetings were all shaped by local folk traditions. Many German immigrants also understood "liberty" in their homelands to mean freedom from governmental interference in religion and village customs. As they brought these concepts with them to North America, they also transferred elements of their distinctively German local mores. These traditions were not equivalent to British understandings of political localism and common law, but Pennsylvania Germans clearly did value their communities' independence within the empire. In the southwestern German states from which many North American immigrants came, no single polity was able to enforce cultural and political conformity. As a result, historian A. G. Roeber

---

Park, Pa., 1999). On how early Americans balanced community and individual interests, see the classic essay by James Henretta, "Families and Farms: *Mentalité* in Pre-Industrial America," *WMQ*, 3d ser., 35 (1978): 3–32, and Allan Kulikoff, *From British Peasants to Colonial American Farmers* (Chapel Hill, N.C., 2000).

3. Middlekauff, *Glorious Cause*, 17 and 27, discusses the local basis of representation in British and colonial government. Linda Colley, *Britons: Forging the Nation, 1707–1837* (New Haven, Conn., 1992), shows the continuation of regionalism in Britain as Britons were constructing ideas of national identity (17, 293–94).

points out, "the traditions of subregional and local autonomy survived, even in the face of the eighteenth-century trend toward absolutism." Thus, while German colonists may have had traditions of localism completely different from those of British provincials, their common commitment to local autonomy allowed the various concepts to coexist and influence each other, if tenuously.[4]

Centering society, politics, and diplomacy around the concerns of the village also made colonists' localist worldviews somewhat comparable to those of Native Americans in the region. Eastern Indians had a long history of valuing local autonomy and traditions. They also were familiar with villages constituting the basic units of larger constituencies, such as "nations"—and, in the case of the six Iroquois nations, a confederation. While Indian villages changed dramatically over time in terms of importance (compared to other locales) and ethnic composition due to migration, war, and shifting alliances, a sense of place was as central to Native as to provincial concepts of community. Thus, in the area called Pennsylvania by European colonizers, all inhabitants shared a broad localism in literal terms. They primarily concerned themselves with the interests of their immediate area, despite the dynamic and rapidly changing nature of communities in the region.[5]

As a result of this prevailing localism, communities were sometimes defined by their members in extremely immediate terms on the eve of the American Revolution. In areas such as Paxton Township, in the south-central part of the colony, residents had difficulty visualizing commonalities with other nearby townships or counties. In some cases, they hardly viewed their own township as a coherent community. They imagined ad hoc communities only when immediate threats, such as military attacks by French or hostile Indian forces,

---

4. On localism in the villages of Germany during the era of colonization in North America, see A. G. Roeber, *Palatines, Liberty, and Property: German Lutherans in Colonial British America* (Baltimore, 1993), 27–132 (quotation from 32). Roeber's work demonstrates how Germans' distinctive notions of liberty and property were "transferred in fragments to North America" (xi) and ultimately transformed into an understanding of civic duty—one informed by British theories—as the protection of the state that grants freedom. On the transference of German ideas of community to America, also consult Mark Häberlein, "Communication and Group Interaction Among German Migrants to Colonial Pennsylvania," and Carola Wessel, "'We Do Not Want to Introduce Anything New': Transplanting the Communal Life from Herrnhut to the Upper Ohio Valley," both in *In Search of Peace and Prosperity: New German Settlements in Eighteenth-Century Europe and America*, ed. Harmut Lehmann, Hermann Wellenreuther, and Renate Wilson (University Park, Pa., 2000), 156–71 and 246–62, respectively.

5. White, *Middle Ground*, 366–412, and Calloway, *American Revolution in Indian Country*, discuss the varying local situations and interests of a number of specific Native villages during the Revolution. On the Iroquois, see Daniel K. Richter, *The Ordeal of the Longhouse: The Peoples of the Iroquois League in the Era of European Colonization* (Chapel Hill, N.C., 1992).

directly touched the region. Inhabitants of other areas had similarly extreme notions of localism. Other than their living in the same vicinity, residents of the upper Juniata Valley were united only by their commitment to traditions of local autonomy and disdain for intrusions by outside authority. Like the colonists in Paxton, they were particularly inwardly focused and expressed very immediate ideas of community interests.[6]

While township or county was the basis of understanding immediate locale, broader regional identities evolved as well. They were usually defined as a result of conflict with people in what was perceived to be a different region. From the perspectives of colonial Pennsylvanians, one of the most salient divisions was that between "eastern" and "western" communities. One reason for this division of regional interests was disproportionate representation in the colonial assembly. In the late colonial period, the populations of new counties and townships in the perceived frontier area grew rapidly, and reapportionment lagged. As a result, westerners resented what they saw as an affront to principles of proper local representation. Not surprisingly, easterners clung to their political advantage. Further intensifying this division between eastern and western colonists were disputes over military service during the era of the French and Indian War and Pontiac's War (ca. 1754–65). Many westerners believed that those in the east cared little for the wartime defense of their "frontier" against hostile Indian groups and the French. The resistance of eastern members of the government, especially Quakers, to funding military measures led many from the war-torn counties to conclude that easterners were selfish. Easterners, in turn, resented these charges, and some feared that western colonists provoked expensive and deadly hostilities with their native neighbors. Moreover, many people from Philadelphia and its environs did not see the imperial wars of the mid-eighteenth century as directly threatening their communities and were somewhat apathetic toward the plight of frontier Pennsylvanians. While these sentiments were not universal in both regions, of course, they were pervasive enough to suggest a clear difference in interests, and they contributed to the development of distinctive eastern and western provincial identities.[7]

6. George W. Franz, *Paxton: A Study of Community Structure and Mobility in the Colonial Pennsylvania Backcountry* (New York, 1989), 42–83 and 271, analyzes the extreme localism of Paxton. On the Juniata Valley, see Tim H. Blessing, "The Upper Juniata Valley," in *Beyond Philadelphia*, ed. Frantz and Pencak, 153–55.

7. Frantz and Pencak, eds., *Beyond Philadelphia*, xii–xvi, show the regional conflict engendered by the underrepresentation of the newer counties and disputes over military service. Alden T. Vaughan, "Frontier Banditti and the Indians: The Paxton Boys' Legacy," in *Roots of American Racism*, 82–102, explains critiques of the frontier inhabitants' treatment of Indians and the provocation of violence.

Other regional conflicts similarly revealed that colonists related their provincial allegiance to their local situation. In two areas, mutual claims to political sovereignty by various colonial polities sharply divided inhabitants. Here, the contest over who constituted the community was determined by allegiance to and land grants from Pennsylvania, Connecticut, and Virginia. In the northeastern Susquehanna River Valley and the fertile Wyoming Valley, Connecticut provincials, under the auspices of the Susquehannah Company, expected to extend their own colony's claim westward. Pennamites—colonists who held land titles from Pennsylvania—resented the influx of the more numerous Connecticut land claimants. In some cases, the Yankee colonists invited Pennsylvanians who were disaffected by the proprietary government's land policies to join them. Just before the Revolutionary War, tensions built and rival claimants sought to remove each other from the area. The land titles issued by the two provinces were often mutually exclusive. These distinctive groups had strong connections to the same place, and the Revolution would, in some ways, be an extension of the struggle that began in the colonial era to determine which group would dominate the region. Armed hostilities broke out between the two factions before the Revolution and later continued under the rubric of civil war between "patriots" and "Tories."[8]

Similar tensions existed in the southwestern part of the province, where both Virginia and Pennsylvania claimed the area around Pittsburgh and parts of the Ohio and Monongahela River Valleys. Like the Yankees and Pennamites, Virginians and Pennsylvanians in this region each claimed (at the other's expense) to constitute the locale's true community. Regional cultural differences between Virginians and Pennsylvanians further exacerbated their border conflict. Both groups remarked on each other's different social practices. While the Virginia-Pennsylvania dispute did not ultimately produce nearly as obvious a Tory-Whig distinction as the contest in the Wyoming Valley, it did lead to distinctive, conflicting definitions of community in the region. These border claims clearly refined people's awareness of perceived regional interests. They also demonstrate that identification with a particular province spoke

---

8. On the jurisdictional disputes among Pennsylvania, Connecticut, and Virginia, see Anne M. Ousterhout, *A State Divided: Opposition in Pennsylvania to the American Revolution* (Westport, Conn., 1987), 230–70. Francis Fox, *Sweet Land of Liberty: The Ordeal of the American Revolution in Northampton County, Pennsylvania* (University Park, Pa., 2000), 42, notes attempts by Susquehannah Company colonists to recruit disaffected Pennsylvanians into their communities. On the conflict between Pennamites and Connecticut claimants in the colonial period, see Frederick J. Stefon, "The Wyoming Valley," in *Beyond Philadelphia*, ed. Frantz and Pencak, 136–51, and Moyer, "Wild Yankees."

more to concerns over access to local lands than strong political allegiance to the respective colonial governments.⁹

Indeed, such contests suggest that colonists' notions of community cannot be simply defined in terms of their connection to a particular region alone. Pennsylvanians also understood themselves in terms of their various group identities *within* a place. In many cases, social conflicts among diverse groups in the province were intertwined with boundary construction within the locale. Dominant and marginal factions struggled with each other to decide who could truly be a part of the community—And definitions of community were further and variously determined by categories such as ethnicity, religion, class, race, and gender.

Ethnicity and religion were vitally important factors in creating cultural boundaries, given Pennsylvania's cultural heterogeneity. In addition to a large native population and a significant number of people of African descent, various European groups, including persons of Scottish, Dutch, English, German, Welsh, and Irish ethnic backgrounds, composed the region's population. This was in large part due to the proprietary government's welcoming immigrants from western Europe, especially the German states. The province's policy of religious toleration for Christian denominations and its lack of an established church proved attractive to a number of European religious sects as well, including Quakers, German pietist sects, Lutherans, Huguenots, Anglicans, Catholics, and Presbyterians, all of whom sought denominational liberty. The result was a culturally pluralistic province. Colonists remained well aware of the differences among them, however. Some communities were dominated by a single ethnic group. While many areas, especially Philadelphia, remained truly multicultural, others took on distinctive ethnic characters. As a result, ethnic identities could blend with regional or local ones. For example, English Quakers tended to live in the oldest (and disproportionately powerful) southeastern counties of Philadelphia, Chester, and Bucks. Scots-Irish Presbyterian provincials, living within a colony largely dominated by English political leaders, often chose to reside in self-consciously Scots-Irish townships and were particularly numerous in Cumberland County. Many German colonists likewise sought the proximity of others with a common background and settled in counties with large German populations, such as York, Berks, and Northampton. German-language newspapers also helped preserve a distinctive identity within

---

9. Ousterhout, *A State Divided*, 230–70. Perkins, *Border Life*, 102–3, discusses the cultural differences, conflicts, and disagreements over slavery between Pennsylvanians and Virginians on the frontier.

the British Empire. What English-speaking neighbors often viewed as boorish clannishness was in reality a reflection of a culture that valued tradition and was fearful of outside or governmental interference with its mores. By the eve of the Revolution, however, mutual distrust between British and German colonists had grown. Germans previously welcomed by the English were increasingly regarded with suspicion and disdain as their numbers increased within the province. As tensions flared among these and other groups, ethnicity became more important as a delineation of identity.[10]

There were, of course, cultural differences within ethnic groups that helped shape colonists' sense of themselves. For instance, factions emerged among Pennsylvania Germans by midcentury. These divisions were most visible in Pennsylvania Germans' political allegiances, but they revealed that denominational identification shaped ideas of community in ways separate from ethnicity. In the colonial period, Pennsylvania politics were defined by competition between two blocs. The largely Anglican descendants of William Penn and their supporters, known as the "proprietary interest," controlled of the executive branch of colonial government. The "Quaker party," whose members included numerous non-Quakers such as Benjamin Franklin, were powerful in the legislature. By the 1740s, increasing numbers of Lutheran and Reformed Germans became active supporters of the proprietary faction, which appeared friendlier to their interests. As a result, they often found themselves opposing German pacifist sectarians. Groups such as the Moravians, Schwenkfelders, and Mennonites largely remained allied with their fellow pacifists, the Quakers, in politics. Religious and political issues, including that of military service, actually created bonds between pacifist and non-pacifist denominations, respectively.[11]

Not all ethnic delineations of community were among Europeans. One of the most significant cultural boundaries in mid-eighteenth-century North America stood between European colonizers and Native inhabitants.

10. Dunn and Dunn, *World of William Penn*, and Sally Schwartz, *"A Mixed Multitude,"* show the cultural, ethnic, and religious pluralism of colonial Pennsylvania. According to Alan Tully in *William Penn's Legacy: Politics and Social Structure in Provincial Pennsylvania, 1726–1755* (Baltimore, 1977), by 1755, Pennsylvania's sixty thousand German residents constituted 40 to 45 percent of the province's population (54). On the growing hostility toward German colonists by the second half of the eighteenth century, consult Arthur D. Graeff, *The Relations Between Pennsylvania Germans and the British Authorities, 1750–1776* (Norristown, Pa., 1939), 31–32.

11. Nash, *Urban Crucible*, 181, describes the movement of mainstream Germans to oppose the Quaker party and the factional divisions among German denominations. On Pennsylvania Germans' participation in colonial politics as an expression of their own interests and cultural values, see Roeber, *Palatines, Liberty, and Property*, 175–205.

Both groups scrutinized each other and remarked upon their respectively different ways of life. Early colonial Pennsylvanians believed Indians to be culturally inferior: most were not Christian, and they did not share European ideas of individual land ownership. Indian land use was also considered backward because of the lack of European-style agriculture and livestock husbandry. Moreover, Pennsylvanians, like other British colonists, remarked on the Indians' gendered division of labor. Indian women were viewed as unfeminine for working the fields. Men were seen as lazy for spending their time in pursuit of hunting, an activity considered primarily a pastime of aristocrats in Europe. Even Pennsylvanians who were theoretically friendly to the idea of Native-European coexistence, such as the Quakers, ultimately took up the Western side of the cultural divide. Conversely, Indians looked at European traditions as foreign and, at times, inferior as well. Indian men viewed colonial men engaged in fieldwork as effeminate. British and German Protestantism appeared intolerant of religious syncretism to many Natives. Indians often saw colonial trade and diplomatic practices as exploitative. European and Native Americans also noted differences among each other's standards of cleanliness, diet, rituals of hospitality, and clothing. As the result of this clear articulation of cultural and ethnic difference, Pennsylvanian and Native communities were usually separate, despite extensive interaction. There were a few exceptions—usually cases of Europeans living among Indians. Some small provincial farmers found that living under the auspices of Indian land use was more promising than seeking land rights from the proprietary government. Colonists, however, rarely welcomed Natives to live among them as equals.[12]

The consistent interaction between colonists and Natives ensured, that general cultural boundaries were not impermeable, though. In fact, Indians and colonists engaged in marked levels of cultural exchange in early colonial

12. On the general early English colonial tendency to comment on Indian cultural differences rather than skin color, see Alden T. Vaughan, "From White Man to Redskin: Changing Anglo-American Perceptions of the American Indian," in *Roots of American Racism*, 7–11. Colin G. Calloway, *New Worlds for All: Indians, Europeans, and the Remaking of Early America* (Baltimore, 1997), 22–23, asserts the importance of the clash of Indian and colonial Anglo-American ideas about individual private property. See Kathleen Brown, *Good Wives*, 42–74, and Stephen Aron, *How the West Was Lost: The Transformation of Kentucky from Daniel Boone to Henry Clay* (Baltimore, 1996), 8–10, on the gendered division of labor. On cultural differences in hygiene, dress, hospitality, and food, see James H. Merrell, *Into the American Woods: Negotiators on the Pennsylvania Frontier* (New York, 1999), 128–40. On "squatter" farmers finding land rights and acceptance under Native auspices rather than those of the proprietary government, see David Preston, "Dispossessing the Indians: Proprietors, Settlers, and Cultural Encounters in Pennsylvania's Contested Borderlands, 1730–1770," in *Friends and Enemies in Penn's Woods*, ed. William A. Pencak and Daniel K. Richter (University Park, Pa., forthcoming).

Pennsylvania. Negotiators, traders, and missionaries in particular took the time to learn European and Indian languages, religions, and customs of diplomacy. Numerous colonists and Natives adopted elements of each other's dress, economies, and ways of living. Some intermarried. Nonetheless, even the various cosmopolitan frontier residents, *métis*, and "cultural brokers" were all well aware of the dangers of too much blurring of Native and European ways: the loss of identity. Those who moved comfortably between colonial and Indian worlds ultimately identified with one group or the other. (Critically, during the early period of relatively peaceful relations with Indians in colonial Pennsylvania, culture remained the primary marker in understanding Native-European difference.[13])

That era of uneasy coexistence was shattered well before the Revolution. Beginning in the 1750s, extensive warfare among colonists and Indians broke out. The French and Indian War and Pontiac's and Dunmore's Wars were all largely fought over the control of lands in the trans-Appalachian west. Long hunters who mixed Indian-style hunting, fur trading, and agriculture lived like their Native neighbors, but they penetrated further into the Ohio country and beyond by the mid-eighteenth century. The growing number of colonial communities in the region appeared to threaten the independence of Native ones. In addition to presenting economic competition in the fur trade, these provincials were committed to the ideology of individual private property rights, an ideology that created conflict. Even more ominous, European immigrants who were primarily farmers (and, in many cases, utterly unfamiliar with Indian culture) poured into the Ohio, Juniata, and Susquehanna Valleys in the same period. As armed conflicts began, many Pennsylvanians fought believing that British victory would allow them to extend their communities further into Indian country. More residents in the region were forced to take up arms as the scale of conflict grew. Increasingly, European Americans began to imagine Natives not as neighbors but as violent and hostile obstacles to their communities. War allowed many colonists of disparate European backgrounds to understand that one of their cultural commonalities (among their diverse local interests) was a desire to expand aggressively into independent Indian lands.[14]

13. See Merrell, *Into the American Woods*, and Jane T. Merritt, "Metaphor, Meaning, and Misunderstanding: Language and Power on the Pennsylvania Frontier," in *Contact Points*, ed. Cayton and Teute, 60–87, on cultural exchange on the early colonial Pennsylvania frontier.

14. On conflicts among Anglo-American long hunters, farmers, and Indians, see Stephen Aron, "Pigs and Hunters: 'Rights in the Woods' on the Trans-Appalachian Frontier," in *Contact Points*, ed. Cayton and Teute, 175–204.

Indians in the region reacted to the expansionism of the British colonists by intermittently creating alliances with each other and European powers. Pan-Indian unity, which would reach its zenith in the American Revolution, had its roots in these colonial wars. Although many Natives tried to stay neutral or allied to the British Americans, the experience of war allowed more Indians to realize a commonality of interests against land-hungry "long knife" colonists. They also came to recognize some shared cultural and spiritual values that became apparent in a series of transnational Native religious revivals in numerous communities in the trans-Allegheny west of the mid-eighteenth century. Awareness of local and ethnic differences among indigenous peoples persisted, then, but at least among some Natives, this awareness was subsumed into a growing cultural identity as "Indians."[15]

Africans and African Americans were the other major non-European ethnic groups in the colony. The mid-Atlantic region of North America had a long history both of African immigration and of slave labor. The British, Swedish, and Dutch all brought Africans and slaves to the area. Some of the earliest slaves were what historian Ira Berlin has termed "Atlantic Creoles"— persons who were familiar with African *and* European cultures before they came to the Americas. Others who came in the mid-eighteenth century were less likely to be familiar with Western ways. Regardless, European colonists initially viewed Africans, like Native Americans, as their cultural inferiors. European Americans imagined Africans to be non-Christian savages. The reality of interaction, however, provided a forum for cultural exchange. To a varying extent, Africans and Europeans mutually influenced each other's ways of life. West Africans who came to North America were themselves ethnically and religiously diverse. They created a common cultural identity by appropriating elements of the colonial culture. Many mastered European languages and became or were born Christian. Yet despite the acclimation of Africans to European culture and the increase in a creole African American population, perceptions of significant ethnic differences remained even as racial ideologies developed. Various African peoples in Pennsylvania would develop a group identity based on their sense of difference from European Americans.[16]

15. Randolph C. Downes, *Council Fires on the Upper Ohio* (1940; Pittsburgh, 1989), 80–120 and 168–69, and Francis Jennings, *Empire of Fortune: Crowns, Colonies, and Tribes in the Seven Years' War in America* (New York, 1988), 200–202, 371–404, and 439–53, give excellent accounts of the colonial wars on the Pennsylvania frontier. Dowd, *Spirited Resistance*, 23–46, explains the growth of Indian unity in this period.

16. See Ira Berlin, *Many Thousands Gone: The First Two Centuries of Slavery in North America* (Cambridge, Mass., 1998), on the process of a shift from "Atlantic Creole" to "African" slave importation.

Pennsylvania's African American population comprised slaves and free blacks. Significantly, Africans' or African Americans' enslavement highlighted their non-European status. Both free blacks and slaves were seen and largely saw themselves as subcommunities within the larger provincial society. Slaves were present in different communities in various capacities as owned chattel. Despite the ubiquity of slavery in the province, however, the institution was not as economically central to the local economy as it was elsewhere. (Unlike the plantation societies in the South, cash-crop monoculture did not develop in the colony, and slaves were not primarily associated with fieldwork of a particular sort). The number of Pennsylvania slaves in 1770 was 5,561, or 2.3 percent of the total population. This was a smaller slave population than those in neighboring New Jersey (8,220, or 7 percent), New York (19,062, or 11.7 percent), and Delaware (7,050, or 20 percent). Still, Pennsylvania's slaves were a significantly large, coherent group. Slavery's creation of a peculiar class status (as goods in perpetuity), its heritable nature, and its application to people of African but not European ethnic descent made slaves aware of themselves as a group quite different from other Pennsylvanian subcommunities.[17]

Free blacks in the province felt the stigma of slavery associated with their ethnic status and clearly developed a sense of separateness within their locale. Members of Philadelphia's visible and growing free black community created their own businesses, churches, and support networks. Also, unlike neighboring New Jersey, the colony of Pennsylvania allowed free blacks to own

---

Berlin's work is particularly useful for understanding the history and centrality of slavery in northern North America and how cultural concepts helped construct race. Edmund S. Morgan, *American Freedom, American Slavery: The Ordeal of Colonial Virginia* (New York, 1976), suggests that the English initially perceived Africans as culturally but not necessarily physiologically different. Mechal Sobel, *The World They Made Together: Black and White Values in Eighteenth-Century Virginia* (New York, 1987), explains the mutual cultural exchange between Africans and Europeans. On the development of a group cultural identity among diverse West Africans living in Pennsylvania, see Gary B. Nash, *Forging Freedom: The Formation of Philadelphia's Black Community, 1720–1840* (Cambridge, Mass., 1988), 13–16.

17. Nash, *Forging Freedom*, 15–37, and Jean R. Soderlund, "Black Women in Colonial Pennsylvania," in *African Americans in Pennsylvania: Shifting Historical Perspectives*, ed. Joe William Trotter Jr. and Eric Ledell Smith (University Park, Pa., 1997), 73–92, offer good general accounts of slavery in colonial Pennsylvania. See Gary B. Nash and Jean R. Soderlund, *Freedom by Degrees: Emancipation in Pennsylvania and Its Aftermath* (New York, 1991), on the nonspecificity of slave occupations (8) and on the slave population of the mid-Atlantic region in 1770 (table on 7). Though slaves resided in all areas of Pennsylvania, they were most visibly concentrated in Philadelphia. Nash asserts that there were 672 slaves and 200 free blacks in the city in 1775 in "Forging Freedom: The Emancipation Experience in the Northern Seaport Cities, 1775–1820," in *Slavery and Freedom in the Era of the American Revolution*, ed. Ira Berlin and Ronald Hoffman (Urbana, Ill., 1986), 5. For specifics on slavery in rural counties, see Frantz and Pencak, eds., *Beyond Philadelphia*, 34, 41–42, 56, 82–83, 119.

property—the Anglo-American philosophical basis for formal community building. While free blacks were proud of their accomplishments within provincial society, they were also painfully aware of their subordinate status. A law passed in 1726 specified that a free African American could be reenslaved if he or she were found to "loiter and misspend his or her time or wander" or to have married a white. There were sound reasons for free blacks to retain a sense of connection to slaves in their midst. Such attitudes are evidenced in an advertisement for the return of Ben, a runaway Philadelphia slave who "is well acquainted in Philadelphia, and is supposed to be secreted by some Negroes there." To hide a slave successfully, these "Negroes" would probably have had to be free and not labor under a master's supervision. In any case, it suggests broad support networks among African Americans. Free blacks realized that the plight of slaves related to their own oppression in the British colony. By the 1760s and 1770s, like Indians and European Americans of the same time, African Americans were aware of belonging to a larger ethnic group.[18]

Cultural identity was not the only social group element that Pennsylvanians used to define community. Class differences and conflict permeated day-to-day life among Pennsylvanians from all regions. Class status related to states of freedom and unfreedom as well as wealth, property ownership, and amount of property. Pennsylvania's upper sorts included wealthy merchants, large landowners, and land speculators. The solid "middling sort," as they called themselves, were propertied freeholders—typically small farmers, shopkeepers, or independent artisans. Persons without substantial property who worked for wages, such as journeymen, laborers, sailors, and paid servants, were considered "lower sorts," or the laboring classes. Unfree servants and slaves, respectively, made up the bottom two rungs of the social ladder. Relations among these unequals in colonial British America were predicated on the paternalistic ethos of deference. Just as children and wives were to obey and respect their fathers and husbands, all colonists were expected to defer to their "betters." The ideology of social deference illustrates how important class gradations were for organizing communities in early America. Such a rigidly hierarchical society, in which people had to be class conscious in order to behave "properly," suggests how crucial one's material conditions were for reckoning identity. In reality, class status and

18. See Nash, *Forging Freedom*, 8–99, on the development of the free black community in colonial and revolutionary Philadelphia; on free blacks' ability to own property in colonial Pennsylvania and the 1726 law on reenslavement, see Nash and Soderlund, *Freedom by Degrees*, 13 (the quotation from the 1726 law is also on 13). Runaway advertisement is in *Pennsylvania Gazette*, January 9, 1766.

deference were contested terrain. Many poorer colonists and even servants and slaves openly and consistently challenged the social hierarchy by refusing to recognize wealthier people as superior. At one level, such rebellion suggested a rejection of elite notions of community and norms. It also suggests class consciousness that rejects subordination. Threats from below to the system of deference were always more acutely felt during times of perceived increasing economic inequality. Such strains manifested the expectation of a system of mutual obligations. If the wealthy prospered while others' status declined, the better sorts were not worthy community leaders.[19]

Just such a growing polarization of wealth and erosion of the status of middling and poorer people characterized the city of Philadelphia during the years preceding the Revolution. Upward social mobility was clearly not the norm for many of the city's poorest inhabitants. Powerful merchants controlled the bulk of the wealth. Compared to that of the elite, the economic status of the lower-middling and lower sorts declined from the late 1760s through the 1780s. Communities defined by class interests became more apparent, as evidenced by a shift in socialization patterns in the city just before the Revolution. Taverns as centers of cross-class dialogues and arguments gave way to taverns and coffee shops catering to more class-specific clienteles. Poor and economically insecure middling-sort urban residents speculated on the causes of their economic grievances in these venues without the presence of elites. Thus, no one was available to contravene their constructions of community by invoking a greater good provided by a deferential social system. Class consciousness and friction—clearly on the rise during the years leading up to the Revolution and inextricably bound up in the political dispute with Britain—created a vital boundary in community definitions in the city.[20]

Class consciousness and conflict were, of course, not limited to the city. The entire colony of Pennsylvania had a large population of servants and

19. John M. Murrin, "In the Land of the Free and the Home of the Slave, Maybe There Was Room for Deference," argues for the centrality of the ideal of deference to colonial class relations, while Michael Zuckerman, "Tocqueville, Turner, and Turds: Four Stories of Manners in Early America," suggests the ubiquity of lower-sort challenges to social deference in certain contexts in colonial America. Both articles appear in *Journal of American History* 85 (June 1998): 86–97 and 13–42, respectively. Alfred Young, *The Shoemaker and the Tea Party*, 20–51, asserts that violations of the ethos of deference in colonial America revealed class consciousness and the rejection of subordination.

20. Foner, *Tom Paine*, 20–41; Nash, *Urban Crucible*, 159–66; and Billy G. Smith, *The "Lower Sort": Philadelphia's Laboring People, 1750–1800* (Ithaca, N.Y., 1990), 147–49, demonstrate the growing polarization of wealth, decline of the lower and middling sorts' standards of living, and class conflict in pre-Revolutionary Philadelphia. Peter Thompson, *Rum Punch and Revolution*, 111–81, shows the increasingly class-specific realm of socialization and the decline of accessible colonial popular politics.

apprentices in both rural and urban areas. Deference toward masters was the expected norm of behavior under the terms of indenture. But with the possibility of economic independence through the paternalist social system appearing to decrease in the years before the Revolution, tensions mounted between servants and masters. In rural areas, a growing group of laborers was becoming a permanent seasonal and migrant working class. For many of these workers, the potential attainment of authentic independence entailed by the ownership of property and land proved impossible. Small family farmers and squatters in frontier regions, too, competed with land speculators. These economic conflicts often had a regional dimension, as many speculators resided in the East. Speculators were an absent elite, unable to assert their membership and dominance in the immediate community directly. In some poorer areas of the colony, such as the upper Juniata Valley, colonists saw themselves as geographically and economically distinct from the rest of the province. Given their squatter traditions, these colonists resented not only the southeastern counties' political domination but their economic power as well.[21]

These material issues fostered myriad class fissures that further sharpened the ways in which Pennsylvanians defined their group identities. Apprentices, for example, constituted a significant subculture within a given town. Colonial regionalism coupled with economic and cultural differences, however, worked to limit trans-regional class consciousness. Seasonal farm laborers developed different senses of their immediate communities than urban journeymen did. In short, class consciousness in late colonial Pennsylvania complicated and further diversified localism.

Nevertheless, one fundamental class divide did permeate the province. The gap between voting citizens and the disenfranchised was based on property-owning status. Pennsylvania allowed only resident men over the age of twenty-one with either landownership of fifty acres or an estate worth fifty pounds the right to vote. Deriving from English conceptions that linked voting rights with freeholding status, the colonial government assumed that only

21. See Nash, *Urban Crucible*, 163–64, on servants and apprentices in the colony and the prewar strain on paternalist social and economic conditions. Paul G. E. Clemens and Lucy Simler, "Rural Labor and the Farm Household in Chester County, Pennsylvania, 1750–1820," in *Work and Labor in Early America*, ed. Stephen Innes (Chapel Hill, N.C., 1988), 106–43, discuss the rise of a rural class of laborers and cottagers in the eighteenth century. On merchant land speculators, see Frederick B. Tolles, *Meeting House and Counting House: The Quaker Merchants of Colonial Philadelphia, 1682–1783* (New York, 1963), 95–96. On squatter-speculator conflict in the greater Pennsylvania frontier region, see Aron, *How the West Was Lost*, 15–21, and Slaughter, *Whiskey Rebellion*, 78–84. On the Juniata Valley, see Blessing, "The Upper Juniata Valley," 153–57.

men with a proper "stake in society" should be able to make political decisions. Those without sufficient property or in conditions of servitude were explicitly excluded from the body politic. Males resident in the province who were not fully naturalized British subjects were also denied voting rights. Naturalization entailed proof of ownership of one hundred acres and an income of ten pounds per year. Thus, non-British residents of Pennsylvania were held to a higher material stake in society: ethnic origins modified class status, as the naturalization requirement was twice the normal property qualification for voting. The property-holding requirements for voting and naturalization caused some resentment among men with lesser holdings who paid taxes to the colony yet were denied franchise. Estimates of voter eligibility among Pennsylvania taxpayers in the pre-Revolutionary period range from 50 to 75 percent. With perhaps close to half of all male taxpayers denied voting rights, the divide between voting and non-voting classes not only defined citizenship but also further refined identities. Self-perceived group membership in colonial Pennsylvania, then, could be an exceedingly complex amalgam of region, culture, and class.[22]

By the mid-eighteenth century, though, the construction of racial ideologies increasingly simplified and clarified provincial concepts of community. Pennsylvanians imagined a world of three fundamental racial groups— "whites," "Negroes," and "Indians"—that created new potential bases for trans-regional solidarities. As previously indicated, the differences among Africans, Native Americans, and Europeans were partly culturally defined, but evidence suggests that racialization, long under way, was becoming a more important mode of defining self and Others. The tortured process by which concepts of ethnocultural difference were systematized as biological difference unfolded over centuries as European imperialism defined the Atlantic world. "Racial idioms," as historian Joyce Chaplin has called them, emerged in the very early colonial periods as Europeans came to understand Indians and Africans as physically different from themselves. Rather than clear systems of racial hierarchy based purely on skin color, there were varying understandings of physical difference related to cultural practices. Late colonial Pennsylvanians similarly conflated articulations of ethnicity and race, and no coherent ideology fully separated the two concepts. Nevertheless, in the era of the French and Indian

22. Robert J. Dinkin, *Voting in Provincial America: A Study of Elections in the Thirteen Colonies, 1689–1776* (Westport, Conn., 1977), 29–38, and Frantz and Pencak's introduction to their *Beyond Philadelphia*, xii, explain voting qualifications in provincial Pennsylvania. On naturalization requirements, see Karen Guenter, "Berks County," in *Beyond Philadelphia*, ed. Frantz and Pencak, 70. On estimates of voter eligibility, see Dinkin, *Voting in Provincial America*, 44.

War (and later), race became a progressively more popular category by which to define identity in the province.[23]

Colonists in Pennsylvania openly moved to a more racialist view of Indians in this period, one that went beyond previous articulations of cultural difference. The outbreak of extensive warfare on the Pennsylvania frontier ca. 1755–74 was a catalyst for this process. As the era of tenuous coexistence was replaced by one of bitter violence, both Indians and European Americans cultivated a growing sense of rigid distinction between them. This is not to say that cultural markers or cultural exchange ceased to be important. In fact, cultural exchange via the unfortunate avenue of military conflict accelerated. Colonists and Indians became mutually acclimated to each others' mores of warfare and developed a common military culture of guerilla raids, attacks on civilians, and scalping. While the scale of such exchange was not as massive for residents of the region as it would be in the Revolution, the results set the stage for what would follow. Pennsylvanians who more typically fought in conjunction with the British army did manage one military raid on their own that was essentially identical to the attacks by Indians on their own communities (attacks they characterized as "barbaric"). In 1756, militiamen surprised a group of Delawares at Kittanning, burned the town, killed close to forty Indians, and destroyed property. In short, the colonists had executed an "Indian-style" raid against their Native enemies and raised an ideological dilemma. For European Americans who interpreted Indian methods of war as significant indications of "savagery," the hybridity of warfare blurred conventional hierarchies. Tragically and ironically, as Indian and colonist cultures converged, race became the fundamental boundary between the two groups. Pennsylvanians in borderland regions became more racist, refusing to differentiate among distinctive Native groups. A provincial scalp bounty facilitated this process and resulted in many colonists attacking Indians regardless of their wartime sympathies. Although financial gain was one motive, indiscriminate scalping also reaffirmed the notion that all Indians were somehow the same, regardless of politics or culture. The clearest demonstration of incipient racism on the Pennsylvania frontier, however, was the attack on neutral Indians at the village of Conestoga by the "Paxton Boys." In response to attacks by hostile Indians during Pontiac's War,

23. On the racial idioms that emerged pertaining to Indians in the English mind as a result of contact and colonialism, see Chaplin, *Subject Matter*. The still classic account of how early modern English people merged cultural and racial concepts of difference when comparing themselves to recently encountered Africans is Winthrop Jordan, *White Over Black: American Attitudes Toward the Negro, 1550–1812* (New York, 1977).

a group of armed colonists from the Paxton region sought vengeance against any available Indian group. The ethnically mixed Natives at Conestoga lived in Lancaster County, far from the base of operations of the Indian anti-British alliance. Many were Christian and had adopted a number of elements of European culture. In December 1763, the Paxton Boys burned Conestoga and killed all six Indians present. Lancaster officials placed the other Conestogans who had not been present during the attack in protective custody at the county workhouse; the Paxton Boys attacked the workhouse a few days later, dismembering and scalping all fourteen Natives. Later, the mob marched on Philadelphia, determined to kill Indians in residence there. Dissuaded from further violence by provincial authorities, the Paxton Boys published their grievances and suggested a racial divide between all Europeans and Indians.[24]

The language that late colonial Pennsylvanians employed to describe themselves and Natives increasingly took on racial overtones. Most clearly, they designated British provincials "white." Although they continued to refer to specific Indian ethnic groups and nations, they also generalized their references to Natives more frequently. For example, in a letter regarding Frederick Stump's 1768 murder of ten Indians, his arrest, and his being freed from the Carlisle jail by a sympathetic mob, the descriptive language suggests a growing racial polarization among frontier Pennsylvanians. The letter sets up a dichotomy of "white people" and "Indians" that suggests the importance of perceived whiteness and its absence as a way of defining community. This development of a "white" identity among diverse European Americans—in opposition to generalized "Indians"—created the possibility of larger communal unity among Pennsylvanians. Indeed, Stump himself, a German American resident of the Juniata Valley, was freed by a mob in heavily Scots-Irish Cumberland County. At this particular moment, in opposition to "the Indians," race trumped ethnicity on the Pennsylvania frontier.[25]

Conversely, Indians were also beginning to construct notions of racial difference between themselves and European Americans. Building on creation narratives that posited separate origins for Europeans, Africans, and Americans, northeastern Indians also began to see peoples of European origin as the same,

---

24. On the Kittanning raid, see Solon J. Buck and Elizabeth Hawthorn Buck, *The Planting of Civilization in Western Pennsylvania* (1939; Pittsburgh, 1995), 85. See McConnell, *Country Between*, 124, on Pennsylvania's scalp bounty and how it encouraged the killing of both friendly and hostile Indians. On the Paxton Boys, see Vaughan, "Frontier Banditti," and Richter, *Facing East*, 203–8.

25. The letter regarding the Stump affair is reproduced in *Pennsylvania Gazette*, February 11, 1768. See Richter, *Facing East*, 213, on the role of ethnicity in the Stump incident.

regardless of their culture or ethnicity. Natives, like Europeans, merged concepts of cultural difference and immutable difference in the mid-eighteenth century that suggested racial idioms. In this period, some Native peoples, particularly in the southeast, used the terms "red," "white," and "black" to designate Indians, Europeans, and Africans respectively. These categories may have denoted cultural designations rather than skin color, however. Indeed, many Natives did not consider all Europeans "white." Some excepted the French from that category. Still, these generalized concepts of difference did influence Indian actions. During Pontiac's War, Indian warriors often spared the lives of African American slaves but killed British colonists. Broader Native identities were in the making. Before this period of warfare and tumult, for example, Ottawas and Delawares might have seen few shared interests, as they considered themselves completely different peoples. Defining themselves in opposition to "white" colonists, though, created common ground. Not surprisingly, such views coincided with the development of pan-Indian consciousness. Like their British colonial neighbors in the region, northeastern Indians began to understand communities in terms of differences that transcended culture alone.[26]

A parallel racialization process occurred in the way that European colonists viewed people of African descent in the province. As Pennsylvania's African population synthesized aspects of European and African culture, purely cultural explanations of difference and subjection to slavery were no longer as effective. Once again, understandings of ethnic differences remained, but they slowly evolved into racialist views—and cultural convergence was a catalyst for racism. If African Americans were Christians and spoke English or German, other rationalizations for hierarchy would be needed. Pennsylvania was well known as one of the early centers of abolitionist sentiment in the mid- and latter eighteenth century, but it is crucial to distinguish between antislavery positions and opposition to racism. Both free and enslaved African Americans encountered laws predicated upon racist assumptions. In the beginning of the eighteenth century, Pennsylvania established separate court systems for blacks and whites: African Americans were not tried by jury and received far harsher

26. Dowd, *Spirited Resistance*, xiii, explains the growing importance of the separate creation stories of Indians and whites to Indian nativist religion during the mid-eighteenth century. Richter, Facing East, 191–201, discusses Native concepts of racial difference as applied to the British as "whites." On the development of Indian "color" consciousness, see Nancy Shoemaker, "How the Indians Got to Be Red," *American Historical Review* 102 (1997): 625–44, and Claudio Saunt, *A New Order of Things: Property, Power, and the Transformation of the Creek Indians, 1733–1816* (New York, 1999), 111–35. On how some Indians spared the lives of slaves in Pontiac's War, see Richter, *Facing East*, 199–200.

penalties than whites for the same crimes. By 1726, the colony had created a "black code" that restricted the freedoms of both slaves and free blacks. The language of these laws specifically evoked early racial designations of "white" and "Negro." Color—rather than culture—was thus institutionalized. Even abolitionist members of the Society of Friends envisioned racially segregated communities in the colonial period, not allowing free blacks or slaves to join the church until the 1790s. While the future of slavery was open to debate in the colony, such discussions clearly did not preclude the racist consciousness that was a vital way in which "whites" defined themselves and Others. In conjunction with the racial Othering of Indians, a growing construct of biological difference in regard to African Americans served to bolster the general Anglo-American colonial identity as "white."[27]

The existence of both slavery and a developing racialist ideology fostered the conscious development of a "black" community among African Americans as well. Largely as a reaction to the racial attitudes of their white neighbors, free blacks and slaves resorted to identities that transcended class, region, and diverse African ethnic origins. As the black codes in Pennsylvania made clear, free, enslaved, African, and American-born "Negroes" were singled out as a uniquely subordinated group. The continuing growth of a creole African American culture no doubt facilitated black understandings of this status on a grand scale. Word spread among North Americans of African descent of their subjection to common oppression throughout the British colonies, and a broad group consciousness emerged. Olaudah Equiano went out of his way in his retrospective 1789 autobiography to discuss the violence and degradation experienced by "Negroes" in the British West Indies and North America. He mentioned that he had heard of free blacks being reenslaved "even in Philadelphia," where, he noted, only "the benevolence of the Quakers" preserved any of the rights "of the sable race." Given primary source limitations, it is difficult to ascertain to what extent most African Americans understood "race" and its relation to skin color or biology in general. What is clear, however, is that European concepts and laws regarding race hierarchy allowed free blacks and slaves to see some degree of common group membership.[28]

27. See Nash and Soderlund, *Freedom by Degrees*, on the racially segregated courts, the Pennsylvania black code, and the quoted racial language from the laws (12–13) as well as the Quaker prohibition on black church membership (29).

28. See Smedley, *Race in North America*, 178–79, on the development of an increasingly racialist view of Africans by European Americans in the mid-eighteenth century. On general racism toward freed and enslaved African Americans in Pennsylvania, see Smith, *The "Lower Sort,"* 18–19. On the development

Nonetheless, ideologies of race remained somewhat amorphous in Pennsylvania's late colonial period. Links between skin color and ethnic origin were often unsystematic. Indeed, the concept of whiteness itself varied greatly. It was by no means clear in the 1750s and 1760s that all Europeans (or even those from northwestern Europe) were "white." One of the most well-known meditations on race in colonial Pennsylvania was Benjamin Franklin's essay from 1751 that offered a very narrow definition of the white race. Franklin asserted: "All Africa is black or tawny; Asia chiefly tawny; America (exclusive of the newcomers) wholly so. And in Europe, the Spaniards, Italians, French, Russians, and Swedes are generally of what we call a swarthy complexion; as are the Germans also, the Saxons only excepted, who, with the English, make the principal body of white people on the face of the earth." In Franklin's view, even the province's non-English Britons and most of its ethnic Germans were not white. This narrow definition of whiteness suggested that racial identity was deeply contested among colonists and that not all Europeans could lay claim to being members of the privileged race in the province. While Franklin's categorization may have been exceptionally exclusive, evidence from the colonial Pennsylvania press further underscores the idea that popular understandings of European and African complexions were far from systematized. The *Pennsylvania Gazette* ran an advertisement regarding a runaway "English servant man," Stephen Archer, who was described as having a "brown complexion." The same paper referred to a runaway Irish servant's "yellow complexion." A "Negroe Man, named Tony" was also reputed to be "of a very yellow complexion." Yet another master described his Irish servant, Brian Roony, as having a "black complexion." Colonial Pennsylvanians were still capable of describing Englishmen as "brown," Irish persons as "black," and Irish and African Americans as "yellow." Biological race in general and whiteness, specifically, were not yet rigid concepts. While race offered the possibility of group identities beyond class and locale, its protean character still held out possibilities for negotiation and further development.[29]

The other social concept that had the potential to transcend the regionalism of colonial Pennsylvania was that of gender. The definition of formal public manhood in the province was both clear and rigid. Voters had to be

of African American culture and community before the Revolution, see Frey, *Water from the Rock*, 5–44, and Nash, *Forging Freedom*, 38–44, as well as *The Interesting Narrative of the Life of Olaudah Equiano, Written by Himself*, ed. Robert J. Allison (Boston, 1995), 107.

29. Franklin's 1751 essay is quoted in Matthew Frye Jacobson, *Whiteness of a Different Color* (Cambridge, Mass., 1998), 40. *Pennsylvania Gazette* references are from July 25, 1775; July 30, 1766; May 7, 1767; and April 10, 1766.

property-owning men. Obviously, this provision clearly excluded women, making full citizenship a masculine domain. Indeed, as historian Linda Kerber has argued, when intellectuals invoked the political community of "men" (voting and non-voting) the term was meant to be gender-specific and not generic. The important implication of this political subjectivity was that all men, at least, had the necessary prerequisite for all the rights of British citizenship. The connection to property holding was a staple of the patriarchal metaphor that organized early modern politics, society, families, and religion. Independent men who owned their own farms or businesses were at the apex of the gendered social hierarchy. Their social and gender status combined to convey political rights. Propertyless men or men with little property, too, could at least aspire to suffrage if their material conditions improved.[30]

Although voting, freeholding status epitomized the public man, masculinity could be expressed in other ways. General European manliness could mean carrying out specifically male labor, such as heavy fieldwork. Regional variations were apparent as well. In frontier regions, some European American men engaged in game hunting for food and trade; hunting had long been a marker of masculinity among Indians of the region, and these European Americans adapted to their neighbors' culture. The tavern was a site where gender identities could be negotiated as well. As places in the province where the larger popular will could be expressed in diverse gatherings of people from all social groups, these institutions only allowed men the opportunity to express political opinions openly. Although women were also present in taverns, the drinking companies were largely men. "Respectable women" rarely frequented Pennsylvania tippling houses, but elite, middling, and poor men all did. In this atmosphere, discussions of politics and what constituted manly behavior could meld, compete, and coexist.[31]

Lower-sort men of the colony, in particular, typically held a notion of manhood that involved exhibitions of physical prowess or fighting. Not fully congruent with more genteel notions of formal patriarchy and property owning,

30. Linda K. Kerber, *Women of the Republic: Intellect and Ideology in Revolutionary America* (Chapel Hill, N.C., 1995).

31. Kathleen Brown, *Good Wives*, 13–74, shows how central fieldwork was to early modern colonial European conceptions of masculinity. On the adoption (from woodland Indians) of hunting as a hallmark of masculinity among European Americans, see Aron, *How the West Was Lost*, 5–28. Peter Thompson, *Rum Punch and Revolution*, shows how taverns emerged as sites in which identity and the popular political will in colonial Pennsylvania were expressed. Thompson also notes that taverns were institutions to be avoided by "respectable" colonial women (75).

this definition of masculinity allowed men of lower social status to create alternative discourses of maleness. Escaped convict John Nailing, for instance, was described as "remarkably talkative, addicted to drinking and swearing, brags much of his manhood, and is a great bruiser." This young Irish immigrant with apparently no stake in society (in the formal colonial sense) took pains to assert that he considered himself a man nonetheless. The description of Nailing's combative nature suggests that he was particularly defensive about this point. A runaway Philadelphia shoemaker's apprentice, James Harrison, was likewise noted to be "very talkative when in liquor, and brags much of his manhood." A state of unfreedom was the ultimate signifier that one was not a patriarch. Still, Harrison—like Nailing—considered the exhibition of his view of male behavior as not only a vital element of his identity but also a source of pride. The fact that the descriptions of Harrison and Nailing link the consumption of spirits with assertions of masculinity further underscores the centrality of a politicized tavern culture to men of all backgrounds.[32]

Obviously, such varied notions of formal and informal manhood further divided Pennsylvanians into more clearly delineated subcommunities. While voting men could engage in the informal codes of martial and physical manliness, disenfranchised men could not avail themselves of the benefits of formal manhood. Poorer men were painfully aware that others viewed them as lesser men. Yet gender identity, like race, held out the possibility of broader commonalities. In a milieu in which basic natural rights political philosophy was predicated on literal manhood, the disenfranchised male was aware that he at least had some rights denied others. Being a man in any sense, therefore, could have larger implications because gender identity in colonial Pennsylvania was so thoroughly politicized. The shared prerogatives of all males, though contested, provided a public sphere for negotiation. This forum on masculinity held out the potential for internal conflict as well as consensus, though. If some men believed in physical masculinity as qualification enough for participation in popular politics, it was possible that poor, disenfranchised residents might ultimately call for some alteration in the definition of citizenship and public manhood. The link between manliness and political action would be reinforced during the debates over imperial taxation: even elites would call on all men in the province to engage in "manly resistance."[33]

32. *Pennsylvania Gazette*, September 18, 1769, and December 14, 1775.
33. Kerber, *Women of the Republic*, shows the connection between natural rights philosophy and masculinity.

These myriad factors in the evolving and situationally varied ideas of community made Pennsylvanians' localism very complex. Intersections of broad identities and narrowly regional ones divided people within a single region. The colony was truly diverse and pluralistic. While race, ethnicity, religion, gender, and class offered possibilities of group membership beyond locale, such consciousness was not independent of the fundamental localism that dominated Pennsylvanians' cosmologies. Concepts of nationalism were even melded with this worldview. The most clearly shared status among Pennsylvanians was that of British subjects in one of the empire's North American provinces. They understood local representation to be at the heart of British liberty. These notions of nationality were profoundly challenged by centralized government in the 1760s and 1770s. Pennsylvanians' reactions to reforms in the British Empire were rooted in their specific colonial situations and identities.

As with the Revolution itself, the colonists interpreted the constitutional crisis over Parliament's right to legislate for the colonies in a variety of ways. There were, however, certain shared terms of discourse. Discussions of the imperial policies of Britain dominated newspapers and tavern discussions for almost a decade before the Revolution. Heated debates over American liberty were commonplace in Pennsylvania. The tropes used by rich and poor, easterners and westerners, German Lutherans and English Quakers were the same. Their common vocabulary was an amalgam of classical republicanism, liberalism, and British Whiggism. Colonists agreed on the importance of balancing order and liberty in a virtuous society. The question was, of course, what constituted proper liberty, order, and virtue. Foreseeably, Pennsylvanians had diverse understandings of this shared political culture. The very plasticity of Anglo-American Whig discourse made it appealing to different groups for varied reasons. Lower- and middling-sort men who would later fight linked their ideas to their identities. Their opposition to Britain's imperial policies stemmed from their own social and political interests. As the constitutional crisis with Britain turned toward open resistance (and later, war), various elites needed to ally themselves with young, unpropertied "white" men in order to consolidate popular support. In the years leading up to the Revolution, definitions of manhood came to embrace political activism and, eventually, soldiering. This process helped the men who took up arms legitimate their social and political visions.[34]

34. On the Anglo-American political vocabulary that was widely shared by colonial Americans during the constitutional crisis with Britain, see Bailyn, *Ideological Origins*, and Gordon S. Wood, *The Creation of the American Republic, 1776–1787* (New York, 1969).

Pennsylvanians became involved in the debate over the empire at various times for distinctly regional reasons. Britain first alienated the province's frontier population with the Proclamation of 1763, which essentially forbade Anglo-American settlement west of the Alleghenies. Parliament hoped to avoid another costly frontier war by protecting Indians from the empire's land-hungry colonists. Although imperfectly enforced and later superseded by other treaty lines, the Proclamation boundary made frontier colonists suspicious of central imperial authority. It appeared to many that the Crown had sold out the very objective for which colonists had fought in the French and Indian War: the opening of the trans-Allegheny west to settlement. The proclamation alarmed wealthy land speculators in the East as well as small farmers in the West. Adding to colonial frustration with the mother country was imperial policy toward the Indians following Pontiac's War. Although they emerged victorious in the war, British authorities learned that they could not treat western Indians contemptuously. The British began to take up the French role on the frontier by distributing gifts to Indian groups, mediating conflict, and engaging in diplomacy rather than blunt coercion—and colonists reacted angrily. A group of Cumberland County vigilantes nicknamed "the Black Boys" attacked pack trains of supplies that were to be used in diplomacy with Indians and besieged the British garrison at Fort Loudon in 1765.[35]

Clearly, these colonists took a jaundiced view of imperial attempts to preserve elements of the old French "middle ground" of negotiation and coexistence with independent Indian groups. While the British sought to do what was best for the overall empire, frontier colonists expressed a more provincial view. They were interested in new lands, particularly given the increase in immigration to the colony in the wake of the previous imperial wars. Many colonists also remained hostile toward Indians in general by virtue of their growing self-definition as "white." They foresaw an expansive British Empire in which the interests of white, not Indian, residents should be protected by the authority of the Crown. British officials did not fully adopt this outlook. They strove to avoid the expense, difficult logistics, and dislocation of frontier war. Economic, diplomatic, and military ties to the Indians of the region protected the welfare

35. See McConnell, *Country Between*, 234, on the Proclamation of 1763; on the reaction of wealthy land speculators to the proclamation, see Marc Egnal, *A Mighty Empire: The Origins of the American Revolution* (Ithaca, N.Y., 1988), 11–15. White, *Middle Ground*, 269–314, asserts that the British learned the lesson from Pontiac's War that they could not ignore diplomacy with western Indians. On frontier hostility to British policy and the Black Boys, see Robert G. Crist, "Cumberland County," in *Beyond Philadelphia*, ed. Frantz and Pencak, 112–13.

of the empire in general and Britain in particular. This is not to say that the British government did not harbor expansionist aims toward the North American interior. Rather, it hoped to acquire new land in a manner that was economical, orderly, and beneficial foremost to Great Britain. Imperial officials often feared that colonists did not attend to any of these larger concerns while pursuing their own interests. Conversely, colonists feared that imperial Indian policy indicated a sinister conspiracy against their freedom to expand territorially. British regular soldiers seemed to be garrisoned at frontier posts as much to police colonists as to protect them. This concern about the redcoats spoke to the traditional Anglo-American anti-army ideology that decried the danger to civilians from a standing army during peacetime. The fact that the troops on the frontier were employed to enforce order among British subjects validated their suspicions.[36]

The debate over Parliament's right to tax the colonies further alienated various groups of Pennsylvanians, particularly those in Philadelphia, from the centralized government. The great seaport city was the center of trade in the province and felt the most immediate impact of the new imperial economic policies. Philadelphia was the center of Pennsylvania's resistance to the Stamp Act, the Townshend Duties, and the Tea Act during the mid-1760s through the mid-1770s. These imperial taxes were all enacted during a period of growing urban poverty in the American colonies. The poorest city dwellers were becoming increasingly impoverished, and some members of the middling sorts feared that their status was in peril. In this period of economic difficulty for common Philadelphians, it is not surprising that many blamed the policies of the British government, especially those that had a direct material effect upon them, such as taxes. Thus, wealthy merchants and the city's lower and middling sorts could unite against British policies that they believed were detrimental to the seaport's overall economic well-being. By the time of the protests against the Townshend Duties of 1767, Philadelphia's artisans were actually leading the non-importation movement and coercing merchants to support it. Master craftsmen—who stood to benefit from the drive for home manufacture— became further politicized in conflict with the mother country. Given the material interests at stake and the growth of poverty in Philadelphia, the city

36. John Shy, *Toward Lexington: The Role of the British Army in the Coming of the American Revolution* (Princeton, N.J., 1965), 207–9, demonstrates provincial fears of British troops in the region. See Lois G. Schwoerer, *"No Standing Armies": The Antiarmy Ideology in Seventeenth-Century England* (Baltimore, 1974), on the general fear of standing armies during times of peace.

became the province's cockpit of resistance to British imperial policy. Internal class issues, however, undergirded this "patriotic" activity.[37]

Interestingly, a number of rural counties in Pennsylvania did not become fully politicized in the constitutional crisis until the 1774 "Intolerable" or Coercive Acts that closed the port of Boston and strengthened centralized British power in the colonies. Apparently these residents of the province did not feel that their well-being had been threatened by earlier British actions, such as the Proclamation of 1763 and the Stamp and Townshend taxes. Although taxation had an economic impact upon the region, it was not as immediately apparent as in the Atlantic trade port of Philadelphia. Nor did the region experience the direct presence of the empire regulating society and intercultural relations, as happened on the frontier. Colonists from the rural areas did, however, seem to find the expansion of centralized authority embodied in laws enacted by Parliament to punish Boston sufficiently menacing that they became active in protesting imperial policy. The specter of widespread military rule in the provinces and the potential economic devastation of Boston alarmed large numbers of rural Pennsylvanians more than debates over Britain's right to tax the colonies. Clearly, different regions of the colony were drawn into the political showdown with the mother country at different times and for various reasons. These local differences suggest that there was no singular unifying ideology of colonial resistance but rather a common language used to protect various communal interests.[38]

Indeed, despite the ubiquity of discussions regarding the constitution of the empire throughout Pennsylvania in the 1763–74 period, some people realized that hyperbole obfuscated the importance of certain issues. John Adlum, who fought in the Continental army during the Revolution, suggested that during the constitutional crisis, some essayists were manipulating the masses to support the patriot side, perhaps for their own material gain. He recalled that "there was a great excitement in the country against the British ministry, and the newspapers were filled with pieces against them to keep the feelings of the

---

37. See Nash, *Urban Crucible*, 209–24, on the effect of growing urban poverty in the constitutional crisis. Thomas M. Doerflinger, *A Vigorous Spirit of Enterprise: Merchants and Economic Development in Revolutionary Philadelphia* (Chapel Hill, N.C., 1986), 167–95, traces the shift from merchant to middling-sort leadership in the non-importation movement over the period from 1765 to 1767.

38. On the Intolerable Acts as the first laws that energized political resistance to British policy in the rural regions of Pennsylvania, see Guenter, "Berks County," 72–73; Eugene R. Slaski, "The Lehigh Valley," 49; Paul E. Doutrich, "York County," 85; and Owen S. Ireland, "Bucks County," 27, all in *Beyond Philadelphia*, ed. Frantz and Pencak.

people alive against taxations and other oppressions real and imaginary." Although Adlum implies a cynical conspiracy to delude the people into revolution, his recognition of the interests of others suggests that he possessed an awareness of his own distinct reasons for supporting the rebel cause. His account also suggests popular awareness of debates over the empire conducted in newspapers, broadsides, and pamphlets. Once a public discussion of liberty, equality, and power was unleashed, no single group could impose their understandings on others. Ordinary Pennsylvanians' social visions could then become thoroughly politicized by incorporation into a broader "patriot" cause.[39]

The ways in which people read or understood these public debates, therefore, could not be wholly circumscribed by the intentions of the authors of particular pieces. For many who wrote essays in the colony's newspapers during the crisis with Britain, the protection of property was equated with the preservation of liberty. Standing up to the actions of Parliament was tantamount to defending American property, the basis of liberty, patriarchy, and representation. One writer denounced British policy by declaring that "liberty—property and life—are now but names in America. Liberty is leveled by the Declarative Act of Parliament to tax us without our consent. Property is now annihilated by the late Act of Parliament [the 1774 Coercive Acts]." While these assertions were entirely compatible with rationalizations by the established colonial elite to protect their property (and their continued social dominance), they were understood differently by others. Middling sorts openly took up the cause, crafting their notions of liberty and property specifically to demonstrate that their group formed the bedrock of virtuous politics. An essay directed "to the Tradesmen, Mechanics, etc. of the Province of Pennsylvania" in 1773 raised the following issues: "The point of the question is whether we have property of our own or not? Whether our property and the dear earned fruits of our labor, are at our own disposal or shall be wantonly wrested from us by a set of luxurious, abandoned, and piratical hirelings, to be appropriated by them to increase the number of such infamous pensioners and support their unlimited extravagance?" Included in this appeal to middling men of property is a critique of British wealth and corruption that could easily be generalized to Pennsylvania. Also embedded in the essay is a labor theory of value, suggesting that those Americans who create material wealth should be entitled to "the dear earned

39. John Adlum, *Memoirs and the Life of John Adlum in the Revolutionary War*, ed. Howard H. Peckham (Chicago, 1968), 5–6.

fruits of our labor." Engagement in the cause of liberty and property could thus seem promising to propertyless laborers as well as established freeholders.[40]

Because these kinds of pleas spoke to imperial *and* to local politics, Philadelphians merged their material aspirations at home with denunciations of British officials. During an election in Philadelphia, the language of class conflict was applied not only to a supposedly corrupt centralized power but also to wealthy provincial candidates. An article warned "respectable farmers, tradesmen, [and] mechanics" to avoid voting for any man "who aspires after wealth and power. . . . Rather than be disappointed; be careful." Although these instructions were aimed at "the laborious farmer and tradesman [who] are the most valuable branch of the community," the growing equation of wealth and Toryism was appealing to the very poor as well. The suggestion that some wealthy Philadelphians might be part of a sinister plot to undermine American liberty allowed impoverished city dwellers to begin to hope that a favorable outcome to the struggle with Britain might bring a level of economic and political change.[41]

In other contexts, discussions of the term "equality" held some of the most radical implications. In 1769, an article in the *Pennsylvania Gazette* called for "an exact equality of constitutional rights among all his Majesty's subjects." While the writer undoubtedly had in mind a federal image of the empire, one in which colonial assemblies were essentially sovereign British legislative bodies in their respective provinces, some readers may have had a different notion. While all residents of the colonies were essentially literal "subjects"—that is, subject to the power of the monarch—not all were active, voting citizens entitled to the rights of a full British subject. A class-based reading of this discourse would have had immense appeal to the unpropertied. The politicization of ordinary Pennsylvanians is suggested by an advertisement regarding a runaway shoemaker's apprentice from Lancaster, Thomas Plunkett, who was "wearing a pair of liberty buttons." "Liberty" to this servant may well have meant something entirely different from "constitutional equality" of the colonies within the empire. Plunkett truly took the issue of freedom into his own hands. Such young men, many of whom would fight in the war, could not help but be aware of the ambiguity of arguments about liberty and equality in a land marked by unfreedom and glaring inequality. They also were aware of the opportunities that their participation in the conflict could create.[42]

40. *Pennsylvania Gazette*, May 18, 1774, and December 8, 1773.
41. Ibid., September 22, 1773.
42. Ibid., January, 19, 1769, and September 29, 1773.

Other discussions of taxation and representation could speak to group identities other than class as well. For example, in addition to being alienated by the abrupt change in British Indian policy, frontier Pennsylvanians in the newer counties could note that they were not properly represented in Philadelphia or in Parliament. Renunciations of Parliamentary arguments for "virtual representation," in which colonial subjects were not directly represented by people from their locale, resonated with people who believed that the east's political dominance of the assembly was somewhat analogous. The politics of the empire easily meshed with those of the province and its regions. In this case, advocates for the Whig cause in the western part of the colony could hope for changes in ministerial policy and in Pennsylvania itself.[43]

Moreover, non-naturalized and naturalized non-British European immigrants could have understood debates on liberty in similarly group-specific terms. Given that their ethnic status singled them out for different citizenship qualifications than those for other colonists, the "exact equality of constitutional rights" was not quite so precise for them. Such inequality was mirrored in British imperial policy. The Stamp Act levied a double tax on all foreign-language newspapers in the colonies. Participation in the patriot cause could hold out the possibility for reform of suffrage requirements that would benefit them. Significantly, mainstream Pennsylvania German–American concepts of liberty shifted dramatically during the very period of the imperial crisis. Spurred by events such as the Stamp Act, many ethnic Germans revised their traditionally "negative" understanding of liberty to a more "positive" one, suggesting that the protection of property demanded public activism. As these colonists took up more visible roles in the province's public sphere, they could more explicitly advocate for their group interests as "patriots."[44]

One possibility for change on the eve of revolution that would affect many groups was the potential for new notions of formal "manhood." Citizenship characterized by an equation of landownership and voting rights was challenged by growing political activism among disenfranchised men. Throughout the troubles with Britain, general invocations of masculinity took on new meanings. Typical of the gendered language used to encourage participation by men of all social ranks in resistance to British policy was a 1773 essay in the *Pennsylvania*

43. See Brunhouse, *Counter-Revolution in Pennsylvania*, 12, on the importance of proportional county representation to radical revolutionaries.
44. See Roeber, *Palatines, Liberty, and Property*, on the double stamp tax on foreign-language newspapers (203–4) and on the general shift among Germans from negative understandings of liberty to more activist ones (175–205, 243–310).

Gazette that called for "manly opposition to the machinations of tyranny." Given the ubiquity of mob actions and boycotts as effective American tools against the enforcement of imperial law, clearly the kind of manly behavior the author had in mind would be compatible with ordinary Pennsylvanians' notions of "informal manhood." In other words, actions that would have been seen previously as apolitical expressions of manhood were being politicized during the crisis with Britain. If "manly opposition" was necessary to preserve liberty in the face of tyranny, many poor men might begin to wonder if they should not have a more formal stake in the body politic. It would be overstating the case to suggest that such rhetoric was equivalent to calls for universal manhood suffrage. Yet this colonial politicization of "informal manhood" continued to develop during the coming war, when poor men acted as soldiers in a Revolutionary army rather than members of a mob opposing taxes.[45]

Even more radical was a growing debate within the province over slavery. In 1774 a number of essayists considered the status of African Americans in the colonies. In light of recent debates about colonial liberty, some were so bold as to suggest that the holding of slaves was a paradox. Unfortunately, European Americans expressing that view were often Quakers, who were becoming increasingly marginalized in Pennsylvania politics as colonial resistance was turning to open rebellion. Abolitionists noted that among the colony's European American population, there was a popular contrary opinion voiced as well: "Negroes are no more fit for, or entitled to liberty, than the brute beasts." Here blacks are equated with "beasts" and not called "men." The net result of an increasingly racialist view among many Pennsylvanians, then, was that African Americans could be denied an "an exact equality of constitutional rights" on the basis of biology rather than politics. This ideology also connected with the colonists' interpretation of Indians as "nonwhites" who were not entitled to the rights of European Americans. Indeed, John Adams described the First Continental Congress in terms of how "three millions of free white people were there represented." Thus, many colonists were making significant links between masculinity in general, "whiteness," and the cause of "liberty." Ominously, a trans-regional commonality was emerging in the patriot coalition: a growing correlation between white manhood and entitlement to natural rights.[46]

45. *Pennsylvania Gazette*, December 8, 1773.
46. Ibid., December 7, 1774; "John Adams to a Friend in London," January 21, 1775, in *Letters of Delegates to Congress, 1774–1789*, ed. Paul H. Smith, Historical Database CD-ROM edition (Summerfield, Fla., 1998), 1:297.

Nevertheless, the fact that some Pennsylvanians made an argument that slavery should be avoided and that free blacks were at least entitled to some rights created a broader discourse that certainly did not occur in the southern colonies. Given the extent of popular knowledge of these political debates, the question of how liberty could coexist with slavery undoubtedly had the potential for a socially revolutionary response among slaves. Blacks who were present in the mobs that intimidated royal officials had an immediate stake in propagating an ideology of liberty. The popular white use of the trope of enslavement—denouncing British attempts to "enslave" colonists—must also have stirred discussion among slaves themselves regarding possible avenues of gaining freedom. It is not surprising, in the light of slave resistance to the institution of slavery in colonial America, that numbers of Pennsylvania's slave population prepared to free themselves whenever the opportunity presented itself in the political and later military tumults.[47]

Thus, various groups in Pennsylvania headed toward the Revolution with different aims and ideals. Patriots from the frontier region could see opposition to British policy as a way of voicing their displeasure over the empire's Indian policy. By stating that they were opposed to taxation without representation, they also directly spoke to their lack of representation at the provincial and imperial levels. Middling-sort radicals in Philadelphia used their attacks on the wealth and corruption of British officials to erode the deferential notion that only the better sorts were fit to govern. The disenfranchised throughout the colony could hope that discussions of liberty and equality, coupled with their political activism, would lead to an enlargement of the body politic. Enemies of the established eastern elite looked to growing rebellion as a way to gain political advantage. Slaves could even use the rhetoric of liberty to serve as a rationale for seeking their own liberation.

Still, some common ground was necessary to unite enough of these diverse interests for the resistance movement—and, subsequently, the Revolution—to succeed. There was, in fact, one concept that most colonists shared during the troubles with the mother country: localism. A majority of Pennsylvanians held a common commitment to a federal view of the empire, one that emphasized the divided sovereignty of local and central government. Elites as well as commoners preferred to be represented directly at the local level rather

---

47. On African American presence in Philadelphia mobs and probable awareness of the ideological implications of the debate over freedom and slavery in the colonial period, see Nash, *Forging Freedom*, 38–45.

than virtually on the national level. This allowed disparate groups to oppose the policies of the Crown for vastly different reasons, all the while protecting what they defined as their communal interests. The meaning of the American resistance was intimately tied to the ways in which people defined these communities. Almost all Pennsylvanians who weighed in during the great debates over the empire sought to identify themselves as the defenders of true local interests. Moreover, this "Whig" perspective addressed early Americans' worldviews and the actual experiences of most Pennsylvanians, while early "Tory" political ideology engendered an essentially imperial outlook. In other words, while the patriot cause could encompass various local and social issues, the loyalist worldview asked British subjects to imagine the greater good of the empire in general as defined by (and meant to benefit) the mother country. The resistance movement, for example, offered frontier provincials the possibility of altering British-Indian relations and opening new lands to settlement. It also provided a discourse through which residents of the region could begin to redress political grievances within Pennsylvania. The British were essentially asking these people to forgo their own short-term interests for the benefit of the larger British Empire. In this formulation, Indian groups with diplomatic ties to the British could be vitally important components of a larger empire. Most expansionist and localist frontier colonists could not tolerate this perspective; the resistance and later Revolutionary movements were able to succeed because they better appealed to people's local interests.

The patriot position also had the advantage of appearing both conservative and progressive. Many colonial Americans held a literal understanding of the term "revolution." It could mean a return to the beginning as well as a complete overturning of the status quo. Virtually all groups harkened back to their versions of an idealized colonial past for their vision of the future. They sought to return to the local autonomy they previously enjoyed and believed was the hallmark of British liberty. Most who opposed British policy in the period portrayed Parliament (somewhat accurately) as the innovators because they attempted to exercise unprecedented powers over the American colonists. Americans could see themselves as better Britons than the British because of their commitment to principles of local direct representation. Indeed, Parliament appeared to be attempting to deprive British colonial subjects of their traditional rights. As Lancaster merchants and traders argued in a 1770 petition, "we . . . cannot sit unmoved at the attempts made to deprive us of the liberty we and our ancestors have so highly esteemed and gloried in." Commitment to the sovereignty of local representative government was the one aspect of a constructed past that colonists shared. Otherwise, they were free to create a history that incorporated present issues and aspirations for the future. For instance, in 1773, middling-sort radicals could see a common present and past in which "the laborious farmer and tradesman are the most valuable branch of the community and have for ages been the support and barrier of liberty." The author of this essay suggested to his audience that the history and the future of British liberty were largely contingent on the interests of the middling classes. The discourse of Anglo-American Whiggism, therefore, provided colonists with recipes to correct what they perceived to be shortcomings in both the colony and the empire. This shared political language was fortuitously malleable enough to encompass a wide variety of group interests.[48]

Resistance to British imperial policy was one thing. Open armed rebellion was quite another. Men who would fight in the coming Revolution would take up arms for many of the same reasons they became involved in popular politics during the constitutional crisis. In other words, they fought when they believed that their communities were threatened or when they had an opportunity for group gain. That is not to say that there was a linear progression from opposing the Stamp Act to joining the Continental army. Rather, the connection is indirect. The politics of the constitutional crisis played into long-standing colonial social conflicts. Popular consciousness of internal provincial issues was transformed by their application to American "liberties" in general. Participation in mob activities, intimidation of royal officials, and boycotts politicized poor Pennsylvanians as active agents in determining the future of America. Revolutionary ideology offered a common vocabulary with which various people could express diverse aims. Still, when war with Britain broke out in Massachusetts in April 1775, it was not clear who would fight and why. Destabilized by the political effects of the dispute with Britain, definitions of what constituted a community were in flux on the eve of the American Revolution. The idea of what America was, is, and would become was contested in ways that it never had been before (or has been since). No outcome was inevitable or impossible. Who took up which side was largely contingent upon how participants saw themselves, their interests, and their communities.

48. *Pennsylvania Gazette*, June 28, 1770, and September 22, 1773.

2

Why They Fought

Early in the Revolutionary War, Alexander Graydon, a Continental officer in the Pennsylvania Line, experienced difficulties in recruiting men from the Philadelphia area. He recalled in his memoirs that, contrary to subsequent popular notions, the initial years of the war were not "a season of almost universal patriotic enthusiasm. It was far from prevalent in my opinion, among the lower ranks of the people, at least in Pennsylvania. At all times, indeed, licentious, levelling principles are much to the general taste . . . but the true merits of the contest were little understood or regarded. The opposition to the claims of Britain originated with the better sort." The question, then, glares: why did thousands of men from the "lower ranks" of society take up arms in or against the Revolutionary cause? Graydon believed that many were manipulated by "sagacious politicians," implying a selfish conspiracy of elites to use the people for their own ends. He also noted the importance of acquisitiveness among the soldiery, declaring, "it appeared that the sordid spirit of gain was the vital principle of this greater part of the army." Graydon suggested that many enlisted primarily for material gain. Because enlisted men typically came from the lowest ranks of society, it appears reasonable that they sought wages and enlistment bounties that might slightly improve their standard of living. Graydon, however, completely dismissed the possibility that the rank and file were actuated by Revolutionary ideology. (His own description of the people suggests otherwise, though: he derisively mentions "licentious levelling principles" among ordinary people.) A nationalist with aspirations to gentility, Graydon denied authenticity to any ideals or "patriotism" that did not fit into his worldview. Yet his own account unintentionally points to motivations among the people not fully appreciated by officers or the upper sorts. Clearly, the soldiery had reasons for fighting that Graydon simply rejected as not relevant to the "true merits of the contest."[1]

Nonetheless, Pennsylvanians of the "lower ranks" entered the war with their own coherent understandings of why they were fighting. The Revolution was not solely a clash between contending elites and the common people they employed to fight. Nor was it simply an opportunity that men used to ameliorate their poverty. Soldiers' motivations were numerous and varied but all firmly rooted in the people's localist outlooks and particular understandings of what constituted their communities. Social issues that were politicized during the constitutional crisis with Britain took on even more urgency during the

---

1. Alexander Graydon, *Alexander Graydon's Memoirs of His Own Time*, ed. John Stockton Littell (n.p., 1969), 134–35, 148. Interpretations of soldiers' motivations are also at the center of a relatively recent debate among historians. One group of scholars has convincingly documented the poverty of average enlisted men and deduced that they served primarily for the material rewards that would in some measure alleviate their extreme indigence. The most convincing of such scholarship includes Lender, "Enlisted Line"; Martin and Lender, *Respectable Army;* Neimeyer, *America Goes to War;* and Papenfuse and Stiverson, "General Smallwood's Recruits." This "economic interpretation" suggests that the Continental army was very much like the standing armies of Europe: officered by gentlemen, the ranks manned by the desperately poor or socially marginal who sought wages. Resch, *Suffering Soldiers;* Royster, *Revolutionary People;* and Robert Middlekauff, "Why Men Fought in the American Revolution," in *Patriots, Redcoats, and Loyalists*, ed. Peter S. Onuf (New York, 1991), 1–16, all argue that soldiers were in fact patriotic and fought as the vanguard of republican virtue even when civilians lost interest in the cause. In contrast to both Graydon and the materialist historians, they assert that soldiers fought for ideological reasons comparable to those of the "better sort." Both sides have their compelling points. Certainly, enlisted men who were poor were interested in economic gain. It is also true that poor people are entirely capable of having and being actuated by ideals. Both economic and ideological motives were important.

war. Military conflict exacerbated prewar animosities and facilitated the decision to take a side. Myriad groups were fighting to protect their vision of community, and it was not readily apparent whose ideas would triumph. Thus, rank-and-file Revolutionaries, loyalists, Indians, and slaves took up arms for comparable reasons. Soldiers were motivated by distinct ideologies that shared certain terms with elite discourse but varied greatly in substance. In this context, commitment to American independence or loyalty to Britain must be complicated by a broader exploration of motivation that situates these issues within American localism and competing identities.

Early War Motivations, 1775–1776

When the war commenced in 1775, Pennsylvanians dubbed their militia an "Association." The name was meant to convey continuity with the boycott organizations during the constitutional crisis. Eligibility for citizen-soldiery seamlessly developed as a wartime extension of popular colonial resistance movements. As was the case in the earlier political protests, common people provided the bulk of membership, making the association a potentially formidable military force. Non-association fines provided an easy way for the wealthy to avoid service in the ranks. Elites tended to seek officers' commissions, eschewing service in what they saw as the vulgar role of enlisted men. As a result, many poor people turned out for militia musters often simply because they had no alternative: they lacked the funds to pay a fine or hire a substitute. Nonetheless, once formed, the militia provided an important social and political forum for all enlisted men. In September 1775, Philadelphia militiamen formed the "Committee of Privates," an institution that was created in other counties in the province as well. The Committee was a quasi-political body of elected militiamen meant to protect both the military and civil rights of enlisted men. Committees of Privates from across the colony quickly became critics of the conservative provincial assembly and proponents of expanded franchise for the poor. Again, the very name—"Committee"—conveyed descent from the extralegal bodies formed during the constitutional crisis that were becoming de facto local governing bodies.[2]

---

2. See Alexander, "Pennsylvania's Revolutionary Militia," 15–19, on the militia and Rosswurm, *Arms, Country, and Class*, 66–72, on the Committee of Privates.

Thus, there were good reasons why the military spirit that swept all the colonies in 1775 made significant headway in Pennsylvania, where the conservative provincial government feared that war would lead to a full break with Britain. Associators were anxious to use their status as soldiers to combine their critiques of Britain with an agenda for change within Pennsylvania. Authorities who took a cautious stand in the war with Britain were the same politicians viewed as responsible for the underrepresentation of frontier regions and the disenfranchisement of many poorer colonists. Additionally, the militia soon became a body that could intimidate unpopular and previously dominant groups. In particular, Quakers who maintained a pacifistic neutrality during the war quickly drew the soldiers' ire. Many Pennsylvanians who lived much of their lives under the Friends' political domination eagerly sought to force the latter to support the war. In November 1775, the Philadelphia militia officers and the Committee of Privates demanded that Quaker pacifists contribute to the state's defense through non-association fines. Unable to resist the chance to ridicule the Friends, they further declared, "we cannot, but with astonishment, [view] the antiquated and absurd doctrine of passive obedience." Not only did the associators suggest that Quakers were not contributing sufficiently to the war, but they also portrayed their spiritual beliefs as alien to the new Revolutionary community. Significantly, the previously powerful were becoming marginal because of their refusal to participate in the military effort. Militia service seemed to offer a public forum through which to affect politics and alter the definition of community.³

Additionally, some members of the Philadelphia militia were motivated to serve by their urban, class-based reading of Whig political discourse. Many of the city's poorer residents hoped that military service would help them lay claim to political equality and equality of economic opportunity in a city where inequality was pronounced. Potential militiamen were attracted to a role that allowed them to criticize any selfish actions of the upper sort as unpatriotic. On October 26, 1775, the Committee of Privates vehemently condemned the wealthy for avoiding service. Their petition to the state government called unequivocally for a fair militia law. The privates also demanded equality of appearance in the ranks. They argued that if associators wore the affordable hunting shirt, "it will level all distinctions." Here was the "leveling" spirit that

3. For the Pennsylvania provincial government's initially conservative and cautious outlook on the war, see Lorett Treese, *The Storm Gathering: The Penn Family and the American Revolution* (University Park, Pa., 1992), 131–56. Militia declarations from *Pennsylvania Packet*, November 13, 1775.

Graydon dismissed as mindless class envy felt by the rabble. In reality, the privates' petition made an explicit connection between inequities in military service and class relations. The committee called on the city's wealthy to engage themselves as active members of the new Revolutionary community by sharing the militia burden. If they did not, the implication was that they would be identified as selfish—possibly treasonous—outsiders.[4]

Still, there was a significant distinction between serving with the associators and volunteering for the Continental army. Alexander Graydon was at least correct that the early part of the war was not a period in which many of the lower sorts in Pennsylvania rushed to engage in combat as members of the regular army. When it came to actually fighting the British at the risk of life and limb, enthusiasm waned. Few stepped forward in the war's early phases. Pennsylvanians were not immediately threatened by British actions in New England, and Philadelphians proved to be reluctant in assisting their neighbors to the north. The city, despite being a hub of communication and the seat of the Continental Congress, failed to send a significant number of men to the new Continental army. The only Pennsylvania battalion to march to camp in Cambridge, Massachusetts, for the siege of Boston was Thompson's Rifle Battalion, which was recruited from the central and western counties of the province. Philadelphians were clearly guarded in their initial response to the overall war effort. When General George Washington passed through Philadelphia on his way to Massachusetts, he was escorted by elements of city light horse and militia, "who went no farther than about five miles when they returned, but the former continued with them and how far they will go is uncertain." Although men were willing enough to join their neighbors in the camaraderie of militia muster, leaving their families and homes to fight hundreds of miles away was another matter.[5]

Interestingly, men from outside the southeastern part of the province reacted differently. They too formed associations, but, in contrast to Philadelphians, quite a number also volunteered for combat with the single Pennsylvania battalion in the Continental army. One possible reason was the close connection that many residents made between martial prowess and manliness. Adapting

---

4. *Pennsylvania Evening Post*, October 26, 1775, 489; "To the Associators of Philadelphia," May 18, 1775, Broadside, Library Company of Philadelphia (hereafter LCP).

5. David Hawke, *In the Midst of a Revolution* (Philadelphia, 1960), 55, discusses Pennsylvanians' anti–New England sentiment as a factor in their apathy toward the Revolutionary cause in the early phases of the war. On the regional origins of Thompson's Rifle Battalion, see Trussell, *Pennsylvania Line*, 28–29. The quotation on the militia is from *Pennsylvania Evening Post*, June 24, 1775.

aspects of Indian cultures that stressed the equation of masculinity and warrior status, these men were anxious to demonstrate their courage as soldiers. Indeed, the assertion of an Indianized warrior identity was pronounced among elements of Thompson's Rifle Battalion. As soldier John Joseph Henry noted, troops appeared dressed in hunting shirts, moccasins, and leggings. They were equipped with rifles, tomahawks, and scalping knives.[6]

Another factor that explains why men from areas beyond the centers of colonial power volunteered for Continental service in 1775 is that the frontier itself remained in an uneasy peace. The great bulk of eastern Indians remained neutral as hostilities broke out between the British and some of their colonists. Most Natives sought to do whatever was necessary to preserve their own independence, and in 1775, cultivating neutrality appeared to serve that aim. Neither the British nor the Revolutionaries wished to draw Native Americans into the conflict, as both hoped for a quick resolution to the war. The result was that a number of Indian groups enjoyed diplomatic and economic patronage from British authorities and from the Continental Congress. Congress, in particular, went out of its way to keep the most powerful northern Indian nations out of the war, using the very frontier diplomacy and gift-giving traditions deplored by many Revolutionaries. Richard Henry Lee, a delegate to Congress, knew that such matters were vital for the war effort. He noted with relief that "we are this day informed in Congress that the six Nations and Canada Indians are firmly disposed to observe a strict neutrality, and I think we shall endeavor to cultivate their friendship." In contrast, the British sought Indian neutrality but also considered open military alliance, often attempting to capitalize on Indian resentment of Anglo-American intrusions on their lands. Native Americans, however, would not be pushed into the war if it was not in their best interest. When, for example, the British official John Butler attempted to enlist Senecas to fight the Revolutionaries in 1776, the war leader Flying Crow responded, "It is true I am tall and strong but I will reserve my strength to strike those who injure [us]." Other groups were equally firm in warning both sides to stay out of their lands. In August 1776 Kiashuta, representing the Mingo, told Revolutionary officials at Fort Pitt, "we will not suffer either the English or Americans to march an army through our country. Should either attempt it, we shall forewarn them three times from the proceeding; but should they then persist, they must abide by the consequence." Significantly, Indians of the region revealed the same commitment to community in their potential motivations to

6. John Joseph Henry, "Journal of John Joseph Henry, 1775," *PA*, 2d ser., 15:65.

fight as their Revolutionary neighbors. Conversely, as long as the war did not spread directly to the frontier, European Americans from the region could afford to fight the British army elsewhere. And given the anger among these Pennsylvanians regarding British frontier policy, they might well have seen the imperial government as the most immediate obstacle to their own territorial expansion in the West.[7]

Meanwhile, the scope of the war was about to widen. As the conflict's first year drew to a close, British strategists realized that they had more than a localized insurrection on their hands. They planned to invade the middle colonies. A broader war promised further direct social disorder in Pennsylvania. Ominously, in December 1775, the royal governor of Virginia, Lord Dunmore, issued a proclamation that freed all slaves of rebel masters—if the slaves would fight for the British. Conceived as a military measure to help win the war, Dunmore and the subsequent British officers who maintained the policy inadvertently transformed the meaning of the Revolution for vast numbers of its participants. For slaves, it was an opportunity to free themselves from chattel bondage. The sheer numbers are staggering. While the standard estimate of free blacks and slaves who served with Revolutionary forces is about 5,000, recent scholarship estimates that between 80,000 and 100,000 slaves attempted to free themselves by running to the British lines over the course of the war. While the British never intended to attack the institution of slavery itself, their policies facilitated a massive slave revolt with profound effects upon the African American and European American communities.[8]

Despite having a comparatively small slave population, news of Dunmore's proclamation greatly affected Pennsylvania. Newspaper coverage of events in Virginia helped make slavery, race, and freedom Revolutionary issues in the province. On December 6, 1775, the *Pennsylvania Journal* published the entire text of the proclamation, preceded by a description of Virginia's royal governor: "Not in legions of horrid hell, can come a devil more damned in evils, to top Dunmore!" Another alarmist piece of news appeared in the *Pennsylvania Evening Post*, in which Lord Dunmore purportedly addressed "the Negroes and Tories of Pennsylvania." It stated that Dunmore intended to "open a safe passage to Philadelphia, where they propose to raise three regiments of black and white

---

7. Richard Henry Lee to George Washington, June 29, 1775, in *Letters of Delegates*, ed. Smith, 1:558; Flying Crow quoted in Calloway, *American Revolution in Indian Country*, 29; speech of Kiashuta printed in *Pennsylvania Gazette*, August 7, 1776.

8. On the numbers of African Americans who fought with the Revolutionaries and who fled to the British, see Gary B. Nash's introduction to Quarles's *Negro in the American Revolution*, xiii–xxiv.

loyal Tories to be officered by Negroes and whites." Such accounts were clearly meant to galvanize fears of social upheaval and threats to the racial hierarchy in Pennsylvania, and they served as propaganda tools and recruiting devices. The idea of white Tories and "Negroes" fighting side by side was menacing. The discussion suggested that while the British cause might be multiracial, the Revolutionary community was, first and foremost, "white." Thus, even non-slaveholders in Pennsylvania could begin to conceive of the war as a struggle to defend the prerogatives of "whiteness." White men who were little moved to fight the British army in Massachusetts might view the social upheaval in the neighboring Chesapeake as more menacing. Dunmore's policy, then, risked creating more armed rebels. Popular press accounts of the freeing of slaves were a double-edged sword, however. As residents discussed the stories, Pennsylvanian slaves became well informed of Dunmore's proclamation, which would affect their own actions when the British army arrived in the region.[9]

By 1776, the other escalation of the war by the British—the invasion of the middle colonies—was under way as well. This campaign spurred a noticeable increase in volunteers for military service among Pennsylvanians. Stirred by General Sir William Howe's landing in New York in the summer of 1776, men from Pennsylvania began to fear for the safety of their own locales. Many volunteered to help defend New York, with the plausible supposition that a British occupation of that region would lead to an invasion of their own state. In particular, the occupation of Philadelphia, the Continental capital, was assumed to be a primary enemy objective. Others with financial and personal connections to the neighboring regions of New Jersey and New York feared social dislocation even if the British did not enter Pennsylvania at all. Not surprisingly, far more southeastern Pennsylvanians stepped forward to fight than in the previous year. Francis Baird, George Nicholas, David Crosby, and John Weller, all residents of southeastern Pennsylvania, "volunteered" for their first tours of duty in the army. By August 1776, Colonel Andrew Kachlein of Bucks County declared that a new battalion was needed to accommodate all the volunteers invigorated by the "public spirit." After the British secured New York and were moving across New Jersey, Philadelphia-area soldiers were likely to reenlist for another tour, fearing that the war was getting uncomfortably close to their homes. Thomas Elton, for instance, a militia volunteer in the New York

9. *Pennsylvania Journal*, December 6, 1775, reprinted in *Diary of the American Revolution: From Newspapers and Original Documents*, ed. Frank Moore (New York, 1860), 1:160–61; *Pennsylvania Evening Post*, November 2, 1776, 550.

campaign, "immediately on being dismissed, enlisted" again into the Third Regiment of the Pennsylvania Flying Camp. Following that tour, he reenlisted and participated in the Battle of Trenton. Jacob Kreider, who volunteered earlier in 1776, offered his services again in December when he feared that "Howe was marching from New York towards Philadelphia." An observer remarked later in the year on how well the militia of Philadelphia and its immediate "environs" were turning out when there was such widespread fear of an attack by the British on Pennsylvania's capital.[10]

To the Pennsylvania troops already serving under Colonel Anthony Wayne at Ticonderoga in upstate New York, the news of British victories near New York City and their sweep across New Jersey caused great consternation. These soldiers, recruited primarily from rural southeastern Pennsylvania, made clear their desire to leave their present posts and protect their homes. Wayne informed General Philip Schuyler that his troops' "anxiety about their friends in the Jerseys and Pennsylvania makes them so impatient to be [led] to the assistance of their distressed country." Wayne implied that his men saw their "country" as Pennsylvania and, more specifically, the communities within the state from which they had come. While these Continental soldiers believed that participation in the war with Britain in general would protect their "country," they also felt that they could not remain where they were while the war came to their neighborhoods.[11]

Some men were even more profoundly localist in outlook than Wayne's troops and were steadfastly opposed to fighting outside their "country." They enlisted with the belief that their primary responsibility was to defend Pennsylvania only. Although New York and New Jersey were close, these soldiers would fight when the enemy actually encroached upon communities. Theodorus Scowden, for instance, enlisted in the Pennsylvania State Troops in 1776. His officers implored the soldiers to leave Pennsylvania to fight the British in order, ultimately, to protect the state. A few agreed to go, but Scowden and others refused. He explained that he was not "willing to do so as [it was] contrary to the terms of his enlistment." Those who were convinced to leave Pennsylvania often came to regret it. Long service away from home and the pos-

10. RWPF, files W3210, S4618, S12626, S22572; Memorial of Colonel Andrew Kachlein, Third Battalion Bucks County Associators, August 2, 1776, Records of Pennsylvania's Revolutionary Governments, 1775–1790 (hereafter PRG), microfilm, reel 10, frame 867; RWPF, files S22228, W10186; Samuel Morris to Samuel C. Morris, December 5, 1776, Strettel-Morris-Milligan Papers, LCP, folder 465.

11. Anthony Wayne to General Philip Schuyler, January 2, 1777, Anthony Wayne Papers, 2:46, Historical Society of Pennsylvania, Philadelphia, Pennsylvania (hereafter HSP).

sible exposure of their families to the enemy led a number of Pennsylvania troops simply to return home in 1776 after their officers violated enlistment promises that their service outside the state would be short. The soldiers informed state authorities that they "did not leave New York for cowardice but for bad usage and we are willing to fight to defend the province where we were enlisted for." Significantly, they explained that they were not abandoning what they believed to be the Revolutionary cause. Rather, they supported the immediate defense of their country, "the province."[12]

Authorities did eventually find that one way to get men to fight in neighboring states was to appeal to their gender identities. As in the constitutional crisis, calls for "manly resistance" to the British proved efficacious in mobilizing large numbers of ordinary men. Conversely, the men who reacted to such gendered discourse saw the promise in "manly" soldiering and hoped to connect such notions to citizenship. Many recruiting efforts, however, were intended to speak directly to protecting the sources of formal patriarchal authority: family and property. For example, officers of Thompson's Rifle Battalion told their men that if they did not reenlist, they risked "our towns laid in ashes and our innocent women and children driven from their peaceable habitations." Obviously, the war was far enough away from the men's "peaceable habitations" that they did not feel unduly alarmed, and this probably explains the lukewarm reception that the officers' pleas elicited. When hostilities moved to the Middle Atlantic, such invocations of "manly" protection of the soldiers' communities became a more potent recruiting measure. The Council of Safety enjoined eastern Pennsylvanians to turn out in 1776 to assist Washington in New Jersey. The Council declared that "a manly resistance" would "secure your property from being plundered, and . . . protect the innocence of our wives and children." The very real possibility of such occurrences was underscored by published narratives of British and Hessian misdeeds against property, women, and children in neighboring New Jersey. This framing of the need for soldiers appealed powerfully to common men's most immediate understanding of what constituted their community: family. Recruiters, essayists, and politicians all made clear that those who fought proved themselves worthy men. Thus, those who defended the community would in some measure determine who was part of it. Also, by explicitly referring to military service as a "manly" role and equating that behavior with patriotism, even soldiers without substantial property

12. RWPF, file S23893; Petition of Pennsylvania Soldiers Returned from New York, September [?] 1776, PRG, reel 10, frame 1052.

could begin to see their own informal gender identities transformed into relatively more institutional ones.[13]

Still, British military activities near the state and calls to "manly" resistance did not completely fill the ranks. Many poor and struggling middling-sort men could not afford to risk economic disaster for their families while serving. To meet their material needs, Pennsylvania authorities began the widespread offering of monetary and land bounties to recruits in 1776, a practice that continued throughout the rest of the war. Modest economic rewards in return for military service were not novel for an eighteenth-century army. When Pennsylvania employed bounties as a recruiting device, it bolstered enrollment in the ranks by making the risks of war somewhat more attractive to poor citizens. Common soldiers were concerned with protecting their communities and families, but the meager bounties helped take the place of sorely needed wages for the lower sort. A group of volunteers for the Pennsylvania Flying Camp demonstrated how important bounties were to them when, in August 1776, they simply "refused to march until they had received their bounties." While such payments rarely approximated the wages they might have made as civilians, they were necessary to ease the general financial dislocation caused by soldiering.[14]

Bounties of land rather than money often were a far more palatable reward for soldiers, especially those with farming backgrounds. Unlike money that was paid initially, land grants were issued after service, thus giving recruits a pecuniary interest in the outcome of the war. The promise of landownership was attractive as an avenue to economic and political independence. John Brown, for example, volunteered when he was promised "one hundred acres of land." John McElnay of York County recalled how land could overcome reluctance to leave local communities. He was a member of Miles's Rifle Regiment, a unit composed of Pennsylvania State Troops raised strictly for the defense of the Commonwealth. When the Pennsylvania government sought to send the unit to New York in 1776, McElnay noted that "as an inducement to go out of

13. Orders: October 26, 1775, Orderly Book of Thompson's Rifle Battalion, HSP; Broadside, Pennsylvania Council of Safety, December 23, 1776, Strettel-Morris-Milligan Papers, LCP, folder 462. For an example of soldiers' familiarity with the myriad atrocity stories about British actions toward women and children in New Jersey, see Anthony Wayne to Richard Stockton, January 3, 1777, Wayne Papers, 2:52, HSP, in which Wayne speaks of the soldiers' knowledge of the British "treating helpless women [and children] in a manner shocking to humanity."

14. Jacob S. Howell to "the Honorable Commissions appointed by the Convention of Pennsylvania to form the Flying Camp," August 19, 1776, Sol Feinstone Collection, DLAR, entry 566.

state, [the men] were promised land equal to the regular troops." The young private was one of many who took the offer and marched across the Delaware.[15]

The militia draft system spoke to additional economic motivations as well. The Pennsylvania militia law of 1777 regulated service by providing eight classes of troops who were drafted in rotation. The law also provided for substitutes to go in the draftees' stead. Those with the financial resources to do so often hired men to serve in their place. Substitution fees provided numbers of poor men with material reasons for serving throughout the rest of the war. The practice was widespread enough in Philadelphia to spawn a lucrative business. Henry Boyer stated that "in July 1777, he was engaged by a man who kept an office for employing substitutes in Arch near Front Street to go as a substitute for a Quaker in a Southwark militia company." Boyer exemplified those who made a career of sorts out of substitution. He served two more tours in the place of other men.[16]

Draftees were also permitted to send family members in their place. This provision spoke to the financial interests of heads of households. In an era when most production centered in familial households, sending younger sons or brothers allowed older, more experienced members of the household to remain at home. Protection of family farm prosperity was especially important during the harvest, when skilled farmers could ill afford to be absent. Examples of such substitutions abound. Young Peter Kessler of Northampton County served as a substitute for his father during the 1778 harvest season. Seventeen-year-old Peter Krumbine of Lancaster County went in place of his father, Leonard, in 1777. Henry Ream fought at White Marsh and Brandywine while serving for his father. Samuel Quigley marched with the Cumberland County militia in place of his father. Jacob Shaffer was twice a substitute for his father. Christian Specht "was a substitute for my brother, Peter Specht." In September 1777, Bucks County resident James Nathan "entered the militia of the United States as a substitute in the place of his brother John." Angus McCoy, who had "no family at that time," explained that "I volunteered and served a tour of military duty in the room or place of my brother, William McCoy, who had charge of a family." Among such substitutes, economic motivation was not purely individualistic but rather reflected some level of self-sacrifice for a greater familial good.[17]

15. RWPF, files S22145, S2788.
16. On the provisions of the 1777 militia law and the social class of Philadelphia substitutes, see Rosswurm, *Arms, Country, and Class*, 135–38, 143; RWPF, file S22129.
17. RWPF, files W2127, S23756, S23863, S4746, S22979, S4873; Dann, *The Revolution Remembered*, 310–11.

During the period of increased need for soldiers in 1776, servants and apprentices, too, flocked to the army for economic and other reasons. In earlier colonial wars, servants represented a rich resource for recruiters in the province. The prospect of wages, bounties, and a nominal state of "freedom" for these unfree laborers was attractive. During the Revolution, such material rewards were coupled with the promise of furthering a cause that could well destabilize conventional social hierarchies. As Americans declared independence as a principle for which they were fighting, many bound laborers understood the term in a way particular to their class. Independence in a social context meant a state in which an individual was free of social and economic dependence on others. For unhappy servants and apprentices who resented their masters, participation in the war represented both a patriotic recourse and an abrupt change in their status. The flow of Pennsylvania servants into the armies throughout the war suggests the level of dissatisfaction with their civilian positions. In 1776, Benjamin Crofts, a Philadelphia painter, complained that his apprentice was enlisted into the service without his permission. Later that year, Benjamin Chew sought the return of his nineteen-year-old servant, John Badger, who "intends to enlist himself." Thomas Dunn, a city tanner, lost his servant (who had already once before "been in the Continental service"). Samuel Dotter of Berks County "left his master and enlisted into the service of his country in the Continental Army." Others were very young men or even children who were probably seeking adventure in addition to the promise of gaining some money and escaping their servitude. Typical was a twelve-year-old Pennsylvania servant who "went off with the Maryland troops." In October 1776, two young city apprentices, probably close friends, ran off together to the military. Young John Mitford, his master believed, quit his status as a servant for a new vocation: "It is supposed his great fondness for fifing has induced him to go off." In 1777, Robert Thornton, an apprentice shoemaker, left occupied Philadelphia. His master angrily noted that "it is supposed his father has taken him to the rebel army, as they were seen going off together." Thornton used the army to escape his apprenticeship, but—by entering the military with his father—he also reestablished direct family ties severed when he entered his master's household.[18]

18. Petition of Benjamin Crofts, January 16, 1776, PRG, reel 10, frame 238; *Pennsylvania Evening Post,* June 8, 1776, 288; *Pennsylvania Ledger,* July 20, 1776; RWPF, file S22735; *Pennsylvania Ledger,* July 27, 1776 and October 19, 1776; *Pennsylvania Evening Post,* April 11, 1776, 183; *Pennsylvania Ledger,* December 10, 1777.

In some areas, the flow of servants into the military was so great that it threatened to disrupt the local economy and notions of social order. These servants obviously saw communal well-being in slightly different terms. Bound workers in Chester County responded well to regular army recruiters in early 1776. Apparently some officers made promises to protect the freedom of recruits from masters who tried to reclaim their servants. Residents complained that Captain Vernon of the Pennsylvania Line enlisted a number of indentured servants "knowing them to be such; gave them cockades and . . . encouraged them to return to him if their masters attempted to correct them . . . [and] he would protect them." Even if officers promised protection, however, masters were legally entitled to recover their laborers. Punishment for absconded servants was often severe in order to discourage the subsequent repetition of rebellious acts. Still, while the promise of better economic status was one element of why apprentices and servants enlisted, liberty from servitude, risky as it could be, was often another.[19]

Recruiting officers often further strengthened their hands by working in taverns, which were centers of social interaction in all regions of the state. They employed a strategy of mixing alcohol, bounty offers, and masculine posturing. Alexander Graydon had his recruiting party meet at a city tavern and made sure that a "number of fellows . . . drank freely of our liquor." While judgment could be impaired by inebriation, this was not the only reason that taverns proved so fruitful for enlistments. As spaces where ordinary men discussed the great political issues of their day, officers could urge speakers to act upon their convictions. Additionally, taverns were places where physical prowess, central to lower-sort views of masculinity, was discussed and enacted. Here recruiters could emphasize connections between manliness and martial prowess in the military. Many veterans openly admitted that they enlisted in taverns, suggesting that they were neither tricked into service nor embarrassed by the circumstances in which they volunteered. Justus Stericher, for example, enlisted "at a tavern, sign of the Buck, in the city of Philadelphia." John and Jacob McVaugh entered the Continental army at "Fulton's Tavern." Moses Moreland joined the regular army "at a public house, sign of the hat."[20]

Thus, by the second year of the war, combinations of material rewards, threats to immediate locales, appeals to gender identity, and offers of potential change in social status drew men to the "patriot cause." Perhaps most significant,

19. William Montgomery et al. to Pennsylvania Council of Safety, February 12, 1776, Wayne Papers, 1:26, HSP.

20. *Alexander Graydon's Memoirs*, 133; RWPF, files S41189, R6815, S7215, S22411.

however, was the solidifying of a coherent Revolutionary ideology in 1776 among the state's poorer residents. The ascendancy of political radicals—drawn from the artisanal and other middling classes—in the state government led to the passage of one of the most democratic constitutions that the English-speaking world had yet seen. The state's Committee of Privates had been instrumental in undermining the conservative, elite-dominated Provincial Assembly in 1776. In June, the members of the Committee of Privates essentially argued that they would not recognize the sovereignty of a body that did not directly represent them. They protested the old assembly's appointment of militia brigadier generals, stating, "Many of the associators have been excluded by this very house from voting for the members now composing it, though this house was applied to on their behalf, and therefore they are not represented in this house. . . . [Also] the counties which have the greatest number of associators have not a proportional representation, and therefore cannot be considered as having an equal voice in the nomination." Here was the articulation of lower-sort and regional critiques of provincial government dating back to the 1760s. As soldiers and members of a powerful political committee, the privates had a public sphere in which to try to redefine the body politic. As the privates suggested, they had long advocated an extension of franchise. The militia was eventually successful in pressuring the assembly to expand voting rights to all associators who paid taxes. The result was the election of a radical conference that declared Pennsylvania's support for the colonies' independence and set up a constitutional convention. Common people found this new frame of government encouraging, because it offered greater hope for direct participation in their own governance. The Pennsylvania Constitution of 1776 provided for a unicameral legislature open to public scrutiny and an executive branch whose power was diffused among members of a Supreme Executive Council. Moreover, the new government purposefully excluded opponents of the radicals and pacifist nemeses of militiamen by demanding an oath of allegiance to the new constitution for all public servants. The promise of greater political participation energized the middling and lower sorts in the state. Poor artisans, farmers, and workers benefited from voting. Westerners quickly sought to gain proportionate power in the state legislature. Participation in the militia and other military service now demonstrated support for the radical order that was firmly committed to independence and to the prosecution of the war.[21]

21. "The Protest of the Committee of Privates," *Pennsylvania Ledger,* June 22, 1776. Hawke, *In the Midst of a Revolution,* 170–73, 184, explains the role of the Committee of Privates in expanding franchise

These events in Pennsylvania coincided with the push for national independence. Occurring at almost the same time as the publication of Thomas Paine's *Common Sense* and the Declaration of Independence, the internal revolution in Pennsylvania attracted scores of common people to the larger Revolutionary cause. These events—the war, military service, national independence, and constitutional and social change—were conflated in the minds of ordinary Pennsylvanians. An understanding of Revolutionary ideology as friendly to the class and local interests of those who were most liable to military duty, coupled with a significant military threat to the region, spurred them to volunteer. Not surprisingly, many recalled entering the war to oppose the British invasion of New York shortly after they heard the Declaration of Independence. John Adlum volunteered after hearing a reading of the document in York County. Jacob Stahley explained, "I resided at Philadelphia in the year 1776 and on the 4th day of July that year, being the day of the Declaration of American Independence, I entered into the service of the United States by signing the association at Philadelphia." Similarly, Robert Scott dated his enlistment July 4, 1776. Griffith Smith, an unfree apprentice, stated that "immediately after the Declaration of Independence," he joined the militia. Actually, most people heard of the Declaration after the fourth of July, which suggests that the date subsequently took on symbolic significance in collective memory. Nonetheless, independence was an important concept to them, one that they rendered relevant to their own lives.[22]

At the center of the convergence of military service and political activism stood the radical Pennsylvania militia privates, especially those in Philadelphia. By 1776, it was clear that they expected the upper sort to share with them both the burden of local defense and the forum of politics. In fact, even associators who could not vote believed that liability to public service entitled them to a public voice and some measure of authority. The Philadelphia Committee of Privates, furthermore, had their say on whom the state should commission as officers in the regular army, declaring that only "those who manifest the most sincere and warm attachment to the cause of liberty," as they

and undermining the respectability of the old state government and the development of the rhetoric of class politics under the new constitution. Wood, *Creation of the American Republic,* 226–37, discusses the radically democratic nature of the 1776 Pennsylvania Constitution and its new frame of government. Brunhouse, *Counter-Revolution in Pennsylvania,* 18, explains the consolidation of radical power and the exclusion of antiradicals by the test oath.

22. Adlum, *Memoirs,* 14; Dann, *The Revolution Remembered,* 116; RWPF, files W3472, W3305, W3467.

defined it, should be appointed. The militia had no formal right to make demands regarding how the state would meet its commitment to the Continental army, but the boldness of the privates' declaration suggests how informally powerful this group had become. Such a voice for poor men—those who had never before had any formal political "say"—undoubtedly made militia service attractive for the disenfranchised. The city's militiamen were also consulted on their views about whether independence should be declared in the summer of 1776. They were, as usual, vocal and not intimidated by their officers. The *Pennsylvania Evening Post* reported on June 11, 1776: "Yesterday the grand question of independence was proposed to the First, Second, Fourth and Fifth Battalions of Associators of the city and suburbs. . . . The lieutenant colonel of the Third Battalion refusing to put the question, gave great umbrage to the men, one of whom replied to him in a genteel, spirited manner: 'How our delegates in Congress may act, we know not, though we have a right to know and intend to promote an inquiry for that purpose.'" The Philadelphia Committee of Privates also expressed its sentiments about the framing of the Pennsylvania Constitution, arguing that in such important matters, "great and overgrown rich men will be improper to be trusted." The militia was on the forefront of attacking the colonial system of social deference. They redefined the community by acting as crucial arbiters of the meaning of Revolutionary ideology. They were in a unique position (with the threat of force of arms) of defining who was a proper citizen in the new republic and who was not.[23]

The same process of politicization was occurring among poor men in rural areas as well. They, too, came to the war invigorated by the ascent of the radicals and their constitution. The promise of broader franchise and proportional representation led these soldiers to create a democratized and egalitarian militia. In Cumberland County, the enlisted men who composed the Committee of Privates submitted a petition to the government that not only called for the usual election of officers but also demanded equality among officers and men in terms of discipline. They further sought to penalize wealthy citizens who avoided their fair share of military duty. The troops contended that without these proposed amendments to the militia law, "the liberties of the Privates of the Association appear to be, in great measure, taken away." In June 1776, the Northampton County Associators expressed their political convictions when they voted in favor of a new constitutional convention and declared the old

23. *Pennsylvania Packet*, February 19, 1776; *Pennsylvania Evening Post*, June 11, 1776, 291; Broadside of the Philadelphia Committee of Privates, 1776, LCP.

conservative state government incompetent. That Northampton was one of the growing and underrepresented counties in the province was probably a major force behind the militia's desire to replace the old government.[24]

Soldiers were aware that the militia offered them an opportunity to remake politics in a way that responded to their class interests. When a company of Cumberland County militiamen who were denied a pay advance refused to march, local official Benjamin Blyth accused the men of breaking the law. The troops responded that "justice and equity were on the side of people getting a month's pay," adding that "justice and equity ought to take place before the law." The animating principle of equality to which these common soldiers steadfastly clung was undoubtedly one of the principles that led them to military service in the first place. Similarly, when the state paid two classes of Philadelphia militiamen only part of their bounty for a tour of duty, the troops made the dispute a matter of principle. An official reported that "they say that all justice and equity will give [the bounty to] them." Although monetary compensation was the focal point of the issue, both militia groups' use of the terms "justice" and "equity" reveals a specifically class-based Revolutionary ideological milieu.[25]

The development of a coherent ideology that fused the internal revolution in Pennsylvania with the cause of American independence in 1776 led to more clearly delineated Revolutionary communities in the state. Obviously, one aspect of this transformation was the enlargement of the formal body politic via the broadening of franchise and the militia's growing politicization. The flip side of this process was both a growing opposition to these changes and the designation of those who disagreed with the new radical order as "outsiders." In other words, while the community was expanding for some people, it was necessarily contracting for others. Those generically labeled "Tories" often were simply constructing counter-hegemonic models of society. As the war continued, it became increasingly difficult for these people to fit into the new notions of community. Henry Juncken, for example, believed that his class status in Reading led the militia to label him a "Tory." Juncken stated that he was "a victim in the early times of the rebellion," because "my misfortune is that I was a popular person possessed of an independent fortune." Often more alienated from

24. "A Petition from the Privates of the First Battalion of Militia in the County of Cumberland," *PA*, 2d ser., 14:470; "Proceedings of a Meeting of the Second Battalion of Northampton Associators," *Pennsylvania Evening Post*, June 1, 1776.

25. Benjamin Blyth to President Joseph Reed, August 6, 1781, PRG, reel 18, frame 919; Sub-Lieutenant George Smith to Joseph Reed, December 20, 1779, PRG, reel 15, frame 627.

the Revolutionary regime than literally loyal to Britain, these people increasingly were pushed into arms against the "patriots." Earlier, in 1775, those who were identified as Tories were usually true loyalists. They supported imperial policies through the 1760s and 1770s and disdained colonial resistance; typically, these loyalists were royal officials who owed their careers directly to authorities in Britain. By 1776, however, the ranks of open loyalists would expand to include many other persons who, during the constitutional crisis, saw themselves as Whigs and were alienated by the course of the war, the radical state government, conditions in Pennsylvania, or independence.[26]

The decision to take up arms against the Revolutionaries was a very dangerous one. Because the Revolutionaries controlled the state and local governments in 1776, there was essentially no alternative to leaving home and running to British lines. The British took possession of relatively nearby New York City and parts of New Jersey in the second half of 1776, and joining the British forces was becoming at least a plausible course of action for Pennsylvanians alienated from the new regime. Still, the risks were great. Acts of treason or seditious speech were punishable by imprisonment. Occupied New York was a considerable distance from Pennsylvania. Loyalists who did travel there left their entire lives behind. A less draconian choice for those defined as potentially treasonous outsiders in their neighborhoods was to leave voluntarily for other regions of the state where they hoped to avoid being forced to take sides. Many chose this safer option. Thomas Majoribank, a Philadelphia baker, "became so obnoxious to the rebels that he was prevented carrying on his trade as usual and removed himself and family out of Philadelphia where he thought to reside in peace without taking up arms." Thomas Yorke fled his native Philadelphia for the countryside in November 1776 "till matters were a little subsided in the city." Joshua Thomas, a farmer from Northampton County who later joined the British army, recalled that he "was obliged to live in the woods." Thomas Hood, another Philadelphian, fled the entire state in October 1776 "to avoid taking an active part on the side of the Americans."[27]

Growing numbers, though, simply fled to British lines in 1776, which was probably the surest way to escape persecution as the "Whig" definition of community continued to become more exclusive. Those who were previously

---

26. American Loyalist Claims Commission Papers, 1780–1835, Public Records Office, Great Britain, Audit Office 13 (hereafter AO13)/71/136.
27. See Henry J. Young, "Treason and Its Punishment in Revolutionary Pennsylvania," *PMHB* 90 (1966): 287–313; AO13/26/280, AO12/38/126, AO12/40/242, AO13/70A/475.

full members of colonial society—and even prominent in their opposition to imperial taxation policy—were regarded with profound suspicion if they did not openly embrace the militia, the new state constitution, or independence. Gideon Vernon, a Chester County farmer who later became an officer in a loyalist unit, recalled how his disdain for the growing democratization of Pennsylvania led to his becoming "obnoxious to the rebel party." He dated his alienation from the Revolutionary community to the moment when he "object[ed] to an alteration proposed by the popular party in the day for choosing sheriffs, assembly men, and other officers." William Hooper, a delegate to the Continental Congress, noted that the radical Pennsylvania Constitution "made more Tories than the whole treasury of Britain could have done." Suddenly, moderate Whigs were defined as Tories. Those who opposed the emerging ideals of revolution in Pennsylvania were informally harassed by their neighbors (if not formally arrested). John Meredith finally left his Bucks County home because of "persecution of the rebel states, [and] he was obliged to take refuge within the British lines at New York." But British lines would soon come to Pennsylvania, and the situation for both Revolutionaries and loyalists changed dramatically.[28]

War Comes to Pennsylvania: Motivation and the British Invasion

The years 1777–78 proved to be the high-water mark for common Pennsylvanians' armed involvement in the Revolution. A British invasion of the southeastern portion of the Commonwealth, the outbreak of bitter war on the frontier, and the escalation of civil war among Pennsylvanians combined to affect almost all residents in some manner. Those who had heretofore been not much moved by British actions in New York and New Jersey, intrigued by the promise of economic gain, or energized by the state's internal revolution were hard-pressed to avoid participation by late 1777. Meanwhile, veterans of previous campaigns found the disorders of war that they had witnessed in other states near their homes. Among those who opposed the Revolution in the state were some who hoped that the presence of the British army would lead to the reestablishment of a society in which they would no longer be considered outsiders. They took up arms as an unprecedented opportunity presented itself.

28. AO12/40/277; William Hooper to Joseph Hewes, October 27, 1776, *Letters of Delegates*, ed. Smith, 5:410; AO12/38/152, AO12/42/350, AO12/40/171.

The British invasion and subsequent occupation of Philadelphia in the autumn and winter of 1777 spurred numerous southeastern Pennsylvanians to military service. A Philadelphian remarked that "the people in general seem determined to oppose [the invasion] with vigor." Sir William Howe, the British commander, corroborated this impression during the initial phases of the invasion: he noted that most people in the region "seem to be, excepting a few individuals, strongly in enmity against us, many haven taken up arms." Indeed, men from the region spent the bulk of their Revolutionary military service fighting against the forces of the Crown threatening the immediate area. John Frailey "entered the Continental service as a volunteer" in August 1777, the very time when Howe's invasion force landed near Chester County. Andrew Shuster volunteered and fought at Brandywine and Germantown. Thomas Elton recalled, "I was then selected as a pilot for Sterling's [sic] Division because I knew the country having been raised in Germantown." Jacob Kreider went out to protect his native Philadelphia as a newly elected militia ensign in the Brandywine and Germantown campaigns. Andrew Keen "equipped himself as a volunteer light horseman . . . while the British remained in Philadelphia." Young Henry Yeager volunteered three times for the defense of the Delaware River in Billingsport. Jacob Sparre, who resided just outside the city, stated that "after the Battle of Brandywine . . . he volunteered . . . to oppose the British as they were coming to Philadelphia." Groups of men who were not even called upon to fight formed militia units as the main British army moved into their neighborhoods. The Pennsylvania government noted, "some of the militia from the southern part of [Chester County], apprehending danger from the enemy, and, in numbers sufficient to form two companies, embodied themselves to prevent any inroad of the enemy." Men from outlying towns feared that in addition to occupying the state's capital, the British might threaten their areas as well. Jacob Long of Lancaster County enlisted "as one of the guard conveying twenty-two loads of powder from Lancaster to Reading . . . which was sent through dread that the British would come to Lancaster."[29]

Once again, Revolutionary authorities employed gendered discourse to facilitate recruitment. With the British operating in the state, exhortations to manly resistance were met with far more enthusiasm than before. Homes and

29. Alexander Nesbit to John Lardner, July 10, 1777, Lardner Family Papers, HSP; General Sir William Howe to Lord George Germain, August 30, 1777, in *Documents of the American Revolution, 1770–1783 (Colonial Office Series)*, ed. K. G. Davies (Dublin, Ireland, 1976), 14:181; RWPF, files S3364, S3898, S22228, W10186, S22343; Dann, *The Revolution Remembered*, 158–59; RWPF, files S23911, S22527; Supreme Executive Council to Chester County Lieutenants, September 4, 1777, PRG, reel 12, frame 953; RWPF, file W3434.

families were actually at stake. In the face of Howe's landing at Head of Elk in Maryland and the impending march on Philadelphia, officers harped upon the need for masculine resistance against a cruel enemy in order to protect property and womanhood in southeastern Pennsylvania. They motivated their men by declaring, "now then is the time for our strenuous exertions; one bold stroke will free the land from rapine, devastation, and burnings and female innocence from brutal lust and violence." Similarly, the Pennsylvania government urged the militia to turn out in language that was rich in appeals to the soldiers' sense of masculinity: "[A] manly effort on the part of our militia will be . . . effectual in destroying the remainder of the King of England's army now under the command of General Howe in Philadelphia, the capital of this commonwealth. . . . If we sit supinely and suffer our enemies to possess our capital without one manly effort for its relief, how disgraceful, how destructive this will be." Ironically, these pleas for manly protection of the community may have worked too well—to the later detriment of recruitment. As the campaign wore on, the British captured Philadelphia and actively raided its surrounding communities. The shocking American defeats at the Battles of Brandywine and Germantown led many men to take the economic and physical threat to their homes and families so seriously that they simply left the army and headed home. Others refused to muster when called. These actions were not necessarily what Pennsylvania Supreme Executive Council President Thomas Wharton called "backward." The soldiers' refusal to join the main army after the enemy had successfully taken over the region was, rather, a logical outcome of their localism: protecting property and families that were vulnerable to the occupying army.[30]

As the occupation continued, however, resentment toward the actions of the British army provided a new source of motivation for Philadelphians to enlist against them. The British army's violence, foraging, damage to property, abuse of civilians, and attempts to intimidate rebels pushed many into the Revolutionary cause. Charles Wallace of Chester County had good reason for personal animus toward the British. After serving a tour of militia duty in Bucks County in February 1778, Wallace and his company were headed home when "he with many others of the company were taken prisoner by a company of the British Dragoons." Wallace recounted how his father, also serving in the militia party, "was with him when the Dragoons came, [and] sought safety in the

30. *Pennsylvania Packet*, September 9, 1777; Circular to the Lieutenants of Several Counties, PRG, reel 12, frame 1280; President Wharton to George Washington, September 12, 1777, PRG, reel 12, frame 1047.

woods. That a Sergeant of the Dragoons (they were called the 17th Light Dragoons) perceiving him, made pursuit and came up with him. The old man, for he was aged, being unarmed, endeavored to avoid the blows of the Dragoons man by dodging around a tree, but eventually was mortally wounded." His father finally died after eight days of agony, and young Wallace underwent harsh treatment while a prisoner in Philadelphia. As soon as he was released, Wallace volunteered in the Ninth Pennsylvania Regiment as a regular soldier, "moved with a spirit of revenge for the death of his father and for barbarous usage while prisoner." Additionally, the British forces inflicted damage to property, threatening to alienate enemies, neutrals, and friends of the Crown alike. Seeking propaganda value from such actions, the Pennsylvania Packet prominently reported the British army's "indiscriminate destruction of Whig and Tory property . . . [which has] increased the resentment of their old enemies and turned the hearts of their friends." Sir William Howe himself feared that when his troops took "property of several of his majesty's loyal subjects" that Tories in the surrounding countryside might become angry enough to refuse support.[31]

Some southeastern Pennsylvanians, however, were so thoroughly alienated from the "patriot" community that the British occupation of Philadelphia, despite its disorders, emboldened them to take up arms. Tories in the city of Philadelphia no longer had to leave their families and property behind to get to British lines. Howe immediately attempted to make loyalism as attractive as possible to a broad range of Pennsylvanians who might have been disaffected from the Revolutionary cause. In October 1777, upon taking possession of Philadelphia, he declared military protection for loyalists and pardons for Revolutionary soldiers who took loyalty oaths. For many Philadelphians, this was the long-awaited opportunity to take up arms against the neighbors who had previously persecuted them. George Drummond, a Philadelphia customs officer, endured "every situation of distress, insult, persecution, and imprisonment until the arrival of Sir William Howe in the year 1777 at which time he joined the army under his command." Nathan Roberts "remained at his father's house until the British army arrived at Philadelphia when he joined them." Alexander McDonald, who had earlier left the city for the frontier to avoid harassment, returned home to fight when the British arrived.[32]

31. RWPF, file W2286; *Pennsylvania Packet,* July 4, 1778; Proclamation of Sir William Howe, British Headquarters Papers, 1747–1783, microfilm, Public Records Office, Great Britain, item 1042, B1.
32. Howe's declaration in *Pennsylvania Evening Post,* October 11, 1777; AO13/71/57, AO12/40/217–18, AO12/40/229.

Men from the area surrounding Philadelphia fled to British lines to become active loyalists as well. Their decision was somewhat more risky, because they left their families behind and their property was immediately subject to confiscation. A new treason act passed by the radicals in early 1777 subjected any armed Tory not only to imprisonment and property confiscation but perhaps also, if captured, to death. Yet many believed that British control of the entire state was at hand. Again, most were persons heavily persecuted by the Revolutionary regime. John Howell's Bucks County farm "was despoiled and plundered of his principal furniture, horses, cattle, and other stock and [illegible] dispossessed of his farm by which he with his wife and family were reduced to great distress and he was compelled for the safety of his person to fly within the British lines at Philadelphia." Isaac Gray of Lancaster ran to the British in Philadelphia after "suffering much from the tyranny of the rebels." Peter Partier, a small Bucks County farmer, explained that he "joined the British army in April 1777 after suffering grievous persecutions and abuses and he immediately enlisted as a private soldier in the 2d battalion of New Jersey Volunteers." Evan Griffith, a Quaker from York County, was so harried by his neighbors that he eventually joined the British Quartermaster General Department in 1778. He conveyed that "it was ever his inclination to join the British, for he could not live at home in peace."[33]

As civil war developed in the region, vengeance became a motivating factor for both sides. Revolutionaries often suggested that they fought specifically to suppress their Tory neighbors. The Pennsylvania government warned General Washington that upon his reoccupation of Philadelphia, "there is reason to apprehend that the provocations which have been given by some of the inhabitants of that city, may have excited a spirit of revenge in the minds of their insulted and abused countrymen." George Simmers specifically recalled volunteering in 1777 for the purpose of "keeping down the Tories." John Hill of Bucks County (who had to be drafted for two previous tours outside Pennsylvania) described how he guarded "the road near Philadelphia to prevent the Tories and others from supplying the enemy with provisions." Hill went out of his way to state, "My services of this time were entirely voluntary and patriotic." Jacob Van Artsalen volunteered at Newtown in Bucks County "to suppress the Tories." William Denniston of Chester County "volunteered in a scouting

---

33. On the 1777 Pennsylvania treason law and punishments for treasonous acts, see Henry Young, "Treason and Its Punishment," 293–95; AO13/70A/482, AO12/40/118–20, AO12/40/295, AO12/42/198–200.

party ... after the Tories." Among loyalists, rebel actions provoked similar responses. In March 1778, a loyalist newspaper reported that exasperated Pennsylvanians "are forming themselves into companies of Volunteers, with a determined resolution to have satisfaction for the unprovoked injuries and cruelties they have sustained" from rebel forces.[34]

Like the Revolutionaries, the British offered common Pennsylvanians economic rewards to facilitate service to the Crown. New loyalist recruits were typically promised "full bounty." In the early phases of the invasion, the British offered rewards for intelligence. James Jeremiah Rice, a tavern keeper, was paid to spy on the American forces and later became a member of the New Jersey (Loyalist) Volunteers. John Jackson remembered that the "day before Brandywine [he] was desired by [Joseph] Galloway to reconnoiter and offered 60 guineas for it." The British also appealed to less affluent Pennsylvanians' notions of masculinity and hopes for economic self-sufficiency. "Spirited fellows" who enlisted in the First Battalion of Pennsylvania Loyalists were offered "50 acres of land, where every gallant hero may retire and enjoy his bottle and lass." Others were drawn into service to the Crown in the hopes of furthering their careers. John Laycock, a journeyman house carpenter, improved his lot in life as he "joined the British army upon their coming to Philadelphia and worked in the Navy Yard." David Tomson similarly found work "as King's carpenter while his majesty's ships lay in the Delaware." Concessions to the Pennsylvanians' localism were used in conjunction with material rewards to solidify Tory support for the British in Philadelphia. Those who agreed to serve on the river galley *Philadelphia*, for example, were promised that it was "for the better defense of the city" and that they would not be forced to leave the area or serve on any other British vessels "contrary to their inclinations."[35]

With the British army in Philadelphia and growing numbers of Tories taking up arms with them, an emerging ideological critique of the Revolutionaries spurred further opposition to the new regime. Capitalizing upon popular Anglo-American Whig anti-taxation sentiment, Tories began appealing to those who felt oppressed by the radical Pennsylvania government's financial and military impositions on citizens. Bernard Page, for instance, appealed to his fellow loyalists to fight because "we are loaded with enormous and ruinous

34. Supreme Executive Council to General Washington, May 27, 1778, PRG, reel 14, frame 134; RWPF, files S22511, W5298, W3894, W2924; *Pennsylvania Evening Post*, March 18, 1778; AO13/70A/482.
35. British Recruiting Broadside, 1778, LCP; AO12/100/356, AO12/40/52; British Recruiting Broadside, 1777, LCP; AO12/101/33, AO12/38/262; British Navy Recruiting Broadside, 1778, LCP.

taxes," arguing that those who joined the British war effort "shall not be subject to any taxes but such as shall be imposed by [our]selves." Page used the traditional colonial argument regarding taxation and representation to bolster the ranks of Tories. Tory newspapers sought to exploit the supposed hypocrisy of the Revolutionary cause as well. In 1778, the *Royal Gazette* noted that the country ironically endured "a burthen of taxes more grievous than she ever even apprehended that Great Britain would have attempted to impose upon her." During the same year, an essay in the *Pennsylvania Evening Post* attempted to mobilize Tory sentiment by pointing out the clear class injustice in the militia burden, portraying Revolutionary leaders as greedy. The author decried those who sent "into eternity so great a number of souls to gratify their thirst after wealth and power." Tories successfully coopted the common Whig discourse for their own purposes. Pennsylvania loyalists appealed to the disaffected by arguing that rebel tyranny destroyed British liberty: "A people in the enjoyment of more liberty and happiness than existed in any other spot on the globe, they have deluded by these unmanly artifices from a state of peace, plenty and freedom to that of WAR, WANT and INEXPRESSIBLE TYRANNY." Such beliefs reflected those of rank-and-file loyalists who believed that tyrannical rebels had destroyed the liberty they had previously enjoyed as members of the community. David Jones, a Philadelphia brewer, decried the "American tyranny and oppression" that led to the persecution of his wife and children who remained after the British left the city.[36]

The British also masterfully manipulated religious, ethnic, and racial tensions in Pennsylvania to their own advantage. Among the primarily Protestant Pennsylvanians in the Wyoming Valley, Bernard Page drew upon anti-Catholicism in his calls to oppose the Revolutionaries. He decried the American alliance with the French, "our popish enemies—the inveterate enemies of our religion and liberties." In Philadelphia, however, the British tried to raise a loyalist regiment that "consist[ed] of natives of Ireland, and of firm and faithful Catholics," by portraying the Revolutionaries as intolerant Protestants. The *Pennsylvania Evening Post* argued that "the common people [in the Catholic Irish community] are exceedingly inveterate against the puritanic descendants of the republicans, who under Cromwell, Ireton, etc. committed so many barbarities upon their ancestors." New Jersey Royal Governor William Franklin also sought to make a connection between the American rebels and the English Puritan army

36. AO13/71, pt. 2/17; *Royal Gazette*, May 30, 1778; *Pennsylvania Evening Post*, February 12, 1778 and January 3, 1778; AO13/71/122.

that devastated Ireland, calling Oliver Cromwell the Revolutionaries' "favorite hero" due in part to his "suppressing what was called a rebellion in Ireland." It is doubtful that many Irish Catholics saw the British as friendly to their homeland or interests, but a number of them could well have been apprehensive about the rise of so many Ulster Irish Presbyterians to prominent positions in the radical Pennsylvania government. Concerned with the protection of their immediate community, when these Irish Catholics were drawn into the war, they sided with what presumably appeared the lesser of two evils.[37]

The presence of a large British army in the state and the disorders of war in general also moved slaves to get involved in the war. Some joined the Revolutionary army when they believed that they had the opportunity to free themselves. For example, the slave Caesar ran away from Philadelphia and went "towards the camp as he is very fond of being a fifer or a drummer and may pass for a freeman." Given the need for men during that period, few recruiters would probably contest his self-identification as free. In 1777, "a Negro lad named Tom" left his master for the Revolutionary forces to "get employ as a fifer to a company, as he went to Trenton six weeks ago with a soldier." American authorities made no blanket promise of freedom in exchange for military service, although it was possible that soldiering could lead to a change in status. Despite the risk of being returned as runaways to their masters, some took their chances in the Revolutionary cause.[38]

Far more slaves believed that their best chance to gain freedom was with the forces of the Crown. Large numbers greeted the British as liberators, despite the fact that other than Dunmore's 1775 proclamation, the royal army had no official policy regarding emancipation. Apparently Dunmore's actions had been sufficient for many slaves to place their hopes for social change in a British victory. In September 1777, the Pennsylvania Lutheran minister Henry Melchior Muhlenberg noted such attitudes in two slaves of his house guests. Muhlenberg stated that "they secretly wished that the British army might win, for then all Negro slaves will gain their freedom. It is said that this sentiment is almost universal among the *Negroes* in America." This comment offers significant insight into how African Americans defined community during the Revolution. Not only does it suggest a communal resistance toward the institution

---

37. AO13/71, pt. 2/17; *Royal New York Loyalist Gazette,* November 8, 1777; *Pennsylvania Evening Post,* January 17, 1778; William Franklin to Lord George Germain, November 12, 1778, in *Documents of the American Revolution,* ed. Davies, 15:252.

38. *Pennsylvania Ledger,* November 16, 1776; *Pennsylvania Packet,* June 3, 1777.

of slavery by slaves and by the entire black community as well. "Negroes in America" were able to imagine some level of common interest—primarily that they would all benefit from the elimination of chattel bondage. The numbers of free blacks who profoundly risked their limited standing in the community by joining the British testify to the growing racial construction of community. George Peters, who was born free, joined the British in September 1777 to help their army ford the Schuylkill and "afterwards [was] employed in different capacities, such as wagoner and laborer to the British army." Jacob Miles, who "[said] he was born free," also joined the British during their Philadelphia campaign. Samuel Edwards, Philip Woodley, and Moses Thompson were other free blacks from Pennsylvania who remained with the British even after their withdrawal from the state.[39]

Male slaves ran to the British forces with the dual purpose of freeing themselves and hoping to fight against slavery. Only a few were actually equipped as soldiers, however. Most ended up employed as laborers for the British army. The promise of freedom proved to be enough nonetheless. Advertisements for runaway slaves abounded in Pennsylvania newspapers during the British occupation of the state capital. In 1778, Tony, "a Negro boy," ran away from his master "the morning the British Army left Philadelphia." In the same year, three slaves ran away together from their master to join the British army. One of them, Toney, "was protected from his master by a Captain Averne of the British grenadiers." In 1778, Jacob Awl of Lancaster County lost his "Negro man named Joe" who "intends to go to Howe's army." Slaves came to British lines from all over the state. Abraham Smith, John Cald, Thomas Nason, Bacchus Erwin, and many others left their Philadelphia masters and evacuated with the British forces from the city. Others came from the countryside and central counties to free themselves. Silas escaped from Bucks County. Thomas Rogers and Isaac Spencer left their Chester County masters in 1778. Edward Christie fled a "Susquehanna Ferry" to join Howe's army as soon as it landed in 1777. In the same year, Thomas York left his master in Reading to assist British forces in Philadelphia.[40]

Moreover, slave resistance was not exclusively male. Large numbers of enslaved women and children fled to the British army as well. Sukey Coleman,

39. Tappert and Doberstein, eds. and trans., *Notebook of a Colonial Clergyman*, 180; AO13/71, pt. 2/49–51; Graham Russell Hodges, ed., *The Black Loyalist Directory: African Americans in Exile After the American Revolution* (New York, 1996), 16, 52, 101, 159.

40. *Pennsylvania Packet*, July 21, 1778; September 1, 1778; and January 14, 1778; Hodges, ed., *Black Loyalist Directory*, 101–2, 188, 49–50, 65, 207, 132, 191.

Lucy Smith, Catherine, Grace, Esther Clark, and Venus Williams all left their masters and gained freedom with the British. Mary was only about twelve years old when she left her master in Philadelphia and "joined the British troops in 1778." David Riddle took his newborn son, Ben, to escape their master when Howe landed. Patterns of communal resistance to slavery within households were also evident. Abbey Moore ran away from her Philadelphia master, Philip Dickinson, in 1776 to seek freedom with the British. A year later, following her example, Sally Miles left the same master. The brief British presence in Pennsylvania created the opportunity for slaves to free themselves and for African Americans in general to express their discontent with their position in the Pennsylvania Revolutionary community. Increasingly classified as outsiders due to their perceived racial characteristics, blacks embraced the British cause in significant numbers.[41]

Such views were fostered by the Pennsylvania government's enactment of two laws in 1777 that made white manhood the prerequisite for citizenship. Henry Muhlenberg, who observed the attitudes of slaves, noted that the state assembly passed "an act which requires all white inhabitants of Pennsylvania, eighteen years or over to swear an oath of allegiance and acknowledge the new government as the lawful authority." A few days later, Muhlenberg learned that the state had also "passed a law requiring all white inhabitants from eighteen to fifty-three years of age to be ready to serve in the militia." More specifically, the law applied to "male white inhabitants" of the state. The laws made support of the revolution more attractive to poor white men and posited "whiteness" in general as central to Revolutionary identity. Conversely, they specifically excluded nonwhites from any claims to loyalty or service to the "patriot" community. Significantly, the law attributed outsider status to Indians as well as African Americans.[42]

War Breaks Out on the Frontier

While the presence of an invading army in the southeastern part of Pennsylvania drew residents from that region into the war, in 1777, widespread warfare enveloped the state's frontier in the trans-Appalachian west as well. Growing

---

41. Hodges, ed., *Black Loyalist Directory*, 28, 104–5, 113, 160, 188, 201, 161, 64, 110.
42. Tappert and Doberstein, eds. and trans., *Notebook of a Colonial Clergyman*, 172–73. On the language of the acts, see *Pennsylvania Gazette*, June 4, 1777 and March 26, 1777.

numbers of Indian groups began to feel that European American intrusions onto their lands threatened their independence. As early as 1776, groups of Mingos attacked Anglo-American settlements in Kentucky. Expansionist colonists in the region were not deterred. U.S. diplomats George Morgan and John Neville observed that "many persons among ourselves wish to promote a war with the savages, not considering the distresses of our country on the sea coast." By April 1777, several Native groups had enough of Revolutionaries' intrusions on their lands and warned that the fragile peace was in serious peril. A Pennsylvania newspaper reported that "the Indians killed one Andrew Simpson. . . . They scalped Simpson and left a tomahawk war belt on him." The victim also had a written warning left on him telling colonists to get off Indian land on the Ohio and Susquehanna Rivers. The document was a copy of the resolves of a meeting of Mohawks, Onondagas, Cayugas, Tuscaroras, Mingos, and Chippewas.[43]

By the summer of 1777, while the British army invaded the Philadelphia area, enough groups of Indians were alienated by the actions of the Revolutionaries that they began taking the war directly to the "long knives." Shawnees began to raid Pennsylvania villages and farms in response to the Virginia militia's murder of their neutralist leader, Cornstalk. Numbers of Iroquois supported British operations in New York. Pennsylvanians, however, may well have initially overestimated the number of Indians united against them. Many groups were split in their allegiances. Some Delawares, for example, remained neutral; some fought against the Revolutionaries; a few aligned with the "patriots." Among the Iroquois Six Nations, Oneidas and Tuscaroras allied with the Revolutionaries. Nevertheless, the assumption that most Ohioan, Iroquois, and Indians in the Great Lakes region were hostile or potentially hostile led Revolutionaries to respond to Indian raids by attacking neutral or friendly groups. This, in turn, motivated larger numbers of Indians to go to war. By 1778, the Revolutionaries on the Pennsylvania frontier faced enemies such as "the Senecas, Cayugas, Mingoes and Wiandots in general, [and] a majority of the Onondagas." Significant numbers among other groups, including Mohawks, Delawares, Miamis, Shawnees, Potawatomis, and Ottawas, were also in arms against "patriot" Pennsylvanians.[44]

---

43. George Morgan and John Nevill[e], Fort Pitt, to Governor Patrick Henry, April 1, 1777, PRG, reel 12, frame 229; *Pennsylvania Packet*, April 8, 1777.

44. Dowd, *Spirited Resistance*, 75–76, discusses the murder of Cornstalk. Consult Calloway, *American Revolution in Indian Country*, on how the war divided various Indian nations internally (26–64; the Indian nations fighting the Revolutionaries are quoted on 46).

The Revolution on Pennsylvania's frontier was essentially a contest over what sorts of communities would dominate the lands in the trans-Allegheny west. While increasing numbers of Indians felt that they had to fight to protect their ways of life and independence, the acquisition of new lands was a major reason many European American farmers became involved in the war. Although some Continental officers tried to prevent Pennsylvanians from occupying Indian lands and thus broadening the scope of the war, their efforts were in vain. For example, in 1779, the Continental commander of the Western Department, Colonel Daniel Brodhead, lamented that "some persons, yet unknown are committing trespasses on the Indian lands near Wheeling." A year later, Brodhead wrote to the Westmoreland County militia lieutenant and complained, "I am informed that some of the people of your county are trespassing upon the Indians' lands." Regular soldiers also had an eye on the fertile lands they saw in the region. Men of the Eighth Pennsylvania Regiment seemed to be using their time in the service to claim land for later use. Their officers chastised those who "presumed to mark trees in the woods with initial letters and their names at large, thereby giv[ing] great uneasiness to our good friends and allies, the Delaware nation." The frontier soldiers' land hunger was even considered by the Pennsylvania government for use as a military strategy. The Supreme Executive Council suggested that "the best and perhaps [easiest] means of protecting the frontiers will be found in the invasion of the Indian country. . . . Perhaps the disposition of the people of Westmoreland County to emigrate into the Indians' country may be diverted and applied to this end." General William Irvine simply observed that among the western Pennsylvania militiamen, "a great majority have no other views than to acquire lands."[45]

Disputes over land also fueled the civil war in this area among European Americans. These disagreements derived from prewar social and political animosities and determined who took which side during the Revolution. People supported the side that coincided with their material interests. In the Wyoming Valley, where violence among rival claimants preceded the Revolution, Connecticut

---

45. Colonel Michael Lyndemood, Fourth Battalion, Berks County, to President Reed, May 6, 1780, PRG, reel 16, frame 47; "To the Inhabitants of Quemchoning Township," September 1, 1780, PRG, reel 16, frame 1071; Daniel Brodhead to Captain Clark, October 11, 1779, Order Book of Daniel Brodhead, Darlington Memorial Library, University of Pittsburgh; Brodhead to Archibald Lochry, April 13, 1780, PA, 1st ser., 12:220; Orderly Book of the Eighth Pennsylvania Regiment, Draper Manuscript Collection (hereafter DMC), microfilm, State Historical Society of Wisconsin, 2 NN 33; Supreme Executive Council to General Irvine, December 17, 1781, PRG, reel 19, frame 301; William Irvine to George Washington, April 20, 1782, in *Washington-Irvine Correspondence*, ed. C. W. Butterfield (Madison, Wis., 1882), 109.

settlers began dubbing their Pennamite neighbors "Tories." The New Englanders used their institutions of local government to define the Pennsylvanians as communal outsiders who may have colluded with hostile Indians to gain control of the region. Nathan Denison, for example, complained that "there are numbers of people in [Pennsylvania who] desire to take the advantage of our distressed situation to get possession of our settlement." The Connecticut claimants used charges of "treason" to intimidate and remove Pennamites. Often, they successfully pushed their local enemies into alliance with their British and Indian enemies. As Bernard Page noted of his conversion to "loyalism," "the lands there were also claimed by Connecticut which sent a posse of their people who by forcible entry took possession of the same and drove [from] their habitations the real proprietors and seized most of their effects." William Vanderlip, George Kentner, Frederick Anger, Michael Showers, William Pickard, and Philip Bender, who fought with Colonel John Butler's Loyalists, all lost property to their New England neighbors. Rather than fighting out of loyalty to Britain, they sought to avenge their losses and defend their communal interests against outside attack. In this localist context, "Toryism" lost most of its traditional connotations: a Pennamite woman angrily complained about "the treatment they [the Pennsylvania residents] had received from the Yankees in taking away their cattle from them," adding that "they were no more Tories than the Yankees were."[46]

In the southwestern region of the Commonwealth, disputes between Virginians and Pennsylvanians divided residents as well. Although civil war between residents who favored one state or the other did not break out as clearly as it did in the Wyoming Valley, both sides did try to paint the other with the brush of Toryism. One observer noted that in the disputed lands the appointment of a militia official caused a "clamor" among one group—"even to the cry of Tory." Tensions between the rival groups ran high, and the specter of violence between them often appeared. Alexander McClean and his party of Pennsylvania militia were met by a "mob or banditti" of men favoring the Virginia claim who were "damning" the Pennsylvanians and were "threatening us to a great degree." Particularly as Pennsylvanians began to dominate local government

---

46. Nathan Denison to Jonathan Trumbull, July 28, 1778, in *The Susquehannah Company Papers*, ed. Robert J. Taylor (Ithaca, N.Y., 1969), 7:48; AO12/42/166, AO12/40/424–25, AO12/40/428–29, AO12/40/335–38, AO12/40/340–43, AO12/40/319, AO12/40/372; Deposition of James Atherton and Son, PRG, reel 12, frame 383; Petition of Cumberland County Residents, Path Valley, May 18, 1778, PRG, reel 14, frame 47.

with the formal establishment of Washington County in 1781, some Virginians resisted the local Revolutionaries.[47]

Interestingly, numbers of fur traders and frontier diplomats tended to oppose the Revolutionaries as well. The influx of new farmers into the region certainly threatened to alter an economy based on the fur trade. Many European American traders who profited from British Indian policies of trade and diplomacy feared that their community, one in which European Americans and Indians necessarily coexisted and interacted, might be destroyed by a Revolutionary victory. Alexander Robertson, an "Indian trader," fled to the British army in 1777. Matthew Elliot, a frontier trader at Fort Pitt, fled the Revolutionary outpost to take up a position in the British Indian department "to retain the Indians in their attachment to His Majesty." Elliot apparently used his skills as a backcountry negotiator to further his career, and the best opportunity for success appeared to be in royal service. Similarly, prominent traders Alexander McKee and Simon Girty believed that personal gain and the preservation of the prewar frontier world lay in siding with the British. After local authorities discovered that he had secretly attempted to recruit other loyalists near Pittsburgh, McKee was confined; he eventually fled the area and led Indian attacks on the Revolutionaries.[48]

Among all the participants—Revolutionaries, loyalists, and Indians—the frontier war's bitterness and character led to vengeful motivations for military service. The conflict in the region was one in which both sides made war not just against each other's military forces but also against civilians and property. Participants raided their enemies' villages, and subsequently, revenge for the killing of kin and neighbors was a major impetus to take up arms. Many Revolutionaries framed their descriptions of their motives as responses to supposedly unprovoked attacks on their loved ones and neighbors. They typically omitted any discussion of their own provocations toward their enemies, mostly describing the war as a reactive one. Revolutionaries indicated that the war was being fought by "whites" against "the Indians" in general. Veterans' memories for details and names while justifying their motives for revenge are striking. Peter Keister recalled the deaths of his neighbors in dramatic detail: "It was an arduous service marked by individual murders and burnings [by] the Indians of our men. I recollect Michael Lamb, John Ebby, John Clinesmith[?], and Jacob

47. Alexander McClean to President Moore, June 27, 1782, PRG, reel 119, frame 814.
48. AO12/40/123, AO12/40/382; on Simon Girty, see *White, Middle Ground,* 380; AO12/40/388–89.

Beekle were killed by the Indians. John Stomilch[?] and his wife were murdered on their farm . . . They were tomahawked and scalped and the old man had seven stab [wounds]." John Dougherty described his motives similarly:

> The Indians were continually committing depredations against the whites and whenever an alarm was given (which was very frequent) . . . I was as willing to go when not drafted as when I was. Some of my relations and acquaintances had been killed by the Indians and I thought it my duty at all times to assist in protecting those that remained. Samuel Dougherty, a relation of mine, was killed at Freeland's Fort. My service and readiness to fight the Indians was well-known at that time.

The result of such "readiness to fight the Indians" was that Revolutionaries' revenge was often as likely to be taken on allied or neutral Indians as hostile natives. As the "patriot" Pennsylvanians widened the war, the number of Indians seeking vengeance for the deaths of kin and fellow villagers grew as well. For Indian warriors as well as the Revolutionaries, retribution was a central motivation. James Duane explained, of Iroquois fighting the Revolutionaries, that "the Senecas and Cayugoes [sic], & the greatest part of the Mohawks, [seek] nothing but Revenge for their lost Friends."[49]

Another similarity between Native and European American motivations was that both groups zealously protected what they viewed as their local interests. Communal solidarity in the face of an immediate threat led many to their first military service of the war. Revolutionaries typically understood their soldiering as a method to preserve the viability of their farms in the face of Indian and Tory attacks. George Wertz "volunteered his services for the defense of his fellow citizens." He guarded families that sought protection and went "scouting through the county and spying after the Indians and marching [to] any place threatened with danger, at any time and on all occasions." John Allen volunteered in Northumberland County "to help people to save their grain." Angus McCoy recounted how he "volunteered to guard [farmers] . . . cutting and gathering their harvest in their collective capacity." John Megaw noted that his "being a single man and not having the charge of a family" made him particularly suited to defending other families. He "volunteered for the term of seven months" to defend members of his community whose farms were protected by a

49. RWPF, files R5819, S12779; James Duane to George Clinton, March, 13, 1778, *Letters of Delegates*, ed. Smith, 9:290.

local fort. Benjamin Alison, a surgeon from Northumberland County, also revealed his commitment to his community, stating that due to his "local situation, there was a necessity of attending the troops that were in the frontier service."[50]

Indian motives to fight revolved around comparable desires to protect their communities. Some groups—typically those in closest proximity to European Americans, such as the Delawares of the Ohio country—tried to maintain neutrality. Increasing pan-Indian unity, however, spurred in part by the rank-and-file Revolutionaries' tendency to refuse to differentiate between Native groups, transformed Indian notions of community. A growing alliance of Indians who were already in arms sought to persuade other groups to join (many times with the threat of force). As the war went on, growing anti-Revolutionary militance, combined with the violent acts of the Revolutionaries, made neutrality increasingly dangerous to the community. Factions within groups often contended to represent the best interests of the people. Among the Delawares, White Eyes, a leader who provided intelligence to the Revolutionaries, noted that his position within his own community was becoming increasingly tenuous. Apparently, in 1778 some young Delaware warriors believed that the best interest of their community warranted joining the growing coalition against the Revolutionaries. White Eyes noted that a continued pro-American neutrality invited attacks by Wyandots, and he pleaded for supplies and gifts so that he could maintain his status among his people. He declared, "I still hold fast to our friendship, but you know that I am weak and am in need of your assistance." He further warned of significant pressures on the Delawares to join the larger militant Indian coalition: "I told you Brother before, that if I should not take the Tomahawk, they would try to force me to it, and now the time cometh that they will do this, therefore you to [sic] consider and to assist me."[51]

As war continued to escalate in the region, all inhabitants—Indian and European American, Whig and Tory—became absorbed with the immediate defense of their communities. Among Revolutionaries, in particular, it became increasingly difficult to get frontier inhabitants to fight in the main eastern theater. Men who had volunteered with the main army before became far more interested in fighting their Indian and Tory neighbors. By 1777, the protection of Philadelphians and other southeastern Pennsylvanians (who had not seemed

50. RWPF, files R11329, S22622; Dann, *The Revolution Remembered*, 310–11; RWPF, file R7099; Memorial of Benjamin Alison, December 6, 1779, PRG, reel 15, frame 569.
51. White Eyes to Colonel George Morgan, July 19, 1778, PRG, reel 14, frames 416–18.

to care much about the safety of the western counties in earlier wars) was not a high priority. Robert Scott, for instance, volunteered in 1776 for the Pennsylvania Flying Camp but did not reenlist for duty in the East. Instead, he served four tours in the frontier militia. John McCaslin volunteered for the New York campaign, but he had to be drafted into service at Valley Forge. He subsequently "went out as a volunteer" under General Clark against "troublesome" Indians. James Morrison volunteered in 1775 and 1776 for service in the East but volunteered for two tours in 1777 on the frontier. Northampton County's Abraham Arnold, who was drafted three times for duty in the East, volunteered twice for duty against the Indians. George Black, who had to be drafted to defend Philadelphia, enlisted for several tours as a frontier ranger. The men of Colonel Barton's Northampton militia were dismissed from Washington's army "being from their local situation exposed to frequent attacks of the Indians." Others, such as John Vandyke, never went east but volunteered every year for frontier duty until the end of the war. Some even served longer than the duration. Westmoreland County militiaman Jacob Deem recalled fighting the Indians from 1781 to 1795.[52]

Some frontier military units simply refused to go east when called into service. They would not abandon their communities while war was raging on their own doorsteps. Samuel Hunter protested the calling of the Northumberland militia to face Howe's invasion in September 1777. He asserted that no one would turn out because "at the present time, the inhabitants of this county are afraid of the Indians coming down upon our frontiers." In 1778, a Bedford County militia company refused to go east because "the savages have made incursions and committed murders on different parts of our frontier." Captain Philip Shrawder of Northampton County told President Joseph Reed in 1781 that it would be difficult to raise recruits for the Continental army, because the militia had "the greatest assurance from the most respectable men of these parts that they should not be taken off but employed for the defense of this county."[53]

Others who did volunteer were blatantly misled about the conditions upon which they joined the Continental army. Many were incensed to find themselves attached to Washington's army when they were promised that their units would be used for the protection of the frontier. Members of the Eighth

52. RWPF, files W3305, S4197, S23816, S6533, W3211; Orders: September 1, 1776, Orderly Book of the Fourth Battalion of Chester County Associators, HSP; RWPF, files W3168, R2838.

53. Samuel Hunter to George Bryan, September 10, 1777, PRG, reel 12, frame 1022; Petition of Inhabitants of Bedford County, January 26, 1778, PRG, reel 13, frame 608; Philip Shrawder to Joseph Reed, September 6, 1781, PRG, reel 18, frame 1154.

Pennsylvania Regiment were angry when they received orders to march east. Lt. Colonel George Wilson of the regiment observed, "as both the officers and men understood they were raised for the defense of the western frontiers, [for] their families and substance to be left in so defenseless a situation in their absence, seems to give sensible trouble." Soldiers from the Wyoming Valley echoed such resentment: "Your petitioners in the year 1776 enlisted in Continental service . . . for the defense of this place and the frontiers, but, contrary to our expectations, were, in a few months after our engagement, called away to join the Continental army under his excellency, General Washington, where we continued almost two years which was so great trouble to us in leaving our families exposed to be ravaged by the savages."[54]

Later War Apathy

As the war progressed and immediate threats receded for some of the state's residents, enthusiasm for military service waned. Even during the period of military crises on the frontier and the British invasion of 1777–78, war weariness manifested itself in the central counties that were never directly touched by fighting. Fewer central Pennsylvanians were anxious to enlist when they perceived that their own locale would not be threatened by the British, hostile Indians, or armed loyalists. The state government chastised the counties of York and Cumberland in 1778 for not coming to the aid of fellow Pennsylvanians, noting, "it must astonish the distant states and the Congress to find the state invaded so very inattentive and backward and the inhabitants of this in the vicinity of the enemy left open to the ravages of the foe by the unfeeling neglect of the more distant settlers." Richard McCalester of York County responded. It was useless to tell men liable for militia service that "the enemy is in the state," he explained, because the men would reply, "we have this story too often. Let the standing army fight, we will stay home and raise bread." Apathy grew over time. In 1780, the Lancaster militia went so far as to declare that they would not turn out "during times of harvest." The excuse of having to take care of their crops was echoed by the York and Cumberland militias, causing President Reed to declare angrily that "these counties [that] suffered least by the enemy have been the most backward in furnishing their proportions of public duty."

54. Lt. Colonel George Wilson to Colonel James Wilson, December 5, 1776, *PA*, 5th ser., 3:305–6; Petition of Wyoming Valley soldiers in *Susquehannah Company Papers,* ed. Taylor, 7:79.

Prospects for enlisting men from the region into the regular army were little better. In 1781, in Lancaster, the "recruiting business" for the Continental army remained "dull." Elsewhere, John Carothers attempted to appeal to the recalcitrant members of the Cumberland County militia by evoking calls to masculine honor. He was "honestly sorry that . . . this county in particular should be found so extremely backward in marching out . . . when one manly effort would, in all human probability, work out our political salvation." Such discourse was not particularly stirring to those who believed that their homes remained secure regardless of whether they fought. Moreover, by the time of this appeal—just before the British evacuation of Philadelphia in 1778—many of the liable men had already served in militia. As far as they were concerned, they had already proved their martial manliness.[55]

Men from this region were also increasingly loath to go to war on the frontier. After the fall of an important fort to hostile Indians, an article in the *Pennsylvania Evening Post* noted "the county of York, having for some time neglected their militia and omitted [rendering] their distressed brethren assistance on a former occasion, have not been called upon now." The paper suggested a remedy for such shame: "as there are doubtless many brave and humane men in that large and populous county, it is expected that many of them will turn out as volunteers." Few "brave and humane men" did so, however. Continental officer John Proctor lamented the lack of support from the central counties in fighting the frontier war. He complained that "the counties of Lancaster, York and Cumberland are so delinquent, they being the three counties in the greatest safety of any in the state."[56]

As the British army evacuated Philadelphia in mid-1778, a similar pattern emerged in southeastern Pennsylvania. The main theater of combat shifted to the South, and the British army in New York remained in a defensive posture. Pennsylvania's capital would not again be directly threatened. In April 1778, when rumors of the impending British retreat were beginning to circulate, recruiting fell off in the countryside. The Supreme Executive Council

55. Supreme Executive Council to the County Lieutenants of Cumberland and York, April 17, 1778, PRG, reel 13, frame 1170; Richard McCalester to President Wharton, May 2, 1778, PRG, reel 13, frame 1265; Samuel Atlee to President Reed, July 30, 1780, PRG, reel 16, frame 809; Joseph Reed to General William Irvine, July 23, 1781, PRG, reel 18, frame 771. The comment on recruiting in Lancaster is in J. Riddle to Dr. Reading Beatty, Surgeon Fourth Pennsylvania Artillery, August 12, 1781, Beatty Family Papers, HSP. John Carothers to Thomas Wharton, April 24, 1778, Papers of the Continental Congress, 1774–1789 (hereafter PCC), microfilm, National Archives, Washington, D.C., reel 83, vol. 1, I. 69, p. 502.

56. *Pennsylvania Evening Post*, August 14, 1779, 201; Colonel John Proctor to President Reed, May 22, 1780, PRG, reel 16, frame 239.

was "a good deal astonished to find that an officer could be six weeks in Chester County and not have it in his power to recruit one man." Nathaniel Burrows of Bucks County recalled that "in the spring of the year 1778, the company under my command became anxious to return home and in the month of June in the year 1778, we quit the army and went home." Significantly, Burrows and his comrades left the service just after the British left the state. The Philadelphia militia even refused to turn out as the British were preparing to leave their city. Many stayed behind to protect their families and property, "having suffered by the depredations of the enemy." Not surprisingly, many Philadelphia-area soldiers left the service and did not volunteer again after the British evacuated the city in 1778. James Hays recalled that "after the British left Philadelphia, he returned to the city and worked for a time at his trade as a carpenter." James Wilkens, of Proctor's Artillery Regiment, enlisted in 1776 and served "until the British left Philadelphia in June 1778." Perhaps the most blunt statement of localism as a motive for an urban soldier was William Fling's. He explained, "after the British evacuated Philadelphia . . . he left the company and returned home, there being no further cause for his services."[57]

Later in the war, more coercive measures were necessary to get Philadelphia-area Pennsylvanians to turn out for the militia and the Continental army. The draft was one solution for the militia. John Fraily, who had volunteered to counter Howe's invasion of Pennsylvania, had to be drafted in August 1780 to do duty out of the state. Frederick Axe, also a volunteer earlier in the war, was drafted in the fall of 1781. Conrad Custard of Bucks County was "pressed to guard the Continental teams to South Carolina" when he entered the army in 1781. In addition to "pressing," recruiters also became more dependent on fraud to collect men for the Continental service. In 1780, Colonel Lewis Nichola was warned about "unfair practices of catching persons by putting [bounty] money in their pockets or such like acts." Despite the ubiquity of high bounties and compulsion in the later years of the war, recruits remained painfully few. An exasperated Major James Parr wrote to President Reed about his failures to raise men in July 1781: "I much fear that my success in the recruiting service will be far short of my own as well as the expectations of Council."[58]

57. Supreme Executive Council to Anthony Wayne, April 2, 1778, PRG, reel 13, frame 1096; RWPF, file S22151; Supreme Executive Council to Philadelphia County Lieutenants and Sub-Lieutenants, May 14, 1778, PRG, reel 13, frame 1363; Lieutenant Archibald Thomson, Philadelphia County, to Supreme Executive Council, June 8, 1778, PRG, reel 14, frame 220; RWPF, files S23681, S40701, S3364.

58. RWPF, files S23641, S23521, S8262; Recruiting Instructions to Colonel Lewis Nichola, July 18, 1780, PRG, reel 16, frame 689; Major James Parr to President Reed, July 26, 1781, PRG, reel 18, frame 796.

many servants. He probably was stirred by the prospect of greater political participation among soldiers. The radical state government, with large numbers of Scots-Irish Presbyterians, was clearly making formerly dominant Quakers marginal by essentially excluding them from the body politic. No longer would Morris be dismissed as a "Scotch rebel." He was a patriot.[61]

61. Ibid.

Men in the southeastern region of the state were just as unconcerned with the war on the frontiers of Pennsylvania. Frontier residents lamented that "living, as it were, on the ends of the American earth, we seem to have been in a great degree neglected by our brethren beyond the mountains." In 1780, President Reed explained to Colonel James Piper of Bedford County that he should expect no help from the east: "many and great are the difficulties in calling out the militia from the inner counties" for duty on the frontier. Such difficulties manifested themselves when eastern officers of several companies of troops protested vehemently against the proposal that "every company in the state ... find two men to serve in the backwoods against the Indians."[59]

Thus the war ended somewhat as it began, with a noticeable lack of zeal for actual fighting. As in 1775, reticence by 1783 was occasioned by the distance of hostilities from many Pennsylvanians' communities (with the notable exception of the frontier). The American Revolution did, however, invigorate the lower and middling sorts that it touched in Pennsylvania. Some enlisted in 1776 out of a desire for political and social change; other men entered to counter communal threats. All joined the war with well-defined expectations, and their beliefs about why they fought determined much of their behavior in the war. Local situations, economic concerns, ideals of manliness, and ideology provided motivation for common people to become involved in the war. This spectrum of reasons for fighting can be primarily understood as a defense of what soldiers imagined to be their communities of interest.

The story of Daniel Morris illustrates this counterpoint to Alexander Graydon's "top-down" view of why soldiers fought. Morris gave a vivid account of motivation that suggests much about soldiers' self-consciously complex reasons for taking up arms. Nowhere does he state that he fought for individual interest alone or that he was manipulated by officers or "sagacious politicians." Morris recalled:

> I lived with [my master] until the time that General Washington was crossing the Schuylkill, about the time the British left Philadelphia, when one Isaac Tyson told me that the American army was pressing all the horses and wagons they could find to take their baggage across the

---

59. Inhabitants of Western Pennsylvania to Brigadier General William Irvine, March 4, 1782, PCC, reel 83, vol. 2, I. 69, p. 403; Joseph Reed to Colonel James Piper, May 8, 1780, PRG, reel 16, frame 63. The eastern officers' protest against sending their men to the frontier is in Entry: May 31, 1780, regarding the protest of "Officers of the Musketry," Diary of George Nelson, 1780–1792, HSP.

Schuylkill. When I went to the house, I told my master, who was a Quaker, of it. He said, "Does thee not wish that they would come and press my horses and wagon and press thee to drive it?" I told him I did. I had a whip in my hand which he took from me and gave me several lashes with it and said, "Thee Scotch rebel, thou was a rebel in thine own country, and now thou has come here to rebel." So I was determined to leave him which I did in about a week from the time he struck me, and then I enlisted in Colonel Preston's artillery, in Captain Rice's company.[60]

Morris was a Philadelphia-area apprentice who entered the army during a military threat to his locale. Taking advantage of the proximity of the American army, he also quit his servitude for the promise of freedom, bounty, and wages in the military. Furthermore, he was able to free himself from an English Quaker master who was clearly disaffected from the Revolutionary cause. Most likely, Morris's master supported neither American independence nor the radical Pennsylvania government that swept the old provincial order from power in the previous year. As a Friend, the master could not take a loyalty oath to the new government, and he could not serve in the militia (although his striking of Morris suggests less than complete pacifism). In contrast, Morris, more than simply running away from an abusive master, was taking up arms in a politicized army. As a white man willing to swear allegiance to the Pennsylvania Constitution and serve in the military, he was making significant progress from unfree subject toward citizen. Ethnic hostility is also apparent. Morris was clearly angered by his master's condescending characterization of Scots in general. Class tensions—as evinced by Morris's open admission of his hope that the army would take his master's property—also enters into the equation. The last straw appeared to be the whipping that physically manifested his social inferiority to his master and lack of independent manhood. And although Morris does not explicitly say so, political issues such as independence and liberty may well have weighed on his mind as he pondered his social situation. The army would allow him to pursue his own freedom and set an example for others. Thus, Morris was defending his own very sophisticated definition of his own community. He was protecting his region (southeastern Pennsylvania) from invasion. He struck a blow against the deferential social order by leaving his master and seeking personal "independence," as did

60. Dann, *The Revolution Remembered*, 163–64.

3

Identity and the Military Community

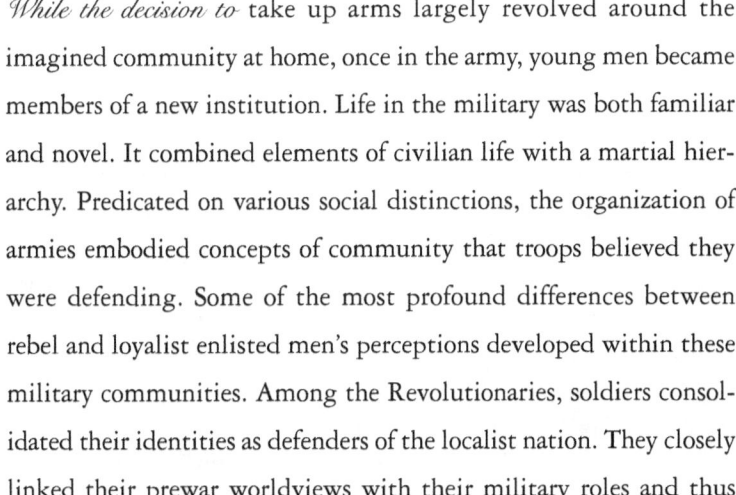

While the decision to take up arms largely revolved around the imagined community at home, once in the army, young men became members of a new institution. Life in the military was both familiar and novel. It combined elements of civilian life with a martial hierarchy. Predicated on various social distinctions, the organization of armies embodied concepts of community that troops believed they were defending. Some of the most profound differences between rebel and loyalist enlisted men's perceptions developed within these military communities. Among the Revolutionaries, soldiers consolidated their identities as defenders of the localist nation. They closely linked their prewar worldviews with their military roles and thus implicitly connected citizenship and soldier status, actually enlarging the prewar view of who was formally part of the community. Just as important, camp life among the Revolutionaries helped transform shared colonial resistance into a basis for a nation predicated on local differences mitigated by an imagined white male identity. Despite myriad internal conflicts among them, groups of soldiers could unite at certain times to effect collective action. The army community, therefore, presciently preceded the body politic of the republic it helped found. In short, military service and soldiers' views of self powerfully influenced the shape of American nationalism.

In contrast, rank-and-file loyalists, who were motivated by comparable localism, underwent an even more pervasive revision of identity. They literally left their prewar worlds behind in order to become part of a multiethnic and hierarchical anti-Revolutionary military coalition. No longer having a community to which to return or to physically defend, these loyalists were typically forced to submit to British war aims and discipline. They also found themselves in alliance with large groups of Americans they previously saw as outsiders, such as Indians and slaves. In order for loyalists to recover the imagined communities they had lost, they had to join a larger military force in which they were admittedly inferior partners. They did not expect to gain greater political privileges within the empire; rather, they hoped that the empire could help them regain their losses. While soldiering among the rebels reinforced narrow, exclusionist definitions of community, then, Tory service broadened the worldviews of loyalist troops by introducing them to larger imperial interests.

Revolutionary Military Life

The Revolutionary militia offered the closest institutional connection between the localism that actuated soldiers and their service. Called upon for short tours during emergencies, militiamen literally served in order to protect their immediate community. Troops were enlisted from the same region of their county and almost always knew each other. In many instances, there were kin ties among men: Isaac Gushert, for example, "went and volunteered in the same company as his brother." David Shields enlisted "under his father, Captain John Shields, at 'Fort Shields' in Westmoreland County."

Further supporting localist outlooks, the militia often performed the bulk of their tours without leaving their immediate environs. In many cases, the nature of their service reinforced distinctive regional identities. Frontier militia typically undertook duties that were similar to those of Indian warriors. When not engaged in combat, they spent a considerable amount of time patrolling the region on reconnaissance missions. Proficiency in scouting necessitated a knowledge of the terrain and an ability to move stealthily. These skills were closely related to those used in hunting, which some had seen as manly behavior before the war. Others further developed military skills they had learned in previous conflicts. The names that such men chose for their units reflected region-specific identities. James McCormick was in a "company by the name of rangers or Indian spies." Abraham Fiscus noted "our company was called Wood Rangers." Daniel Livingston was part of a "company [that] was on duty seven months, engaged not only in occupying the fort, but on scouting expeditions through the various parts of the country."[1]

Regionalism sometimes led to conflict when large numbers of militia units served together or were attached to the main army. Arguments could quickly escalate into insubordination. In 1777, for example, the Chester County militia debated with Philadelphia militiamen about the fair allocation of labor duty. When officers sided with the urban soldiers, the rural troops refused to comply with their punishment. More ominously, discord broke out along ethnic and local lines in Feree's Battalion of Lancaster militia. Even though the soldiers were from the same county, the very heterogeneity of the region that they defended seemed to have fostered disagreements about "real Americans." The conflict reached such a disabling level that a number of privates complained, "the battalion is . . . divided in a most shocking manner, so bad as some parts of it threaten to disarm other parts by force. . . . It has got so bad one society [is] against another; one nation against another." While underscoring the military inefficiency of citizen-soldiers in the eyes of officers, such disputes also highlighted the potential volatility of the Revolutionary coalition and the localist nation itself. It is not surprising that such antagonisms manifested themselves in militia camps, given the disparate views of community that moved men to defend their homes. One of the salient aspects of the Revolution that surely was illustrated by the soldiers' experiences in Feree's Battalion was how very different many of their neighbors and comrades were. Nonetheless, these internecine disputes symbolized the nation itself: a union of potentially conflicting localisms.[2]

    1. RWPF, files S22804, S22989, S23886, S7860, S8881, W2778, S22361.

    2. Orders: February 28, 1776, Orderly Book of the Fourth Pennsylvania Battalion, HSP; RWPF, file W2286; Daniel Brodhead to Captain Joseph Irwin, October 13, 1779, PA, 1st ser., 12:169–70; Remonstrance of Private Associators, Colonel John Feree's Lancaster Battalion, September [26?], 1775, PRG, reel 10, frame 79.

There were also aspects of militia service that created stronger bonds among men. Militiamen soon learned that collective action united the soldiery and could enhance their status within both the military and the state. Thousands of Pennsylvanians from comparable social backgrounds participated in the most radically democratic militia in Revolutionary America. Through their influence on civil affairs, these men felt that they had a stake in the political as well as the military outcome of the war. Privates voted for officers, were represented at courts-martial, and had their own committees to further their political and military interests. Most of this formal military say and informal political power developed through the Committees of Privates. The organization was one that represented the interests of enlisted men and was raised, like the militia itself, on a countywide basis. The rank interests of the soldiers, then, intersected with their other identities. The committees adhered to Anglo-American Whig traditions of local representation while making troops aware of their shared status and interests. Militia privates petitioned the state to change voting qualifications from property ownership to liability to military service. Service was often a school for political action: voting on military matters set important precedents for relatively poorer men, many of whom had never before had a formal say in any kind of election.[3]

As a result, electing officers was one of the most important things that militiamen did. Most saw themselves as the true community in arms, and the selection of leaders was therefore vitally important. Given that the colony of Pennsylvania did not have a long militia tradition, the election of junior—let alone senior—officers was novel. Having a say in who would lead them was a major concern among Pennsylvania associators throughout the war and apparently consumed much of their attention. In August 1775, men of the Fifth Battalion of York County militia contested the outcome of an election by declaring it undemocratic. They argued, "Matthew Dill, Esq., being chosen colonel of said battalion, this raised an immediate dissatisfaction (as the majority of [the men] were not apprized of the measure)." Also in 1775, a company of Berks County militia called for new elections after an officer referred to Germans in derogatory terms. Berks had a large German ethnic population; the slur was not a politic move for someone who owed his position to his men. In the following year, militiamen from Cumberland County declared that they were willing to

3. See Foner, *Tom Paine*, 63–66; Nash, *Urban Crucible*, 243–44; and Rosswurm, *Arms, Country, and Class*, 55–108, on the radicalism and politicization of the Pennsylvania militia. Consult Brunhouse, *Counter-Revolution in Pennsylvania*, on the militia's role in politics throughout the state.

march "to the immediate defense of the middle states upon the condition they should have the liberty of electing out of their own number a major to command." What the men meant by "their own number" might have been that the major would be selected from the pool of enlisted men. More likely, though, the troops sought someone who was defined as a social "insider" and friendly to their local view of what they believed to be the true Revolutionary cause. Unsurprisingly, many militiamen remembered officer elections as one of the most significant aspects of life in the army. Henry Greninger's participation in the election of Adam Sheafer as his captain figured prominently in his pension deposition. Similarly, Robert Gray and James Alworth clearly recalled—more than forty years after the Revolution—how they elected their officers.[4]

Such activities often took on both social and political overtones. In 1777, men from Chester County demanded "a free and fair election of officers." They wished to allow all troops to vote without any undue pressure from more prominent men in the community who perhaps were less friendly to the new radical Pennsylvania government. In other cases, militiamen made certain that all who voted for officers had properly taken the oath of allegiance to the new state constitution. In April 1779, men from a Chester County battalion were furious that some of those who voted for officers had not taken the "test [oath]." At other times, militiamen refused appointments of officials they had not approved. The Eighth Battalion of York County militia were "much aggrieved" when "a certain John McKinley (a most avowed enemy of our constitution) was imposed [upon] us as wagon master for this battalion." In these cases, the men served as both defenders and definers of the community. Soldiers were still enthusiastically participating in officer elections even toward the end of the war, as clear military threats from the British were fading. In 1781, the Bucks County militia arranged their vote at "the most advantageous and agreeable time for the people . . . [which] will give them an opportunity of conferring one with another upon the subject." While the war may have been winding down in the southeastern part of the state, the process of defining "the people" and giving them a voice was still significant.[5]

4. Petition of the Fifth Battalion of York County Militia, August 31, 1775, PRG, reel 10, frame 53; Laura Leff Becker, "The American Revolution as a Community Experience: A Case Study of Reading, Pennsylvania" (Ph.D. diss., University of Pennsylvania, 1978), 334; Resolution of the Cumberland County Committee, August 20, 1776, PRG, reel 10, frame 921; RWPF, files S10764, W4446, S2208.

5. Recommendations for the Election of Militia Officers, Chester County, May 29, 1777, PRG, reel 12, frame 367; Timothy Matlack to Sub-Lieutenant Lewis Gronow, April 28, 1779, PRG, reel 14, frame 1209; Petition of the Eighth Battalion of York County Militia, March 13, 1778, PRG, reel 13, frame 983; Lieutenant Joseph Hart to President Reed, September 7, 1781, PRG, reel 18, frame 1172.

Militiamen's election of officers and activism in the day-to-day activities of their units shaped their lives as soldiers. Not surprisingly, relations between officers and enlisted men were far less authoritarian than those in the Continental army. As was the case with the regular army, however, there was an informal assumption that the rank hierarchy was related to the social one. Privates, despite the citizen-soldier ideal, tended to come from the lower and middling sorts. Officers were generally more affluent than their men and were concerned about their reputations both as military leaders and as prominent members of their communities. Nevertheless, because soldiers elected many of their officers, popularity with the rank and file was a necessity. Ties to the soldiery helped officers consolidate the image of a particular region in arms that at times overcame class and even rank identities. One well-known result was that discipline was not nearly as harsh in the militia as it was in the Continental army. Officers could not afford to alienate their men by brutally punishing them. In 1775, Pennsylvania militiamen sought to ensure that "no penalty shall be inflicted . . . [on troops] other than degrading, cashiering, or fining." This radical demand sought to eradicate corporal punishment and apply sanctions typically administered to officers to all members of the militia.[6]

Another result of militia structure was that officers sometimes made common cause with their men against other officers or officials. For example, in 1779, a number of militia boatmen went on strike for higher wages and refused to continue their work in support of Sullivan's expedition against the Iroquois. Colonel Adam Hubley of the Continental army reported angrily that "some of the [militia] officers are concerned as they seem equally dilatory [as] their men." In 1781, a similar incident took place with a Cumberland County militia officer who stood by his men's demand for pay advances. Captain Bentley of Chester County even went so far as to quit the militia "without permission" with "several men of his company." Militia officers essentially replicated their local roles as social leaders, speaking for the best interests of the men to whom they owed their rank status. Although Continental officers would also try to represent their men's interests, militia officers were more willing to engage in collective action with their men.[7]

6. *Pennsylvania Magazine*, Supplement, 1775, 616, American Periodical Series I, reel 24.
7. Colonel Adam Hubley to General Edward Hand, June 23, 1779, Hand Papers, HSP; Benjamin Blyth to President Joseph Reed, August 6, 1781, PRG, reel 18, frame 919; Entry: November 6, 1777, Orderly Book of Captain Peter Brown's Company of Philadelphia Militia Artillery, Early American Orderly Books, microfilm, New-York Historical Society, New York, New York (hereafter NYHS).

The community replicated in most militia units was typically white and male. As the 1777 Pennsylvania militia law made "every male white person . . . capable of bearing arms" liable to the draft, the assumed prerequisite for liability to service, other than being a man, was "whiteness." The provision was an important one in constructing Revolutionary identity. It defined white men as de facto insiders, excluding everyone else from formal membership in the new public sphere of militia service. The growing militiaman ideal—a white male—also helped consolidate support for the cause among the state's ethnically diverse European population. On the frontier, this identity as "white Americans" was defined in opposition to "Indians." Throughout the state, the presence of African Americans made the racial element of militia service a significant aspect of soldiers' identity. Despite manpower shortages during the war, Pennsylvanians appeared very reluctant to allow even free blacks to serve in the militia. The attempt to limit African American militia service suggests that the group was excluded from the imagined community, entitled neither to represent it nor to take up the important and growing political power inherent in citizen-soldiery in the state.[8]

Many discovered common ground in the cause of independence and support for the radical Pennsylvania Constitution of 1776. A visible manifestation of militiamen's politicization came in 1781, when the Revolutionary government in Pennsylvania acknowledged its need for their support. During the Yorktown campaign, President Joseph Reed was reluctant to order the militia into the field because the men would be unable to vote in civil elections. Reed feared that "the election will fall into the hands of [those] unfriendly to [the radical] government if the militia do not return." Thus, one of the most significant roles of the militia in the state was not necessarily in the field but in local musters, where politics could be discussed.[9]

This politicization of the militia affected how units enforced order at home and projected their image of a just community. In many cases, militiamen's views of citizenship in that community related to their class interests. In Philadelphia, most notably, the militia formed the backbone of a number of extralegal price-fixing committees. They attempted to limit the profits of monopolizers and keep inflation at an acceptable level for the city's lower sort. For these men, part

---

8. *Pennsylvania Gazette*, March 26, 1777; on the paucity of African Americans in all the state militias, see Neimeyer, *America Goes to War*, 85. Steven Rosswurm only found one African American on extant Philadelphia militia muster rolls in *Arms, Country, and Class*.

9. Joseph Reed to General Lacey, October 3, 1781, Papers of Joseph Reed, microfilm, NYHS, reel 3.

of their role as soldiers was to guard the economic interests of their class and community. The Third Battalion of Philadelphia militia, for example, demanded that "tanners, shoemakers, weavers, and other tradesmen . . . regulate their prices" by rates given by the committee of the militia battalion. These city troops engaged in a formal Revolutionary version of economic regulation previously enforced extralegally by the mob. The militiamen's association with the new government gave their social aspirations a formal political tincture—and, of course, the threat of armed coercion always lurked behind their declarations regarding price controls.[10]

In the famous 1779 "Fort Wilson Riot," Philadelphia militiamen took it upon themselves to besiege the house of James Wilson, who opposed price controls. The troops, fearing that their views on economic policy were being ignored by the state government, fired on Wilson's house and were eventually put down by the city's upper-class troop of light horse. The incident at "Fort Wilson" demonstrated discord within the imagined Revolutionary community in a single locale. The elite light horse troops were defending their notion of community from threats posed by the lower-sort militiamen, who, in turn, were protecting their vision of Revolutionary justice. While cross-class alliances could exist for the sake of the war, there was always the potential for conflict that could not be deflected by shared white male privilege. Furthermore, the riot illustrated some of the limitations of lower-sort activism in the militia. Other county militias did not come to the assistance of the besiegers. These militias were engrossed in enforcing order in their own communities and left the Philadelphians to themselves. The very localist structure and role of the militia hindered soldiers' support for men of comparable social status in other regions.[11]

There also was overlap in membership between the regular army and the militia. The localist and politicized experience of citizen-soldiers was something that former militiamen carried to the Continental army. There were also similarities in camp experiences, as the militia and army often operated together. The Continental army, however, offered a different sort of military role and community. Even more clearly than the militia, the regular army's very structure represented the new nation. Regular soldiers were organized into state lines, with constituent units of the Pennsylvania Line raised at a regional level. Entire regiments were recruited from several counties, usually in close

10. Broadside of the Committee of the Third Battalion, Philadelphia County, LCP.
11. See Foner, *Tom Paine*, 174–78, and Rosswurm, *Arms, Country, and Class*, 205–27, on the Fort Wilson affair.

proximity. Captains of the Continental companies usually raised the majority of their men from their own immediate neighborhoods. Thus, localism was affirmed at the small unit level. Continental service, though, almost always entailed joining with men from many different areas and states to constitute an army. The army, then, enacted the localist nation. It comprised diverse Americans fighting for different reasons in a single institution. Regulars' terms of service were far longer than militiamen's, leading to extensive and sustained periods of time present in military encampments. The Continentals were also more apt to serve farther from their immediate environs, altering the perception of how they defended the community. Finally, the Continental army was a far more hierarchical and disciplined military body than the militia. As a result, soldiers began to construct identities and interests very distinct from those of their officers.

Localism in the army could potentially lead to conflict within the ranks, as it did in the militia. Quarrels among men from different states—quarrels deriving from regionalism and unit pride—were pronounced. In 1775, the officers of Thompson's Pennsylvania Rifle Battalion condemned such infighting and declared, "it is hoped that all distinction of colonies will be laid aside, so that one and the same spirit may animate the whole." A year later, officers of the Fourth Pennsylvania Battalion continued to plead for harmony among men from different states and various Pennsylvania units. They decried "the foolish distinction between the troops of one colony and another, and that between different regiments." While these rivalries were not conducive to good order in the army, ironically, they may have created bonds among the men by visibly illustrating their common worldviews. In other words, the Continental army instilled nationalism in troops by providing a forum for them to understand their shared desire to protect diverse notions of community.[12]

A construction of "whiteness" remained one powerful way to create imagined shared interests within the army and mitigate regional conflict. African Americans were not explicitly excluded from Continental service (as they were from the Pennsylvania militia draft), but their numbers in the regular army remained very small compared with those of European Americans. Manpower demands and war weariness led most northerners and some southerners to accept the idea of using limited numbers of African Americans as soldiers. Because there was no consistent American policy of emancipation for military service, however, slaves were far less likely to join the Revolutionary

12. Orderly Book of Thompson's Rifle Battalion, HSP; Orders: May 11, 1776, Orderly Book of the Fourth Pennsylvania Battalion, HSP.

forces than the British. Estimates of the total African American presence in the Continental army run to about 5,000 soldiers. Numbers of blacks in the Pennsylvania Line were rather negligible, compared with the larger contingents among New England troops. John Trussell, in his study of the Pennsylvania Line, found in his sample of a return of the Continental army in August 1778 that of the 755 African American soldiers present in fourteen brigades, there were only 37 in the two Pennsylvania brigades, which contained a total of 2,480 enlisted men. At about 1.5 percent of these Pennsylvania regulars, blacks in the ranks were clearly the exception rather than the rule. Soldiers coming to the army who assumed that white manhood was the prerequisite for citizenship in the new nation would not be significantly challenged by the racial composition of the Pennsylvania Line. Indeed, the presence of African Americans may have fostered racist nationalism. Alexander Graydon commented that the numbers of New England "Negroes" had a "disagreeable, degrading effect" on white soldiers unused to serving with nonwhites in the army.[13]

Indians in the Pennsylvania Line were even more rare. Trussell found only one Shawnee and one Mohawk, the only Native Americans to appear on any regular muster roll in the state. The most famous group of Indians attached to the main Continental army, the Stockbridge of New England, were decimated by heavy casualties in a skirmish with the British near Kingsbridge, New York, in 1778. Although they continued to serve with Continental forces, their numbers remained small. Pennsylvania Continentals were most likely to encounter Indians not as members of their army but as allies. They operated at times with these Indian allies and scouts, but they rarely fought or camped with large numbers of Indians. The number of Indians friendly to the Revolutionaries paled in comparison with the large numbers of Indians allied with the British. Indians simply were not a major component of the Pennsylvania military community.[14]

Soon, other major similarities beyond "whiteness" would become apparent to soldiers. While part of the army, soldiers lived under a system of rank hierarchy undergirded by early American social distinctions. Officers were assumed to be gentlemen, and the rank and file were treated as the lower and lower-middling sorts. The enlisted men were given duties and living conditions

13. See Neimeyer, *America Goes to War*, 82–83, on the numbers of African Americans in the Continental army. Quarles, *Negro in the American Revolution*, 68–93, addresses the large proportion of free blacks and the majority of black troops coming from New England. Trussell, *Pennsylvania Line*, 248–49; Graydon quoted in Quarles, *Negro in the American Revolution*, 72.

14. On the Stockbridge, see Calloway, *American Revolution in Indian Country*, 83–107.

supposedly commensurate with their low rank and social status. Privates were all confronted with more dirt, disease, and labor duty than their superiors. One of the hallmarks of army culture was the filth in which enlisted men lived. These conditions derived mostly from the soldiers' resistance to the most rudimentary sanitary practices advocated by their officers. Poor men from the city were already familiar with cramped, dirty living conditions. Many rural and frontier troops were unused to living in large gatherings of people and saw no reason to clean up after themselves at camp. That soldiers from all regions of the state flouted regulations regarding hygiene throughout the war suggests that they rejected the imposition of officers' standards upon them. It also reflected common American resistance to European regular army–style discipline, as their British enemies maintained relatively more hygienic camps. Most important, the rank and file's living conditions indicated a continuation of their civilian way of life in the military. Enlisted men believed cleaning to be women's work. They were willing to die—literally—rather than submit to such unmanly labor. Officers' constant orders to their men regarding conditions at camp demonstrate the depth and persistence of lower-order resistance to their dictates. Pennsylvania soldiers, for instance, continually defied the purpose of latrines. In 1776, officers of the Third Pennsylvania Battalion ordered that "no person on any account will be suffered the use of any other place than the necessary house." Still, the men resisted and "would ease [themselves] about the camp." Officers of the Thirteenth Pennsylvania commented upon a "stench" that had "arisen from such places [that is] extreme[ly] offensive to the camps and to the passengers of those roads." The town major of Philadelphia was so appalled by the soldiers' quarters in the city that he complained to the state government in 1776 that the barracks houses were "generally as dirty as a pigsty, with human ordure in the garrets, cellars, outhouses, yards, etc., the stench of which is intolerable and threatens a pestilence if not remedied." Two years later, soldiers had not professionalized much in terms of living conditions, and their officers were "again necessitated to repeat the order for keeping the camp clean."[15]

Other aspects of military identity were imposed upon soldiers from above. Tedious labor duties underscored the common lot of the soldiery. Officers typically engaged men in roles related to their prewar occupations. For example,

15. Orders: July 21, 1776, Orderly Book of the Third Pennsylvania Battalion, HSP; Orders: May 26, 1777 and July 24, 1777, Orderly Book of the Thirteenth Pennsylvania Regiment, HSP; Memorial of Lewis Nichola, Town Major of Philadelphia, December 1776, PRG, reel 11, frame 675; Orders: August 20, 1778, Orderly Book of the First Pennsylvania Regiment, PA, 2d ser., 11:318; Orders: August 15, 1777, Orderly Book of the Thirteenth Pennsylvania Regiment, HSP.

skilled artisans were likely to be called upon to perform their trade at camp. Mariners might well operate bateaux. Additionally, the few African Americans who joined the Revolutionary Pennsylvania military were apt to receive the worst tasks, such as burying the dead or acting as servants; Levi Burns served as a waiter in the Tenth Pennsylvania Regiment. All troops, however, shared certain laborious roles, such as long, dull guard duty. Michael Teter of the Fifth Pennsylvania Regiment was at his post when his fingers froze and "afterwards [were] taken off by the surgeons." Troops also typically built earthworks and boats and were employed in other labor details. Members of the Pennsylvania Line were sent to repair roads and were "directed to be particularly careful to remove rocks and stones and all other obstructions from the road." Such drudgery was the lot of enlisted men who worked while officers supervised. This kind of duty reinforced the congruence between class and rank status in the army.[16]

Soldiers who worked and lived together began to socialize as well. As they did so, they brought prewar notions of manly behavior to the army that, over time, politicized previously informal constructs of manhood. Soldiers recreated aspects of tavern culture within the army. Companionable drinking and ensuing political discussions in camp were the wartime equivalent of prewar tippling. Issues of liquor were common in all eighteenth-century European armies and would be important in the Continental army as well. Rations would typically include the ubiquitous "gill of rum or whiskey" along with hard bread and meats. Quantities of alcohol were increased to celebrate holidays and military victories or to alleviate the aches caused by fatiguing duty. Daniel Deall, for example, dutifully recorded in his diary how he went and drew his "four gills" following his work on barracks construction. Drinking was so ubiquitous within the ranks that officers of the Second Pennsylvania Regiment were warned "not to let the soldiers have such a quantity [of rum] as may injure them." Officers engaged in companionable drinking as well, but unlike the mixed social class patronage of prewar Pennsylvania taverns, soldiers and officers drank in rank-specific social circles. While the men drank inferior spirits, such as grog

16. John William Kreuger, "Troop Life in the Champlain Valley Forts During the American Revolution" (Ph.D. diss., State University of New York at Albany, 1981), 162–67, discusses the assignment of particular camp tasks to men with comparable prewar occupations. Quarles, *Negro in the American Revolution*, asserts the tendency of the American army (as well as the British) to assign tasks to African Americans that were typical of the labor performed by slaves and also corresponded to the low status accorded such soldiers. On Levi Burns, see Quarles, *Negro in the American Revolution*, 77. Petition of Michael Teter, August 19, 1779, PRG, reel 15, frame 242; Orders: June 23, 1779, Orderly Book of the Fifth Pennsylvania Regiment, Early American Orderly Books, microfilm, NYHS.

or rum, officers bought expensive wines and spirits from sutlers for entertaining fellow officers. The pattern of rank- and class-specific drinking in the army appears to mirror the process that Peter Thompson has identified in Philadelphia taverns during the Revolutionary era, a process in which social groups ceased larger social and informal political interaction in common spaces.[17]

Enlisted men seamlessly transplanted to the army not only their wonted drinking culture but also their informal notions of manly behavior that often accompanied it. James McCalister from the Fifth Pennsylvania Regiment had a tendency "when in liquor [to] boast much of Burgoyne's capture," according to a desertion notice. The fact that officers characterized the soldier in this way suggests that they were quite familiar with McCalister's behavior when drinking and his masculine posturing. Significantly, this depiction of McCalister echoes descriptions of marginalized colonists who associated drinking, violence, pride, and informal manhood. During the colonial period, lower sorts often bragged of their manhood in fights, and once they became soldiers, they could refer to their battles in the service of the country as members of the Revolutionary military. Other advertisements for deserters further suggest that officers were well aware of their men's social habits, which attests to the centrality of social drinking in military life. Samuel Marler was described as a man who "dearly loves company where liquor is plenty." James Reily was "no enemy to strong liquor, and when brim full vomits oaths and blasphemy very liberally."[18]

Some troops brought specific regional variations of masculinity to the army. A number of soldiers were apt to hunt while in the military, and for some, the warrior/hunter ideal was especially important. Adopting these norms of masculinity from Indians, these men expected that prowess in marksmanship and hunting would enhance their status within the military community. The killing of game also had the obvious attraction of supplementing often meager rations. Troops who were able to hunt effectively did so regardless of whether they had permission. Francis Johnston remarked that many of his men avidly hunted whenever given the chance. Among the frontier soldiers of the Eighth Pennsylvania Regiment stationed at Fort Pitt, this activity interfered with the army's ability to function properly. Colonel Daniel Brodhead chastised one of

17. The typical order for the men to receive the gill of liquor is from Orders: August 6, 1778, Orderly Book of the First Pennsylvania Regiment, *PA*, 2d ser., 11:300; Entry: September 25, 1776, Diary of Daniel Deall, in RWPF, file W6999. On the transformation of tavern life to a class-specific arena of interaction, see Peter Thompson, *Rum Punch and Revolution*, 110–46.

18. Orders: November 10, 1778, Orderly Book of the Second Pennsylvania Regiment, HSP; *Pennsylvania Packet*, May 23, 1778; *Pennsylvania Evening Post*, May 10, 1777.

his officers for allowing his men to "frequently go a hunting." While Brodhead saw such activity as a threat to proper military order, his men probably saw it as the entirely reasonable occupation of warriors.[19]

Not all men in the army were as familiar with firearms, though. Numbers of soldiers had never owned or discharged a weapon in their lives, and the prospect of suddenly being armed must have been empowering. The idea of the army as a kind of embodiment of citizens in arms politicized the simple fact of bearing arms. Indeed, early American culture strongly linked arms, men, and citizenship in the institution of the militia. For very poor soldiers who had never before been able to afford to arm themselves for service, the issuing of firearms suddenly placed them on equal footing with others. The significance that men attached to being armed is attested to by myriad instances of the unauthorized firing of weapons within the army. Orders against the practice were issued, largely in vain, throughout the war. In 1775, men of Thompson's Rifle Battalion were warned to desist from discharging their weapons when not in battle because "no other end is answered but to waste their ammunition and expose themselves to the ridicule of the enemy." The scale and persistence of disorderly firing among the Revolutionaries (which was in fact more pronounced than among the British and loyalists) suggests, however, something more than a lack of discipline. The practice was dangerous to the soldiers themselves, yet they continued it. Orders for Hand's Rifle Regiment stated, "the constant firing in the camp, notwithstanding the repeated orders to the contrary is very scandalous and seldom a day passes but some persons are shot by their friends." Even as the Continental army continued to professionalize, the disorder continued. In 1778, the exasperated officers of the First Pennsylvania Regiment excoriated their men for how "the camp is continually disordered both within its own limits and its vicinity, by a disorderly firing."[20]

The presence of large numbers of women in camp further refined soldiers' identities by presenting a feminine counterpoint for military masculinity. Wives who accompanied their spouses to the army allowed their husbands to be efficient soldiers while reaffirming patriarchal family relations in camp. These women were usually junior partners in the family production units of early America and assumed a similar role while attached to the military. They cared,

---

19. Francis Johnston to Anthony Wayne, October 7, 1776, Wayne Papers, 1:109, HSP; Orderly Book of the Eighth Pennsylvania Regiment, 2 NN 37, DMC.

20. Orders: August 4, 1775, Orderly Book of Thompson's Rifle Regiment, HSP; Orders: August 30, 1776, Orderly Book of Hand's Rifle Regiment, HSP; Orders: August 19, 1776, and September 14, 1778, Orderly Book of the First Pennsylvania Regiment, PA, 2d ser., 11:347.

cooked, and sewed for their spouses. They also accompanied their husbands' units and received rations. In essence, the family unit, the centerpiece of early modern communities, was transplanted into the American army defending those communities. Troops and their wives entered, lived in, and left the military together. John Hawkins noted in his journal that noncommissioned officers, in particular, resided with their wives. Jane Taplin was typical of the wives who accompanied their spouses to the army. As she put it, she "came with my husband to Philadelphia since he was a drummer in Captain John Lucas' Company." John White's "wife was with him" when he ran away from the Seventh Pennsylvania Regiment. Abraham Goss recalled how his "father and mother returned from the army and took him . . . along with [them] to the army." Goss's entire family entered the army together and truly symbolized the community in arms in defense of the nation.[21]

Officers' spouses served a similar role in their husbands' construction of military identity by helping to equate class and rank status. Few women married to officers actually went to camp, and when they did, it was usually for short periods. Unlike poor soldiers who needed their wives to care for them, officers could hire servants or camp followers. They largely chose not to expose their wives to the ugliness of the army. When they did come to camp, these women, especially the wives of senior officers, offered a genteel model of femininity and submission to male authority. Rather than washing, cooking, and sewing, they concentrated on planning and carrying out social events as would befit women of their class. Their presence in camp was visible evidence for the soldiery that here, as at home, gender and class status intersected.[22]

In contrast, the bulk of female camp followers came from the lower orders of society and did tasks that were seen as the domain of their gender and class. Most were single wage-earning women from the region in which the army was operating. Nonetheless, even these female laborers helped create a shared sense among soldiers from all regions about what constituted masculine duties in camp. For example, women would, for a fee, wash the men's clothes, a task that soldiers did not see as particularly manly. Colonel William Irvine of the Second Pennsylvania Regiment warned women to do their duty at a reasonable rate, declaring, "should any woman refuse to wash for a soldier at the above

21. On the continuity of family roles and labor in the military, see Holly A. Mayer, *Belonging to the Army: Camp Followers and Community During the American Revolution* (Columbia, S.C., 1996), 138. Entry: February 11, 1779, Journal of John H. Hawkins, HSP; Petition of Jane Taplin, n.d., PRG, reel 10, frame 205; *Pennsylvania Packet*, March 4, 1778; RWPF, file S22799.

22. See Holly Mayer, *Belonging to the Army*, 15 and 147, on the role of officers' wives at camp.

rates ... [officers are] to dismiss her [from] the Regiment." Another important role of women in camp, as at home, was sewing and making clothes. Captain Joseph Stiles was directed to employ "a number of women to make into shirts, all the linen in your possession." Moreover, the language of orderly books makes it clear that women were considered a constituent part of the Continental army. Typical orders regarding women, for example, declared that "no woman shall be permitted to ride in any of the wagons without leave in writing [from] their brigadier to whose brigade *she belongs*" [emphasis added]. Yet it was also understood that these prostitutes, wives, lovers, and laborers constituted a distinctly feminine part of the army. They were not soldiers. That special role was to be filled (at least officially) only by a man. A very small number of women blurred gender lines and served as soldiers, but this was noted by troops with astonishment. Distinct roles for men and women within the military community underscored modified continuities between civilian life and the national army.[23]

If the presence of women extended aspects of the prewar community and gender order into the military, the rank hierarchy did the same for social distinctions. Officers, patterning their identities after those of European regular officers, cultivated an image of gentility that transcended regional differences. Such pretensions instilled a sense of "rank/class consciousness" among the officers that eventually spread to the soldiers. The rank and file used common regional and class backgrounds, friendship, unit pride, and shared experiences as low-ranking troops to define what it meant to be a soldier. Their superiors saw honor, professionalism, and airs of superiority toward their men as the hallmarks of their military identities. Although American officers lacked the aristocratic backgrounds of their European counterparts, they saw themselves as gentlemen. They were, therefore, virtually obsessed with their military reputations. A commission was an avenue to genteel manhood in the military, and when officers were denied what they believed to be a just promotion, they would rather leave the army than continue. Major Ennion Williams resigned in February 1777 when, he said, "the several promotions above me renders my station no longer honorable." Similarly, Captain Andrew Porter left when he failed to receive the rank of major, to which he "conceived myself entitled." Junior and senior officers believed that their commissions denoted superior social status

23. Orders: October 7, 1778, Orderly Book of the Second Pennsylvania Regiment, HSP; Supreme Executive Council to Captain Joseph Stiles, May 5, 1778, PRG, reel 113, frame 1304; Orders: July 4, 1777, Orderly Book of the Thirteenth Pennsylvania Regiment, HSP. A very few women served as soldiers by posing as men in the army. See, for example, Linda Grant DePauw, *Four Traditions: Women of New York During the American Revolution* (Albany, 1974).

and entitled them to respect. Alexander Graydon's reaction to the possibility that he might be drafted as an enlisted man in the militia shows how closely linked class and officer status were: "after having held the rank of captain in the Continental army, he confesses that his feelings would have been wounded by being obliged to perform the duty of a private centinel in common with a set of men (the peasantry of the country) with whom from their education and manner of life he could not associate."[24]

In order to solidify their claims to social superiority, Continental officers sought better living conditions than those of their men. They set themselves off from their men by living in separate quarters, and they expected better provisions. Isaac Craig, a Pennsylvania officer in the Marines, was shocked in 1776 when he was served the same rations as the men, "some salt beef and old bread." He noted, "we the officers concluded we had a right to something better than altogether salt provisions." The conspicuously better life enjoyed by the officers served to reinforce both class and rank differences. For example, John Lardner, an officer in the Philadelphia Lighthorse, sought out accommodations befitting his status while serving in New Jersey. He informed his mother that "we have got one of the best houses in Amboy . . . five stables for our horses, a man to take care of them, and a negro wench to cook and wash for us." Officers could easily see their manner of life as a transplantation of a deferential community from home into the military. In a sense, they attempted to recreate the prewar imagined community. Obvious differences in living conditions over the long term—when compared with the short tours of the militia—graphically illustrated material inequities in the rank system, however.[25]

Day-to-day practices in the army enacted and underscored differences between the officers and men. In the Fourth Pennsylvania Battalion, officers wore certain cockades to distinguish their rank before uniforms became standardized. Officers also tried to deny the men any physical characteristics, such as long hair, that might connote military gentility. They attempted to enforce uniformity of appearance on the men to reaffirm both groups' military status.

24. Major Ennion Williams to President Wharton, February 4, 1777, PRG, reel 11, frame 1203; Captain Andrew Porter to Supreme Executive Council, March 12, 1782, PRG, reel 19, frame 567; Memorial of Alexander Graydon, October 5, 1780, PRG, reel 16, frame 1223.
25. Isaac Craig to the Marine Committee, November 5, 1776, Isaac Craig Papers, Craig Collection, microfilm, Carnegie Library, Pittsburgh, Pennsylvania, reel 1; John Lardner to Mrs. C. Lardner, August 14, 1776, Lardner Family Papers, HSP; Orders: July 21, 1776, Orderly Book of the Third Pennsylvania Battalion, HSP.

Such expedients reinforced the soldiers' status as common men and common soldiers. For the Second Pennsylvania Regiment, "the hair of all the non-commissioned officers and privates [was] to be cut short and alike." Colonel Lewis Nichola declared that proper discipline could only be accomplished through "impressing soldiers with a high idea of the superiority of their officers over them, supported not only by force, but also by every reasonable mark of distinction which reminds them of that superiority." If such social and professional pretensions created solidarity among the officer corps, it also undoubtedly reinforced bonds among common soldiers who defined themselves in opposition to their superiors.[26]

Further highlighting the enlisted men's common lot and their differences from officers was the process of military justice. In the regular army, especially, punishment for breaches of discipline illustrated the logic of class and rank. The exercise of army law over enlisted men reflected the eighteenth-century Anglo-American legal tradition of bodily punishment for lower-class lawbreakers. The system operated selectively along class/rank lines: trials, sentences, verdicts, and pardons were in the hands of officers. Although punishment in the American forces was almost always lighter than in the British, as the war progressed, penalties for enlisted men became more harsh. Pennsylvania officers used flogging as the most common penalty. By 1776, the standard punishment for desertion was thirty-nine lashes. As the Continental army became more professionalized and officers came to see themselves as similar to their European counterparts, stiffer penalties followed. Roger Curry of the Third Pennsylvania Regiment received one hundred lashes for stealing "a pair of white worsted stockings" from an officer's tent (a heavier penalty than for desertion). In 1778, Alexander Dinney of the Fourth Pennsylvania Regiment suffered one hundred lashes for "repeated desertion." John Mullen of the Second Pennsylvania received the same punishment for "leaving his post and getting drunk." Members of the Eighth Pennsylvania who were out of camp after retreat were subject to twenty-five lashes. At the same court-martial session, Thomas Cunningham, a soldier, was sentenced to one hundred lashes for desertion. Death by execution was another element of military justice for particularly disorderly soldiers. In 1780, James Coleman of the Eleventh Pennsylvania was sentenced to death for "repeated desertion, forgery, and disposing of his arms."

26. Orders: March 31, 1776, Orderly Book of the Fourth Pennsylvania Battalion, HSP; Orders: April 6, 1778, Orderly Book of the Second Pennsylvania Regiment, HSP; Lewis Nichola to Edward Hand, May 26, 1781, Feinstone Collection, DLAR, item 1025.

In the same year, Jacob Justice and Thomas Brown of the Seventh Pennsylvania were "under sentence of death for plundering."[27]

Such corporal punishment against soldiers served to create a spectacle by which military authority was upheld. Borrowing the concepts of "majesty, justice, and mercy" from English criminal law, officers remained in total control of the ritual of punishment. They reinforced their rank status by ordering floggings and executions. Such scenes preserved military order by suggesting the fate of all who might defy it. Officers hoped that soldiers who witnessed punishments would be deterred from committing comparable offenses. Colonel William Butler spoke for many Pennsylvania officers when he declared that "public examples" should "be made of . . . these villains." Senior officers also granted discretionary pardons. Like a monarch, the commander-in-chief could remit a sentence. Such majestic power allowed officers to give selective mercy. Last-minute reprieves were received by many a Revolutionary soldier while on the gallows. Such spectacles were designed to make patently clear the omnipotence of the rank hierarchy.[28]

In contrast, officers received quite different penalties than enlisted men for comparable offenses. The disparity must have been glaring to soldiers. Officers were far more likely to receive acquittal. If convicted, their punishment was usually a form of dishonor. Corporal punishment for an officer was virtually unheard of in the Revolutionary army. Their punishment was primarily psychological. Shame was the specter that followed officers who violated the codes of military propriety. Lieutenant Anderson of the Eleventh Pennsylvania was

27. Robert Harry Berlin, "The Administration of Military Justice in the Continental Army During the American Revolution" (Ph.D. diss., University of California, Santa Barbara, 1976), 124–29, explains that officers filled the role of judges in all matters of military justice in the Continental army. On the eighteenth-century legal system that tended to punish lower-class lawbreakers physically, see E. P. Thompson, *Whigs and Hunters: The Origins of the Black Act* (New York, 1975), 197, and Douglas Hay, "Property, Authority, and Criminal Law," in *Albion's Fatal Tree: Crime and Society in Eighteenth-Century England*, ed. Douglas Hay et al. (London, 1975), 45–48. Orders: July 7, 1776, Orderly Book of Hand's Rifle Regiment, HSP; Orders: August 8, 1778, and October 5, 1778, Orderly Book of the Second Pennsylvania Regiment, HSP; Orders: November 10, 1778, Orderly Book of the First Pennsylvania Regiment, PA, 2d ser., 11:384; Orders: May 1, 1780, Orderly Book of the Second Pennsylvania Regiment, HSP; Orderly Book of the Eighth Pennsylvania Regiment, 2 NN 7, 2 NN 41–43, DMC; Orders: May 9, 1780, Orderly Book of the Second Pennsylvania Regiment, HSP.

28. Hay, "Property, Authority, and Criminal Law," asserts that "majesty, justice, and mercy" are the centerpieces of English criminal law (26, 40–48). Louis P. Masur, *Rites of Execution: Capital Punishment and the Transformation of American Culture* (New York, 1989), 27–34, notes this tradition's persistence in the United States. Colonel William Butler to General Edward Hand, November 10, 1778, Hand Papers, 1:48, HSP; on pardons as majestic largesse, see E. P. Thompson, *Whigs and Hunters*, 262, and Royster, *Revolutionary People*, 80.

discharged for "behaving in a manner unbecoming the character of an officer and a gentleman." Another punishment for an officer found guilty of assault was "to be severely reprimanded by Colonel St. Clair." Captain Theopolis Parke was found guilty of "defrauding his men of their pay and bounty" and was sentenced to be "cashiered with infamy." Captain Hector McNeil was found guilty of "drunkenness and ungentleman-like behavior . . . discharged from the service with disgrace." Lieutenant Foster deserted to British-occupied Philadelphia and was "to have his sword broken over his head," to be cashiered, and to have his name published in newspapers. Officers of the First Pennsylvania absent without leave were implored to return to camp or risk "the blush that such a stigma thrown on their characters would give." It would be a mistake, though, to assume that the punishment of officers was light. Humiliation cut to the very heart of their class and rank status by tainting honor.[29]

In courts-martial relating to conflicts between officers and men, the class/rank-based disparities of military justice were most manifest. Not surprisingly, the officers who ran the court usually sided with their own. Typically, officers found guilty of physically abusing their men would be acquitted by virtue of justifiable circumstances. The ability to strike enlisted men at will was considered a privilege of rank. It was rarely denied to officers, no matter how dubious the use of physical force appeared. Lieutenant James Armstrong of the Third Pennsylvania Regiment was tried for "beating a number of persons." The court decided "that the provocation was, in some degree, equal to the offense." Adam Gilchrist, a foragemaster, was found guilty of "abusing and threatening to take the life of a soldier." The court declared, "as the nature of the insult received by him rendered instantaneous chastisement necessary, the court is of the opinion he is pardonable." In 1779, Captain Lee was found guilty of "wounding Luke Jolly, a private in the Tenth Pennsylvania Regiment." The result was similar. The court found that "the conduct of Captain Lee was rash, but considering the vexation occasioned by losing the horses, and being forced to walk so far and supposing the man to have stolen the horse and hesitating to go back when ordered is a sufficient excuse for his conduct." In September

---

29. On the disjunction between officers' and soldiers' punishments, see Robert Berlin, "Administration of Military Justice," 111. Berlin notes that the worst penalty for convicted soldiers was death, while their officers were subject, at worst, to dismissal and shame. Orders: April 3, 1778, Orderly Book of the Ninth Pennsylvania Regiment, HSP; Orders: August 21, 1776, Orderly Book of the Fourth Pennsylvania Battalion, HSP; *Pennsylvania Packet,* April 18, 1780; Orders: November 26, 1777, Orderly Book of Brown's Philadelphia Militia Artillery, Early American Orderly Books, NYHS; *Pennsylvania Packet,* October 23, 1779, and February 25, 1778.

1778, Lieutenant McFarlin of the First Pennsylvania Regiment was tried for "unmercifully beating James Welch, soldier in the Seventh Pennsylvania Regiment, without provocation." The officers trying the case concluded: "the court are unanimously of the opinion that Lieutenant McFarlin did not unmercifully beat James Welch and that he had a sufficient provocation to strike him."[30]

The courts were not as understanding when the defendants were enlisted men who did violence to their officers. One of the most ominous transgressions a soldier could commit was to strike a superior. Such action threatened the very stability of the class/rank system. Reaction in courts-martial was quick and decisive. John McCarty of the First Pennsylvania Regiment took matters into his own hands when his superior threatened him. McCarty grumbled about guard duty, and his sergeant replied that "he would be obliged to strike him and make him go." The soldier then answered, "if you do, you must take what follows." McCarty was found guilty of "abusing and threatening" the sergeant and an officer. For the transgression against the noncommissioned officer, McCarty was sentenced to fifty lashes. Significantly, he was supposed to get one hundred lashes for his insubordination toward his officer. The punishment indicated that an equal offense against a commissioned officer was seen as twice as heinous. Others received comparably harsh sentences for not respecting their officers. Thomas Temmington of the Seventh Pennsylvania Regiment was found guilty of "disobedience of orders and attempting to shoot Captain Beting" and was sentenced to one hundred lashes. Neal McGonnagel of the same regiment was to suffer death for "threatening Captain Scott's life." Perhaps in some conflicts with officers, soldiers took justice upon themselves, aware that military justice would not protect them from abusive superiors. When enlisted men did seriously injure their officers, the punishment was rapid and severe. There was no inquiry into whether the situation merited the action. The preservation of discipline and the rank hierarchy necessitated harsh penalties for insubordination in any guise.[31]

The rituals of rank, coupled with enlisted men's reaction to them, helped construct a subcommunity identity of soldiery within the Continental army,

30. Orders: August 1, 1778, Orderly Book of the First Pennsylvania Regiment, PA, 2d ser., 11:294; Orders: April 13, 1778, Orderly Book of the Second Pennsylvania Regiment, HSP; Orders: July 4, 1779, Orderly Book of the Fifth Pennsylvania Regiment, Early American Orderly Books, NYHS; Orders: September 10, 1778, Orderly Book of the First Pennsylvania Regiment, PA, 2d ser., 11:342.

31. Proceedings of a Court-Martial, May 10, 1780, Irvine Papers, 3:15, HSP; Orders: May 8 and 11, 1780, and January 3, 1779, Orderly Book of the Second Pennsylvania Regiment, HSP; Orders: August 11, 1778, Orderly Book of the First Pennsylvania Regiment, PA, 2d ser., 11:309.

especially within companies and regiments. Common interests grew out of similar class, regional, and rank status among Pennsylvania enlisted men of the Continental army. Belonging to an institution that was considerably less democratic than the militia, the Continentals primarily emphasized their material rights. The men came from different regions, but they shared assumptions about what constituted a moral economy in both army and civilian life. They presumed that the bare necessities of life would be available at camp on a fair basis for all. In fact, many probably recalled politicized mob actions in which they engaged before the Revolution to defend the economic interests of their immediate community against imperial policy and life in the army. They expected to receive promised pay and bounties on time. Troops also demanded that their basic material needs (food, clothing, shelter, and so on) be met. Although soldiers endured privation on a level that few European professional soldiers would, there was a limit. When they felt that the government or their officers treated them unfairly, soldiers took matters into their own hands and reacted to blatant violations of what might be termed their military moral economy. They developed comparable understandings of what sort of treatment they deserved and developed strategies against mistreatment. Such actions took the form of petitions, individual and mass desertions, and isolated uprisings against the authority of officers, culminating in the revolt of the entire Pennsylvania Line in 1781.[32]

Material complaints about the lack of supplies were salient throughout the war. Soldiers often attempted to effect action by petitioning the state government. In late 1776, a number of privates of the Pennsylvania Line complained to the state about how their captain abused them and seemed to be withholding the men's bounties and supplies. Similarly, in 1777, privates of the Third Battalion stated, "your petitioners having suffered severely during the late actions they served in, were in hopes to find some comfortable refreshment from the fruits of their hazardous labor." They demanded their back pay and supplies, complaining that their colonel was "using us with ill treats, unbecoming

32. See E. P. Thompson, "The Moral Economy of the English Crowd in the Eighteenth Century," *Past and Present* 50 (1971): 76–136, on the moral economy as a basis for popular politics in eighteenth-century Anglo civilian society, and see James Kirby Martin, "A 'Most Undisciplined, Profligate Crew': Protest and Defiance in the Continental Ranks, 1776–1783," in *Arms and Independence: The Military Character of the American Revolution*, ed. Ronald Hoffman and Peter J. Albert (Charlottesville, Va., 1984), on the Continental rank and file's development of a moral economy within the military community. M. S. Anderson, *War and Society of Europe of the Old Regime* (New York, 1988), 54–55, notes the European level of tolerance among regulars for material deprivation and the omnipresence of mutiny.

a gentleman." The men of an artillery company petitioned in 1780 that they were "in great distress for regimental clothing and that their pay is by no means sufficient to furnish them with the least article of that nature." The men of the Pennsylvania Continental Artificers declared that they had "been a long time without pay and under great necessity for clothing." General Anthony Wayne noted how the absence of liquor for the men "begins to make them murmur." Another officer reported, "my people are growing very clamorous having no prospect of bread for some days." Ominously, on the eve of the 1781 revolt of the Pennsylvania Line, Anthony Wayne observed that "the distressed situation of the soldiery for want of clothing beggars all description." Both officers and men knew that the soldiery would not tolerate such severe hardships for long without developing their own remedies.[33]

For regular troops already in the army for a long tour of service, unfair withholding of pay often occasioned simple desertion. Leaving the army without permission was, in part, an individual decision. But when men did it *en masse*, it demonstrated solidarity among the soldiery. Deserting or threatening to do so was one way to force authorities to address the soldiers' material situation. Even officers were forced to admit that the cause of desertion in their ranks was poor supply or overdue wages. In 1777, Colonel William Cook noted: "This hard duty without a proper allowance of rum and want of pay to provide necessaries, I believe, occasioned a number of the soldiers to desert." Colonel William Butler explained about his men that "nothing but their naked situation induces any of them to leave me." Anthony Wayne stated that in the face of shortages of clothes, blankets, and other necessities, the soldiers "unhappily think any change will be far the better and too many have therefore risked desertion." Officers noted that David Kennedy, a private in the Ninth Pennsylvania, was openly "threatening to desert as soon as he got shoes." Francis Johnston commented that during the particularly harsh winter of 1779–80, "desertion prevails considerably." By spring 1780, the situation had not improved. General William Irvine wrote: "Desertion still prevails to a vast degree . . . want of provision and other hardship I believe are the leading causes—together with the little value of their pay." In early 1781, General Arthur St. Clair anxiously

33. Petition of Soldiers of the Continental Line, PRG, reel 11, frame 706; Petition of the Privates of the Third Battalion, PRG, reel 12, frame 32; Petition of Captain W. E. Godfrey's Artillery Company, July 27, 1780, PRG, reel 16, frame 789; Petition of Captain H. Mathews and Men of the Pennsylvania Continental Artificers, January 1, 1781, PRG, reel 17, frame 305; Anthony Wayne to Colonel A. Dunham, December 7, 1780, Wayne Papers, 11:27, HSP; Major Reid to William Irvine, January 2, 1780, Irvine Papers, 2:90, HSP; Anthony Wayne to Francis Johnston, December 30, 1780, Wayne Papers, 11:89, HSP.

observed of the Pennsylvania regulars under his command the "great uneasiness prevailing among the soldiery; occasioned by the detention of their bounties.... It has been represented to me that unless they are soon made easy on these heads, it is like to end in a general desertion." Given the above evidence, it also appears that Pennsylvania Continentals saw their service in contractual terms. If the state government or army was unable to provide them with the necessities of life allowing them to function as soldiers, they apparently found it completely acceptable to break their part of their voluntary agreement and go home.[34]

Another method of seeking redress was mutiny. A risky and radical tactic in the military, collective actions by soldiers must have seemed fairly compatible with mob actions popular during the prewar crisis with Britain. Rebellions by the rank and file were typically in reaction to the deeds of officers or egregious violations of the military moral economy (and often both). Although mutinies were common in early modern European armies, Revolutionary ones differed slightly. Continental soldiers were not lifetime professionals. Few fled to the enemy after mutiny or desertion. They were not simply striking for better wages. Most had their own stake in the localist nation and simply wanted to be treated as valued participants in the military community. In the highly charged political atmosphere of the American Revolution, such uprisings could take on ominous overtones in the eyes of elites. Men took up arms with expectations unique to their classes and locales. The troops' belief in their own variants of liberty and equality provided contexts for the discussion of equitable treatment in the army. When a rebellion erupted among the Revolutionary soldiery, it caused elites to fear a possible political faction emerging among the armed lower sort.[35]

Mutinies occurred regularly among Pennsylvania troops throughout the war. Soldiers resorted to collective resistance when other avenues appeared futile. They rebelled against authorities who had demonstrated themselves, in the troops' view, unfit to lead. In early revolts, collective action was typically confined to one or a few small units. In 1775, a few men of Thompson's Rifle

---

34. Colonel William Cook to Supreme Executive Council, April 23, 1777, PRG, reel 12, frame 291; Colonel Richard Butler to President Wharton, March 28, 1778, PRG, reel 13, frame 1059; Anthony Wayne to President Wharton, May 4, 1778, PRG, reel 13, frame 1295; General Orders, February 22, 1778, in *The Writings of George Washington*, ed. John C. Fitzpatrick (Washington, D.C., 1933), 10:500; Francis Johnston to Joseph Reed, March 5, 1780, Reed Papers, NYHS, reel 2; William Irvine to Joseph Reed, May 2, 1780, PRG, reel 16, frames 13–14; Arthur St. Clair to Joseph Reed, April 3, 1781, Arthur St. Clair Papers, microfilm, Ohio Historical Society, reel 1, frame 532.

35. See M. S. Anderson, *War and Society*, 53–54, on mutinies in eighteenth-century European armies.

Battalion mutinied when some of their comrades were court-martialed. A few months later, some Pennsylvanians in the northern army under Francis Johnston were in a state of "great disturbance and mutiny." These uprisings originated in small units, and they illustrate how men from the same locale were quick to recognize their common interests and mount resistance to their officers. As the war went on, ties grew and so did the numbers and significance of mutinies. On August 27, 1776, members of the Pennsylvania militia posted in Philadelphia refused "to obey the general marching orders [and] their officers" and behaved in a "riotous" manner. The disorder spread to the Pennsylvania Line on the same day, and officers of the Fourth Pennsylvania Battalion cautioned their men "not to carve out remedies for themselves if they are injured." Mutiny occurred again among the Pennsylvania Continentals in the northern theater in September 1776. Lewis Farmer described how "three battalions mutinied and appeared on the parade under arms. . . . As to their complaints: the want of pay, the want of clothes, the want of blankets, the want of particular species of rations." In January of the following year, "the Sixth Regiment of Pennsylvania assembled and refused duty." These actions were on regiment and battalion levels, involving hundreds of men. Officers, fearing that their authority was in jeopardy, typically reacted quickly and put down these early rebellions. Negotiations were rare. Persuasion and, at times, the threat of force ended soldier strikes.[36]

The most famous mutiny of the Revolution was that of the entire Pennsylvania Line in January 1781. Again, soldiers' commitment to protecting their own interests within the military moral economy was the central motive. Men were angry that their superiors construed their "three years or the duration of the war" enlistments to mean that they were to serve at least three years. The troops obviously believed that they were to serve three years at the most. Soldiers were also upset about their lack of material supplies and the high bounties being paid to new troops. This time, however, the unrest began with a single regiment

36. Henry J. Young, ed., "The Spirit of 1775: A Letter of Robert Magaw, Major of the Continental Riflemen to the Gentlemen of the Committee of Correspondence in the Town of Carlisle, Dated at Cambridge, 13 August 1775, with an Essay on the Background and the Sequel," *John and Mary's Journal* 1 (1975): 15–50; Orders: September 3, 1775, Orderly Book of Thompson's Rifle Battalion, HSP; Nicholas Haussegger to Francis Johnston, March 18, 1776, Wayne Papers, 1:37, HSP; Francis Johnston to Anthony Wayne, February 26, 1776, Wayne Papers, 1:29, HSP; Orders: August 27, 1776, Orderly Book of the Fourth Battalion Chester County Associators, HSP; Resolve of the Pennsylvania Council of Safety, August 27, 1776, PCC, reel 83, vol. 1, I. 69, p. 221; Orders: August 27, 1776, Orderly Book of the Fourth Pennsylvania Battalion, HSP; Lewis Farmer to President Wharton, September 14, 1776, PCC, reel 83, vol. 1, I. 69, pp. 291–92; Anthony Wayne to Philip Schuyler, January 26, 1777, Wayne Papers, 2:74, HSP; Anthony Wayne to Philip Schuyler, February 12, 1777, Wayne Papers, 2:86, HSP.

and quickly spread to the entire line. This expression of soldier solidarity was truly cross-regional, involving regular enlisted men from throughout the state and different units. Troops felt strongly that their actions were the only possible recourse against the injustice shown by the state and their officers. Christian Moser of the Fourth Pennsylvania Regiment was certain enough about the rectitude of his participation in the mutiny to recount it in his pension application. He recalled: "The Pennsylvania Line to which deponent belonged, revolted and marched from Morristown to Trenton.... Deponent's term of enlistment expired in April 1780, but he was detained in the service till the revolt. This unjust detention was the cause of the revolt of deponent and others." Jeremiah Murray explained that he served under General Wayne "until their revolt." Dennis Carrol declared the mutiny to be "occasioned by keeping the men in the army after their times had expired." Carrol was on furlough when the unrest broke out, agreed with his comrades, and simply failed to return to his unit.[37]

As the January 1781 mutiny progressed, it became apparent that many of the soldiers were also angry with their superiors. The initial outbreak of the revolt resulted in violence between officers and their men. As usual, officers sought to crush the rebellion. They were unsuccessful. The solidarity among the soldiers was too extensive. Anthony Wayne reported to George Washington that "every possible exertion was used by the officers to suppress it [the mutiny] in its rise, but the torrent was too potent to be stemmed." Franz Dido, a private, recalled the men's reactions to Anthony Wayne's initial attempts to intervene in the revolt. He noted how "the soldiers [were] pointing [at Wayne] and crying shoot the damned rascal." Dido also described how "Colonel [Walter] Stewart was driven out of camp at the point of the bayonet." When the mutineers were camped at Princeton, a group of officers attempted to approach the men but "were stopped by a guard and treated with a great deal of insolence and turned back." As President Joseph Reed of the Pennsylvania Supreme Executive Council was negotiating to settle the dispute, the men continued to express their displeasure with their officers. Colonel Craig was "exceedingly insulted by some of his regiment who presented their firelocks and threatened to take his life." Years of resentment over the officers' class pretensions and mistreatment of the men exploded in 1781.[38]

37. Carl Van Doren, *Mutiny in January* (New York, 1943), 16–17; RWPF, files S22912, S41023, S2117.

38. Anthony Wayne to George Washington, January 2, 1781, Wayne Papers, 11:101, HSP; RWPF, file W7017; Major Thomas Moore to Anthony Wayne, January 5, 1781, Wayne Papers, 11:125, HSP; Samuel Atlee to Joseph Reed, January 16, 1781, Reed Papers, NYHS, reel 3.

Still, the soldiers did not rebel against the Revolutionary cause, in which they had their own stake. It was a mutiny against injustice and other principles that they believed to be at odds with the very ideals for which they were fighting. When the British heard of the Pennsylvanians' actions, they immediately sent word that the Crown would offer a pardon in exchange for laying down their arms and declaring their allegiance to Great Britain. They added "that pay due to them from Congress [will be] faithfully paid to them [by the British] without any expectation of military service." Despite the promise of material gain, the troops refused to negotiate with the enemy. Anthony Wayne noted that "the soldiery in general affect to spurn at the idea of turning *Arnold* (as they express it)." Franz Dido declared with satisfaction, "I remember the hanging of the spies who had been sent to us by the British." Far from betraying the spirit of the Revolution, the mutineers felt that they were upholding it. They believed their cause was just and had no desire to flock to the British standard.[39]

The significance of the mutiny of January 1781 is not only that most of the Pennsylvania Line soldiers united across unit and regional distinctions but also that they won. Their negotiations with the state government resulted in discharges on the enlisted men's terms. They had successfully identified their common interests as soldiers and defended them against their officers. The mutineers expected to be treated fairly as men and as defenders of their country. Troops rejected the rank and class authority of officers who appeared unfit to lead. The rank and file neither shrank from confronting their superiors with force nor abandoned their own vision of the Revolutionary cause. The Pennsylvania Line mutiny was a moment in which their shared concerns as soldiers overrode others. As rank-and-file defenders of the localist nation, they guarded their vision of their military community and interests. Despite sympathy from some troops from outside Pennsylvania, however, the deep regional divisions within the nation and soldiery quickly reappeared. Mutiny broke out in the New Jersey Line soon after the Pennsylvania revolt, and Washington purposefully used New England troops to crush it. The fact that the New Englanders were willing to do so demonstrates the limitations inherent in the developed identity among "brother soldiers" in the ranks. Apparently these men were unwilling to stand up for the particular interests of the troops of another state line.[40]

---

39. "Copy of Proposals of the British to the Pennsylvania Troops," January 1781, PCC, reel 170, vol. 2, I. 152, p. 499; Anthony Wayne to George Washington, January 8, 1781, Wayne Papers, 11:114, HSP; RWPF, file W7017.

40. On the suppression of the New Jersey revolt, see Neimeyer, *America Goes to War,* 152–53.

Mutinies continued among Pennsylvania troops, but they never again attained the level of solidarity of January 1781. In spring 1781, Anthony Wayne brutally suppressed a potential mutiny on the march to Virginia by executing "ringleaders." When discontent among Pennsylvania troops serving in the southern army manifested itself, Nathanael Greene used a similar tactic and punished supposed leaders. The last uprising involving Pennsylvania troops occurred in June 1783, when elements of the state's Continentals mutinied in Philadelphia over back pay, forcing Congress to flee the city. The militia did not turn out in numbers sufficient to crush the revolt, and the Continental army—essentially in the process of disbanding—was also unable to respond. Once again, negotiation with the soldiers ended the dispute.[41]

In conjunction with the politicization of the militia and the Fort Wilson riot, the collective actions taken by Pennsylvania Continentals in 1781 and 1783 must have appeared ominous to the state government. Although the radicals owed their ascension in part to support from ordinary soldiers, they also realized that could not always control this politicized military force. Conversely, soldiers were conscious of their agency in creating the republic. Both the militia and the Pennsylvania Line represented and enacted the nation that they were helping create. Diverse groups protecting various imagined communities served together, and military life, rather than nationalizing soldiers, appeared to refine their localism. Particularly within the Continental army, the rank hierarchy helped soldiers construct a subcommunity within the camp. Prewar class differences codified by rank distinctions graphically demonstrated differing rank/class interests within units. Soldiers' views of who they represented and what they were fighting for narrowed even further. Continued significant regional differences prevented full trans-regional class consciousness in the army, as witnessed by the lack of support for the lower-sort Philadelphia militia at Fort Wilson and the continued use of Continentals from other states or units to put down mutinies. Yet the riot and mutinies suggested growing power for poorer white men. Revolutionary military life, like the emerging United States, was simultaneously pervaded by a contentiously pluralistic localism and a promise for white males.

41. See ibid., 153–57, on subsequent Pennsylvania mutinies, and on the 1783 revolt, see Mary A. Y. Gallagher, "Reinterpreting the 'Very Trifling Mutiny' at Philadelphia in June 1783," *PMHB* 119 (1995): 3–35.

Tory Military Life

The experience of armed loyalists in their military communities was decidedly different. Those who chose to fight against the Revolutionaries typically had to flee their homes, often leaving their families behind, unless the main British army operated in their immediate area. For southeastern Pennsylvanians, the British occupation was short-lived; Tories in the region left in the evacuation. The anti-Revolutionary forces that they joined were varied. Some were recruited in loyalist units on an equal footing with British regulars. Within the main army, these men served alongside British troops and large numbers of German auxiliaries. European American Tories also encountered large numbers of slaves who fled to British lines in the hope of freeing themselves. While only a few of these African Americans served as troops, the imperial forces utilized runaways for labor and support duties. Frontier loyalists saw limited numbers of British regular troops in the backcountry. More prominently, they served in alliance with the large numbers of Indian forces who resisted the Revolutionaries. What was clear to most European Americans who fought against the rebels was that the imperial coalition was hierarchical, with British (rather than loyalist) aims being paramount to the royal officers and officials who coordinated the war effort. As the conflict progressed, most Tories came to understand that the only way they would ever be able to return to their former lives would be with a complete imperial victory that would change American society. British victory would at least temporarily preserve eastern Indian independence. It would also probably free large numbers of slaves and destabilize the institution of slavery in North America. Joining the imperial cause literally forced loyalists to take a broader view of community, one that would reluctantly have to include non-European groups.

Military life for Tories almost invariably involved leaving their locales and possessions behind in order to serve. Jasper Harding was typical: he was forced "from his attachment to British government [to abandon] his property" early in the war in order to reach British lines. Hugh McNeil of Bedford County spent his time early in the war organizing a sort of underground railroad for Tories through the heavily Whig backcountry area, "assisting young men to escape to the British army." After a prison term for his actions, McNeil left his community for good "upon the army landing at the Head of Elk . . . and has remained with them ever since." Margaret Lenox was left behind in Philadelphia after her husband made his way to Montreal to join the British. John

Loofbourrow "was obliged to save his life, to abandon his family and property and to seek for refuge with the British army." The dislocation of families was so great among such men that the royal forces at one point raised money "for the benefit of the women and children" of loyalists. Unlike the rebel militia, Tories did not usually serve short tours in the immediate vicinity. The fortunes of the war demanded that they leave their areas and serve where British authorities deemed necessary. Even more galling must have been the fact that the rebel militias remained in control of the communities that Tories left.[42]

Pennsylvania loyalists also served in units in which the connection to their specific locale was not always clear. They served in various provincial forces, only a few of which were raised on a purely geographical basis. The limited number of loyalist units organized and the shortage of men often made a specific local character impossible. The Bucks County Dragoons and Philadelphia Light Dragoons were raised largely in the southeastern part of the state during the British invasion. The local affiliation of troops in these units often varied, however. Owen Roberts, for example, joined the Bucks County Volunteers after leaving his home in Northampton County. Peter Partier, a farmer from Bucks County, served as "a private soldier in the 2d battalion of New Jersey Volunteers." Loyalist militias were rare enough that men who served in them came from regions outside the area they purported to represent. Charles Holmes fled Philadelphia for New York and served in a New York loyalist militia. Some Tory units raised in the state were organized along ethnic lines, such as the Volunteers of Ireland and the Black Company of Pioneers. Others had no specific regional or national composition; Butler's Rangers, for instance, was composed of various loyalists from Pennsylvania and New York. The Queen's Rangers had initially been recruited in New York and Connecticut to serve on frontier duty, but they were used with the British army in conventional operations. In the early Philadelphia campaign, about one hundred men from the southeastern Pennsylvania region joined the unit. Additionally, numbers of the Rangers' officers were southerners who had served under Lord Dunmore in Virginia, and the ranks also contained large numbers of Scottish highlanders from North Carolina. The Associated Loyalists evolved from a "Refugee Club" of Tories forced to leave their homes all over North America in occupied New York.[43]

42. AO13/96/367, AO12/40/262, AO12/100/345, AO13/71/175; Paul Leicester Ford, ed., *Orderly Book of the Maryland Loyalists Regiment, June 18, 1778–October 12, 1778* (Brooklyn, N.Y., 1891), 88.

43. AO13/71, pt. 2/241, AO12/40/295, AO12/100/346. Consult Robert S. Allen, ed., *The Loyal Americans: The Military Role of the Loyalist Provincial Corps and Their Settlement in British North America, 1775–1784* (Ottawa, Ontario, 1983), 11–12, on the various loyalist units. J. G. Simcoe, *A Journal of the*

The British invasion of Pennsylvania appeared to offer the best hope of local service. Indeed, during the British occupation of Philadelphia, approximately 1,400 Pennsylvanians who had not yet fought for the British enlisted into loyalist units. Circumstances would, however, remove most of these soldiers from their immediate areas. The British occupation of southeastern Pennsylvania lasted less than a year. When General Henry Clinton evacuated Philadelphia in June 1778, he took roughly 3,000 loyalists with him. Those actively employed as part of the army would not serve in this region again. Most retreated and served in New York City, which, over the course of the war, became a staging area of various refugees from Revolutionary power. Pennsylvanians mixed and joined together with Tories from all over British North America who had made their way to the occupied seaport. Later, Maryland and Pennsylvania loyalists were consolidated into the United Provincial Corps and sent for duty in Florida. In fact, by 1779 large numbers of Pennsylvania loyalists were fighting in Florida and Jamaica, decimated by disease and poorly supplied but still engaged in the larger cause of empire as the Revolution became, from the British point of view, a larger imperial war with Spain and France. The Volunteers of Ireland fought in Virginia and the Carolinas, and most of the native Pennsylvanians in the unit never saw their homes again. For the rest of the war, most active Pennsylvania loyalists (with the exception of some on the frontier) were operating and camped outside of their neighborhoods. It was becoming increasingly obvious that they could not simply hope for a quick victory to restore royal control of their locales. The only way they could possibly go home was in the case of complete British victory in a war against the French, Spanish, and American rebels all over the eastern seaboard of North America. Slowly, provincial localism was giving way under the weight of participation in a larger imperial war effort.[44]

Even the British army itself was a hodgepodge of different ethnicities and nationalities. Scottish Highlander units served alongside British infantry.

Operations of the Queen's Rangers (New York, 1968), 17–18, discusses the composition of the Queen's Rangers. On the Associated Loyalists, see Edward H. Tebbenhoff, "Associated Loyalists: An Aspect of Militant Loyalism," in *Patriots, Redcoats, and Loyalists,* ed. Onuf, 125.

44. Wilbur H. Siebert, *The Loyalists of Pennsylvania* (Columbus, Ohio, 1920), 41–42, gives the number of loyalists who enlisted during the Philadelphia campaign, and Middlekauff, *Glorious Cause,* 420, gives the number of loyalists who evacuated with Clinton's force. On New York as a staging area for refugees, see Robert Ernst, "A Tory-Eye View of the Evacuation of New York," in *Patriots, Redcoats, and Loyalists,* ed. Onuf, 378. Allen, ed., *Loyal Americans,* 11–12, discusses the transfer of Pennsylvania loyalists to Florida. Brigadier General John Campbell to General Sir Henry Clinton, 10 February–21 March 1779, in *Documents of the American Revolution,* ed. Davies, 17:56–57, makes clear the poor condition of Pennsylvania loyalists in Florida and Jamaica.

During operations in the middle colonies, German troops made up a sizable portion of the regulars. There was the potential for conflict, but all were united—if not by a purely common cause, then by strict British military discipline. In 1778, when British sailors "attacked and with knives wounded and defaced three Hessian soldiers" in New York, a loyalist newspaper expressed both surprise and regret. The *Royal Gazette* decried such acts that "raise a spirit of discord between nations, who have always lived together, whether in camp or garrison, with remarkable cordiality and affection." While this account may have overstated the bonds between Hessians and British, it does evoke the orderly multinational ideal of the regular army. Moreover, the presence of large numbers of German troops may have been responsible for the recruitment of German American Tories. Justice Walker, for instance, a Hessian-born Philadelphia tallow chandler, fled to British lines because he was persecuted "for upholding and clothing some of the band of musick [*sic*] belonging to the Hessian Corps in the service of his majesty." For sympathizing with fellow German-speaking members of the imperial coalition rather than obeying the mores of his new community, rebels forced Walker to side with the enemy. A number of loyalist units, including the British Legion, Volunteers of Ireland, and Queen's Rangers, were also "placed on equal footing with British Regular regiments." Thus, the "regulars" of the British army included not only Britons but also Germans and Americans.[45]

Another aspect of loyalist military life that differed from that of the Revolutionaries was the ubiquity of African Americans in support roles and occasionally as soldiers among the imperial forces. Given various British emancipation policies and the hope of freeing themselves with the forces of the Crown, the number of African Americans with the British dwarfed that of African Americans allied with the Revolutionaries. An estimated 80,000–100,000 slaves fled to British lines, and the black component of the army must have been apparent in camp. As with the Revolutionaries, they were usually employed in labor details. George Peters, a Pennsylvania free black and a miller by vocation, served as a "wagoner and laborer to the army." While free blacks and runaway slaves were often treated by British troops and American Tories with disdain and condescension, they were increasingly present in the imperial military community. Some Pennsylvania Tories served with African American soldiers. Samuel Lindsay left his farm in Chambersburg in early 1776 to join the nearest British force, Lord Dunmore's in Virginia. Lindsay suddenly found himself a part of a

45. *Royal Gazette*, February 14, 1778; AO12/38/9–11; Allen, ed., *Loyal Americans*, 12.

force composed of Tories, runaway servants, and the Ethiopian Regiment of freed slaves of rebel masters. Pennsylvanians who saw action in the southern campaign served with even larger numbers of African American allies and auxiliaries. The Volunteers of Ireland, raised by the British in Philadelphia, served in Virginia and in the Charleston campaign in South Carolina. These Tories would have been part of a diverse imperial force in that region, one described by rebels as

> consisting of two battalions of Highlanders (the 71st Regiment), two regiments of Hessians, 1 battalion of the 60th, 2 regiments of North American new levies, Col. Brown's corps of dragoons or light horse; to which were attached a large body of the most infamous banditti and horse thieves that perhaps ever were collected together any where, under the direction of McGirt (dignified with the title of Colonel) a corps of Indians, with negro and white savages disguised like them.

John Peebles, a British officer who participated in the attack on Charleston, remarked matter-of-factly on the constant flow of slaves coming to British lines to augment the anti-Revolutionary force. In one instance, he noted, "five Negroes came in to us having made their escape over the works." In another entry in his diary, he explained how African Americans immediately described their willingness to fight: "some Negroes come in from the town who say they intended to have made a sally."[46]

As was made clear in the description of the diverse army attacking the rebels in Charleston, the anti-Revolutionary military community consisted of large numbers of former slaves and also had numerous Indians. Indeed, Native Americans fighting to preserve their independence constituted the great bulk of the force fighting the Revolutionaries on the northern frontier. Loyalist units in the region, such as Butler's Rangers, served alongside significant allied Indian forces. Sometimes, Indian war leaders such as the Mohawk Joseph Brant commanded combined attacks. "Captain Brant" was praised by the loyalist James Rivington for leading "large bodies of refugees and Indians and occasion[ing]

46. On the numbers of slaves who fled to the British, see Frey, *Water from the Rock*, 211; AO12/102/25, AO12/40/19. See Holton, *Forced Founders*, 133–63, for the operations of Lord Dunmore and the Ethiopian Regiment. Mark M. Boatner III, *Encyclopedia of the American Revolution* (Mechanicsburg, Pa., 1994), discusses the operations of the Volunteers of Ireland (1156–57). The description of imperial forces at Charleston is in *Pennsylvania Gazette*, August 18, 1779; Ira D. Gruber, ed., *John Peebles' American War: The Diary of a Scottish Grenadier, 1776–1782* (Mechanicsburg, Pa., 1998), 356–57.

tremendous alarms in the back settlements." British forts such as Niagara served as staging areas for raids on the Revolutionaries and as refugee camps where displaced loyalists and Indians lived together. Although they belonged to separate groups, they were in close enough proximity that they constituted a singular military community. Once again, coordinating this larger war effort were the British commanders of posts and officials in the Indian Department. From the British and loyalist perspective, at least, the structure of such posts graphically represented their view of the imperial endeavor: a large British-led coalition of many different groups, including vast numbers of Indians. Loyalists were forced by necessity to make common cause with British frontier authorities and with Indians battling to maintain their independence.[47]

This is not to say that such service made Tories see their Native neighbors as equals in the empire. Before the war, most rank-and-file loyalists shared colonial hostility toward Indians generated by earlier imperial wars. Many carried their suspicions of Indians as an entire group into the Revolution. Philip Buck, of Butler's Rangers, complained that "the Indians had his other cattle in 1778" that the rebels did not take. Buck's use of the term "Indians" suggests that he, like most Revolutionaries, refused to differentiate among Native groups. Numbers of Tories omitted mentioning their association with Indians by stating that they served as loyalists under British command. Edward Turner, a Pennamite settler, described how "there were families of Loyalists [who] came away to join the British. His father came with him, joined the rangers [and] died in service." Specifically, men such as Turner explained their service as joining the British cause, not siding specifically with the Indian struggle for independence.[48]

Others, however, openly recognized the military importance of Indian allies. When rumors flew among the Queen's Rangers that they would be transferred for duty in the West Indies in 1778, Lt. Colonel John Simcoe requested "that he might be permitted with his corps, and other loyalists to join the Indians and troops under Colonel Butler." Also, Pennsylvanians active in prewar frontier trade easily made the transition to the British Indian Department, where they were responsible for day-to-day trade and diplomacy and Indian raids on Revolutionaries. Matthew Elliot, for example, had blankets and other items

---

47. James Rivington to Richard Cumberland, November 23, 1778, in *Documents of the American Revolution*, ed. Davies, 15:267. On Fort Niagara as a refugee camp and heterogeneous community, see Calloway, *American Revolution in Indian Country*, 130.

48. AO12/40/349, AO12/40/366.

marked for trade with Indians that he refused to surrender to the Continental army. Elliot made his way to the British post at Detroit and engaged in Indian Department service "to retain the Indians in their attachment to His Majesty." The well-known Simon Girty defected from the rebel side as an interpreter and later led several Indian attacks on Revolutionary forces. His brothers, George and James, were both frontier traders who took up arms with the Indians against the Revolutionaries and fought as members of the Indian Department. George lived among Delawares, and James was with Shawnees. Their military community was essentially that of Native warriors. Alexander McKee also joined the Indian Department and led Indian raids against his erstwhile neighbors. John Depue, a Pennamite, served first in Butler's Rangers and later took an appointment in the Indian Department, thus making common cause with Indians against his Connecticut enemies. Solomon Secord, another Pennamite farmer, "and two brothers joined the British army with their father [James]." Like Depue, they served as rangers and in the Indian Department. These Pennsylvanians' role in the imperial military hierarchy was clear. They served as American intermediaries between British officials and Indian allies. While the role was not new for the Girtys or for McKee, men like Depue and Secord were farmers who participated in a community in which the existence of powerful Indian nations was no longer a hindrance but a necessity for the reconstruction of their prewar worlds. Loyalist military service broadened their worldview, and they became more accepting of centralized power directing the war and of ethnically inclusive alliances.[49]

It was also clear that British aims were paramount, especially when British officers presided. Anglo-Americans who cherished local autonomy submitted to central authority—and had no alternative. In the Tory military community, they could not seek an enlargement of rights within the empire but were forced instead to demonstrate subordination to authority. Loyalists recalled their service as being on behalf of "government" rather than their own narrow interests. Jasper Harding noted his "attachment to British government." John Wormington also clearly mentioned "attachment to British Government." Lieutenant James Moody raised five hundred "friends of government" to fight the rebels in New Jersey. George Sinclair of Chester County "was employed in many

---

49. Simcoe, *Operations of the Queen's Rangers*, 73–74. On the Girtys, see Boatner, *Encyclopedia of the American Revolution*, 434–35, and Colin G. Calloway, "Simon Girty: Interpreter and Intermediary," in *Being and Becoming Indian: Biographical Studies of North American Frontiers*, ed. James A. Clifton (Chicago, 1989), 38–58; AO12/40/402, AO12/40/407, AO12/40/388, AO12/40/376, AO12/40/410.

secret and dangerous services for government." While declaring service to government became a trope of loyalist expression, its use demonstrated a recognition of a British-led coalition and the importance of central government.[50]

British officers often attributed motives of "attachment to government" to their Indian allies, who were willing to let the British characterize them as subject to imperial government in exchange for military support. Frederick Haldimand, royal governor of Quebec, lauded "Joseph Brant whose attachment to government, resolution, and personal exertion, makes him a character of a very distinguished kind." Haldimand also described the Seneca war leader Schenderachta as "brave, prudent, and perfectly attached to government." Even though Indians were clearly fighting to preserve their communities and cultures, they were willing to metaphorically submit themselves to a coordinated war effort in consultation with British "fathers." The discourse of frontier diplomacy was rich in familial metaphors, of course, which the British and loyalists could easily adapt to their patriarchal notions of centralized authority. Prominent Indians like Brant, conversely, skillfully pursued their own interests under the rubric of their "attachment to government."[51]

American forces in the imperial coalition did not lose their regional identity entirely. While some loyalist units, including the Queen's Rangers and the Volunteers of Ireland, were raised on an equal footing with the regular regiments, the Associated Loyalists and others clung to Anglo-American antimilitarist ideals. The Associated Loyalists were willing to be part of the larger war effort and submit to British direction, but they declared that they "were unwilling to become soldiers by profession, though ardently inclined to take up arms, and contribute their aid towards reducing the rebels." They indicated their role as American contributors to a larger cause—namely, "reducing the rebels"—as temporary provincial soldiers. The British offered other concessions to local American military traditions as well. Sometimes this proved beneficial, such as when loyalist desertion was excused in light of the men's "anxious desire to see their absent families," thus sparing them the usual brutal punishment for such behavior.[52]

50. AO13/96/367, AO12/38/162; James Moody, *Lieutenant James Moody's Narrative of His Exertions and Sufferings* (New York, 1968), 7; AO13/22/261.

51. Frederick Haldimand to Lord George Germain, October 24, 1778, and Haldimand to Lord Germain, September 13, 1779, both in *Documents of the American Revolution*, ed. Davies, 15:231 and 17:211, respectively. See White, *Middle Ground*, on the misunderstandings about the nature of diplomatic familial relations as a basis for common ground in frontier alliances in general.

52. On loyalist units raised on an equal footing with regulars, see Allen, ed., *Loyal Americans*, 12; Declaration by the Board of Directors of the Associated Loyalists, *Royal Gazette*, February 3, 1781; Ford, ed., *Orderly Book of the Maryland Loyalist Regiment*, 83.

Nevertheless, the stricter discipline expected by the British distinguished loyalist camp life from that of even the Continental army. The commander of the Queen's Rangers, Lt. Colonel John Simcoe, noted that his men's "regularity in messing and cleanliness in every respect, conduced to the health of a soldier." Sometimes, like the rebels, unfamiliarity with the military led some Tories to try the patience of their officers and of the British. Officers of the Maryland Loyalist Regiment decried the "sorry, scandalous, and irregular behavior of some disorderly soldiers." They also had to order that "no officer or soldier is permitted to discharge fire arms in the neighborhood of the camp." When attached to the British army, however, loyalists soon found that breaches of discipline were met with the brutal punishment that was commonplace in the regular army. Soldiers convicted of theft received one thousand lashes, far more than the typical punishment in the Revolutionary forces. As a result, loyalists' resistance to discipline and mutiny were relatively rare, compared with the Revolutionaries.[53]

The presence of women with the British army also served to underscore an emerging imperial military identity. Like the loyalist soldiers, American women who chose to attach themselves to the British army found themselves subject to harsh discipline. Elizabeth Clark was fortunate that her conviction on plundering charges only resulted in one hundred lashes "on her bare back." The broad military community of women with the imperial forces was also diverse. While Anglo-American women such as Clark acclimated themselves to a European professional army, the regulars also brought British women with them. Some officers' and soldiers' wives accompanied them all the way to North America. Thus, even the female imperial military community was made up of Americans and Europeans. Typically, the most genteel women with the imperial forces were British officers' wives, which tended to underscore not only class but also national hierarchy within the army. At the bottom of the British military hierarchy stood the tens of thousands of slave women who sought freedom behind British lines. Many times bringing children and kin with them, these potential sources of labor were too attractive for the British to ignore. Judith Jackson, for example, labored for the British throughout the war. She explained, "I was in the service a year and a half with Mr. Savage, the remaining part, I was with Lord Dunmore, washing and ironing in his service." Women who facilitated the operation of British and

53. Simcoe, *Operations of the Queen's Rangers*, 22; Ford, ed., *Orderly Book of the Maryland Loyalist Regiment*, 83, 46, and 90.

loyalist forces were a feminine mirror of the hierarchical military coalition they served.[54]

On the frontier, Indian women were an important part of the military community, especially among the Iroquois and other groups in which women had a significant say in whether to fight or continue wars. The Mohawk Molly Brant, for example, departed for Fort Niagara in 1779 to urge members of the Indian alliance to keep fighting. Governor Frederick Haldimand noted that Brant was "thinking it may be in her power to be useful in keeping up the spirits of the Indians and preventing them from coming to terms with the rebels." Elsewhere, in refugee communities such as the one around Fort Niagara, Indian women were vital in sustaining bases of operation in order to continue the war effort. Moreover, these Native Americans brought non-European standards of manly and feminine behavior with them to British lines.[55]

Loyalist soldiers also retained elements of colonial concepts of masculinity. For example, while Lt. Colonel Simcoe of the Queen's Rangers tended to disdain constant patrolling, he found that "the inclinations of the Americans, though averse from tactical arrangement, had always been turned to patrolling, in their antiquated dialect, scouting: the Indians, their original enemies, and the nature of their country, had familiarized them to this species of warfare." And like the rebels, loyalists enjoyed some continuity of informal male tavern culture in the British army, such as drinking and gaming. Given that British soldiers were looked down upon as the "dregs" of society, most Pennsylvanians who fought the rebels did not believe that their service would transform their informal notions of manly behavior into political manhood. Indeed, most British troops were poor and disenfranchised, and the loyalist rank and file raised on an equivalent basis risked the same social stigma. When loyalists accepted their secondary role in defending "government," they essentially accepted the social and political hierarchy already in existence in British North America in exchange for imperial help in preserving their communities.[56]

54. Ford, ed., *Orderly Book of the Maryland Loyalist Regiment*, 27. For an example of British soldiers' wives accompanying the army, see John Andre, *Major Andre's Journal* (New York, 1968), 30. On the presence of large numbers of runaway slave women with the British army, see Frey, *Water from the Rock*, 118–19, 121–22. Petition of Judith Jackson, former slave, September 18, 1783, in *The Price of Loyalty: Tory Writings from the Revolutionary Era*, ed. Catherine S. Crary (New York, 1973), 258.

55. On Indian women present in Indian war expeditions and at imperial posts, see Calloway, *American Revolution in Indian Country*, 55; Governor Frederick Haldimand to Lord George Germain, September 14, 1779, in *Documents of the American Revolution*, ed. Davies, 17:214.

56. Simcoe, *Operations of the Queen's Rangers*, 75. On views of British soldiers, see Sylvia Frey, *The British Soldier in America: A Social History of Military Life in the Revolutionary Period* (Austin, Tex., 1981).

Indeed, manliness among loyalists was sometimes defined by heroic sacrifice for government and adherence to order. James Smither, for example—a spy in Philadelphia for the British army—praised the "manlyness [sic] and fortitude" of his contact in protecting him from rebel authorities. In 1778, John Simcoe's public orders to his Rangers appealed to their sense of honor in trying to keep his troops orderly in New Jersey. He declared that plundering indicated a "cowardly ruffian," while disapproval of such illegal activity marked a soldier as "truly brave." He further stated that they should continue the behavior that "has left a favorable impression of the Queen's Rangers on the minds of such of the inhabitants of Pennsylvania." During the Philadelphia campaign, Sir William Howe characterized his soldiers as orderly and restrained. He promised locals that the royal force was ordered to adhere to "regularity and good discipline" and would not engage in plundering. Instances of plundering obviously did occur, but it was clear that in such a professional force, ideal manly behavior was characterized by submitting to authority. In fact, among Tories, masculinity often related to the ability to sacrifice home, kin, and community to fight for a larger cause. Lieutenant Colonel John Peters, who led loyalists with Burgoyne's expedition in 1777, remarked that his men "had the courage to leave their wives and children, their friends and property, and turn soldiers." This was the inverse of Revolutionary formulations of martial masculinity that defined courage as specifically protecting the locale—and interpreted this very practice, across regions, as constituting a larger cause.[57]

Also evident among the loyalist troops was a pronounced lack of the kind of collective action taken by Revolutionary Pennsylvanians. The threat of brutal punishment and the premium placed on submission to orders were partial explanations. More significantly, the British army was typically better equipped and more regularly supplied than its enemies. Soldiers rarely believed their military moral economy to be violated. And with their property often confiscated by rebel authorities, simply going home and leaving the army was not a realistic possibility. Orderly membership in the military effort appeared to be the only way to recover their lost communities. Perhaps one of the most compelling explanations for the lack of collective action among loyalists was the structure of their units. As the war went on, local ties between soldiers were sundered, and regional Tory units received new recruits or were combined with

57. AO13/25/454–56; Simcoe, *Operations of the Queen's Rangers*, 62–63; Howe's proclamation reproduced in *Major Andre's Journal*, 38–39; Lieutenant Colonel John Peters to [?], December 9, 1779, in *The Price of Loyalty*, ed. Crary, 309.

others. The imperial military community itself tended to break down the ties of localism that united many Americans. Finally, the draconian discipline of the British army made anything approaching mutiny very dangerous. Elias Boudinot reported to the Continental army how "a mutiny was raised by the new troops from England under Lord Rawdon, to quell which cost 100 men killed & wounded."[58]

One documented case of loyalist mutiny among Burgoyne's forces in 1777 derived from the British general's apparent violation of service conditions with both his Indian allies and Tory auxiliaries. Burgoyne promised that the Indians could "fight the enemy in their own way" and that the provincials would serve "under their own officers." When he tried to rein in traditional Indian methods of warfare, numbers of warriors simply left the army. According to Lieutenant Colonel John Peters, "the general next told the provincial officers that as they know not the art of war, his sergeants and officers should take command of their men. . . . Upon which a mutiny sprung up among the Americans and they resolved to follow the Indians sooner than submit to the order." The British backed off and allowed the loyalist officers to lead the men, but without formal commissions. The Tories, still unhappy, "rejoined the royal army." Interestingly, the mutiny seemed to relate not only to violated terms of service but also to Burgoyne's suggestion that loyalist officers were not fit to lead in an orderly army, which the Americans clearly resented. Despite their anger at Burgoyne and repeated condescension from him, the Americans remained, reluctantly obeyed their orders, and, to their minds, continued to make heroic and unrecognized sacrifices for "government."[59]

Loyalists' willing submission to authority demonstrated a divergence in worldviews fostered by differences between Revolutionary and Tory military life. While Revolutionary soldiers constructed identities as defenders of the localist nation, loyalists came to see themselves as inferior constituent parts of the empire. Tories typically sought to protect their imagined communities, but in order to do so, they left behind their locales and joined a multiethnic, hierarchical, imperial war coalition. British leaders demanded obedience and respect in exchange for military assistance. While those deemed Tories by their Revolutionary neighbors may have disdained this inferior position, they often had little choice but to embrace it. Disenfranchised from their immediate

58. Elias Boudinot to James Caldwell, August 11, 1781, in *Letters of Delegates,* ed. Smith, 17:498.
59. Lieutenant Colonel John Peters to [?], December 9, 1779, in *The Price of Loyalty,* ed. Crary, 307-8.

community, their only real hope of recovering their past was in a larger imperial victory. They served in conjunction with large numbers of Indians and freed slaves, British and German regulars, and loyalists from outside their region. Slowly (and perhaps reluctantly), they adopted a view of community that was imperial in nature, focusing on the larger best interests of the British Empire. Other groups' interests, significantly, were vital to the cause as well. While Anglo-American loyalists often looked down upon their Indian and African American allies and auxiliaries, they at least recognized them as a key contingent of the war effort. Tories who fought with Mohawks and Senecas against Revolutionaries, for example, had to envision a victory and a future shared with their Native allies. Indian independence in the region would serve, in the short term, mutually beneficial imperial interests.

In contrast, the Revolutionary military community reinforced the notion of a nation founded upon diverse localisms. By the very constitution of the Continental army and militia, soldiers represented and defended specific locales. Moreover, the experience of army life, with its system of rank and military manhood, made soldiers aware of their common status and, eventually, their power to act collectively. The definition of the formal community was thus reinforced and expanded. Soldiers became aware of their vital roles in the localist nation and believed that their informal notions of manhood, politicized by melding with military manhood, should be recognized. While not all collective actions were as violent as Fort Wilson or as successful as the mutiny of the Pennsylvania Line, together, they sent a striking signal to elites that soldiers were capable of defining and defending class-specific views of community. The increasing emphasis on white manhood as a de facto prerequisite for citizen-soldiering helped blunt this potential conflict, but soldiers' collective actions also demonstrated a commitment to a relatively egalitarian view of the army.

Loyalist military service, then, tended to foster identities among soldiers as members of a hierarchical, ethnically inclusive imperial army. Meanwhile, camp life among the Revolutionaries validated localism and the exclusion of racial Others, simultaneously creating self-perceptions of public men protecting their particular communal interests. The structures of the British and Revolutionary forces had some similarities, however. Both were larger forces composed of various regional and ethnic components. Among the British forces, the role of these constituent elements was to preserve and serve the imperial polity. Among the Revolutionaries, the locally raised units represented the

Revolutionary cause and the nation itself. Although identity forged in camp life was important, ultimately, military violence was one of the greatest forces in shaping perceptions. Encounters with those seen as the enemy were just as significant as interaction with comrades, and fighting the enemy was, of course, the primary duty of soldiers. It is in the context of these bloody encounters that various enlisted men further defined American identities.

4

The Meaning of the War Against the British

On September 11, 1777, one of the largest land battles of the Revolution was fought in southeastern Pennsylvania—the Battle of Brandywine. The main British army invaded Pennsylvania from the Chesapeake at Head of Elk and slowly made its way toward Philadelphia. General George Washington, although reluctant to risk the Continental army in battle against a superior force, was equally concerned about protecting Philadelphia, the seat of the Continental Congress and symbol of the new nation. Reinforced by militia, Washington prepared to fight on the east bank of the Brandywine Creek near Chadd's Ford, blocking the main road into Philadelphia. Early in the morning of September 11, Sir William Howe, the British commander, prepared to attack. German mercenary, loyalist, and

British troops under General Wilhelm Knyphausen began a secondary attack on the American center, while British troops under Lord Cornwallis tried to turn the rebels' right flank. By about 2:30 in the afternoon, Cornwallis succeeded in fording the Brandywine and outflanking the Continental and rebel militia forces. Revolutionary units under General John Sullivan quickly and desperately made a new line perpendicular to the creek and prepared to face the British assault on the relatively good defensive ground of a small plowed hill.[1]

Cornwallis calmly deployed his columns into lines. According to historian Robert Middlekauff, "once the British were ready, they did nothing but stand in the sunshine, their bayonets sending off flashes when they caught the light. Perhaps they hoped to unnerve the Americans; if so, they failed, but they did impress them." When the British advance began, a gap in the American line became apparent and it appeared that the battle would be quickly over. Elements of General Nathanael Greene's brigade were quickly rushed in to plug the hole. By 6:00 in the evening, they had arrived. Smoke soon obscured the battlefield and made proper unit cohesion and maneuvering difficult to maintain. As the British regulars slowly closed with the rebel forces, the Revolutionaries began to give way. The American "retreat" was starting to look a bit like a rout, as some soldiers left the field without orders to do so. Washington himself had arrived at the scene of the action about 5:30 P.M. and, while he allowed Sullivan to continue to direct his units, the commander-in-chief and the Marquis de Lafayette rode up and down the line to rally the troops and discourage disorderly retreat. Nevertheless, the entire American right flank was collapsing and retreated east on the road to Chester. Lafayette was wounded in the leg and the withdrawal was proving difficult to control.[2]

Meanwhile, troops under Knyphausen crossed the creek at Chadd's Ford under heavy Revolutionary fire. For a while, the Brandywine ran red with blood. Despite stiff resistance and a barrage of grapeshot, the British force, with the elements of the 71st Highland Regiment and Queen's Rangers leading the attack, made its way toward enemy lines. They eventually succeeded in capturing several artillery pieces and soon turned them on the rebels. Eventually, Revolutionary forces near Chadd's Ford were forced to retreat as well. Washington

1. See Russell F. Weigley, *The American Way of War: A History of United States Military Strategy and Policy* (Bloomington, Ind., 1973), 11, on Washington's strategy of avoiding major engagements with the main British army and his reluctant commitment to fight at Brandywine to make a show symbolically of protecting Philadelphia. On the Battle of Brandywine, see Middlekauff, *Glorious Cause*, 386–87, and Howard H. Peckham, *The War for Independence: A Military History* (Chicago, 1979), 69–70.

2. Middlekauff, *Glorious Cause*, 387–88; Boatner, *Encyclopedia of the American Revolution*, 108–9.

managed to withdraw his defeated force toward Chester. Cornwallis's forces met those of Knyphausen at about 7:00 P.M., and Howe established a new headquarters at the town of Dilworth. Darkness began to descend and, fourteen hours after the first troop dispositions of the day, the battle was over. The Revolutionaries fielded 11,000 troops that day. They suffered between 800–900 killed and wounded, roughly an 8 percent casualty rate. Approximately 400 Americans were captured, as were eleven of their field pieces. The British employed about 12,500 troops and lost 577 killed and wounded. While the British won the field that day, they again failed to destroy Washington's army completely.[3]

The perspectives of those who participated in the battle differed in tone from the general historical accounts. A British officer, Lieutenant John Peebles, echoed a description of the tactics and troop dispositions but put a slightly more human face on the battle. Peebles explained that "the army [was] put in motion by the break of day." He was attached to Cornwallis's flanking movement. After crossing the Brandywine and proceeding "by the road leading to Dilworth," Peebles noted that the Second Light Infantry skirmished with the rebels at about 9:00 A.M., slowing the advance. As they were getting closer to enemy lines, weariness from marching became a consideration. About a mile from the village of Dilworth, Peebles explained that, "after having marched 15 or 16 miles; here the General refreshed." This was the British perspective on the slow, deliberate deployment. Rather than purposefully attempting to unnerve the enemy, the royal force literally needed time to catch its breath and prepare for a difficult assault against what eventually proved to be formidable Revolutionary defensive positions. Between 4:00 and 5:00 in the evening, the British attack began. Peebles described the confusing melee as best he could:

> The British troops formed their respective corps and moved up to the enemy under a heavy fire mostly from behind fences, and after giving them a few rounds charged them with such spirit that they immediately fled in confusion leaving several pieces of cannon in the field and playing those that were more distant. Our troops pursued the fugitives through the woods and over fences for about 3 miles, when they came upon a second and more extensive line of the Enemy's best troops drawn up and posted to great advantage. Here they sustained a warm attack for some time and poured a heavy fire on the British troops as they came up, who were by this time much fatigued with a long

3. Middlekauff, *Glorious Cause*, 388–89; Boatner, *Encyclopedia of the American Revolution*, 108–9.

march and a rapid pursuit. Notwithstanding these disadvantages we briskly attacked the enemy and after a close fire for some minutes charged them again and drove them into the woods in the greatest confusion; when the weariness of the troops and the night coming on prevented any further pursuit and saved thousands of the rebels.

Peebles concluded his account of the battle by explaining, "in this day's action the whole rebel army were drawn out and posted to the greatest advantage, on all the high grounds from the north side [of Chadd's] Ford to the westward of Dilworth village (a space of 4 miles) being 20,000 strong and confident of victory, but were beat and totally routed by about 5000 British troops."[4]

Obviously, Peebles grossly overestimated the size of his opponents' forces. The flanking force was about 5,000 strong, but the actions of Knyphausen also contributed to the general rebel defeat. It is possible that he exaggerated the numbers to magnify the importance and scope of the British victory. It is equally plausible that he was honestly confused about the number of troops deployed. As a junior officer, he was not fully privy to the information that field commanders had. His calculation of a strong American force may also have been shaped by the arduousness of the battle. Literally exhausted by marching and executing the offensive against well-defended positions may have made the rebels appear to be far more numerous than they in fact were. Peebles was a professional soldier and his account reflects the view of a junior officer. Specifically, he focused upon the small unit tactics in the advance on the rebel right. One gets an impression from his diary entry of the toll of the march, the brutality of the fighting, and the effects of the fog of war on the participants.

Another striking account of Brandywine offers yet another perspective. On September 11, 1777, Jacob Ritter, a private in the Bucks County militia, was about to get his first and only taste of combat in the American Revolution. His recollection is brief and lacks tactical details. Nevertheless, it remains deeply affecting in terms of the insight it gives to the experience of enlisted men in battle. Ritter recalled that "general orders were given for every company to maintain its ranks and each man to keep his place." This must have been disquieting for the troops, as it was clear that they were about to absorb an attack. Given that the key to success for an eighteenth-century army was for the soldiers to maintain formation and discipline despite the carnage surrounding them, Ritter and his comrades would have been bracing for the worst. When the British

4. Gruber, ed., *John Peebles' American War*, 132–34.

forces were slowly forming and recovering from their march, Ritter noted that "an awful pause preceded the engagement and some of us stood in solemn silence." The precision movements of the British regulars and the fearsome glints of light reflecting off their bayonets was disconcerting to green soldiers such as Ritter and clearly presaged the close combat to come. While not unnerved enough to disobey stern orders and flee the field, one can easily imagine that the prospect entered many soldiers' minds as they "stood in solemn silence." The sight of the British troops preparing for battle did indeed leave an impression.[5]

Soon enough, the eerie quietude was punctuated by movement and firing. Ritter described how

> bombshells and shot fell round me like hail, cutting down my comrades on every side, and tearing off the limbs of the trees like a whirlwind; the very rocks quaked, and the hills that surrounded us seemed to tremble with the roar of cannon. . . . Towards evening, (for the battle lasted from sunrise to sunset,) our battalion was ordered to march forward to the charge. Our way was over the dead and dying, and I saw many bodies crushed to pieces beneath the wagons, and we were bespattered with blood.

When finally ordered to retreat, Ritter simply fled into the woods. The exhausted young militiaman, separated from his unit and part of a general rout, found shelter in the underbrush and fell asleep. The next morning, he was captured by a group of Hessians, making him one of the four hundred prisoners of war that the British army claimed. For Jacob Ritter, the Battle of Brandywine was a shattering experience. The memory of that September day haunted the veteran for the rest of his life. The violence he witnessed so horrified him that he became a pacifist. When he returned home, he left his pro-Revolutionary Lutheran congregation and became a Quaker.[6]

Ritter's narrative clearly differs from those of historians and those of officers such as Peebles. Although his conversion to pacifism was exceptional, other aspects of his perspective on combat against the British are representative of other enlisted men's. Most salient is the emphasis on the human toll of battle. Men of the ranks typically remembered particular instances of violence,

---

5. Joseph Foulke, ed., *Memoirs of Jacob Ritter, A Faithful Minister in the Society of Friends* (Philadelphia, 1844), 12–16, 18–27 (reproduced in RWPF, file S9080).
6. Ibid.

especially deaths and injuries among comrades. Given that their role in the army was to fight, this is not surprising. Discussions of unit dispositions, tactics, and strategic significance were more the purview of officers, who were charged with coordinating troop movements and overseeing performance in battle. Another key element of Ritter's account is the marked absence of attributing responsibility for the bloodshed. The enemy was not a band of inhuman monsters. Ritter does not blame the British army for the carnage inflicted upon the rebel force. Rather, he implies that it is part and parcel of the horrors of war. Thus he recoils from warfare in general rather than decrying specific deeds committed by one side or another. Again, while few other soldiers reacted so radically by denouncing military service, most of the Pennsylvania rank and file seldom expressed specific hostility toward their counterparts in the British regular army.

At first, this attitude toward the military forces of George III may appear surprising. It is consistent, however, with the outlooks of Revolutionary soldiers. For the most part, Pennsylvania enlisted men viewed their imperial counterparts variously with empathy, apathy, and only rarely with enmity. The British army was not viewed as a direct threat to the community before it operated near the soldiers' homes. Early on, soldiers were able to separate their antagonism toward British policy from their attitudes toward the rank-and-file European soldiers. Indeed, many realized that they were of similar ethnic, (perceived) racial, and class backgrounds. Enlisted men were then able to see potential common ground, because they shared some fundamental notions of identity and community. As rank-and-file soldiers, they held similar military and social status. Moreover, they developed mores of manly martial behavior as they interacted that did not require rendering the enemy into a radically negative reference point in the construction of identity. The prevailing ideology of European "limited war" demanded that formally constituted European military forces be treated respectfully as fellow soldiers. As the British made the momentous decision to fight a largely conventional war against the rebels (as they would have fought any other European opponent), notions of eighteenth-century limited war framed the rules and defined exceptions. The Revolutionaries' war against the British army was not one between groups with contending ideas of community. It was premised on shared assumptions about what constituted proper behavior among the fraternity of soldiers.[7]

7. M. S. Anderson, *War and Society*; Christopher Duffy, *The Military Experience in the Age of Reason* (New York, 1988); and John Childs, *Armies and Warfare in Europe* (New York, 1982), discuss the shared Anglo-American view of limited war—that is, focusing conflict upon military forces and attempting to avoid violence against civilians.

Ultimately, Pennsylvania troops viewed their British counterparts as culturally similar and holding common concepts about what constituted "honorable" warfare, even if both sides did not always adhere to them. Therefore, in some ways, European enemies were positive references for the construction of soldierly identities among the rebels. Revolutionaries saw European regulars as respectable "white" enemies who were not social outsiders or traitors to the imagined community, as American foes were. On one hand, European soldiers were members of a "racial community" that was of fundamental importance to the rebels. On the other, British troops had no initial connection with the Revolutionaries' locales at all, thus exempting them from local animosities. Except for the brief time in which the British invaded the southeastern part of the state and in a few frontier actions, royal regulars did not usually disrupt soldiers' communities. Pennsylvania may have been exceptional among many states: Howe's roughly ten months of operations and occupation was not long enough for the British rank and file to earn the lasting enmity of the rebels in the region. Although strains were present during the invasion, the mutual military culture of European warfare that both regular armies practiced largely persisted. The brief intrusion of the British army into Pennsylvanians' localist nation did little to fundamentally alter their notions of self and community.

Anglo-American Military Culture

Ironically, this community of military culture based on professional European standards of soldiering evolved among a people with a strongly anti-army history. The Anglo-American Whig political tradition provided a vocabulary with which to critique the actions of a standing army during times of peace. Indeed, many rank-and-file Revolutionaries were moved to fight when the British army appeared to threaten the well-being of their imagined communities directly, as was the case on the prewar frontier when the army was seen as protecting and supplying independent Indian nations. Nevertheless, a class-biased strain of this anti-army sentiment appears to have primarily affected elites' views of British soldiers during the war. Many officers and other prominent Revolutionaries specifically condemned the British army because they believed it was composed of the jetsam of European society and motivated solely by the prospect of pay. Pennsylvania officer John Morris, for example, compared the American army—which supposedly comprised "brave citizens fighting for their liberties"—favorably to the British forces, who were "mercenary soldiers fighting for pay only and void of every principle." Colonel Daniel Brodhead referred to the enemy army as "mercenaries, and slaves of Britain." Even more derisively, a writer in a Pennsylvania newspaper condemned the British army as "block-headed, half-starved, half-naked, half-paid, mongrel banditti, composed of the sweepings of the jails of Britain, Ireland, Germany, and America." Obviously, many Revolutionary soldiers who came from the lowest orders of colonial society would have contested the notion that poor people were incapable of holding "principles." Furthermore, Revolutionary officers often referred to their own men as derogatorily as they did the British. General Anthony Wayne of the Pennsylvania Line referred to his troops as "food for worms . . . miserable, sharp looking caitiffs, hungry lean faced villains." Other Revolutionary officers called their men "the sweepings of the York streets" and "a wretched motley crew." In short, officers who despised the British army for its "banditti" often held a similarly contemptuous opinion of their own enlisted men. Not surprisingly, this was an anti-army prejudice not easily translatable among the Revolutionary rank and file. Such rhetoric might well have drawn attention to the comparable class status of soldiers in both armies.[8]

Furthermore, Revolutionaries who were drafted and did not have the economic resources to avoid service could easily sympathize with poor men forced to serve as soldiers in order to make a living far from their homes. Many German mercenaries were essentially forced to fight in a war in which they had no direct stake when the sovereign of their particular state hired them out to the British. Johann Conrad Döhla, for example, explained that his Bayreuth Infantry regiment was ordered to fight "by the gracious order" of the Margrave of Brandenburg, who had sold their services to George III. While officers may have consistently denounced the motivations of British soldiers and German mercenaries, Revolutionary Pennsylvania soldiers were conspicuously silent on the issue.[9]

8. For conclusions about general prewar perceptions of the British army based primarily upon elite-generated documents, see Bailyn, *Ideological Origins*, 112–19; John Morris to Samuel C. Morris, July 27, 1776, Strettel-Morris-Milligan Papers, LCP, folder 472; Daniel Brodhead to Nathanael Greene, September 6, 1780, Woods Collection of Western Pennsylvania Documents, Historical Society of Western Pennsylvania, Pittsburgh, Pennsylvania; *Pennsylvania Evening Post*, May 8, 1777, 254. The article is entitled "A tar . . . to General Howe." It is patently suspect that an average sailor in Revolutionary Philadelphia was quite so eager to condemn the British army based on its soldiers' low class status. While the author's identity is unclear, the piece speaks to the perspectives of officers and civilians of some substance—not to tars. Anthony Wayne and the other officers are quoted in Neimeyer, *America Goes To War*, 9.

9. On the impressment of mostly poor men into the German auxiliary units, see Neimeyer, *America Goes to War*, 54–55; Johann Conrad Döhla, *A Hessian Diary of the American Revolution*, ed. and trans. Bruce E. Burgoyne (Norman, Okla., 1990), 3. The lack of ideological disdain for common British soldiers might have been affected by their army's short period of operation in Pennsylvania, but there is evidence that soldiers

Fraternization among European regulars and Pennsylvania troops attests to the early lack of hostility between the groups. Indeed, it may even indicate developing notions of broader soldierly communities. As early as 1775, the men of Thompson's Rifle Battalion were chided for "continually conversing with the officers and soldiers of the enemies." In 1776, despite the defeat and capture of many Pennsylvania soldiers at Fort Washington in New York, the rank and file engaged their captors in what appears to be relatively polite conversation. John Adlum of the York County Flying Camp recalled that after their surrender, "a great many Hessian under-officers and sergeants came to converse with us. There was a majority of our regiment Germans or rather sons of Germans, consequently the conversation was in their own language." Adlum, an English speaker, managed to strike up a discussion with one of his guards about the battle both had fought. Adlum explained, "I had a curiosity what they had thought of our defense and observed to him that they made a great haul of us that day, to which he replied yes but it could not well be otherwise as our lines were not half manned." Rather than insult Adlum, the soldier spoke almost respectfully to the rebel, recognizing that the shortage of manpower more than anything else explained the British victory. British officers also noted the interaction between opposing enlisted men. Lieutenant John Peebles recorded in his diary that during the Pennsylvania campaign, the Revolutionaries "have a guard just opposite to us here who asked for a truce for a day, which was agreed to by our guard, and they chatted to one another."[10]

As evidenced by Adlum's account of interaction between German auxiliaries and German Pennsylvanians, some soldiers could identify with their European opponents by virtue of similar ethnic heritages, vital reference points in ideas of communities. The large number of Pennsylvanians with Scottish, Irish, or German ancestries shared cultural backgrounds with soldiers serving the Crown. These non-English British soldiers might feel as apathetic toward the cause of empire as their Revolutionary opponents. Some Irish captives, for example, were transported to the colonies and essentially forced to serve in the British army. These troops would experience antipathy toward British policies and share cultural origins in common with large numbers of Irish American soldiers. Instances of men meeting each other and discovering that they could

---

of other states exhibited similar views. Lender concludes in his study of New Jersey Continentals that "they collectively did not evince a fervent hatred—and certainly not a political hatred of the [British regular] opponents" (see "Enlisted Line," 156).

10. Orderly Book of Thompson's Rifle Battalion, 19, HSP; Adlum, *Memoirs*, 75, 81; Gruber, ed., *John Peebles' American War*, 137.

speak the same language or dialect and shared regional origins opened common ground. It was no accident that the Hessian soldiers at Fort Washington sought out their German-speaking counterparts among the Pennsylvania prisoners. These troops probably had more in common culturally with these Pennsylvanians than with their British comrades. Socialization among enemies could occur at times as men faced each other across lines and pickets. Samuel Graff, a Pennsylvania German soldier, recalled that one time, "while he was on guard . . . he conversed with the British guard, a Hessian, being about twenty rods apart. The Hessian held up his bottle and told deponent to come and get a drink." As the war went on, more and more German auxiliaries began to desert British service, and some reenlisted in the Revolutionary forces. As almost a quarter of the Pennsylvania Line was first-generation German American, these deserters could easily find a home among the state's military.[11]

Furthermore, as Pennsylvania Revolutionaries increasingly equated European ethnic heritage with perceived white identity, common ethnocultural backgrounds allowed soldiers to see each other as members of a single racial group. In the popular press, writers made clear racial designations of European regulars to distinguish them from nonwhites. In 1779, for example, an account of an attack on Freeland's Fort near Sunbury noted that it was carried out "by about 200 Indians and 100 Whites, who called themselves Regulars." Whiteness, a fundamental prerequisite for consideration as a member of Revolutionary communities, was an attribute that Pennsylvanians believed European regulars shared with them. The result of this perception was that European members of the British army were treated as whites who had no direct stake in the internal definition of community that was being articulated in Pennsylvania during the war. These racialist notions also help explain some of the absence of hostility toward enemy regulars.[12]

Soldiers of the two main armies also shared certain concepts of social behavior and military masculinity. For example, members of the Philadelphia militia were enjoined by their officers that "no indecent language [is to be] exchanged with our enemy." These soldiers were probably engaged in a taunting contest with their counterparts. Given the ubiquity of profanity among men of

11. See Neimeyer, *America Goes to War*, 34, on Irish captives forced into the British army during the Revolution; on the Hessians and German-speaking members of John Adlum's Pennsylvania unit interacting through a common language, see Adlum, *Memoirs*, 75; RWPF, file W7566; Neimeyer, *America Goes to War*, 52–64, explains the growing desertion rate of German troops from the British army and the German component of the Pennsylvania Line.

12. *Pennsylvania Gazette*, August 4, 1779.

the ranks, the exchange of obscenity with the enemy could be an expression of mutual respect and a battle of verbal wits. Another instance of taunting via threats and insults was Peter Tritt and his York County comrades' experience in monitoring the British invasion fleet off the coast of Long Island in 1776. Tritt was so close to the enemy ships "that by speaking loud[ly], we could converse with them from the water's edge." After speaking for a while, the redcoats made a request. Apparently used to friendly relations with the rebel rank and file, the British soldiers offered the Pennsylvanians money if they would bring them fresh cherries from nearby trees. Perhaps the Revolutionaries were insulted by the implication that they should in some manner serve the British. In any event, Tritt and his comrades replied with a challenge to the redcoats, stating that "if they would come on shore we would give them *cherries* and charge them nothing." The result was an exchange of fire by both sides anxious to prove their martial prowess.[13]

Other shared rituals of martial manliness demonstrated simultaneous jeering and a sense of respect among opponents. "Huzzahing" each other was common among British, Hessian, and Revolutionary soldiers. Many times it was a recognition of a victory over an opponent, as in 1776, when Alexander Graydon recalled that the American surrender of Fort Washington was "announced [among the British] by an huzzah." At Long Island, Michael Graham recalled that the British were "huzzahing when they took prisoners." The Americans were able to get revenge not only in substance but also in ritual later in the same year. At the Battle of Trenton, a group of captured Hessians were brought "to the ferry and huzza'd." The huzzah was also used to mark mutual admiration among adversaries before the terrible necessity of bloodshed. John Joseph Henry recounted that he and his comrades had been drawn up in formation in front of Quebec under the eyes of the city's defenders, and "they [the British] gave us a huzzah! We returned it and remained a considerable time huzzaing." This action served to augment unit pride and to recognize the martial manliness of the opponent. Henry so respected this enemy force that he recalled them as "that fine body of men, the Seventh Regiment."[14]

In general, Pennsylvania enlisted men looked upon the faces of their European adversaries when the war broke out and saw fellow soldiers. This

13. Orders: July 23, 1776, Orderly Book of the Third Battalion of Philadelphia Associators, HSP; RWPF, file S23974.
14. *Alexander Graydon's Memoirs*, 208; Dann, *The Revolution Remembered*, 50; Brigadier General John Cadwalader to Council of Safety, December 26, 1776, PRG, reel 11, frames 612-13; Henry, "Journal," 115, 155.

grudging respect and common cultural background sustained an Anglo-American military culture based on the mutual desire for limited war between the main armies. Soldiers believed that their experience fighting the British would be in accord with the martial conventions of eighteenth-century Europe. Indeed, much of the fighting between the regular armies of the Revolution took on an only slightly modified European form. The forces of the Crown learned to utilize small formations and light infantry to fight more efficiently in the North American environment. Conversely, the Americans emulated the linear tactics and methods of campaigning utilized by the British. To be sure, the Continental army was unlike its regular British counterpart in that enlistments were short and discipline was often weak. Furthermore, the bulk of the American reserve forces came from the militia, an undisciplined group of short-term soldiers raised during emergencies. At times, the militia acted as irregulars. They fled battle while keeping control of the countryside where the British army was not able to exert its presence. Nonetheless, Pennsylvanians served in campaigns that were marked by large armies maneuvering and seeking (or avoiding) that centerpiece of limited war, the battle. Small-party skirmishes and raids on outposts were also common, but even these were considered normal support operations in European war. As long as the main target of violence remained the enemy's military force, limited war was a concept embraced by both sides. These ideals were generated from a shared cultural heritage among Europeans and European Americans and were predicated on respect between enemies.[15]

Of course, the context in which soldiers could have mutual expectations of European conventions of war was shaped by how both governments and their military commanders viewed the war. Congress's creation of a regular military force, the Continental army, in 1775 transformed the war from a local Massachusetts uprising to a united colonial armed resistance movement. By the end of the year, the British government and its field commanders believed that they had a conventional war on their hands. Throughout the Revolution, for the most part, the British and Continental armies fought each other as two national armies in Europe would have fought. As Sir William Howe, the British commander from 1776 to 1778, made clear, "the common soldier taken in

15. On the British tactical adaptation to the conditions of the North American continent, see Duffy, *The Military Experience*, 286, and Frey, *British Soldier*, 96–103. See John Shy, "The Military Conflict Considered as a Revolutionary War," in *A People Numerous and Armed*, 213–44, on the role of the militia in the American Revolution.

arms against his King, guilty as he is of the crime of rebellion, shall not become the object of a retaliating punishment." The British decision to treat the enemy army as a respectable opposing standing army had momentous implications for both Revolutionaries and loyalists. Essentially, they were offering a sort of military recognition of American independence. The British treated captured Americans as prisoners of war, not treasonous rebels. Thus they were subject to martial—but not civil—law for their actions in the field. Given the scale of the rebellion, this was an act of expedience that would diminish the possibility that Revolutionary authorities would brutalize British prisoners.[16]

Taking captives and treating them as prisoners of war was, then, a vital convention of Anglo-American military culture. The expectation among such combatants was that the defeated members of an army could rely on the mercy of the victors. In fact, some Revolutionaries went out of their way to ensure that if they were forced to surrender, they would do so to the British and not American loyalists. The officer William Irvine, for example, sought out the British when his men were surrounded by Canadian militiamen. He feared that the Canadians would not abide by European conventions of war, so he and his officers "concluded it would be better for us to deliver ourselves up to the British officers than run the risk of being murdered in the woods by the Canadians." Some officers received respectful treatment from their European captors. Colonel Samuel Miles explained that after his capture at Long Island, "we have been treated as genteelly by the Hessian and Highland officers as we could expect." Captain John Nice explained that at the Battle of Long Island, "we clubbed our firearms, followed our colonel, and received good quarters from the colonel of the Highlanders." Though "British officers and soldiers insulted" Nice and his men later, they were eventually "turned over to a battalion of Hessians who used us very well." As indicated in Nice's account, however, officers were particularly sensitive to verbal insults. Their pretensions to class status through their commissions in the Continental army were sometimes disdained by Europeans, who had a truly aristocratic officer corps. Captured Continental officers were easily offended by verbal attacks on their honor. Colonel Samuel Atlee recalled surrendering with his troops at Long Island and "receiving as we passed through the right wing of the British army, the most opprobrious and scurrilous language." Still, the surrender of Atlee, Nice, and their men was

16. On the shift in British strategy toward the prosecution of a conventional war, see Shy, "Military Conflict," 223–25. Sir William Howe to General George Washington, February 21, 1778, *Documents of the American Revolution*, ed. Davies, 15:51.

accepted according to eighteenth-century limited-war norms. Common soldiers captured in battle were happy to receive quarter, food, and lodging. Enlisted men tended to fear ill physical treatment. Indelicate language and taunts were not as damaging to their collective psyches as to those of their superiors.[17]

The treatment of enlisted men varied widely. While captive officers could expect fairly decent quarters, soldiers were typically separated and sent to less desirable holding areas, such as churches or the infamous prison ships in New York. The physical abuse or neglect of soldiers strained relations between Revolutionaries and the forces of the Crown. In particular, those Pennsylvania soldiers captured in the New York campaign and imprisoned on hulks and in the city came to resent their guards. Ill use while a helpless prisoner of war was something few would forgive. Thomas Boyd and William Darlington, both privates in the Pennsylvania Flying Camp, were captured at Fort Washington and complained that while imprisoned in New York, they received inedible rations and, in Boyd's words, "were severely flogged for imaginary faults." Similarly, James Reed, also captured at Fort Washington in 1776, recalled painfully that he had spent "thirteen weeks and three days" on a British prison ship. Upon his release, he "immediately enlisted as a soldier for three years." Lambert Dorland "suffered extreme hardships with cold and hunger" while confined. David Kennedy condemned the "savage and inhuman treatment he received while in captivity." John Craven of the Fifth Pennsylvania Regiment recalled that during his captivity in British-occupied Philadelphia, he had "endured his full share of sufferings and privations." These men's subsequent attitudes toward the British were tainted by the experience of mistreatment. European conventions (in theory) held that prisoners of war were to be provided for as well as the situation would allow. The British treatment of some of these captives threatened to break the tenuous understanding between armies regarding prisoners.[18]

Nevertheless, there is evidence to suggest that the identification among European and American enlisted men persisted despite the British ill treatment of prisoners. Common soldiers apparently attempted to alleviate the sufferings of their enemy counterparts. In 1777, a congressional committee investigating

17. William Irvine[?] to [?], May 25, 1776, Irvine Papers, 1:47, HSP; Samuel Miles to Joseph Reed, Samuel Miles Papers, 1776–1802, American Philosophical Society, Philadelphia, Pennsylvania; Diary Notes, August 26–27, 1776, Captain John Nice Papers, 1776–1864, HSP; Colonel Samuel Atlee's Journal, *PA*, 2d ser., 1:516.

18. Depositions of Thomas Boyd and William Darlington in *Pennsylvania Evening Post*, May 3, 1777; RWPF, files S16236, S42171; Petition of David Kennedy, February 8, 1780, PRG, reel 15, frame 827; RG-2, reel 54, frame 499.

British military conduct concluded: "Sometimes the [British] common soldiers expressed sympathy with the [American] prisoners and the foreigners more than the English." The implication was that the officers were less interested in the plight of prisoners than enlisted men. Once again, soldiers appeared to identify with each other in terms of class and rank, despite deplorable prison-camp conditions. It was also not surprising that troops from Germany, Ireland, and other non-English regions apparently sympathized even more with the rebels than their English counterparts.[19]

In the end, the British and Americans also believed strongly enough in each other's adherence to European rules of war to grant parole to captives. Because feeding and housing prisoners could become a great expense, authorities often released officers, soldiers, and even entire units to go home or remain free in an area as long as they promised not to participate in the war. Samuel Atlee noted that numbers of British prisoners were paroled to live without supervision in Lancaster in 1778. In the same year, Colonel Robert Magaw returned to his home in Carlisle "on parole." Enlisted men also were granted the privilege of waiting out the war at home. Jacob Burkhart went home to Reading on parole in 1776. Philip Duck of the Fifth Pennsylvania Battalion stated that "the enemy permitted him to go at large, on his parole of honor in the power of the enemy for about two years and five months." John Adlum recalled, "I got a parole to go home" from confinement in New York. In 1780, Adlum refused to submit to the militia draft because his officers could not produce evidence that he had been exchanged.[20]

Revolutionary enlisted men conversely recalled most especially their victories over the main British army in which prisoners were honorably taken. Anxious to prove themselves soldiers (rather than lawless rebels, as loyalists often characterized them), the rank and file proudly took charge of enemy regulars who sought quarter. Garret Kroesen of the Pennsylvania State Troops, for example, was pleased that his unit in 1776 "took eight regulars of the enemy and eight Hessians which was supposed to be the first of the Hessians that were taken." Jacob Eyler, a Philadelphia militiaman, described the Battle of Princeton simply as "a considerable engagement in which we captured about three hundred prisoners." Ebenezer Pyott, a Chester County militiaman, recalled that

19. *Pennsylvania Packet,* April 29, 1777.
20. Samuel Atlee to Elias Boudinot, May 9, 1778, Ferdinand J. Dreer Autograph Collection, Soldiers of the Revolution, vol. 49:1, p. 18, HSP; Robert Magaw to General Gates, August 17, 1778, ibid., vol. 51:2, p. 103; RWPF, files S22150, W3230; Dann, *The Revolution Remembered,* 118–20 (Adlum is quoted on 118).

the culmination of his skirmish with the enemy was that they "took a party [of] fourteen Hessians and about thirty British." Jacob Shaffer confined "about a dozen mounted British and their horses."[21]

Moreover, British forces were not the only ones who sometimes failed to live up to expectations for proper care of prisoners. Treatment of captives varied. Enemy German troops, in particular, were singled out for benign handling in the hope that they would perhaps join the Revolutionaries. English soldiers did not always fare so well. Thomas Wileman complained of his rations at the Lancaster jail: "bread . . . so very bad that it occasioned a continual drought and such an inflammation in the mouth that the skin came partly off." Wileman also heard that another group of British captives nearby had been punished for being suspected of starting a fire. He noted that "rebel soldiers with bayonets killed eight and wounded eighteen of them." Sir William Howe also quietly rebuked General Washington by asserting that "the severity exercised against the British prisoners in general has been often a subject of fruitless remonstrance." Nonetheless, the commanders of both armies were engaged in a dialogue about alleged abuses of prisoners, which demonstrates a shared milieu of what Howe termed "the rules of war." Obviously, both sides knew the attendant consequences of violations and sought to minimize the risk of "the savage principle of indiscriminate retaliation."[22]

Other shared rites of campaigning further demonstrated cultural understanding among soldiers serving with the main armies. Burial of the enemy's dead, for example, reflected a respect for opponents. Because these foes were seen as white Christian soldiers doing their duty, they were believed entitled to a decent interment of their remains when killed in action. Near New York in 1776, a group of Edward Hand's Pennsylvania Continentals took charge of a number of grievously wounded Hessians after a skirmish. They also took the time to bury the Hessians' dead. Captain John Nice noted in his journal that after the Battle of Monmouth, "a strong party was sent to bury the dead of both armies." Often the enemy dead were buried amid the pomp befitting their ranks. Private John Hendry helped bury a British officer "with the honors of war" after the Battle of Princeton. John Joseph Henry was completely satisfied that the British had lived up to the rules of war when they buried General Richard

21. RWPF, files S22866, S8451, S32460, S22979.
22. See Neimeyer, *America Goes to War,* 155–63, on the recruitment efforts among the British-employed German troops and the treatment of prisoners. Deposition of Thomas Wileman, Seventeenth Dragoons, February 18, 1778, British Headquarters Papers, item 948, 2. Sir William Howe to General George Washington, February 21, 1778, *Documents of the American Revolution,* ed. Davies, 15:50–51.

Montgomery, an officer with the Continental army, with honors in Canada. Caring for the dead and wounded after a battle was a duty performed under truce. A British major, John Andre, noted that two days after the Battle of Brandywine, his army went so far as to allow "surgeons . . . from the rebel army to attend their wounded" behind enemy lines.[23]

Obviously, cease-fires proved beneficial to both armies. Important social functions such as the exchange of mail, prisoners, and supplies for prisoners between sides continued throughout the war. The flag of truce was a recognized European tradition adopted, and for the most part respected, by Revolutionaries. Violations of such a code of honor were seen as unsoldierly. Flags also assured that the two sides would be able to communicate with each other despite the ongoing war. As John Peebles noted, opposing enlisted men on guard duty "asked for a truce" with each other in order to converse. Courtesy was even routinely extended to an opponent during hostilities to allow the enemy to supply his own prisoners. To some extent an economizing effort, the measure also demonstrated an American and British commitment to preserving European conventions of war, at least in the main theaters. Captain James Christy of the Third Pennsylvania conducted British officers to Lancaster to carry "clothing for the British prisoners."[24]

Among the shared Anglo-American expectations of actions for the main armies, there were some regional variations. Frontier and rural soldiers often fought in the major conventional campaigns equipped in a manner that suggested a more truly "American" way of war. Their use of rifles suggested that they expected to be employed in ways other than line and musket volley tactics. Many Revolutionaries, even from the East, believed that the use of riflemen would tip the military balance in their favor. Philadelphian Samuel Morris was struck by the "hearty, fine troops, with their rifles in their hands," marching to reinforce Washington in 1776. Some, like Neal McKay, came east in units composed of sharpshooters. McKay proudly recalled that "we were known by the name of 'Paxton Rifle men.'" Other facets of frontier soldiers' equipment suggested an alternative to European military culture. James Fergus arrived in New York from Cumberland County with a tomahawk. John Joseph Henry and his comrades marched to Quebec armed with tomahawks and scalping

---

23. *Pennsylvania Packet,* November 5, 1776; Military Journal, June–August 1778, 2–3, Nice Papers, HSP; RWPF, file S13381; Henry, "Journal," 155; *Major Andre's Journal,* 47.

24. Gruber, ed., *John Peebles' American War,* 136–37; Deposition of Captain James Christy, February 3, 1778, PRG, reel 13, frame 667.

knives in addition to their rifles. In 1775, an observer in Connecticut noted the passing of "a number of Paxton Boys, dressed and painted in the Indian fashion." The use of term "Paxton Boys" surely conjured up images among the Revolutionaries of the infamous Indian murderers of the 1760s and suggested that perhaps they would show a similar mercilessness toward their British enemies. Their appearance was meant to project a truly American identity, that is, a "white" hybrid of Indian and European military cultures that would intimidate their foes. Additionally, such carefully constructed imagery was a further articulation of particular communal identities.[25]

When attached to the main army, these soldiers sought to utilize their region-specific martial skills against the British. Some believed that their familiarity with small-party guerrilla tactics qualified them to be in elite units of scouts in any theater. In 1776, the Pennsylvania government informed General Washington that the frontier militia "have applied to us for liberty to act as scouting parties of irregulars—this mode of waging war they say is more adapted to their genius." In such reconnaissance parties, men were anxious to demonstrate their stealth and fulfill the vital role of providing intelligence. Edward Coen, who was earlier drafted to fight in the East, volunteered when "a call was made [among the soldiers] to turn out as scouts." Robert Beer of Northampton County served with the main American army, "often on scouts in detached parties." James McMaster served "with forty other riflemen to scout."[26]

Occasionally, when soldiers attempted to use frontier tactics that were considered perfectly acceptable against Native American opponents, they were quickly criticized by easterners as violating the rules of war. Many from the eastern regions of the state, especially officers, had no wish to see the conventions of limited war break down into a vicious conflict of destruction and revenge. With their homes threatened most by the main British army, they did not seek to escalate hostilities unless the redcoats first violated the perceived norms of combat. During the New York campaign, Alexander Graydon made his feelings about frontier tactics known when he explained how a rifleman sought to snipe at guards in the British camp and how he had "considerable

25. Samuel Morris to Samuel C. Morris, August 20, 1776, Strettel-Morris-Milligan Papers, LCP, folder 482; RWPF, files S22899, W255573; Henry, "Journal," 65. The observer of the Paxton Boys is quoted from Henry M. M. Richards, *The Pennsylvania German in the Revolutionary War, 1775–1783* (Baltimore, 1978), 21–22.

26. RWPF, files S17356, S2064; Council of Safety to General Washington, December 25, 1776, PRG, reel 11, frame 605.

difficulty restraining" him. Graydon declared, "carrying a rifle is too apt to create an appetite for the savage mode of warfare which does its work in concealment; and makes a merit of destroying the enemy whenever and wherever he may be found."[27]

Overall, however, most Pennsylvania soldiers acted in ways that were within the pale of Anglo-American military culture. Despite some men's wishes to be employed in a manner of fighting with which they were most familiar, they had no desire to upset the tenuous understandings upon which limited war depended. By about 1777, most frontier troops believed that the conflict in the West was their primary war, and they did not seek to begin a cycle of revenge violence against a powerful European army. In contrast to their actions on the frontier, they did not mutilate or scalp their European foes, and they usually offered them quarter. John McCasland was a soldier who exhibited a representative frontier reaction to the war in the East. McCasland's unit was primarily engaged in interdicting Hessian foragers in southeastern Pennsylvania. On one memorable occasion, they located a group of Hessians in a Bucks County house. McCasland recalled that his company designated him to shoot a single enemy soldier. He stated, "I did not like to shoot a man down in cold blood. The company present knew I was a good marksman, and I concluded to break his thigh. I shot with a rifle and aimed at his hip." The rest of the Hessians attempted to surrender, but unable to speak English, they sent one of their number "out of the cellar with a large bottle of rum and advanced with it at arm's length as a flag of truce." McCasland did not kill the European, for whom he clearly felt pity, though he well knew he could have. Instead, he inflicted enough damage to take the prisoner in a way consistent with Anglo-American military culture while demonstrating his prowess as a sharpshooter. Interestingly, McCasland displayed no such scruples about killing in cold blood when he fought against Indians later in the war. Ultimately, the frontier soldiers' contribution to Anglo-American military culture proved to be regional variants on the theme of European-style war. The case of several Pennsylvania riflemen in the Battle of Long Island illustrated this process as they sighted their enemy, who "gave them three huzzas." The Americans knew that these yells signified both a challenge to and respect for opponents and answered back with their frontier version of the cheer. The riflemen "returned [the huzzas] with the Indian war whoop."[28]

27. *Alexander Graydon's Memoirs*, 172–73.
28. Dann, *The Revolution Remembered*, 156; *Pennsylvania Evening Post*, July 6, 1776, 338.

The Experience of Battle

For soldiers from all regions of Pennsylvania, conventional battle was the defining event of limited war. Confrontations with military violence in the main theater came mostly in actions between armies or skirmishes between units. Until the Revolution, the majority of young men from the state had not taken part in a conventional European-style battle. As a result, they romanticized combat. Many hoped to prove their manliness as soldiers and gain fame for their imagined martial prowess. Indeed, conventional battles were seen as peculiarly male arenas of interaction; women of the army and other camp followers were usually ordered to the rear of the lines. Recruits' anxiousness to see combat was typically related to their inexperience with the horrors of war. Before the crushing defeats of the New York campaign, the green troops of the Philadelphia militia were described by one of their officers as "in high spirits, and longing for an opportunity to have skirmish with [the British]." Later in 1776, John Cadwalader was loath to retreat after leading his Pennsylvania militia across the Delaware because they "were twice disappointed" in their hopes of engaging the enemy in battle. Some soldiers who never fought in a battle expressed disappointment in missing their chance to prove their bravery. Often, their most vivid memory of the war was how close they came to fighting the enemy. John Hipple explained that his unit was marched "into a field, expecting an engagement with the enemy, but [they] were disappointed." Alexander Logan heard noises one night and expected a battle with the British army. He stated, "we were prepared to give them a warm reception if they had advanced. This was the nearest chance I had of being engaged with the enemy and I think I felt as a soldier ought to feel."[29]

When enlisted men were unlucky enough to face the British army in combat, they did not typically have a chance to think clearly about how to gain everlasting fame as soldiers. For the rank and file, the most memorable part of European-style battles was the horrific violence. Soldiers' accounts concentrated on their confusion, fear, and revulsion toward the death and injuries suffered by those around them. Battles in the American Revolution were quite similar to those in eighteenth-century Europe. Soldiers formed into lines on a battlefield. The attackers moved forward to meet the defenders. Because of the limited range of muskets of the period, volleys were exchanged at fairly close quarters. The soft lead balls fired from the infantry had a fearsome effect on their targets.

29. *Pennsylvania Evening Post,* July 25, 1776, 369; John Cadwalader to George Washington[?], December 27, 1776, Reed Papers, NYHS, reel 1; RWPF, files S4373, W2821.

They shattered bones and ripped flesh apart rather than leaving the clean entry and exit wounds of modern rifles. Wounded soldiers could lie in the field in agony for hours before they died. After the volleys, fighting between infantry was decided in hand-to-hand combat with bayonets and musket butts. In order to fight successfully under these conditions, soldiers had to operate in tight formations and attempt to ignore the suffering around them. Such discipline proved impossible for many of the young Revolutionaries, who had never seen such a spectacle. American officers, like their British counterparts, attempted to dull the nerves of their men by plying them with alcohol. Typically, extra liquor rations were issued just before and after battle. One Pennsylvania sergeant openly admitted that he had to use "powder and rum on Long Island to promote courage." For most of the rank and file, however, even strong spirits could not ease the disquieting experience of risking life and limb while comrades and foes dropped around them. For the Philadelphian Jacob Zumbro, fear defined his experience in battle. He recalled being "several times exposed to danger under heavy cannonading" in New Jersey. At Germantown he "shared all the danger of the field." For many such as Zumbro, the realization that they could be killed or wounded at any time in a massive battle fueled not only fear but also a sense of helplessness. It was impossible to see the direction from which death might be coming. Officers barked orders to stand firm or move forward. All Zumbro clearly recalled of the two major battles in which he participated was that he was constantly in "danger."[30]

Understandably, many enlisted men described battles in terms of wounds they received. While a number of soldiers believed that proving disabilities caused by war would strengthen their pension applications (though it was not a necessary requirement for most pensions), it is also likely that being injured was their most significant memory of combat. Jacob Hefflebrower explained that he received "a severe wound in his forehead" at Princeton and that the brass front of his cap had fortuitously deflected the ball enough to save his life. Harmenius Thornton, who served in an artillery regiment, was wounded by his

---

30. Consult John Keegan's classic, *The Face of Battle: A Study of Agincourt, Waterloo, and the Somme* (New York, 1978), on how common soldiers perceived battles as a jarring, confusingly violent experience; on the eighteenth century specifically, see M. S. Anderson, *War and Society*, 142–64, and Duffy, *The Military Experience*, 190–97. An example of the Continental army's officers giving their men spirits before and after an engagement occurred in 1777, when the general orders make clear that all soldiers who were to fight at Brandywine were to receive immediately their full ration of rum. See the *Valley Forge Orderly Book of General George Weedon* (n.p., 1971), 42–43. The sergeant is quoted from the "Diary of Sergeant R—," in Richards, *The Pennsylvania German*, 124; RWPF, file S23087.

comrades at Germantown "by a cannon running over him." Samuel Gilman "received a wound in the left arm" at Paoli. William Kelly was injured at the hands of British troops in close combat. He stated, "I was wounded with a saber on the forehead which fractured my skull, also on the arms. I received the wounds on my arms defending my head." John Miller fought at Trenton, where he "received a slight wound in the left hand . . . [and] he saw many dead and wounded." Others, such as Samuel Amburn, recalled how close they had come to death in battle. Amburn marveled over how he had fought at Trenton and Brandywine and was lucky enough to escape "unhurt, though at one time, a ball passed through the clothing near his neck."[31]

The violence visited upon comrades was also a disturbing sight. Many described battles solely in terms of the men they knew who were killed or wounded. Even in these cases, though, they again did not exhibit anger at the British and Hessians for inflicting the casualties. Jacob Krider wrote home to his parents about his first jarring experience with combat in the New York campaign. After attacking a British position, his unit was forced to retreat, suffering only one casualty. Krider explained in excruciating detail that this man was "shot through the cheek . . . and, as he fell, one of the men stepped up saying you're done for, with that, one of our men said he shot him through the head." Even years after the events, veterans retained vivid memories of who was killed or wounded and how. Jesse Fulton stated that he "fought in the battle of 'Chestnut Hill' when his Captain Patrick Marshall was killed." William Boyd was engaged at White Marsh, where he recalled that "one of our men was on this occasion wounded in the hand by the sword of a British horseman. The name of the man thus wounded was Martin Stilaman[?]." Frederick Hesser "remember[ed] that Major Solomon Bush received a wound in the thigh in a skirmish with the Hessians at the White Horse." John Byrne described how he "was in the Battle of Brandywine in which his Captain, McClintock[?], and his ensign, Matthew Langwall, were killed and deponent received a bayonet wound in the right side." Also at Brandywine, Jacob Strembeck watched in horror as "Lieutenant Bowde was killed." Moses Moreland recounted how "at the Battle of Germantown, affirmant's company was on the left. Two of our company were killed and two wounded by the enemy's picket guard."[32]

31. RWPF, file S5501; Comptroller General Records, Record Group 4, Pennsylvania State Archives, item 119; RG-2, reel 155, frame 204; RWPF, files W3692, R7207, S32095.
32. Jacob Krider to his parents, August 1776, in RWPF, file W10186; RWPF, files S23645, S22127, S22292, S2408, S4896, S22411.

Some soldiers left extraordinarily detailed accounts of the disorder of battles. A sergeant in the Battle of Princeton surveyed the butchery among his comrades around him and found, "My old associates were scattered about groaning, dying and dead. One officer who was shot from his horse lay in a hollow place in the ground rolling and writhing in his blood, unconscious of anything around him. The ground was frozen and all the blood which was shed remained on the surface, which added to the horror of this scene of carnage." John Heneberger, a Lancaster militiaman, described the Battle of Germantown: "The battle began about daybreak. Our company only gave one fire. The Hessians fired at us from a cornfield, but they shot too high. The bullets rattled among the trees above our heads. We were not much engaged in the battle, but there was one man wounded by a cannon shot within a rod of me. The battle lasted until two o'clock in the afternoon back and forward." Both accounts convey well the chaotic, frightening experience of enlisted men in a conventional eighteenth-century battle. Some even commented upon the physical harm visited upon their European enemies. Sergeant Young felt sympathy for the wounded Hessians he saw after the Battle of Trenton. He saw "one of them with his nose shot off and all of them in a wretched condition." In the context of these accounts, Jacob Ritter's revulsion toward military violence at Brandywine does not appear quite as exceptional as it does at first glance. Because soldiers were the men in the army charged with killing the enemy, they absorbed most of the blows in combat. It is not surprising that their understanding of combat was most focused on its human toll. The killing and maiming of other men in their units and among enemy soldiers led to a heightened awareness of the fragility of life for enlisted men once fighting began.[33]

Troops were often amazingly candid about how their will to live overwhelmed their devotion to duty. Many recounted how their units retreated in disarray. Neal McKay explained how fear overcame the majority of his comrades in the Battle of Brandywine: "when the British troops came up about one half of our brigade retreated" without firing a shot. Asa Thomas, a Bucks County militiaman at Brandywine, noted that "there was some firing between our advance and the enemy's guard; we retreated." The same sergeant who was horrified by the bloodshed at Princeton recounted how in the early stages of the battle, "I looked about for the main body of the army which I could not discover—discharged my musket at part of the enemy and ran for a piece of wood at a little distance where I thought

33. "Diary of Sergeant R—," 122–23; RWPF, file S22824; Entry: December 27, 1776, Sergeant Young Journal, HSP; Foulke, ed., *Memoirs of Jacob Ritter,* 12–16, 18–27.

I might shelter." Borick Bechtel recalled of Brandywine that "on this day, they were once fired upon by the British artillery, when he is very positive the whole regiment ran." John Hawkins wrote in his diary of the same battle that he threw down his knapsack full of supplies which "was very cumbersome . . . when running."[34]

Officers saw unauthorized retreats among the enlisted men as dishonorable and unprofessional. They expected their men to stand in battle but often found themselves abandoned in the field. In one particular instance—a battle at Edge Hill—officers lamented that the ranks broke, leaving a senior officer to be captured. John Armstrong wrote: "we have lost the use of our good officer and friend, General Irvine, three of his fingers being shot off, he fell from his horse and none of his men gave him the least assistance, being, at that time, broke and running." Elias Boudinot added of the action, "the Pennsylvania militia greatly disgraced their country—turning away at the first fire from half their number." Soldiers who were present saw the battle differently. George Hays, a Cumberland County militiaman, recalled the British attack at Edge Hill as more significant. He described how "we were attacked at that time by the British troops from Philadelphia four times and [were] driven from our encampment four miles in awe of the attacks and Colonel William Irvine from Carlisle was taken prisoner." Even with numerical superiority, the militiamen did not have the discipline and experience of their foes in conventional battle.[35]

In further contrast with enlisted men, officers saw battles primarily in tactical rather than human terms. They were charged with leading their men in combat and measured success by how their troops fought. They paid keen attention to unit formations, movements, reinforcements, and the manner of retreats. Thus, their focus was on the course of battle rather than its violence. Also, being privy to military objectives and the movements of the army, they had a more coherent overview of battles than their troops did. Leaders were able to understand the progression of a large action, whereas soldiers typically viewed it as a confusingly violent jumble of movements, firing, and close combat. Officers' views of battle reflected the simple fact that they were the directors of military violence, not its primary participants. Tactical descriptions of battles abound in the accounts of officers. Lieutenant James McMichael offered the following account of the Battle of White Plains:

34. RWPF, files S22899, W3475; "Diary of Sergeant R—," 121–22; RWPF, file S23542; Entry: September 11, 1777, Journal of John H. Hawkins. The entry is, interestingly, crossed out but still legible.
35. John Armstrong to Thomas Wharton, December 7, 1777, and Elias Boudinot to Thomas Wharton, December 9, 1777, both in the Reed Papers, NYHS, reel 2; RWPF, file W2937.

> We were attacked by their right wing (all Hessians) and after keeping up an incessant fire for an hour, we were informed by our flanking party that their light horse was surrounding us, when we retreated to the lines. Their left wing attacked a party of ours at an advanced post on a hill. Our troops behaved with great fortitude, but being overpowered by numbers, were obliged to fall back to the lines. The enemy attempted to force our right wing in the lines, but were driven back, and finally retreated.

The description contains many of the classic concerns of an officer with battle. McMichael, a junior-grade officer charged with carrying out tactical maneuvers, is primarily concerned with the movements and manners of engagement of his own troops and the enemy. He felt the need to assert that his men performed well in the combat but were simply overwhelmed before an unwise flanking movement by the British brought about a draw. A quite similar description was given by Colonel Samuel Atlee in his journal of the Battle of Long Island:

> I ordered [the troops] not to advance but maintain the possession of the hill, (which answered at this time every necessary purpose). The order was immediately obeyed when we found by a heavy fire from the fence that it was lined as I expected. The fire was as briskly returned by my brave soldiers. The enemy finding it too hot and our fire too well directed, retreated to and joined the right of this wing of their army.... I having left, for the security of my right flank and to protect my rear in case of retreat, a company in a wood on my right.

Clearly, Atlee was more interested in advertising his own tactical prowess than gauging the horror of violence that his men had to endure while holding hills and taking "heavy fire." When officers did mention individual casualties, they were invariably suffered by other officers, usually of comparable ranks. For example, Atlee rued the loss of "Lieutenant Colonel Parry, whom, in the midst of the action and immediately after he fell, I ordered to be borne by four soldiers off the field." Fallen enlisted men would not receive a great deal of notice from officers, much less such special treatment for their bodies.[36]

36. Diary of Lieutenant James McMichael, *PA*, 2d ser., 15:201; Colonel Samuel Atlee's Journal, 513-14.

Officers were also obsessed with maintaining their sense of honor in battle. They feared being labeled incompetent or, worse yet, craven. Officers warned the men of Hand's Rifle Regiment that any who fled the enemy would be severely punished so that "the brave and gallant part of the army may not fall a sacrifice to the base and cowardly part or share their disgrace in a cowardly and unmanly retreat." Even though common soldiers found nothing "unmanly" about running from what they deemed an overwhelming force, clearly their superiors did. In another case, Colonel Samuel Miles wrote an account of his participation in the Battle of Long Island years after the fact. It was intended to answer his critics—those who suggested that Miles's poor officership was one of the factors in the American defeat. Miles's retrospective account gives the usual incredibly detailed tactical account of the battle (a memory apparently undimmed by the passage of years). Then the retired colonel issues his apology for the capture of his command. Seeking to engage the enemy, Miles's troops were overwhelmed and taken prisoner. Yet he and his officers decided that they must seek battle rather than being "blamed for not fighting at all and perhaps charged with cowardice which would be worse than death itself." Such a concern with martial honor was the particular realm of officers. They did not consult their already exhausted and terrified troops about whether to press an engagement. Indeed, Miles's soldiers, unburdened by the demands of genteel officers' honor, probably sensed the battle already lost and would have welcomed retreat. In any case, it is safe to assume that few troops wished to risk their lives merely to protect the reputation of their colonel, much less see his dishonor as "worse than death itself."[37]

The one common factor officers and enlisted men did share was their acceptance of enemy deeds when they were seen as within the conventions of limited war. Both believed that the military violence of the large eighteenth-century European-style battle was a grim duty that soldiers had to pursue. Therefore, as long as the British and their German auxiliaries fought without killing in an "unfair" manner, they were not held personally responsible for the bloodshed that ensued. In fact, the Americans hoped that the enemy would similarly view them as honorable soldiers. The carnage of battle was terrifying, certainly, to many participants, but soldiers respected the lots of the enemy counterparts who faced the same violence in conventional engagements. It was when one side or the other breached the accepted norms of European warfare that some

37. Orders: September 20, 1776, Orderly Book of Hand's Rifle Regiment, HSP; Samuel Miles, Autobiographical Sketch, Miles Papers, American Philosophical Society.

combatants finally viewed each other with vehement hostility. These violations, however, were seen as precisely that: exceptional strains on a common military culture. Both sides, of course, used breaches of the mores of warfare as propaganda. Just as important, they hoped to control the destructive aspects of the war by appealing to shared sensibilities about "honorable" behavior in combat.

Strains on Conventions

Given the importance of conventions regarding prisoners of war, mistreatment of captives in the field was decried and threatened retaliation in kind. Failure to grant quarter to those who had clearly surrendered to the mercy of the enemy could mark either side as "uncivilized" in the other's eyes. When Alexander Graydon's men threw down their weapons to signify their surrender at Fort Washington, they found that the British "either did not or would not take the signal." Upon the approach of a British officer who cried out that no prisoners should be taken, Captain Graydon was able to shame him into following the conventions of European war when he declared, "Sir, I put myself under your protection." The worst that Graydon's men would have to suffer that day was the enemy's insults (rather than their bayonets). Urich Gandee recalled that when his comrades heard that the British had hanged an American captain as a spy rather than treat him as a prisoner of war, "the soldiers were much exasperated at this inhuman treatment towards their unfortunate countryman." General Anthony Wayne described his anger over British actions in New Jersey, noting that the enemy "refused any quarter and in cold blood, most barbarously and wantonly put to the bayonet men naked and unarmed, begging for mercy, incapable of resistance." Thomas Davis, a Chester County soldier at the Battle of Princeton, openly threatened his foes with revenge for deeds he considered unconscionable. He and his comrades found an officer who "was shot in the eye and bayoneted in many parts of his body. We brought him down and showed him to the British prisoners, telling them they should be treated the same way." Such atrocities—considered beyond the pale of "civilized" warfare—obviously imperiled any empathy soldiers might have felt toward their adversaries. Indeed, sometimes violations of European martial conventions did bring about immediate retribution in kind. Sergeant Young witnessed at Princeton how "a young lad that was wounded they stabbed three times in his side with his bayonet, which so exasperated our men that, seeing two Hessians behind a tree, ran at them, shot one and [ran] the other through."[38]

Other breaches of Anglo-American military conventions threatened, at various times, to undermine limited war. During "quiet" periods in a campaign, members of the main armies were able to see each other, particularly sentries. The unwritten assumption among soldiers of both sides was that it was unmanly and dishonorable to pick off guards. Killing such members of the enemy's army was sure to invite vengeance. Officers went to great lengths to suppress firing on enemy guards. William Moore remembered that in New Jersey "a member of the rifle corps fired across the river at the Hessians which was returned by a shot. . . . This being against orders, the rifleman who fired was put under guard." Henry Miller witnessed one of his comrades kill a British guard across the Hackensack River "with a kind of rifle gun made apparently for that purpose carrying about a one ounce ball. [Miller] saw the guard when he fell. . . . They were afterwards ordered and prevented from using it by the officers." Sometimes, killing a sentry set off a chain reaction of similar acts. Jacob Long recalled that the uneasy truce between picket guards around Philadelphia could quickly devolve into a war of revenge among soldiers who were not meant to engage the enemy but to observe them. Long's picket was "repeatedly fired on by the enemy. One man belonging to the piquet above them had his leg shot off. The captain of deponent's piquet, in a spirit of retaliation attempted to have one of the enemy's sentinel[s] shot."[39]

Refusals to recognize flags of truce were also decried by both sides as heinous violations of the rules of war. In January 1778, Thomas Wiggins of the Sixteenth Regiment of British Light Dragoons gave his account of how the rebels refused to respect his safety while he carried the white flag. He encountered a party of Americans and,

> notwithstanding his trumpet was sounding and his flag was in full view when he came within sixty yards of them, one of the light dragoons discharged his piece at him, upon which he told them he was a flag of truce. That immediately after he perceived the riflemen presenting their pieces at him, whereupon he again informed them repeatedly in a still more

---

38. *Alexander Graydon's Memoirs*, 205–6; RWPF, file R3890; Anthony Wayne to Thomas Hartley, October 5, 1778, Wayne Papers, 5:86, HSP; RWPF, file S23597. Entry: January 6, 1777, Sergeant Young Journal.

39. RWPF, files W25718, W2838, W3434.

audible voice that he was a flag, but all that did not avail in preventing a great number of them discharging their guns at him.

Similarly, George Thompson told of how some British soldiers carrying supplies to prisoners were made prisoners by a party of Americans who refused to recognize their flag. They told the Europeans that they would be tried as spies. A loyalist paper also reported in 1777 that a party of rebels, plundering the houses of Tories, robbed a British officer who was under a flag of truce. British and Revolutionary officers typically took their complaints to each other in an attempt to control the actions of their men. In February 1778, Sir William Howe sought to allay George Washington's concerns about the "absurdities" he heard regarding the treatment of American prisoners and those under flags of truce while inquiring into "the severity exercised against British prisoners."[40]

Officers were often even more frustrated in their attempts to limit thefts during the war. Soldiers on both sides sometimes looted the dead and wounded. Those who did the plundering felt that it was an acceptable practice. Poor enlisted men could justify taking the spoils of war by viewing it as a supplement to their meager pay. Samuel Graff of the Lancaster militia was utterly unabashed in his description of robbing a dead foe. He recalled that he "took from him his musket, sword, two dollars in silver, a guinea, and silver watch." Alexander Graydon lauded the "bravery" of "an Irish lad of about eighteen, who belonged to my company, killed a British soldier and brought off his arms." In a skirmish with the British in 1780, William Irvine attempted to make officers the final arbiters of what constituted proper war booty. He approved of "lawful plunder" but threatened death for those who took matters into their own hands and confiscated items without the approval of their officers.[41]

Pennsylvania troops were angered when they witnessed elements of the British army engaging in the same sorts of confiscation. Andrew Long was appalled after the Battle of Brandywine when he "saw the British women plundering the dead and wounded of both sides." Perhaps it particularly galled the soldier that the women of the enemy army—not even the troops—were taking

40. Petition of Thomas Wiggins, Sixteenth Regiment, Light Dragoons, January 3, 1778, British Headquarters Papers, item 837, 2–3; Deposition of Sergeant George Thompson, Sixty-third Regiment, February 16, 1778, ibid., item 945, 2–3; *Pennsylvania Evening Post*, December 18, 1777; Sir William Howe to General George Washington, February 21, 1778, *Documents of the American Revolution*, ed. Davies, 15:49–50.

41. RWPF, file W7566; *Alexander Graydon's Memoirs*, 187; Orders to March, January 14, 1780, Irvine Papers, 2:116, HSP.

the war prizes. The image of dying men having their few possessions stolen by women was emasculating. Isaac Anderson had a quite personal experience with the practice of plunder. At the Battle of Edge Hill, he was "shot through the head, stripped, and left on the field for dead." He was finally taken prisoner, wounded and naked "after lying twenty-four hours in the snow." John Adlum was horrified as he watched his comrade, Ensign Jacob Barnitz, "shot through both legs" and left "on the field of battle all night naked, having been stripped by the Hessians or their trulls." Others recalled the essence of the service in terms of their material losses to the enemy when captured. John McElnay recalled with disgust that when he surrendered at Long Island, "he had a good deal of money in his pocket, having received his pay and been . . . saving." The British "took all his money from him." Captain Michael Simpson of the First Pennsylvania Regiment was incensed when his British captors "took my clothing, great coat, and boots." Abraham Eschelman helped take the prisoners at Trenton, noting that "this affair gratified us exceedingly because the Hessians had assisted in taking our blankets and tents at Fort Lee." Alexander Nisbet was furious with the British because "our men had drawn three days provisions and had taken it into the country to get cooked when the enemy came upon them and took it all."[42]

All the above instances strained the limits of Anglo-American military culture. In a number of cases, acts of revenge followed that generated more hostility and a desire for retribution. Yet these occurrences were not enough to shatter completely the conventions of limited war. It was when members of the British army injected themselves into local hostilities by raiding, destroying, and confiscating property in the Revolutionaries' communities that views of enemy regulars began to change. Such acts earned the British and Hessians the enmity of Whigs, neutrals, and sometimes even Tories in the region. Revolutionary troops reacted especially angrily to British threats to their homes. No longer were the European regulars seen as fellow white Christians engaged in their vocation; rather, they were very tangible threats to the imagined community. As soon as the war moved into the Middle Atlantic region in 1776, troops from the southeastern part of Pennsylvania realized that the occupation of Philadelphia and its environs would be an enemy objective. Quickly, apathy or empathy toward forces of the Crown turned to fear and anger. As British

42. RWPF, files W8063, W4628; Dann, *The Revolution Remembered,* 118; RWPF, file S2788; Captain Michael Simpson to Supreme Executive Council, January 12, 1779, PRG, reel 14, frame 915; RWPF, files S22757, S22422.

forces moved across New Jersey late in the year, Pennsylvania newspapers filled with atrocity stories portraying European regulars as a dangerous threat to both property and manhood in Pennsylvania. Redcoats and Hessians were depicted as marauding robbers and libidinous monsters. Stories of plunder, rape, and beatings in neighboring New Jersey abounded as the British took up positions on the Delaware. Suddenly, enemy soldiers were no longer civilized Europeans. On December 18, 1777, the *Pennsylvania Packet* reported that "the progress of the British and Hessian troops through New Jersey has been attended with such scenes of desolation and outrage as would disgrace the most barbarous nations." The paper also stated that three New Jersey women "had been all very much abused and the youngest of them, a girl about fifteen, had been ravished that morning by a British officer." Nine days later, the *Packet* reported that British troops in Pennington, New Jersey, had chased fifteen women into the woods and raped them. It noted that "one man had the cruel mortification to have his wife and only daughter (a child of ten years of age) ravished." Late in 1776, the Pennsylvania Assembly printed a broadside that warned, "every species of ravage and calamity have already marked the footsteps of our enemy and they are now within a few miles of your metropolis [Philadelphia], waiting to cross the Delaware to glut their inordinate lust and rapine and desolation in plunder of that rich and populous city." Such accounts, of course, were meant to galvanize resistance against the British and to frighten hesitant neutrals. Regardless of whether the reports were exaggerated, they were effective recruiting devices because they emphasized violations of military conventions near Pennsylvanians' homes.[43]

These images were soon appropriated by anxious southeastern Pennsylvania soldiers. In 1776, the Philadelphia militia declared its resolve to stand up to "a bold and inhuman soldiery [who] are ready to ravage our country. Their footsteps are marked with cruelty unpracticed by civilized nations for near a century past." Implicit in the description of the British was a call for the enemy to reform itself. By conjuring up the specter of the Thirty Years' War in Europe, the militia suggested that if enemy troops continued to act "uncivilized," they might expect brutal responses. "Cruelty" in war also applied to the destruction of property, something that acutely concerned many soldiers in the region. In January 1777, for example, Sergeant Young noted in his journal: "while I pass through this country [New Jersey], I could

43. *Pennsylvania Packet,* December 18, 1776, and December 27, 1776; Pennsylvania Assembly Broadside, December 24, 1776, LCP.

not help taking notice of the devastation done by those sons of blood and murder."[44]

Predictably, southeastern Pennsylvania soldiers' attitudes toward enemy regulars hardened when the British actually invaded the state in 1777. With hostile occupation looming, the state government employed anti-British propaganda in a local context to motivate the soldiers. It predicted "scenes of plunder, devastation, and cruelty upon the people in the enemy's reach and the complete ruin of those who exerted themselves in this country's cause." Soldiers were more likely, however, to become embittered when the British did start raiding and confiscating property in their immediate region. Arthur Andrews of Chester County recalled how he defended "the inhabitants from the ravages of the British soldiers who were stationed at the city of Philadelphia at that time." Similarly, William Sanders of Philadelphia remembered with anger his "pursuit of the British who were destroying the property of the inhabitants." Ensign Bradford of Chester County was furious at the British for robbing houses near Haverford, and he declared them to be "merciless wretches." As the enemy occupation continued, anger mounted toward British acts against civilians and their property in Philadelphia's environs. Captain McLaw watched in horror as Howe's forces were "burning and laying waste [to] all the farms from the Rising Sun Tavern . . . to the city." One resident saw the British march through Germantown "sparing neither friend or foe; burning, robbing, stealing all the way they went." Such behavior was condemned by the Germantowner as the "shame of the British nation," suggesting that the soldiers had failed to live up to the expectations of "civilized" warfare and, therefore, were not behaving in a truly "British" manner.[45]

In order to limit the alienation of Pennsylvanians from the forces of the Crown and to save the honor of the "British nation," Sir William Howe issued strict orders against plundering and threatened brutal punishment. Nevertheless, officers could not always control their men. Major John Andre reported that soon after the invasion of Pennsylvania began, "great complaints were made of the plunder committed by the Troops—chiefly by the Hessians." A few weeks later, he discussed the fates of those found guilty of such deeds: "two men, one of the Light Infantry and one of the Grenadiers, were executed at Lord Cornwallis's

44. To "Fellow Soldiers," 1776, Broadside, LCP; Entry: January 17, 1777, Sergeant Young Journal.
45. Supreme Executive Council and the Pennsylvania General Assembly to Congress, April [13?], 1777, PRG, reel 12, frame 277; RWPF, files S23517, S4663; Entry: December 8[?], 1777, Extract of the Journal of Captain McLaw, Reed Papers, NYHS, reel 2; Entry: December 8, 1777, Germantown Journal, microfilm, NYHS, reel 2.

camp for plunder." Clearly, the British hoped to control their own violations of martial laws in order to weaken the propaganda value of such actions for the rebels. Yet the Revolutionaries sometimes wearied of the British promises to attempt to limit plunder and took actions into their own hands. John Peebles reported that "2 men of the 71st [were] found in the wood yesterday with their throats cut, and 2 Grenadiers hang'd by the rebels with their plunder on their backs." Significantly, Peebles casts no further judgment upon the rebels, leaving readers of his diary to assume that he expects the enemy to protect their property from marauders.[46]

Perceived British violations of combat norms against Pennsylvanians could become especially dangerous amid these growing tensions and bring about brutal retaliation. One of the most infamous occurrences was dubbed the "Paoli Massacre." In late September 1777, British regulars surprised Pennsylvania troops under the command of Anthony Wayne with a night attack using only bayonets. The attack was one that the European regulars saw as conventional, orderly, and well executed. The Pennsylvanians saw the engagement as cowardly and shockingly violent, and they regarded it as a harbinger of British misbehavior to come when the redcoats occupied parts of the state. (Wayne actually learned from the assault and launched a similar one against British forces at Stony Point, New York, in 1779.) At this point in the war, many American troops were largely unacquainted with such tactics. Most were so taken by surprise that they never fully woke up before they met their deaths or were badly wounded. The memory of this action was a particularly bitter one for those who survived. Nathaniel Irwin remembered the "night of the 20th of September, 1777 where many of the Americans were bayoneted" as a "massacre." Thomas Dickey recalled that his "company which at first consisted of 190 men were all killed including the officers at Paoli except only eighteen men." John Hawkins condemned "the bloody Highlanders," who "in the night" attacked Wayne's troops and "bayoneted them in a most shocking manner." Andrew Wallace "narrowly escaped the savage brutality of the foe by taking refuge in a cluster of chestnut oak sprouts." John Frailey of Philadelphia called Paoli "a spot of ground that will never be forgotten by Americans," one where "they came in contact with the British and were dispersed and driven off in a very deplorable manner."[47]

46. *Major Andre's Journal*, 42, 47; Gruber, ed., *John Peebles' American War*, 129.
47. See Middlekauff, *Glorious Cause*, 389, on the action at Paoli, and Peckham, *War for Independence*, 128–29, on Wayne's later bayonet attack on Stony Point. RWPF, files S4418, S2175; Entry: October 10, 1777, Journal of John H. Hawkins; RWPF, files S3466, S23641.

As word circulated among the Pennsylvania troops of the British action at Paoli, their anger grew. The combination of British misdeeds in combat and the profound threat that they physically presented to rebel communities proved explosive. A few days later, at the Battle of Germantown, some of their frustration boiled over in the form of atrocities against British forces. One observer declared that "the rebels had used the British troops barbarously." Anthony Wayne slyly winked at his men's actions during the battle. He reported that "our officers exerted themselves to save many of the poor wretches who were crying for mercy—but to little purpose. The rage and fury of the soldiers was not to be restrained for some time—at least not until great numbers of the enemy fell by our bayonets." Fortunately, both armies retired into winter quarters before revenge slaughters could occur in another major engagement. The next large battle did not take place until that at Monmouth, New Jersey, as the British forces withdrew from Pennsylvania.[48]

Still, the British army's continual scouring of the southeastern Pennsylvania countryside for forage during its occupation led to a number of bitter skirmishes. Many troops defending their homes adamantly resisted any enemy forays into their neighborhoods. John Andre noted that the local rebels were consistently attempting to raid small posts of the British army. He explained that on one occasion, "the militia, of which there were skulking parties about the right of our encampment, wounded three or four men and two officers of Wemy's Corps." European regulars sometimes responded even more violently in an attempt to intimidate the local rebels. One practice was "the burning of the houses of those who act vigorously in the militia." One atrocity was far more horrid. On May 1, 1778, near Crooked Billet, Pennsylvania, a militia force under General John Lacey was defeated in a skirmish with British light infantry and the Queen's Rangers. Following the action, a number of local residents found that the American prisoners had met a gruesome death. One witness heard the redcoats boast of having "bayoneted some of General Lacey's men after they had surrendered themselves prisoners, others they threw into heaps of buckwheat straw while alive and burnt them to death." Colonel Frederick Watts and Samuel Henry of Bucks County corroborated the story when they explained how they found "the bodies of the dead used in a most inhuman and barbarous manner . . . burnt to that degree that some of them could not be

48. Jonathan Clark Jr. to George Washington, October 6, 1777, George Washington Papers, microfilm, Library of Congress, 4th ser., reel 44; Anthony Wayne to Polly Wayne, October 6, 1777, Wayne Papers, 4:31, HSP.

known. We viewed the corpses of the dead and saw only two as we remember that escaped the most cruel barbarity that had ever been experienced by any civilized nation, nay savage barbarity in its utmost exertion of cruelty would not equal it." Ominously, this British action was considered so beyond the pale of limited European-style war that it once again raised the issue of "savagery." The attack did cause much resentment, but mercifully for southeastern Pennsylvanians, the British army began its withdrawal from the state a few weeks later. A cycle of revenge violence was not sustained for the long term.[49]

Ultimately, the main British army was not in the state long enough for total war to break out on a sustained level. After nine months of occupation, the new British commander, General Sir Henry Clinton, retired from Philadelphia to New York. With the passage of time, some Pennsylvania soldiers again resumed their previously respectful view of their European counterparts. A few, however, were affected for life in terms of their views of the British. Young Nathaniel Boileau, whose family farm was the site of the Crooked Billet action, enlisted in 1781 as soon as he was old enough to fight. More typically, anger for past deeds remained but, with the passage of time, slowly became less immediate. What facilitated fading hostility among Pennsylvanians was the simple fact that the main British army was no longer directly threatening their lives, livelihoods, and property. From late 1778 onward it became apparent that the king's forces were in a defensive posture in New York City and that the main theater of operations was shifting to the southern states. With the royal troops safely out of their state and the probability of their return remote, enemy regulars were rarely again characterized by Pennsylvania soldiers as savages. By 1780, socializing with European counterparts was again rampant among the entire Pennsylvania Brigade, whose officers lamented that "the practice of going into the vicinity of the enemy . . . is all too common."[50]

Clearly, hostility toward the troops of the British army was limited and situational. A common European culture, shared ethnic backgrounds, and comparable class status among the soldiery helped mitigate tensions from the outset of the war. Consistent reference by both sides to "civilized" military behavior

49. *Major Andre's Journal*, 53; Joseph Reed to [?], October 30, 1777, Reed Papers, NYHS, reel 2, contains the quotation about the burning of militiamen's homes. Deposition of Thomas Craven and William Stayner, May 15, 1778, PRG, reel 14, frame 6; Deposition of Colonel Frederick Watts and Samuel Henry, May 14, 1778, PRG, reel 13, frame 1358.

50. See Ruth L. Woodward and Wesley Frank Craven, eds., *Princetonians, 1784–1790: A Biographical Dictionary* (Princeton, N.J., 1991), 335–49, on Nathaniel Boileau. Division Orders: June 10, 1780, Orderly Book of the Second Pennsylvania Regiment, HSP.

was meant to reaffirm shared Western conventions of warfare—even when they were violated. Critiques of enemy actions served as propaganda but often aimed, as well, to shame the enemy into acting within the realm of accepted norms. Even witnesses to the Crooked Billet slaughter discursively employed Manichean polarities of "civilization" and "savagery." By invoking the experience of "any civilized nation" and decrying British "savage barbarity," they tried to humiliate anyone in the British army with pretensions to civility. Furthermore, common sets of beliefs about what constituted "civilized" warfare and what was an atrocity allowed both sides to criticize each other using a common vocabulary. The British and the Revolutionaries typically tried to defend themselves against charges of violations of norms, thus demonstrating that they had some concern over whether the enemy viewed them as honorable. In the end, American adversaries drew the most sustained ire from Pennsylvania troops. Violent as the war against European regulars was, it was consistently less brutal and characterized by more restraint compared to that prosecuted against other residents of the region. In the cruel crucible of war, ideologies of race, criminality, community, and citizenship were forged in bitter bloodshed among Americans.[51]

---

51. Deposition of Colonel Frederick Watts and Samuel Henry, May 14, 1778, PRG, reel 13, frame 1358.

Race and Violence on the Frontier

There was a clear dissonance between the popular Revolutionary mythology of Indian violence and the brutal actions of Pennsylvania frontier soldiers. A key instance involved the following description of militia action that appeared in the *Pennsylvania Evening Post* in April 1782. The account told the story of an effective raid in response to enemy Indian attacks:

> Parties of Indians, striking the settlements so early in the season greatly alarmed the people, and but too plainly evinced their determination to harass the frontiers and nothing could save them but a quick and spirited exertion. They [the local militia] therefore determined to extirpate the

aggressors, and, if possible, to recover the people that had been carried off. . . . They proceeded to the towns on the Muskingum, where the Indians had collected a large quantity of provisions, to supply their war parties. They arrived at the town in the night undiscovered, attacked the Indians in their cabins, and so completely surprised them, that they killed and scalped upwards of ninety (but a few making their escape) about forty of whom were warriors, the rest old men, women, and children. About eighty horses fell into their hands, which they loaded with the plunder, the greatest part furs and skins and returned to the Ohio without the loss of one man.[1]

What the story does not fully reveal is that this "expedition" was the infamous March 1782 "Gnadenhütten Massacre." The Indians were mostly Christian Delawares, Unamis, and Munsees (along with a few Shawnee) who had been converted by Moravian missionaries in the Ohio country. Not only were they pacifist neutrals, but they had also, to a large extent, adopted numerous aspects of Anglo-American culture. They were Christian farmers who lived in wood cabins. Additionally, Moravian missionaries in the area had been passing intelligence on hostile Indian military dispositions to the Revolutionary authorities. The villages had thus assisted the U.S. war effort. As a result of this activity, the Moravian Indians were removed from their villages in 1781 by northern Indian neighbors who viewed them as potentially dangerous and too friendly toward the Revolutionaries. The movement was so sudden that many Moravian Delawares left corn crops in their fields and were eventually conducted back to their towns when winter food supplies ran low. This was when the Pennsylvania militia struck. Near the town of Gnadenhütten, in the Muskingum Valley of present-day Ohio, the *métis* Joseph Shabosh, son of a Moravian missionary, first encountered the Revolutionaries. After he attempted to identify himself as a friend, the militia literally cut him to pieces. Upon arriving at the village, the Pennsylvania troops informed the other Indians that they intended to move them closer to Fort Pitt to protect them from Native groups allied with the British. Other Pennsylvania soldiers invited Moravian Delawares from the nearby town of Salem to join the others at Gnadenhütten to prepare for the same move. The militiamen then deliberated among themselves and decided to execute the Moravian Indians, whom

---

1. *Pennsylvania Evening Post,* April 16, 1782.

they deemed enemy warriors. There were, of course, no warriors in the pacifist community. The men and women of Gnadenhütten prepared for their grim fate by singing hymns until soldiers conducted the Indians to their "cabins" and proceeded to bludgeon them to death, using mallets. Some of the victims were scalped while still living; the corpses of others were cut up by a number of soldiers.[2]

The *Pennsylvania Evening Post* account omitted these significant details, but it did clearly suggest that a surprise attack on an Indian village in which ninety men, women, and children were killed and scalped was an acceptable military action. The report also noted that the soldiers then plundered the Indian community with great success. What was certainly obvious to readers in the 1780s was the similarity of the militia's military practices to those deemed atrocities when committed by Indians. For example, Thomas Rees, a Northampton County militiaman, recalled of his military service that "whenever we heard of any outrages committed by the Indians, we marched to the place in pursuit of them." Like most of his comrades, he refers to his enemies as a single, undifferentiated group—"the Indians"—and suggests that they provoked hostilities. The "outrages" mentioned by Rees were excruciatingly detailed by other Revolutionaries, such as Colonel Hosterman of the Northumberland County militia, who reported how he and his troops discovered "Peter Smith's wife shot through, stab[bed], and a knife left by her and scalped. William King's wife tomahawked and scalped. She was sitting up this morning, but leaned on her husband when [he] came to her and expired immediately. She appeared sensible but did not speak. A little girl killed and scalped. A boy same. Snodgrass shot through the head, killed and scalped, tomahawked, stabbed, etc. Campbell shot in the back, tomahawked, stabbed, and a knife left in him." Yet, as evidenced by Gnadenhütten, the Revolutionaries killed and scalped their enemies, many of whom were noncombatants. They also were capable of attacking both neutral and allied Indians. On the one hand, Revolutionaries condemned Indian warfare as "savage," but on the other, they fought in the same ways and aggressively escalated the conflict. A cultural double standard emerged that appears, superficially, to be intellectually vacuous.[3]

---

2. On the Gnadenhütten Massacre, see Buck and Buck, *The Planting of Civilization*, 197–98, and Dowd, *Spirited Resistance*, 85–87. My description and analysis of the Gnadenhütten incident particularly builds upon Slaughter, *Whiskey Rebellion*, 75–78.

3. RWPF, file S7377; Colonel Hosterman to Lieutenant Samuel Hunter, June 10, 1778, PRG, reel 14, frame 241.

The ways that Revolutionaries described the frontier war were, however, neither contradictory nor hypocritical. War in this region between Indians and European Americans was responsible for a fundamental shift in self-perception and for the construction of a national identity that reconciled these apparent inconsistencies in Revolutionaries' descriptions of military actions. Although violence on the Revolutionary Pennsylvania frontier engendered few attempts at restraint (unlike the regular armies), it was, like the war against the British, also the product of a shared military culture among combatants. Because the stakes were high—namely, the future of the trans-Allegheny west—there was neither empathy between opponents nor attempts to limit war. Fighting predominated among the region's residents and both sides prosecuted war against entire peoples rather than only military forces. Prisoners received no quarter and were mutilated and/or tortured. Scalping signified manly victory over a foe. Noncombatants, property, and food sources were valid targets in raids meant to cripple the enemy's social infrastructure. In short, the military cultures of both European Americans and Indians in the region evolved via martial exchange so as to be nearly identical. This interaction rendered problematic previous European American notions of cultural superiority over Indians. As the frontier war progressed, a notion of physiological "whiteness" increasingly became the key explanation for Indian inferiority and a cornerstone of American national identity. This concept created unity among ethnically diverse Revolutionaries and implicated Indians as "nonwhite." The development of white racial consciousness emerged in Pennsylvania during the colonial wars of the 1750s and 1760s, but, during the War for Independence, race became central to the definition of "American-ness." Revolutionaries then adapted Indian culture, especially methods of warfare, with no peril to their belief in their superiority. "Other" and self on the Pennsylvania frontier were no longer primarily defined according to cultural differences but by perceptions of skin color. Racism fueled and escalated military violence and fostered the development of a biological definition of national citizenship.[4]

4. See Hirsch, "Collision of Military Cultures," on war as a medium for cultural exchange in the colonial period. See Daniel K. Richter, "'Believing That Many of the Red People Suffer Much for the Want of Food': Hunting, Agriculture, and a Quaker Construction of Indianness in the Early Republic," *Journal of the Early Republic* 19 (Winter 1999): 601–28, and Elise Marienstras, "The Common Man's Indian: The Image of the Indian as a Promoter of National Identity in the Early National Era," in *Native Americans and the Early Republic,* ed. Frederick E. Hoxie, Ronald Hoffman, and Peter J. Albert (Charlottesville, Va., 1999), 261–96, on Indians as negative reference points in American identity, despite actual cultural similarities.

The Development of Frontier Military Culture

A salient difference between the Revolution on the frontier and earlier colonial wars in Pennsylvania was that combat was carried out primarily by frontier residents. With the exception of Sullivan's 1779 Continental army expedition and a few other operations, most military violence was prosecuted by the Revolutionaries with local militias and locally raised Continental units. Indeed, militiaman John Struthers recalled the war in the Ohio River Valley as essentially the people fighting in and for communities. He stated, "it was admitted by everyone at the time that the only security of the people along the river and adjacent settlements was the vigilance of the [local] volunteers." Conversely, Indian nations in the area, regardless of which side they took, typically fought to protect their independence and way of life. Quite simply, the war between villagers often translated into a contest of which village would prevail and persist in the region. The stakes and animosity in the fighting were both high.[5]

Some of these residents had experienced previous intercultural interaction and warfare. Long hunters, "Indian traders," and missionaries had long shared a common economic and social milieu with their Indian neighbors. Although these European Americans fought on both sides in the Revolution, numbers became "loyalists" to protect their immediate material interests—that is, trade with Native Americans and the British-sponsored imperial system. The influx of new residents into the perceived "hinterland" of Pennsylvania in the mid-eighteenth century typically consisted of people who saw themselves as "settlers" or "inhabitants." In other words, they sought to possess the land and cultivate it in the traditional European sense, with the primary male role being fieldwork. These new farmers had little desire to interact with Indian neighbors but did covet their lands. Unlike traders or missionaries who had compelling reasons for direct interaction with Native Americans, new colonists saw Indians as obstacles to the possession of the land and its proper "settlement."[6]

---

5. In *The Planting of Civilization,* Buck and Buck describe how Pennsylvania frontier residents carried out much of the war (175–203). Struthers is quoted in Dann, *The Revolution Remembered,* 258. Richard White employs the apt phrase, "the contest of villagers," to describe the Revolution on the frontier in *Middle Ground,* 366–412.

6. See Aron, *How the West Was Lost,* 5–57, on long hunters' and traders' interactions with Indians, and Merrell, *Into the American Woods,* on cultural "negotiators." On Pennsylvania "Indian traders" who chose to side with local Indians and the British against the Revolutionaries, see Chapter 2 of this volume. On the mid-eighteenth-century migration of "settlers" to the Pennsylvania frontier, see Fischer, *Albion's Seed,* 633–39, and R. Eugene Harper, *The Transformation of Western Pennsylvania, 1770–1800* (Pittsburgh, 1991), 17–57. Peter C. Mancall, *Valley of Opportunity: Economic Culture Along the Upper Susquehanna, 1700–1800* (Ithaca, N.Y.), 69–93, explains the process of how new farmers superseded earlier Indian traders.

A few of these Pennsylvania farmers had memories of earlier colonial wars that framed their primary understanding of cultural interaction with Indians in terms of warfare. Their recollections of previous Indian military actions colored their perceptions of the Revolution and provided for an imagined continuity of general Indian hostility toward Anglo-Americans. They thus incorporated discussions of earlier wars into their narratives of the Revolution. Robert Scott, a volunteer in the Revolutionary frontier war, noted that his anger toward his Native enemies in the War for Independence stemmed from the French and Indian War, in which "his father and family were banished by the Indians" from their Northampton County farm. Similarly, Archibald Loudon, a Cumberland County Revolutionary soldier, formed his opinion of Native Americans as a young man when, "after Braddock's defeat by the Indians, they began to murder the inhabitants of Sherman's Valley where we lived." William Jones simply attributed responsibility for a past act of military violence to all Native Americans and fought in the Revolution because his "father was killed by the Indians when he was a boy, after which time, he became their settled enemy."[7]

More recent immigrants missed these earlier tumults and based their preconceptions about Indians on secondhand sources. Although new to the frontier, these colonists were exposed to a literary genre that colored their expectations of Indians and neatly fit with their neighbors' views of continuous Native violence and hostility. Stories of Indian military actions in previous wars—and captivity narratives in particular—were familiar to the immigrants. If they did had not read the stories, in an oral culture, they undoubtedly heard them. These tales all stressed the supposedly brutal methods of Indian war, especially in regard to the treatment of women and children. Indian cultural inferiority was constructed in terms of Natives' supposed violence vis-à-vis European Americans. Additionally, by the mid-eighteenth century, popular narratives of frontier war justified land appropriation by killing hostile and supposedly "brutal" Indians. Such messages assuaged the consciences of land-hungry farmers by positing Native Americans as a single hostile group posing an obstacle to "civilization." Depriving them of their lands was viewed as both defensively and culturally necessary.[8]

7. RWPF, files W3305, S4573, W2124.
8. For a prime example of the captivity narrative genre, see Mary Rowlandson, *The Narrative of the Captivity and Restoration of Mrs. Mary Rowlandson* (Boston, 1930). Rowlandson's seventeenth-century tale was the first one published and among the most popular in the genre. Significantly for the Revolutionary War generation, it was republished twice in 1773. On the colonial legacy of Othering Indians in terms of their supposedly brutal methods of warfare and treatment of captives and how this changed over time in

Given this frame of reference, frontier Revolutionaries articulated their version of Native American "savagery" by condemning specific Indian military acts. Not surprisingly, their accounts prominently feature terms such as "savage" and "barbarities." John Struthers described his "pursuit of the savages who had committed . . . barbarities." Troops from the Wyoming region angrily related how "the savages . . . made incursions and, in a most barbarous and inhuman manner, killed numbers of our parents and friends." Sergeant Theobald Coontz of the Pennsylvania Rangers also described Indians as "the savages." Lorentz Holben served "for the protection of the inhabitants of that newborn land against the savage Indians." John Dougherty described going to Indians' "haunts"—thereby suggesting that Indians were incapable of living in "villages" or "settlements," but rather merely frequented certain areas. William Moore recalled that his unit helped assure that the Indians would "not again infest" the frontiers. Additionally, as these accounts suggest, soldiers framed their own actions as simply reactive and the Indians' acts as provocations. Of course, the situation was far more complex than such a formula would suggest. It ignores the reality that not all Indians were hostile to the United States; moreover, many of the supposedly "peaceable inhabitants" were in fact colonists who trespassed on Indian lands. Soldiers simply neglected to mention that their intrusions proved bellicose, as witnessed by a publicized prewar Iroquois and Chippewa warning that "insist[ed] on our quitting their lands immediately, and not make any excuse."[9]

Other terms specifically used to describe military actions in the region are telling as well. Revolutionaries described themselves as "killing" the enemy while commonly stating that Indians committed "murders" or "massacres." This linguistic strategy suggested that Indians, as a singular group, were inherently violent, and it also justified their conquest as being necessarily provoked by "atrocities." In pension applications, soldiers went out of their way to describe Indian warfare as murderous. Benjamin Lewis described how "there were many massacres committed by the savages in the neighborhood of Northumberland." Christian Acker fought "against the Indians who were at that time murdering the inhabitants." Peter Wolf accused Indians of "murdering," and in battle, he said, they "slaughtered a number of our troops." George Vanzant of

---

various historical contexts, see Jill Lepore, *The Name of War: King Philip's War and the Origins of American Identity* (New York, 1998), 173–90. On the "land imperative" narrative of the mid-eighteenth century, see James Levernier and Hennig Cohen, eds., *The Indians and Their Captives* (Westport, Conn., 1977), xii.

9. Dann, *The Revolution Remembered,* 254; the Wyoming soldiers are quoted in Susquehannah Company Papers, ed. Taylor, 7:79; Petition of Sergeant Theobald Coontz, December 20, 1782, PRG, reel 19, frame 1282; RWPF, files S22309, S12779, W25718; *Pennsylvania Evening Post,* April 16, 1782.

Bedford County served to "prevent the savages from murdering and plundering the inhabitants on the frontiers." Similarly, Andrew Myers of Washington County condemned Indian "outrages on the frontier inhabitants." Lawrence Konkle of Westmoreland County recalled that Indians committed "many murders and depredations." Thomas Rees decried the "great number of murders by the Indians." This linguistic maneuver was also popular during the war itself. William Maclay, for example, wrote of the situation on the Revolutionary frontier: "we are told every hour of more and more murders committed by the straggling savages." In 1778, a Bedford County militia company spoke of how Indians "made incursions and committed murders on different parts of our frontier."[10]

The linking of terms such as "outrages," "murder," "massacre," and "savages" with "the Indians" was crucial in developing a negative reference point. That Indian military violence was often dubbed "murder" by Revolutionaries was significant during a period when narratives of murder in America suggested the inhumanity of those who committed the act. The genre no longer attributed the perpetrators' culpability to the human condition, deriving from original sin (as earlier colonial crime tales did). Rather, murderers came to be seen, in the words of historian Karen Halttunen, as "something other than human," violent creatures lacking morals. Notably, "murder" typically signified any Indian military action, not only the killing of non-soldiers. In other words, the discourse of depraved crime, not warfare, was applied to enemy acts. This ominous suggestion of all Indians having a proclivity to murder implied a less-than-human enemy. The conflation of crime, inhumanity, and "Indians" as a singular group was powerful. The Westmoreland militia, for example, spoke fearfully in a petition of leaving "our families exposed to be again ravaged by the Indians and probably all murdered." The soldiers also used the term "ravage," clearly adding sexual as well as economic violations to their litany of criminal charges; they went on to state that Indians killed in an "inhuman manner." The implication was that "the Indians" were collectively responsible for inhuman murder rather than military violence.[11]

---

10. RWPF, files S13746, S22073, S7963, S23042, W5155, S22341, S7377; William Maclay to Timothy Matlack, July 12, 1778, *Susquehannah Company Papers*, ed. Taylor, 7:47; Petition of Inhabitants of Bedford County, January 26, 1778, PRG, reel 13, frame 608.

11. On the shift in eighteenth-century conceptions of murder, see Karen Halttunen, "Early American Murder Narratives: The Birth of Horror," in *The Power of Culture: Critical Essays in American History*, ed. Richard Wrightman Fox and Jackson Lears (Chicago, 1993), 67–101, quotation on 85; Petition of Westmoreland Militia, January 23, 1781, in *Susquehannah Company Papers*, ed. Taylor, 7:79–80.

These links in the minds of Revolutionaries among Indians, inhumanity, and murder were important, especially as the military cultures of both groups converged. While the two groups fought in increasingly similar ways, such visceral formulations maintained images of Indian difference. In reality, however, the Indian and Revolutionary ways of warring were very similar. Both sides, for instance, developed comparable total war aims. Initially, many Revolutionaries assumed that the object of Indian hostilities was to terrorize and remove all European American settlement in the trans-Allegheny west. In spring 1778, Northumberland militia officer James Potter articulated that "the Indians are determined to clear the two branches of the Susquehanna." Revolutionaries used the same sorts of war aims and the same terror tactics against Indian communities but rationalized them as a response to Indian actions. Archibald Lochry, for example, asked the state government to allow him to mount a Westmoreland County militia raid to destroy the towns and crops of hostile Indians. Lochry argued that "the enemy are almost constantly in our country killing and captivating the inhabitants. I see no way we can have of defending ourselves other than by offensive operations." The total war aims of Revolutionaries were thus justified as "defensive-offensive" operations. This formulation masked the desire for Indian-controlled lands by projecting aggressor status on the enemy. Indian leaders, of course, knew better and long understood American war aims. The Seneca sachem Sayenqueraghta described in 1779 "the rebels, who, notwithstanding their fair speeches, wish to extirpate us from the earth, that they may possess our lands, the desire of attaining which we are convinced is the cause of the present war."[12]

Such "offensive operations" were not directed against the enemy's war parties but their societies. Like Indian raids, Revolutionary forays were terror campaigns in which noncombatants were attacked and the Native economy disrupted. Pennsylvania soldiers hoped that such blows against the enemy's homes would destroy Native American communities and open up new lands. Although Revolutionary enlisted men called raids against their communities despicable acts of savage enemies, they saw their attacks as honorable, even brave. David White of Washington County "volunteered three different times to go to the Shawnee towns." Northumberland County soldier Joseph Keefer proudly recalled how his unit "had a skirmish with the Indians and burnt and

12. James Potter to Major General John Armstrong, May 7, 1778, PCC, reel 83, vol. 1, I. 69, p. 537; Archibald Lochry to Joseph Reed, July 4, 1781, PRG, reel 18, frame 547; Sayenqueraghta quoted in Calloway, *American Revolution in Indian Country*, 132–33.

destroyed their town." George Reem accompanied General John Sullivan's 1779 Continental expedition into Iroquois country. Reem stated that he assisted in "destroying the cornfields and burning the Indian villages. I was at the burning of Chemung, Newtown, Catherine's Town, Gennesse Castle, and three other small villages." Westmoreland ranger Jacob Rudolf "assisted in taking the Muncy towns and destroying the corn of the Indians." John McCaslin, the soldier who could not bring himself to shoot a lone Hessian sentinel during the Philadelphia campaign, went on two destructive tours of duty against Shawnee towns. He related how, in one case, "we defeated and routed [the Shawnees]—cut their corn down and burnt their houses." On the second tour, McCaslin again "burnt [the Shawnees'] corn which was gathered and burnt as many as seven little towns—took five Indians (women and children) prisoners and killed five or six warriors."[13]

Like Indians, Revolutionaries also killed civilians. George Roush candidly described how his unit, under the command of Captain Samuel Brady, ambushed a hunting camp: "We fired and killed three, one of which was a squaw, and then approached the camp. . . . Whilst we were examining their guns, an Indian boy, which we supposed to be of the age of fifteen or sixteen years, came near and halloed to us and said, 'Unhee, what did you shoot at?' And a man by the name of Fulks answered in the Indian language and said, 'A raccoon.' The Indian came across the creek, and when he came in shooting distance one of our company shot him." The account suggests that the soldiers were well aware that this was not a war party; the Indian boy, missing the ambush, was trusting enough of the soldiers to come over to them. Roush apparently saw nothing dishonorable or unmilitary in killing the hunting party, the woman, and the young boy. Occasionally, officers at least professed to be horrified by these actions of frontier Revolutionaries who killed those assumed to be innocent civilians. For example, the infamous "Squaw Campaign" of 1778 was a projected expedition into the Ohio country against hostile Indian towns and was primarily carried out by Westmoreland County militia. When held up by flooding on the Beaver River, the troops attacked a village of neutral Delawares. The commanding Continental officer, General Edward Hand, found to "his great mortification" that "the men were so impetuous that I could not prevent their killing the man and one of the women. Another woman was taken and with difficulty saved." In another Indian settlement, Hand was again unable to dissuade his men from killing all the Indians they found. The troops attacked

13. RWPF, files S22586, R5815, R8633, S4164; Dann, *The Revolution Remembered*, 157.

"four women with a boy, of these, one woman only was saved." During this "campaign," Samuel Murphy recalled how "a small Indian boy . . . was discovered and killed and several claimed the *honor*." Murphy also recounted how another militiaman scalped an elderly Indian woman.[14]

In battle, as in raids, frontier soldiers used tactics essentially identical to those used by Indians (tactics that they characterized as unfair). Revolutionaries consistently described Indian warriors' behavior as unmanly by emphasizing their supposed tendency to flee from manly face-to-face combat after raids. Indian attacks were variously described as unmanly, dishonorable, cruel, and cowardly. Abraham Eschelman saw Indians as cowards who "generally retreated before us." Similarly, John Swisshelm was disappointed to find that his foes, "after having committed many depredations, fled." In the common frontier military culture, however, Revolutionaries did the same thing: they would ambush Indian war parties and retreat rapidly before they could be attacked by a larger force. Veterans proudly recounted the successes of their own surprise attacks. William Campbell explained how his patrol "discovered a light, three of us went to see what it was and found four Indians encamped. We f[e]ll on them and killed them all without firing a shot, they being asleep." John Hutson recalled how he and his comrades "espied the Indians kindling a fire . . . then retired . . . and stayed there until they . . . would be in their first sleep." Hutson's company planned to "surround the Indians and tomahawk them without giving any alarm."[15]

Indians, conversely, sometimes expressed frustration at the tactics of the Revolutionaries. Joseph Brant, a Mohawk war leader, denounced what he believed to be the cowardice of enemy soldiers who hid in their system of frontier forts posted near settlements. In one case, he explained how a recent battle had resulted in a victory and the taking of prisoners, but Brant lamented, "the reason we could not take more of them, is as owing to the many forts about the place, into which they were always willing to run like ground hogs." Here Brant echoes the attitudes of his foes by likening his enemy to cowardly animals fleeing danger when confronted with a superior force. In addition to a shared military culture of battle, it was clear that both sides had a common vocabulary

14. Daniel K. Richter, "War and Culture: The Iroquois Experience," *WMQ*, 3d ser., 40 (1983): 528–59; Roush quoted in Dann, *The Revolution Remembered*, 260–61. On the Squaw Campaign, see Buck and Buck, *The Planting of Civilization*, 188–89. Edward Hand to Jasper Ewing, March 7, 1778, and "Recollections of Samuel Murphy," both in Reuben Gold Thwaites and Louise Phelps Kellogg, eds., *Frontier Defense on the Upper Ohio, 1777–1778* (Madison, Wis., 1912), 215–16 and 219–20, respectively.

15. RWPF, files S22757, W8300, R1638; Huston quoted in Dann, *The Revolution Remembered*, 266–67.

with which to critique and demean the enemy. Additionally, Indians used the same rationale of revenge for brutal attacks on civilians that the Revolutionaries used to justify their own acts. Another Mohawk war leader, Captain William Johnson, explained Iroquois actions in the Cherry Valley campaign of 1778 by stating, "rebels came to Oughquago when we Indians [warriors] were gone from our place, and you burned our houses, which makes us and our brothers, the Seneca Indians angry, so that we destroyed men, women, and children at Cherry Valley." Clearly a shared culture of vengeance-motivated warfare created a cycle of violence among the region's inhabitants.[16]

Scalping was another shared custom in frontier war. Eastern Indian cultures traditionally valued the taking of the crown of the scalp as evidence of a manly triumph over an enemy and as a tangible manifestation of served vengeance to bring back to the community. In some cases the enemy's scalp represented the restoration of departed spirits of kin or members of the nation. They also could be used effectively in diplomacy. In 1780, Kayashuta, a Seneca, used a scalp bedecked with wampum for just such a purpose, explaining in a council, "Brothers! This is the flesh of a Virginian taken by the Shawnese and Delawares of Sciota, which they have sent to you to replace your chief *Sekanade*, that he may once more be among you." Scalping was also a rite that had long been adopted by European Americans in warfare against Indians. In fact, the Pennsylvania government offered scalp bounties in both the French and Indian War and the Revolutionary War. In addition to the economic impetus, European Americans used the custom in much the same way as Indians: to demonstrate manly triumph over an enemy and to acquire a trophy that proved revenge.[17]

As was the case with other acts of violence, Revolutionary accounts portrayed the practice as a savage atrocity when committed by "the Indians." Rebel narratives always closely focused not just on the killing of women and children but, typically, on their being scalped as well. In October 1777, word reached Fort Pitt that Native warriors "killed one Smith and daughter and tomahawked his son, a boy about six years old and, after scalping him, left him." In the following year in the frontier region of Cumberland County, an officer reported:

16. Joseph Brant to Lieutenant Colonel Bolton, July 29, 1779, British Headquarters Papers, 1747–1783, microfilm, Public Records Office, Great Britain, item 2156 (6); Johnson quoted in Barbara Graymont, *The Iroquois in the American Revolution* (Syracuse, N.Y., 1972), 190.

17. James Axtell, "Scalping: The Ethnohistory of a Moral Question," in *The European and the Indian: Essays in the Ethnohistory of Colonial North America* (New York, 1981), explains the cultural role of scalping in Native and European American communities. Kayashuta is quoted in Graymont, *Iroquois in the American Revolution*, 232.

"Jacob Stanford and his wife were inhumanly killed and scalped." In 1779, the *Pennsylvania Evening Post* reported that "three children were . . . killed and scalped by the Indians." Reports from Westmoreland County stated, "two children at Palmer's Fort . . . killed and scalped." By portraying Indians as the aggressors and initiators of such actions, Pennsylvanians could then see their own practice of scalping as necessary revenge against a "savage" enemy. As a result, Revolutionary soldiers commonly and proudly sought their war trophies. In 1779, Colonel Daniel Brodhead stated that he "sent out one scalping party toward the Mingo towns." Captain Samuel Brady was recommended for promotion following a skirmish in which he "brought in a[n] . . . Indian's scalp." In 1781, a Northampton militia made up of "spirited volunteers" reacted to an attack by tracking down the perpetrators and taking "one Indian scalp." For these soldiers, the taking of scalps was perceived as necessary, just as it was among their Indian enemies.[18]

The treatment of prisoners provided another forum for cultural exchange in regard to military mores. Revolutionaries, not surprisingly, portrayed Indian treatment of prisoners as evidence of barbarism. For the many recent immigrants to the region who had no firsthand experience with Indians, knowledge of captivity narratives informed their understandings of how Indians handled their prisoners. The assumption was that death or torture were likely ends for those who surrendered, with adoption being the least violent outcome. Others who had previous experience with frontier wars knew what to expect. In virtually all cases, however, Revolutionary soldiers consistently complained of Indian treatment of prisoners. Following the 1778 attack on Wyoming, Captain Alexander Patterson reported his horror that the Indians and Tories spared few lives after soldiers surrendered. He claimed that "the enemy had treated such as fell into their hands with the greatest cruelties and that upwards of two hundred had been scalped." Ezekiel Lewis noted that following a skirmish, the "Indians killed a great number of said prisoners." Joseph Pipes of Washington County complained that he "was treated with great severity by the Indians almost all the time he was with them" as a prisoner. James Thompson recalled

18. Colonel John Gibson to Edward Hand, October 22, 1777, in *Frontier Defense,* by Thwaites and Kellogg, 142; Colonel Arthur Buchannan to John Carrothers, May 11, 1778, PRG, reel 13, frame 1335; *Pennsylvania Evening Post,* May 11, 1779; Thomas Galbraith to President Wharton, PCC, reel 83, vol. 1, I. 69, p. 439. On European Americans imagining scalping as a necessary response to perceived savagery and Indian scalping, see Axtell, "Scalping," 209, 229. Daniel Brodhead to General Washington, June 5, 1779, *PA,* 1st ser., 12:127; *Pennsylvania Evening Post,* May 11, 1778; Brodhead to Washington, June 29, 1780, *PA,* 1st ser., 12:243; *Pennsylvania Packet,* June 31, 1781.

his captivity in terms of it being the result of a surprise attack on an innocent civilian (despite the fact that he was in the militia), noting, "the inhabitants principally had fled, and I removed my family to Penn's Creek and was returning to my house for more necessary articles for the family, when I was taken by four Indians who were secreted in a wood near a path along which I was passing." Thompson then explained that "they had not taken me very far until they also took a young woman of the name of Mary Young a prisoner." Here he expressed a popular theme in early American literature—the captivity of an innocent, vulnerable, white woman by Indians, supposedly demonstrating their "savage" ways of war. Thompson recounted the hardships of their journey; at one point, at night, he "got the ropes loose and got up and could have effected my escape but could not bear the idea of leaving the girl with them." Thompson unsuccessfully tried to kill his captors with stones. His portrayal of the experience, however, revealed his sense that the taking of women as war prisoners (at least when done by Indians) violated his understanding of the rules of war.[19]

Revolutionaries rarely considered the Indians' reasons for taking these captives and for treating them as they did. Indeed, the taking of prisoners was a central element of Indian military culture. Killing prisoners was an accepted way of assuaging grief over the death of community members. Furthermore, adopted captives could also fill a deceased person's place in society. Many European Americans found themselves compelled to join an Indian community, but in many cases, they willingly did so and were eventually reluctant to return to their old communities. Payment of ransom for prisoners of war taken by Native warriors was a custom that encouraged many Indians to increase the number of captives they took.[20]

Despite the prevalence of the taking and killing of prisoners among Indians, in many cases, stories of mistreatment were also blatantly exaggerated or falsified by the Revolutionaries. The combined Indian and Tory victory against Connecticut claimants in Wyoming generated numerous untrue charges of atrocities. The battle was popularized in the pro-Whig press as the

19. Deposition of Captain Alexander Patterson, 12th Pennsylvania Regiment, July 6, 1778, PCC, reel 55, I. 53, p. 59; RWPF, files S4631, S11245; Dann, *The Revolution Remembered*, 283–84.

20. See James Axtell, "The White Indians of Colonial America," *WMQ*, 3d ser., 32 (1975): 55–88, on Indian motives and the treatment of European Americans adopted into their communities as well as the often favorable view that the captives developed of Indian culture; see Graymont, *Iroquois in the American Revolution*, 232, on the Native American tradition of killing prisoners of war, especially the wounded and weak who were not candidates for adoption. Ian K. Steele, *Betrayals: Fort William Henry and the "Massacre"* (New York, 1992), describes the centrality of taking prisoners to Indian warfare and the effects of the market for European ransoms.

"Wyoming Massacre" in order to suggest to readers that the attack involved the slaughter of helpless people. This use of language helped justify the most destructive elements of Sullivan's subsequent punitive raid into Iroquoia by the Continental army in 1779. Discussions of "atrocities" at Wyoming circulated among the regulars on Sullivan's expedition. William Rogers, a chaplain with the Pennsylvania troops, noted in his diary, "it is said Queen Esther [Esther Montour], of the Six Nations, who was with the enemy, scalped and tomahawked, with her own hands in cold blood, eight or ten persons. The Indian women in general were guilty of the greatest barbarities." Even though the stories of the women's presence among warriors were false, the account was designed to suggest the unacceptability of Iroquois military culture by constructing it as a world in which gender norms were turned upside down. Furthermore, calling women "guilty of the greatest barbarities" suggested the plausibility of treating enemy Iroquois women with similar severity.[21]

The exaggerated atrocity tales regarding Wyoming also enraged Indians who participated in the attack and believed that they had been markedly generous and restrained in their treatment of the enemy who surrendered. In the major attack on Wyoming, Loyalist Major John Butler reported that "227 scalps [were taken] and only five prisoners: the Indians were so exasperated with their loss last year near Fort Stanwix that it was with the greatest difficulty I could save the lives of those few." Nonetheless, the Indians did not take out their vengeance on these few captives. Blacksnake, a participant in the battle, later told historian Lyman Draper that he could not recall any burnings of prisoners in the action. Additionally, Major John Butler, Sayenqueraghta, and other leaders of subsequent attacks on various forts in the Wyoming region negotiated articles of capitulation that offered quarter for Revolutionaries who surrendered in exchange for pledging to stop fighting in the war. This, of course, was a very European notion of "parole" adopted by some Indian leaders. As Revolutionaries continued to accuse Indians of "atrocities" at Wyoming in order to justify terror raids on hostile and neutral villages in Iroquoia, anger grew. Further frustrating some Iroquois was the presence in these actions of Colonel Nathan Denison, who earlier had been paroled and had promised future neutrality. The result was that many Iroquois were so irritated by Revolutionary

21. On the fabrication of atrocity stories from the Wyoming attack, see Fon W. Boardman, *Against the Iroquois: The Sullivan Campaign of 1779 in New York State* (New York, 1978), 15; on the false atrocity stories and the fact that women were not present in the attack on Wyoming, see Graymont, *Iroquois in the American Revolution*, 174, 181; Journal of Reverend William Rogers, *PA*, 2d ser., 15:260.

characterizations of them and brutal actions against their towns that during the combined Indian-Tory attack on Cherry Valley, New York, in November 1778, they indiscriminately killed and plundered numerous Anglo-American residents of the region. The cycle of violence was completed as both sides abandoned any pretense to restraint in the war and in their treatment of prisoners on Pennsylvania's northern frontier and in the Mohawk Valley.[22]

In actuality, frontier Revolutionary soldiers were far less interested than Indians were in taking prisoners after battle. European American soldiers did not wish to adopt captives into their communities or receive material rewards for their exchange. In fact, the state's scalp bounty encouraged the killing of prisoners. In the few instances when Indians were taken prisoner following battles, it was usually in the hope that they would provide information about enemy military strength. Revolutionaries anxious for vengeance on any hostile Indian would even endeavor to kill prisoners who could give intelligence. Such was the case in June 1780, when Colonel Matthew Smith recommended moving a Native prisoner from a frontier jail in Sunbury to a more secure region in Lancaster County. He explained, "It appeared not to be safe to leave him at Sunbury. The people are so exasperated there w[ere] several attempts made to shoot him while confined." As the war went on, Revolutionaries rarely bothered to take any Indian prisoners at all. By 1782, a group of Iroquois complained that while British troops could expect quarter from the rebels, "we have no mercy to expect, if taken, as they will put us to death immediately, and will not even spare the women and children."[23]

It was torture, however, that drew the loudest cries of Indian barbarity from Revolutionary soldiers. The brutal physical torment of captives was an important communal ritual among eastern Indians. It had deep spiritual significance in addition to being an acceptable form of vengeance against enemies. Warriors who were tortured struggled to keep from calling out in pain in order to demonstrate their spiritual mastery over their bodies, thus refuting their enemies' attempts to portray them as weak. Those who went stoically to their deaths during torture proved their manliness and courage to their tormentors. Stories of the brutal torment of captives that actually occurred, however, were

22. See Graymont, *Iroquois in the American Revolution*, 157–91, on the Wyoming region actions of summer 1778, Revolutionary accusations of cruelty, and Indian anger over such charges (which ultimately fueled their actions at Cherry Valley); Major John Butler to Lieutenant Colonel Mason Bolton, July 8, 1778, in *Documents of the American Revolution*, ed. Davies, 15:165–66.

23. Colonel Matthew Smith to Joseph Reed, June 26, 1780, PCC, reel 83, vol. 2, I. 69, p. 252; the Iroquois complaint of killing prisoners is quoted in White, *Middle Ground*, 391.

also typically disseminated among Revolutionary soldiers without reference to the Indians' motives. The ritual was explained not in terms of vengeance but as a horror story about the innate violence of all Indians. For example, when Lieutenant Thomas Boyd and his reconnaissance party fell into the hands of vengeful Iroquois during John Sullivan's 1779 expedition, most of Boyd's troops were killed; the officer was marked for torture to alleviate the grief of those who had suffered at the hands of the invading rebel army. Boyd's comrades were undoubtedly appalled to hear General Sullivan report that the Indians "whipped him in the most cruel manner, pulled out Mr. Boyd's nails, cut off his nose, plucked out one of his eyes, cut out his tongue, stabbed him with spears in sundry places, and inflicted other torture which decency will not permit me to mention." David Freemoyer, one of Boyd's soldiers who managed to escape, witnessed his comrades the next day "putting together the body of Lieutenant Boyd, which the enemy had severed in five pieces—the head cut off, the body then split in twain, and then each cut into again." No one, however, mentioned that Boyd was tormented to avenge the sufferings of Iroquois who lost family or had their villages burned by Sullivan's troops. In fact, the retelling of Boyd's fate was carefully used to further dehumanize Indians and justify the actions of Sullivan's soldiers.[24]

Another highly publicized incident of torture was that of Colonel William Crawford in 1782. Dr. Knight, a military surgeon on Crawford's expedition against Sandusky, recounted his commander's treatment at the hands of a group of Delawares. Knight explained that the colonel was stripped naked, and seventy shots of powder were fired at his body. Indians then cut off his ears, prodded him with burning sticks, and tossed hot embers at him. Crawford then

> continued in the extremities of pain for an hour and three quarters or two hours longer, as near as I can judge, when at last, being almost totally exhausted, he laid down on his belly; they then scalped him and repeatedly threw the scalp in my face, telling me "that was my great captain." An old squaw . . . got a board, took a parcel of coals and ashes and laid them on his back and head, after he had been scalped, he then raised himself upon his feet and began to walk around the post; they

24. See Calloway, *New Worlds for All*, 97, and White, *Middle Ground*, 387, on the role of torture in Indian warfare and worldviews. On the torture of Boyd, see Graymont, *Iroquois in the American Revolution*, 217. Sullivan is quoted in *Pennsylvania Packet*, October 9, 1779; Freemoyer is quoted in Dann, *The Revolution Remembered*, 296.

next put a burning stick to him as usual, but he seemed more insensible of pain than before.

The *Pennsylvania Packet* reported that, upon hearing of Crawford's fate, the western Pennsylvania "militia are greatly enraged and determined to have ample satisfaction." The frontier soldiers ignored the idea that Crawford had been tortured in retribution for the slaughter of the Moravian Delawares at Gnadenhütten. Indians in the Ohio Valley region were infuriated by the action at Gnadenhütten, viewing the premeditated beating of neutrals to death with coopers' mallets to be a form of torture. Gnadenhütten led to a revival of burnings and torture among these western Indians—modified to punish specifically those who were guilty of the atrocity. In 1782–83, Revolutionaries who were known to have been at the massacre were subject to immolation or worse at the hands of Indian captors. In fact, the Delaware leader, Wyngenund, explained to Crawford before the torture that he might have been spared had his expedition not included Colonel David Williamson, who led the action at Gnadenhutten. Significantly, these Indians indicated that Crawford's fate was the result of the Revolutionaries' brutal behavior. Frontier militias, however, simply ignored the message.[25]

Clearly, the experience of the Revolutionary War was a process in which Native and European Americans learned from and reacted to each other's military actions and cultures. The result was the employment of strikingly similar methods of warfare. Such a "hybrid" European American mix of martial customs was hardly novel, as colonists and Indians had been engaging in intermittent violent cultural exchanges for centuries at that point. Yet the pervasiveness and scale of the process was unprecedented. Over the course of the war, most eastern Indian nations were drawn into the conflict in order to protect their interests. A few sided with the Revolutionaries, some groups split and engaged in civil war, others sought neutrality, and most fought in coalition with the British Empire. Significantly, as the war went on, more and more Indian groups were alienated from the Revolutionaries. While war broke out on the frontiers of most Revolutionary states, it was perhaps most brutal (and with the highest stakes) on the greater Pennsylvania frontier, a region that would

25. "Narrative of Dr. Knight," *PA*, 2d ser., 14:714–15; *Pennsylvania Packet*, July 27, 1782; on the motives of Indians in Crawford's torture, C. Sipe Hale, *Fort Ligonier and Its Times* (n.p., 1971), 560, and Dowd, *Spirited Resistance*, 87–88; Governor Frederick Haldimand to Brigadier General Sir John Johnson, February 6, 1783, in *Documents of the American Revolution*, ed. Davies, 21:152.

prove a conduit for Anglo-American expansion into the trans-Allegheny west. For many Pennsylvania farmers who happened to be relatively new to the area, their most meaningful and sustained cultural exposure to Indians came in warfare. The other factor that made the Revolutionary frontier war unique in the history of Indian-colonist warfare was that it coincided with the creation of the independent American republic. The nature of armed conflict thus shaped concepts of U.S. citizenship and identity.[26]

The Consolidation of Wartime "White" Identity

The appropriation of "Indian-ness" for the purposes of defining American identity vis-à-vis Europe also had a long history in colonial North America. The Revolutionaries who arrived for service with tomahawks, scalping knives, and Indian apparel were asserting their difference from European regulars. The concept of the Indianized Indian-fighter, however, was a construction of self that was fraught with cultural peril. Given that the Anglo-American tradition of denigrating Indians as "savages" had a central strain that emphasized the supposed barbarity of native methods of warfare, European Americans who adopted such customs risked the accusation that they themselves had descended into savagery. In part, they responded by simply justifying their actions as retribution in kind for imagined unprovoked acts of brutal violence. In the end, though, this strategy proved insufficient. Indians and even other Revolutionaries were fully aware that this was not exactly the case. Continental officers and diplomats in the region noted the aggressive European American intrusions onto Indian lands as provocative. They also consistently condemned frontiersmen's attacks on neutral and allied Indians as unjustifiable and dangerous. Given their desire to coordinate a larger strategy focused primarily upon gaining independence from Britain, they saw such acts as selfish at best and evidence of cultural savagery at worst. The intellectual solution to these issues for the rank-and-file soldiers was a full-blown development of incipient ideas about racial identities. In particular, they carefully constructed concepts of "whiteness" that created community, defined others, and justified

---

26. John E. Ferling, *A Wilderness of Miseries: War and Warriors in Early America* (Westport, Conn., 1980), shows the long history of hybrid warfare in early America. Dowd, *Spirited Resistance*, 65–89, demonstrates that the massive extent of Indian involvement in the war was meant to protect their interests and independence.

apparently irrational acts against non-belligerent Indians. It is only in this context that the brutality of the war prosecuted by frontier Revolutionaries becomes fully comprehensible.[27]

Critically, when soldiers spoke of perceived physiological identity, they referenced themselves. The rank and file purposefully omitted mentions of Indian skin color and consistently called their own "white." While this process created community, it also implicitly "Othered" Indians via biology. Soldiers' mentions of "whiteness" in their retrospective accounts of the war were pronounced. John Dougherty, for instance, recalled how "the Indians were killing the white people wherever they could find them," thus suggesting the imagery of a simplistic race war. John Foster stated that Indians "massacred the whites." Adam Wolfe was a guard "between the Indians and whites during the holding of a treaty at Pittsburgh." Andrew Myers explained that "the Indians . . . [were] determined not to yield to the white people." John Struthers referred both to prisoners taken by Indians and his militia party that sought to recover them as "the whites." James Huston remarked upon the presence of "a white man" among an Indian war party. David Freemoyer, a militiaman from nearby New York who served on Sullivan's expedition, decried Indians' "predatory incursions upon the whites."[28]

Although these men retrospectively recalled "white" identity, there is ample evidence that their memories derived from popular perceptions of "whiteness" on the Revolutionary frontier. Reports published in Pennsylvania newspapers frequently referred to "whites" and "Indians." Like the soldiers' narratives, the accounts did not connect Indians with a specific color. In 1776, the *Pennsylvania Gazette* reported, "The Indians have scalped two or three white people on the Ohio." The same paper also discussed the capture of a young woman by "three Indians and twenty seven white savages." In 1779, the *Gazette* published an account of a sortie by "Captain Brady of the 8th Pennsylvania regiment, with 20 white men." Daniel Brodhead's expedition into Indian country

27. See, for example, Philip J. Deloria, *Playing Indian* (New Haven, Conn., 1998), 10–37, on the role of the appropriation of "Indian-ness" for elements of American identity in the colonial and Revolutionary periods. General William Irvine noted that among the frontier residents involved in the war, "a great majority have no other views than to acquire lands" (William Irvine to George Washington, April 20, 1782, in *Washington-Irvine Correspondence*, ed. Butterfield, 109). Timothy Pickering raised the specter of frontier cultural degeneracy, noting that Anglo-American frontier residents were "little less savage than their tawny neighbors and by similar barbarities have in fact provoked them to revenge" (Timothy Pickering to General Washington, May 19, 1778, PRG, reel 14, frame 54).

28. RWPF, files S12779, S23637, S4731, W5155; Struthers, Huston, and Freemoyer are quoted in Dann, *The Revolution Remembered*, 256–57, 265–66, and 304, respectively.

had a vanguard described as "consisting of 15 white men (including the spies) and 8 Delaware Indians."[29]

Other contemporary accounts suggested the growing centrality of a shared white identity. Joseph Martin suggested a white-Indian polarity in a letter warning Revolutionaries that "I found out a plan . . . is forming between the Northern and southward Indians. . . . They were seen by a white man." Additionally, the presence of "whites" was consistently remarked upon when they were found among Indians who fought against Revolutionaries. Lieutenant Erkuries Beatty, a Pennsylvanian on General John Sullivan's 1779 expedition into Iroquoia, noted in the journal he kept while campaigning that "we received word from Captain Graham that he had caught one squaw and killed one and had taken two or three children and one white man." In a petition to Congress, Connecticut residents in the Wyoming Valley critiqued "the Indians with a number of white people, enemies to these states committed repeated depredations." Like those offered by the pension applicants, none of the above accounts identifies Indians by a specific color, but they do state that anyone of European descent was "white" in an essentialist way. This was a crucial moment for a people who had previously nonsystematically discussed skin complexions as only partly related to ethnic origins. The Revolution yielded a new, popular worldview in which identities were simply polarized: whites and nonwhites.[30]

Definitions of "whiteness," of course, were both arbitrary and sometimes confusing. The equation of cultural origins with a pale skin complexion compared to Indians often proved difficult to demonstrate outside of a European American social context. Lieutenant Beatty told of a striking incident that he observed while in a Seneca town: "A young child, I believe about three years old [was] found running about the houses, which one of our officers picked up and found it to be a white child but it was so much tanned and smoked that we could hardly distinguish it from a[n] Indian child and was exceedingly poor, scarcely able to walk. It could talk no English; nothing but Indian, and I believe but little of that." Interestingly, Beatty and his comrades were startled to find a "white" child so "tanned" and out of his cultural context. Their account suggests that "whiteness" could be physically obscured, and

29. *Pennsylvania Gazette,* March 13, 1776; May 19, 1779; July 14, 1779; and October 20, 1779.
30. Joseph Martin to Col. B. Logan, 20 February 1783, 46 J 74, DMC; Lieutenant Erkuries Beatty, Journal of an Expedition to Onondaga, *PA,* 2d ser., 15:223; "Petition of the Inhabitants of Westmoreland to the Continental Congress," March 12, 1778, *Susquehannah Company Papers,* ed. Taylor, 8:38; "Governor [Henry] Hamilton's Journal of His Vincennes Expedition From Detroit, 1778," 45 J 17, DMC.

without cultural cues, identity was slippery. The soldiers, however, arrived at the conclusion that the child was "white." They do not mention precisely what characteristics led them to make this decision, but as there were no cultural clues (such as language), they must have based it on physical characteristics. Another incident further suggested that being white trumped ethnic heritage. George Roush enlisted as an "Indian spy" and was ordered "to tan his thighs and legs with wild cherry and white oak bark." Roush and his comrades adopted a "nonwhite" appearance as well as the cultural trappings of an Indian warrior (he painted his face with Indian markings signifying war and wore "a breechcloth, leather leggings, moccasins"). Significantly, the "Indian spies" did not believe the disguise could fully work without "tanning" their skin and obscuring their whiteness.[31]

European Americans did not create these constructions of race in a vacuum. Rather, they affected and were affected by Indian views. Historian Nancy Shoemaker found convincing evidence that in the early eighteenth century, southern nations, such as the Creek, Cherokee, and Chickasaw, employed the term "white" to denote European Americans while conceiving themselves to be "red." She argues that these Indians constructed their color-based identity in conjunction with southern colonists who defined Africans and African Americans as "black" and themselves, in opposition, as "white." The color "red" had various cultural connotations among southern nations (especially the Cherokee) that it did not among northern groups. There was, therefore, no concrete connection between symbolic redness and skin color. Shoemaker also finds that few northeastern Indians described themselves as "red" during the same period. There is nonetheless evidence that these groups were also creating racialized worldviews in the eighteenth century. Gregory Evans Dowd has elucidated a pattern of Indian spiritual revivals during the 1745–75 period that led to the development of a militant nativist movement. Nativist leaders, even in the Northeast, began to discuss their self-conception in essentially race-based terms. As Dowd points out, they "taught that all Indians were a single people, separately created," suggesting that differences between Natives and European Americans were more than purely cultural. While many Indians in the region saw ethnic and cultural differences as signifiers, they still commonly employed the term "white." Shikellamy, an Oneida, asserted in 1745 that "we are Indians . . . and don't wish to be transformed into white men." Shikellamy's statement suggests cultural adaptation could alter identity. Such

31. Beatty, Journal, 242; Roush quoted in Dann, *The Revolution Remembered*, 259.

Native characterizations of European Americans as "whites" informed the Revolutionaries' own self-conceptions.[32]

Popular understandings of white identity were also influenced by its use as a de facto basis for liability to militia service and oaths of allegiance in the Revolutionary state. Nascent notions of racial identity had, of course, been growing in importance during earlier colonial wars. At midcentury, however, they remained one possible strain of thought in terms of what it meant to be a British colonist. The exigencies of the War for Independence itself, which began to create a Revolutionary equivalence of whiteness with the cause of the new nation, had important implications. One major reason for the construct's prevalence on the frontier was that it formed a basis for imagining some level of common interest among diverse and often competing communities. The Pennsylvania frontier was particularly ethnically heterogeneous just in terms of its European American population. People in the region were previously related not by common cultures, languages, or religion, but simply by a shared identity as British subjects. In addition to the coincidence of various localisms, the perception of whiteness, contrasted with "the Indians," was one of the few shared characteristics of Revolutionaries in the area. When war began in 1775—and when independence from the British Empire became a reality in 1776—these residents could no longer fall back on their common identities as British subjects. They could call themselves "Americans," but it was not immediately apparent what constituted a true American. "Whiteness," then, became an intellectual construct that encapsulated the European heritage as a physical characteristic. Inhabitants of the frontier, divorced from their specific areas of origin in Europe, imagined themselves as a common group of people in the "new world," defined as whites by Revolutionary laws.

Racialist discourse among frontier Revolutionaries served another function: it justified the double standard applied to frontier military actions. Soldiers were able to assimilate elements of Indian warfare without fear of seeing themselves as "savage," because race, rather than culture, became the definitive boundary between European Americans and Indians. Thus they did not believe that they were hypocritical when they denounced Indian violence and praised their own. Among "whites," military culture was not the issue. Perceived racial characteristics now defined de facto "civilization" among whites as well as "savagery," which was seen as innate to Indians. Revolutionaries who

---

32. Nancy Shoemaker, "How the Indians Got to Be Red," 625–44; Dowd, *Spirited Resistance*, 47–89, quotation on xiii; Shikellamy quoted in Merrell, *Into the American Woods*, 104.

fought as Indians did need not defend their actions. They only had to assert who they were, as they believed "whites" to be biologically superior to their opponents. This "Indianized" white Indian-hater identity among Revolutionary soldiers also embodied one of the contradictory elements of an emerging American national identity: a simultaneous loathing of and desire for the Indian Other. By employing the term "white," the longing for cultural similarity was fulfilled, because arbitrarily constructed biological difference created racial hierarchy. Ironically, the massive Revolutionary collisions of military cultures in the greater Pennsylvania frontier region created a situation in which, as Native and European Americans became increasingly similar in their ways of war, racism emerged as a clear ideology.[33]

The converse side of this articulation of "whiteness" was, of course, that Indians were viewed as "nonwhite" Others. As rank-and-file frontier Revolutionaries did not specify Indian skin color, the process appears to have been primarily one of self-identification; Natives were racial outsiders because of their perceived lack of "whiteness." Continually (and ominously), soldiers referred to their enemies not by the names of their nations or ethnic groups, e.g., Mohawk or Shawnee, but rather simply as an undifferentiated group—"the Indians." Benjamin Lewis, Jacob Rudolf, George Wertz, John Megaw, Thomas Black, Andrew Dougherty, William Elliott, John Vandyke, George Swagers, William Moore, Lorentz Holben, John Dean, John Gray, and Stephen Oliver were just a few of the myriad veterans who referred to their wartime opponents in their pension applications simply as "the Indians." Petitions from the region authored during the war exhibit the same attitude toward hostile Indian nations as simply being "the Indians" in general. The men of the Fourth Battalion of Northampton militia explained that they were fighting "against a cruel enemy, the Indians." The Westmoreland militia in the Connecticut settlements of the Wyoming region also described "incursions from the Indians."[34]

The net result of this wartime consolidation of white identity, its equation with the Revolutionary cause, and the view of various Indian nations as a

33. On the "Indianized" Indian hater, see Richard Slotkin, *Regeneration Through Violence: The Mythology of the American Frontier, 1600–1860* (Middletown, Conn., 1973), and White, *Middle Ground*, 368–75. On the role of race and simultaneous, contradictory desire for and repulsion toward the Other in the construction of national subjectivity, see Smith-Rosenberg, "Dis-Covering the Subject," 843–48.

34. RWPF, files S4164, S13746, R11329, R7099, S22651, W2078, S16378, W2457, W25718, S22309, S12751, S23669, W9610; Petition of the Fourth Battalion of Northampton Militia, PRG, reel 14, frame 990; Petition of the Westmoreland Militia, January 23, 1781, in *Susquehannah Company Papers*, ed. Taylor, 7:80.

singular nonwhite group was the racist brutalization of warfare. While indiscriminate killing of Indians regardless of their wartime sympathies characterized colonial frontier conflicts, its scale in the Revolution and the linking of these actions to American identity were, once again, unprecedented. Throughout the war, often to the chagrin of Revolutionary authorities, frontier rank-and-file soldiers killed allied and neutral Indians. As soon as conflict broke out, diplomats and officers had their hands full trying to prevent the widening of the war via the slaughter of Indians. In March 1777, George Morgan, an official at Fort Pitt, worried that local inhabitants would "massacre our known friends at their hunting camps." The same year, Colonel Edward Hand, the Continental army commander at Fort Pitt, remarked that "the people here are well-disposed, savage-like, to murder a defenseless unsuspecting Indian." Colonel John Gibson informed Hand that one of the Revolutionaries' Delaware allies, White Eyes, was "in danger of being killed" because of recent hostile Indian attacks and that "it was with the utmost difficulty [that] I prevented one of the men who escaped [from a recent battle] from killing the Delawares." After another hostile Indian attack killed a single militiaman, Gibson again suggested to Hand that it was "not safe for the [friendly] Delaware to pass unless you send a party down to escort them to Fort Pitt to treat." Hand passed the information on to local Indians and declared, "Brothers the Delaware—I lately told you it would be dangerous for any Indians to come near this place [Fort Pitt] owing to the foolish conduct of the Mingos and Wyandots." In September 1777, the situation deteriorated further when Virginia soldiers murdered the Shawnee leader Cornstalk, a proponent of neutrality, while he was being held as a hostage in a fort. Militiamen killed Cornstalk in response to a hostile Indian attack and thereby alienated the few Shawnees who did not advocate war with the United States. Captain John Stuart, who witnessed the act and explained how the militia generalized their hostility and need for vengeance, described how the men retrieved the body of a comrade. He noted that "the corpse of Gilmore was scalped and covered in blood. . . . The cry was raised let us kill the Indians in the fort and every man with his gun in his hand came up the [river] bank pale as death with rage."[35]

35. Morgan quoted in Dowd, *Spirited Resistance*, 75; Edward Hand to Jasper Yeates, October 2, 1777, in *Frontier Defense*, by Thwaites and Kellogg, 119; Colonel John Gibson to General Edward Hand, August 1, 1777, ibid., 35; John Gibson to Edward Hand, August 1, 1777, Edward Hand Correspondence, 1777–1785, Darlington Memorial Library, University of Pittsburgh; Edward Hand to the Delaware, September 17, 1777, in *Frontier Defense*, by Thwaites and Kellogg, 86; Portion of the "Narrative of Captain John Stuart," ibid., 159.

Violence continued to worsen against non-belligerent Indian groups as the war continued. In 1778, the Coshocton Delaware leader, White Eyes, died under unclear circumstances and was most likely killed by militia while carrying messages for the Revolutionaries. In the following year, troops continued to single the Delawares out as subjects for revenge for deeds committed by other Indian groups. Among the men of the Eighth Pennsylvania Regiment (raised primarily in the state's frontier counties), a soldier disrupted discipline and diplomacy in western Pennsylvania by having "fired a gun at one of the friendly Delawares." Also in 1779, the President of Pennsylvania's Supreme Executive Council, Joseph Reed, refused Colonel Daniel Brodhead's request for supplies for his Delaware allies in an expedition against hostile Iroquois. Reed noted, "so violent are the prejudices against the Indians . . . [among] the people in the back counties" that Brodhead could expect no support for Indian allies. In 1780, a group of pro–United States Delawares directly under Brodhead's protection at Fort Pitt was almost put to death by Westmoreland County residents furious over attacks by other Indians. Brodhead noted that "upwards of forty men from the neighborhood of Hannah's Town have attempted to destroy them [the Delawares]. . . . I suppose the women and children were to suffer an equal carnage with the men." Such actions among rank-and-file Revolutionaries continued to erode Native neutrality. Increasingly, Indian communities began to split as militants left to fight against the Revolutionaries. In April 1781, Brodhead decided to attack Coshocton, one of the last remaining significant neutral Delaware communities, as a preemptive strike after a faction less friendly to the United States appeared to be ascendant. The village was essentially razed by Continentals, militia, and a few Coshocton Delawares who served as guides, including the pro-Revolutionary leader Killbuck. Some of the Delawares attacked in Coshocton earlier served under Brodhead during his expedition against the Seneca in support of Sullivan in 1779. The victors executed fifteen prisoners, and the survivors of the raid retreated to Sandusky, where they joined Wyandots and Delawares already in arms against the Revolutionaries.[36]

Such behavior, coupled with incipient Indian notions of racial difference, led at least a few Indians to view all European Americans as the same and potentially dangerous as a group. In a well-publicized 1778 incident in Bedford

36. On the murder of White Eyes, see Dowd, *Spirited Resistance*, 77–78. Orders: July 29, 1779, Orderly Book of the Eighth Pennsylvania Regiment, 2 NN 108, DMC; Joseph Reed's description of the prejudice of frontier residents toward Indians is quoted in Downes, *Council Fires*, 250; Daniel Brodhead to Joseph Reed, November 2, 1780, PRG, reel 16, frame 1273. On the attack on Coshocton, see Dowd, *Spirited Resistance*, 81–83.

County, a group of loyalists set out to join the attacks on the Revolutionaries but, according to one account, "the Indians suspecting some design in the white people," killed one leader and forced the other Tories to flee. The employment of racialist discourse in the letter is intriguing. It is not clear whether the author of the report—John Piper, a Bedford County Revolutionary militia official—was summarizing the witnesses' testimony of Indian behavior or his own impression. The use of the terms "the Indians" and "the white people" reflected prevalent Anglo-American racism. The account also underscores popular perceptions of race war (and it probably further solidified white identity). There is, however, some evidence to suggest that the behavior of the unidentified Indians in this affair illustrated a growing group consciousness that Piper attributes to them. Richard Weston, one of the loyalists, testified that the party was "met by Indians and that one of them shot his brother and another of them scalped him. That after his brother was shot, McKee[?] pulled a letter out of his pocket that he had got from an English officer in Carlisle gaol and with the letter displayed a handkerchief crying peace, peace, brother, but that the savages ran off without giving attention." Although the Indians might well have expected a party of "long knives" to be potentially hostile, it is striking that they fled after the attack even when the party of European Americans did not fight back or attempt to avenge the death of Weston's brother. Furthermore, the cries of peace and the exhibition of the English officer's letter were clear attempts to associate them with British authorities that the war party simply ignored. It seems plausible that the experience of indiscriminate Revolutionary violence against Indians affected their notions that there could be various motives and factions among European Americans in the region. The development of wartime white identity, then, appears to have fostered both pan-Indian unity and self-identity. This process, in turn, when reported, served to consolidate white racism and confirm stereotypes that all Indians were the same and innately hostile to whites. This incident ultimately proved exceptional, as Indians fought in coalition with large numbers of Tories as well as the British. Nonetheless, rebel authorities made sure that it was well known to those social outsiders who still wondered if their communal interests might be best served by fighting with hostile Indians against the Revolutionaries.[37]

Indians fighting the Revolutionaries could ill afford to develop the same sort of full-blown racialist consciousness as that held by the rebels. Many

37. Lieutenant John Piper to President Wharton, May 4, 1778, PRG, reel 12, frame 1286; Examination of Richard Weston, May 22, 1778, PRG, reel 14, frame 93–94.

nations that took up arms against the United States had formidable factions of accommodationists who sought not only to ally themselves with European imperial power but also to embrace the cultural and economic exchange that had already transpired. In the Revolution, it was also apparent to even the most militant of Indian nativists that the war effort would require assistance from the British. Thus, it was never very practical to dismiss all "whites" as exactly the same. It appears that at least some Indians specified only Anglo-American frontier residents as all the same: dangerous, aggressive, and brutally violent "long knives." As a result, the military violence prosecuted by groups such as the Iroquois, Delawares, Wyandots, Miamis, Mingos, and others was not nearly as indiscriminate as that of their adversaries. They could not afford to kill their Tory and British allies on a wholesale level to rid the region of all whites; few envisioned an Indian-only postwar order. The "long knives" themselves, however, did generalize all Indians as a single inferior, hostile (or potentially hostile) group. The behavior and discourse generated by ordinary frontier Revolutionaries suggests that many did indeed anticipate a world purged of "the Indians." In 1783, when the Treaty of Paris formally ended hostilities between the Americans and the British, General William Irvine lamented that some Indians were still fighting and that their continued resistance "will give force to a temper already pretty prevalent among the back settlers, never to make peace with the Indians . . . till the whole of the western tribes are driven over the Mississippi and lakes, entirely beyond American lines."[38]

This "temper" explains the Pennsylvania soldiers' behavior at Gnadenhütten in 1782. The massacre marked the apotheosis of "white" racialist identity and the brutalization of frontier war. Indians in the region, the British, and loyalists all vehemently decried the incident as cold-blooded, unjustified, and mindless murder. Significantly, a number of Revolutionary authorities criticized the action as a "massacre" as well. General Irvine, the Continental commander at Fort Pitt at the time, denounced the actions of the militia, informing George Washington that "they found about ninety men, women, and children all of whom they put to death, it is said, after cool deliberation and considering the matter for three days." Continental Congress delegate David Howell also openly criticized "the Massacring of the Moravian Indians." Some western Pennsylvanians attempted to defend the action by arguing that it was necessitated by the

38. See Dowd, *Spirited Resistance*, 47–89, on the alliance between pro-British accommodationists and nativists during the Revolution; William Irvine to George Washington, April 16, 1783, in *Washington-Irvine Correspondence*, ed. Butterfield, 149.

belief that the Moravians were harboring hostile war parties in their communities. The militia had also heard that one of the Moravian women was wearing the dress of a white captive. Finally, the militia themselves argued that the presence of metal utensils, china, and pots was clear evidence that these Delawares were dealing in war spoils from hostile raids.[39]

The situation was considerably more complex, however. Most of these arguments were made by frontier residents in response to their critics from outside the region. The Washington County militia party led by Colonel Williamson was more fully aware of the unique position of the Moravian Delawares than they openly admitted. They understood that these neutral, Christianized people literally lived on the spatial and cultural boundary between communities of Revolutionaries and Indians actively resisting them. Missionaries among the Delawares such as David Zeisberger forwarded intelligence to Americans at Fort Pitt. The Moravians had to respect the power and wishes of their Indian neighbors to the north, though, who did in fact send war parties through their villages. In the end, most militiamen knew that these Moravian Indians were not a serious military threat and that killing them would only further alienate neutrals. The logic employed by the militia at the Gnadenhütten Massacre was undergirded by the *weltanschauung* of white frontier racial identity. They asserted that they were seeking "just revenge" against Indians who raided "white" communities by killing "Indians" in general. The choice of the Moravian Delawares as the target of vengeance was a significant one. Like the Conestoga Indians killed by the Paxton Boys in 1764, the Moravians were, in some ways, more European in their culture than the frontiersmen who attacked them. They were Christian, they employed a European-style gendered division of labor in their agricultural fieldwork, they used European goods, and they were pacifists. The militiamen, meanwhile, adopted many aspects of Indian military culture. Again, like the Paxton Boys, the militia at Gnadenhütten were probably subconsciously troubled in regard to their own identity by this cultural inversion. They assuaged their concerns by embracing the apparent cultural paradox to vindicate racial identity. Thus, Indianized Europeans violently illustrated supposedly immutable, noncultural differences between whites and nonwhites by attacking Europeanized Indians. The missionary John Heckewelder noted how the men,

39. William Irvine to George Washington, April 20, 1782, in *Washington-Irvine Correspondence*, ed. Butterfield, 99; David Howell to Moses Brown, November 6, 1782, *Letters of Delegates*, ed. Smith, 18:448. On the rationalizations for killing the Moravian Delawares, see Buck and Buck, *The Planting of Civilization*, 197, and White, *Middle Ground*, 390.

women, and children (who did not resist) went to their deaths singing Christian hymns. He also described how the militiamen torturously beat them with mallets and then took "off their scalps." One Delaware survivor witnessed in horror as "the blood began to run a stream." Heckewelder recorded that several militiamen wanted to burn the Indians alive, a customary torture among Indians. As Heckewelder described the incident, based on witnesses' testimony, Gnadenhütten resembled the staple Anglo-American narratives of Indian barbarity against whites in warfare—with the roles simply inverted. The Revolutionaries appear to be the savages; the Delawares, the stoic Christian victims.[40]

What Heckewelder portrays as tragic irony, the militia saw as an intentional assertion of region-specific American white identity. The soldiers graphically enacted their conviction that race had superseded culture as the primary signifier of difference on the frontier. They did not feel the need to defend their actions, as they viewed themselves as "white" and therefore superior to any Indian. They proudly utilized Indian traditions such as torture and scalping of the enemy as evidence of their mastery of frontier warfare and their victory over foes. It did not matter to the soldiers that their victims were pacifist Christians. They were inferior beings and generally culpable for enemy attacks, as were all Indians. Race was innate, unaffected by cultural exchange. In fact, in one interesting moment of exchange, the Moravian Delawares pleaded their friendliness toward the Revolutionaries and the militia responded by pointing out that pots, kettles, tools, and other implements that they had were "things as were made use of by White People and not by Indians." While ostensibly this appears to be a rationale for attributing the Delawares' possession of these goods to theft and involvement in raids, the soldiers knew that these people did indeed use such items and had done so for a long time, even before the war. The militiaman's statement suggests that Indian use of these goods was not appropriate. Only "white people" could properly use them. In other words, identity was not formed so much in the use of the implements themselves but in *who* was using them. Indians could utilize a plow and still be Indians. It would not mitigate their fate at the hands of white enemies. White people could wield a tomahawk and still be white people. It did not diminish what the militia saw to be the fundamental marker

---

40. On Moravian Delaware cultural similarity, see Slaughter, *Whiskey Rebellion*, 75–77. My interpretation of Gnadenhütten builds upon Thomas Slaughter's analysis of the Paxton Boys' 1764 massacre of the Conestoga in "Crowds in Eighteenth-Century America: Reflections and New Directions," *PMHB* 115 (1991):18–21. On Heckewelder and the survivors' accounts, see Paul A. W. Wallace, ed., *Thirty Thousand Miles with John Heckewelder* (Pittsburgh, 1958), 189–99 (quotation on 195).

of superiority: whiteness, not culture. The Revolutionary militia was intentionally declaring and prosecuting race war.[41]

According to historian Gregory Evans Dowd, it was also clear that the attack on Gnadenhutten was "no spontaneous outbreak of frontier frenzy" regarding recent hostile Indian attacks. In 1781, the local militia had planned an assault on the Moravian towns that was opposed by Continental authorities such as Colonel John Gibson, who asserted that the residents were helpful to the U.S. cause. Additionally, as Irvine pointed out in his letter to Washington, the militiamen discussed at length what to do with the Moravians. They then purposefully deceived the Delawares by stating that they only meant to move them closer to Fort Pitt to protect them from hostile Indians. Some militiamen went to another Moravian village, Salem, and brought the inhabitants back to Gnadenhütten. Heckewelder noted that "the militia having in those parts no further opportunity of killing innocent people and no stomach to engage with warriors, set off [for] home . . . and afterwards falling upon the peaceable Indians on the north side of the Allegheny River opposite Pittsburgh, killed several of those." These "peaceable Indians" were in fact Killbuck and his party of Coshocton Delawares who had remained allied to the United States, even participating in the 1781 raid on Coshocton itself. These methodical slaughters were meant to send a message. The militia explicitly demonstrated that they would use the common military culture of the frontier in all its brutality against all Indians. Indeed, they were embarking on a war designed to remove Indians from the region. The militia party's essentially genocidal behavior marked the full expression of frontier "American" identity. As whites, they were essentially making war on all of their enemies—the Indians.[42]

This worldview, while prevalent, was not universal. A few frontier soldiers recognized that not all Indians were the timeless enemies of "whites." Henry Woods, for example, recalled that during the Revolution "the Indians were then hostile" and that they "took part with the British," suggesting at least that Indians were not innately hostile. Another soldier, Theodorus Scowden, recalled that a group of his neighbors was killed "by the Indians who were then at war with us and were allies of the British." Implicit in his statement is

41. Wallace, *Thirty Thousand Miles*, 193.
42. Quote by Dowd in *Spirited Resistance*, 86; on the same page, see Dowd's discussion of the 1781 planned militia attack on the Moravian towns and Gibson's response. Regarding the militia's premeditation and deception of the Moravian Delawares, see Slaughter, *Whiskey Rebellion*, 76, and White, *Middle Ground*, 190–91. Wallace, *Thirty Thousand Miles*, 197; on the attack on Killbuck's party, see Dowd, *Spirited Resistance*, 86.

the possibility that he may be referring to certain groups, not all "Indians." Still, Scowden did not explicitly bother to differentiate nations. Perhaps one of the most exceptional cases was that of John Struthers, a Washington County militiaman. While he too employed descriptions of "the whites" and "the Indians" who "committed several murders," he also suggested that not all Indians should be treated as enemies. When Colonel Williamson attempted to raise an expedition against the Moravian towns in 1781, Struthers refused "taking a part." In the attacks on Gnadenhütten and Salem the following year, he condemned the killing of "nearly a hundred of all ages and sexes" and noted, "in this, also, I refused to be concerned." Nonetheless, Struthers did note that his refusal to attack neutral Delawares was done "at the risk of my popularity as a soldier." Obviously, his exceptional actions were enough to cast aspersions onto his own membership in the imagined community of Revolutionaries.[43]

The frontier American identity that underpinned a man's "popularity as a soldier" was a region-specific imagining of the new nation. For these frontiersmen, the Revolutionary cause was embodied by the "whites" who fought "the Indians" using Indian methods of warfare. Soldiers consistently referred to their skills as "woodsmen," "rangers," and "Indian spies." They asserted their frontier martial prowess as evidence of cultural superiority to Europeans and Eastern U.S. residents and remained assured of their "biological" superiority over Indians due to their perceived "whiteness." As prototypical white Indianized Indianfighters, they saw themselves as the most American of the Americans. Henry Dickerson, a private from Washington County in the Eighth Pennsylvania Regiment, cultivated a reputation as "a good marksman and woodsman." Martin Orner of Northampton County "became an experienced woodsman." John Elder was in a "company of Indian scouts." Fauntley Muse of Westmoreland County explained that because of his "familiarity with Indians' warfare and habits [he] was employed as spy."[44]

Implicit in this identity was a favorable comparison of "white" frontier military culture to that of Europe and that practiced by Revolutionary soldiers from the East. Frontier troops believed that they had developed wartime skills that easterners presumably lacked. Soldiers from the East occasionally arrived to help on the frontier, and local troops could then clearly see the regional differences in military culture. They must have viewed the eastern Pennsylvania soldiers' ineptitude at frontier fighting with satisfaction. When Colonel Thomas

43. RWPF, files S23893, S22604; Dann, *The Revolution Remembered*, 254–57.
44. RG-2, reel 34, frame 155; RWPF, files S23829, W24117, W8480.

Hartley's troops (raised predominantly in the eastern rural areas of Pennsylvania) were tested in battle against Indians, their inexperience in frontier war was painfully evident. Hartley compared his men's military acumen with that of the local militia accompanying them. He explained, "Captain Murrow, from his knowledge of Indian affairs and their mode of fighting was serviceable. His men were marksmen and were useful." Hartley juxtaposed this analysis with an evaluation of his regulars: "The men of my regiment were armed with muskets and bayonets. They were no great marksmen and were awkward at wood fighting." While Hartley's Continentals fought well enough in the East against the main British army, men who fancied themselves seasoned Indian-fighters saw these regulars' martial methods as more European than American.[45]

Indeed, eastern Pennsylvanians who served in brief frontier tours never assimilated frontier military culture to the extent of their western counterparts. They typically viewed frontier tactics as "uncivilized" violations of European martial conventions. Although eastern troops in the region were charged with total war aims (attacking Indian societies as well as their military forces), they were usually deployed in large regular European-style formations. Many of these soldiers had their previous military experience in large battles against the British, and they centered their condemnation of Indian inferiority on the warriors' failure to meet in open battle. Colonel Hartley, for instance, expressed his growing frustration with his and his eastern regulars' assignment in north-central Pennsylvania by noting, "we shall gain little honor on these frontiers as the Indians will not come to action with us fairly." And because the easterners' communities were not being raided, they did not describe the war in terms of vengeance for specific attacks. Rather, they tended to describe Indian warfare as strange and unfathomable. As one participant in Sullivan's expedition stated, it was a "dark and bloody method of prosecuting war." Thus, eastern soldiers tended to construct a military image of Indian enemies as unknowable "savages." In this context, frontier skirmishes were often portrayed as nightmarish for eastern soldiers inexperienced with the locale and local military tactics. George Stewart, of rural York County, found that an inferior knowledge of such combat almost cost him his life. After being defeated decisively in battle by a group of Indians, Stewart's unit attempted to retreat. To Stewart's chagrin, "the Indians got in advance of us." York County men not familiar with the frontier or fighting in it were mystified by enemy ambushes. Seasoned regular soldiers who had

45. On the regional composition of Hartley's Regiment, see Trussell, *Pennsylvania Line,* 139–43; Thomas Hartley to the Continental Congress, October 8, 1778, PCC, reel 96, vol. 11, I. 78, p. 346.

learned how to stand up to the British army were also frightened of the prospect of battle with an elusive Indian enemy. Colonel Hartley explained that after the Indian and Tory attack on Wyoming, "I never saw so great a panic with a part of my own regiment."[46]

There was some degree of adaptation to frontier military rituals, however. The mutilation of foes was common among troops from the East. Such behavior would have been considered unacceptable against enemy European regulars. Eastern soldiers also learned to scalp. On Sullivan's expedition, following a battle in which the Continentals routed their Indian and Tory opponents with cannon fire, an observer "saw eight of their warriors' scalps taken on the spot." Significantly, the Tories were not scalped. Other easterners took war prizes in this 1779 campaign that demonstrated their unfamiliarity with frontier military culture. They took trophies that were not scalps and probably would not have been seen as respectable tokens of victory by either Indians or frontier soldiers. Lieutenant Beatty of the Fourth Pennsylvania Regiment noted that in an Indian burial ground, "there were about 100 graves, some of which our men had dug up." These troops were apparently looking for war souvenirs in addition to exhibiting a morbid curiosity about an Indian culture that seemed very foreign to them. An even more blatant illustration of how some eastern soldiers considered any portion of a dead Indian's body a legitimate war trophy occurred among the New Jersey troops: Lieutenant William Barton explained that his men found dead Indians and "skinned two of them from their hips down for boot legs; one pair for the major and the other for myself." Ironically, frontier Revolutionaries as well as Indian warriors would have found this "trophy" to be an unacceptable substitute for the scalp of an enemy. These easterners demonstrated by their actions that, while they certainly saw Indians as subhuman opponents deserving none of the European conventional martial treatment, they did not as fully adapt to frontier military culture as frontier residents had done.[47]

Unspoken but clearly suggested in these understandings of frontier war among eastern troops was the notion that frontier Revolutionaries, by fighting in an Indian manner, were little more "civilized" than their enemies. While eastern soldiers appeared to appreciate the acumen of their western comrades

46. Thomas Hartley to Anthony Wayne, Wayne Papers, 5:85, HSP; *Pennsylvania Packet,* August 24, 1779; RWPF, file W3365; Thomas Hartley to Anthony Wayne, September 2, 1778, Wayne Papers, 5:85, HSP.

47. *Pennsylvania Packet,* September 7, 1779; Beatty, Journal, 235; "Journal of Lieutenant William Barton," in *Journal of the Military Expedition of Major General John Sullivan Against the Six Nations of Indians in 1779,* comp. G. S. Conover (Freeport, N.Y., 1972), 8.

as woodsmen and effective irregulars, they exhibited little desire to emulate it. Thus, they maintained a distinct sense of their own regional identity. Their version of American identity seemed to imply that at least in terms of military mores, they were culturally superior to Indians and whites who lived in the region. Service on the frontier graphically demonstrated to these men that Americans in "settled" regions away from contact with independent Indian nations were further removed from "savagery" than their frontier counterparts were. Furthermore, easterners' regional situation shaped their perceptions of their enemies. Soldiers from the other regions of the state had little personal stake in local frontier conflicts. Their own communities and families were threatened primarily by the British regular army and local Tories. The frontier war was not their immediate concern, and they never developed the impetus to respond to Indian attacks in kind. Indeed, some eastern enlisted men only thinly veiled their contempt for the frontier war and its stakes. William Iddings, a veteran of the "conventional" campaigns who moved from Chester to Northumberland County during the war, demonstrated an eastern rank-and-file perspective that belittled the importance of the war on the frontier, characterizing battles as "several brushes with the Indians."[48]

Militia and Continental officers, who tended to come from more socially prominent backgrounds than their men, exhibited a view of Indians during the war that differed from both the eastern and frontier rank and file. Constructions of race varied by both region and class. The beliefs of Continental commanders provide insight into how the upper and upper-middling sorts saw Indians. Most of the high-ranking Continental officers in the Pennsylvania frontier area were from the eastern parts of the state; for that matter, even high-ranking officers from the frontier regions usually identified with other officers' views of Indians. In this instance, class outlooks tended to be stronger than local ones. Upper-grade officers almost always believed the Indians to be inferior and mindless enemies who were spurred to fight by British machinations. This condescending and paternalistic view assumed that Indians were unable to prosecute war on their own accord and contrasts with the belief held by rank-and-file

48. On the difficulty of getting eastern soldiers to leave their own regions to protect the frontier, see, for example, Joseph Reed to Edward Hand, April 21, 1779, Reed Papers, NYHS, reel 2, in which Pennsylvania President Reed explains that he understands "complaints made by the inhabitants of the frontiers of being neglected by us [eastern Pennsylvanians]." Also see Joseph Reed to Colonel James Piper, May 8, 1780, PRG, reel 16, frame 63, in which Reed explains that help will not be forthcoming to the frontier because "many and great difficulties occur in calling out the militia from the inner counties." RWPF, file S22849.

frontier Revolutionaries, who understood that Indians were fighting for their own reasons and held them responsible as a racial group. Pennsylvania Colonel Edward Hand, a commander of the Continental Western Department, revealed that he believed Indian attacks to be largely actuated by Europeans. He informed Jasper Yeates that "you will see how busy the British are to engage the savages to depopulate the frontiers." Colonel Daniel Brodhead, Hand's successor, also believed that hostile Indians were manipulated by agents of the Crown. He observed that "the Mingoes are again prevailed on by English goods and address to disturb our repose." The state government echoed Brodhead's sentiments when it declared, "the invasions of the savages will probably continue as long as British art and cruelty continue to excite them." Similarly, Reverend William Rogers, a chaplain with the Pennsylvania troops on Sullivan's expedition against the Iroquois, believed that the British had "influenced the savage tribes to kill and wretchedly torture to death, persons of each sex and of every age." Such views also evinced a more cosmopolitan and nationalistic elite outlook on the Revolution. High-ranking officers took the main British army to be the most important enemy and held that hostile Indians were merely the Crown's pawns. Colonel Brodhead said as much when he rued what he believed to be the secondary importance of his frontier command. He wrote to General Anthony Wayne, "Damn my fortune for leaving the Grand Army and coming to serve where, if I do all I can, little of laurels or credit can be expected."[49]

Such officers were far more likely than their soldiers to construct a view of racial difference based on the appearance of Indians. They repeatedly remarked on Indians' skin color. As educated Anglo-American elites of the late eighteenth century, these officers were struck with perceived physical differences of Others, and they tended not to subscribe to the self-referential white-non-white bifurcated view found among ordinary frontier soldiers. Daniel Brodhead referred to Indians variously as "yellow boys," "black rascals," and "black caitiffs." Reverend Rogers called the Indians "tawny." The more cosmopolitan frontier officers also viewed Indians' complexions as their most outstanding characteristic. Michael Huffnagle, an officer from Westmoreland County, referred to Native warriors as "blacks." Such reactions to Indians allowed easterners and some frontier officers, such as Huffnagle, to navigate the cultural differences between

49. Edward Hand to Jasper Yeates, July 12, 1777, in *Frontier Defense*, by Thwaites and Kellogg, 19; Colonel Brodhead to President Reed, May 13, 1780, PRG, reel 16, frame 122; *Pennsylvania Evening Post*, November 10, 1780, 139; Journal of Reverend William Rogers, 265–66; Daniel Brodhead to Anthony Wayne, October 19, 1778, Wayne Papers, 5:122, HSP.

themselves and Native Americans. Curiously, several officers mark Indians' skin color as black. One possible explanation for these observations is that they racialized Native Americans by likening them to African Americans. In any event, what was clear was that officers were not shaping their identities in terms of "whiteness." As property owners already secure in their status as full voting citizens, their racist constructs revolved around the perceived appearances of Indians and others. Frontier soldiers, coming largely from the ranks of the poor and politically disenfranchised, were creating a new white American identity that would eventually supersede the virtuous freeholder as the model of citizenship.[50]

Officers' racism was also paternalistic rather than violent. Because many could not conceive of Indians acting independently, they assumed that Natives were lured into the war and could just as easily be convinced otherwise. Charged with frontier diplomacy and coordinating grand strategy, high-ranking officers were, therefore, more likely to differentiate among friendly, neutral, and hostile Indians. Continental commanders in the West took care to cultivate Indian allies and condemned white attacks on friendly groups—not so much out of authentic concern for the victims but because they wished to avoid widening the war. They realized, in the context of the grand strategy of the war, that Indian alliances or neutrality were vital. The commanders of the Continental Western Department, headquartered at Fort Pitt, all had to negotiate with Indians and coordinate the Revolutionary War effort on the frontier. Some officers displayed a grasp of the subtle differences among Native groups in regard to their wartime sympathies. Colonel Brodhead wrote in 1779, "The Wyandotts of Sandusky and the Mingoes of Tankhonnetick and the Peckawee and Chilacoffee tribes of the Shawanese nation continue their depredations . . . but the Delaware inform me that most of the other nations to the Westward and Southward are friendly to the United States." General William Irvine was alarmed by Gnadenhutten and worried for the safety of his own Delaware scouts. Seeing the war primarily in terms of defeating the British, such officers sought to counter the diplomacy of the Crown in the West rather than eliminate all Indians.[51]

50. Daniel Brodhead to Captain Samuel Morehead, May 8, 1779, Order Book of Daniel Brodhead, Darlington Memorial Library, University of Pittsburgh; Brodhead to Lieutenant Nielly, April 30, 1779, ibid.; Daniel Brodhead to Nathanael Greene, September 6, 1780, Woods Collection of Western Pennsylvania Documents, Historical Society of Western Pennsylvania; Journal of Reverend William Rogers, 278; Michael Huffnagle to President Moore, July[?], 1782, PRG, reel 19, frame 930.

51. Daniel Brodhead to Timothy Pickering, November 3, 1779, *PA*, 1st ser., 12:179–80; William Irvine to George Washington, April 20, 1782, in *Washington-Irvine Correspondence*, ed. Butterfield, 99–106.

Because of the tension between negotiating with Indians and controlling violently racist Revolutionary soldiers, elites also marked the differences between themselves and "white" frontier inhabitants. They commented on frontier military culture as being uncivilized and implied their own superiority. True Americans, they believed, lived in regions where such horrendous violence was absent. Here, the officers evoked an identity that was simultaneously genteel, eastern, and racist. Officers from the settled regions saw frontiersmen as scarcely more civilized than the Indians, redeemed only by their "whiteness." Timothy Pickering, commenting on the war on the Pennsylvania frontier, exemplified this view. He called for disciplined regulars to fight in the region because "the inhabitants appear, many of them, to be a wild, ungovernable race, little less savage than their tawny neighbors and by similar barbarities have in fact provoked them to revenge." Edward Hand called frontiersmen who were constantly killing all Indians "savage-like." These men clearly saw the ordinary residents of the region to be only a step removed from Indians. Yet that step was their skin color and European heritage. As Pickering suggested, savagery was a commonality among Indians and frontier inhabitants; "tawny" skin color was not.[52]

Hence, the proliferation of regional identities in the frontier war mirrored constructions of American identity in general: competing localisms palliated by the concept of race. Frontier soldiers believed that their mastery of Indian tactics demonstrated their cultural superiority to Europeans, while their construction of "whiteness" in opposition to "the Indians" created a rationale of biological superiority that justified essentially genocidal attacks. Eastern rank-and-file men never fully assimilated the military culture of the region, and they differentiated themselves from Indians and from frontier "whites" by emphasizing "savage" martial norms. Officers and diplomats in the region espoused an elite paternalistic racism that pointed to the skin color of Indians rather than solely focusing upon a trans–European American self-identification as "white." Taking a broader view of the war, they strategically distinguished among groups of Indians and were consistently annoyed by frontier Revolutionaries who attacked neutrals and allies. Such inhabitants seemed to exhibit an inexplicable Western "savagery" in the minds of officers who could not fully understand the identity constructed by frontier troops. In the end, however, it is apparent that the one element that held these groups together as "Americans"

52. Timothy Pickering to General Washington, May 19, 1778, PRG, reel 14, frame 54; Edward Hand to Jasper Yeates, October 2, 1777, in *Frontier Defense,* by Thwaites and Kellogg, 119.

was the concept of racial identity—specifically, the assumption that they were all "whites." Few Revolutionaries in the region seriously entertained the notion that "nonwhite" Indians would have a place in the postwar republic. In other words, all Revolutionaries predicated their image of who was part of the nation on "whiteness." Although some looked upon frontier soldiers as almost "savage" themselves, perceived skin color was always a prerequisite for shared identities as Americans. During a war in which the United States was born, regional and class-based national identities emerged that shared general assumptions of European American racial superiority. The Revolution, to an extent hitherto unrecognized, forged a view of American-ness rooted in "whiteness" that specifically stood in opposition to Indians.

The war, of course, altered the way Indians viewed themselves and their neighbors as well. Pan-Indian alliances and identities were bolstered by indiscriminate violence perpetrated by the Revolutionaries. While most Indians continued to differentiate among groups of "whites" and sought British and Tory assistance in the war, they increasingly came to see U.S. citizens as one singularly dangerous group of whites. Ultimately, while the majority of northeastern Indians envisioned a postwar world where contact with Europeans and European Americans would be inevitable and perhaps desirable, they did not seek inclusion in the Revolutionaries' imagined communities. The actual desires of Natives were of little import to the Revolutionaries, who believed that whites could consciously choose sides but all Indians were, by definition, communal outsiders—Others. While race and violence created boundaries in the frontier war, Pennsylvanians who underwent civil war and contested the nature of their communities were viewed and acted upon in quite different ways than Indians.

Civil War and the Contest for Community

On July 30, 1778, the *Pennsylvania Gazette* reported on the so-called Wyoming Massacre and singled out the "villainous Tories" for particular criticism. One of the most striking stories was that of "Partial Terry," a loyalist who left his Revolutionary family behind. He purportedly "several times sent his father word, that he hoped to wash his hands in his heart's blood." During the attack, according to the report, "the monster, with his own hand murdered his father, mother, brothers and sisters, stripped off their scalps, and cut off his father's head." Later, during Sullivan's 1779 expedition, Reverend William Rogers recorded a story told by Colonel Zebulon Butler about internecine violence in the Wyoming region. Butler told the story of two brothers, John and Henry Pensell, who were on opposite sides of the Pennsylvania civil war. During the battle, the Revolutionary soldier Henry lost his weapon and found himself at the mercy of his Tory brother, John. As Henry pleaded for his brother to spare his life, John coolly loaded his gun. According to Butler's account, Henry asked, "'You won't kill your brother will you?' 'Yes,' replied the monster, 'I will as soon as look at you, you are a damned rebel.' He then shot him and afterwards went up and struck him four or five times with a tomahawk and scalped him." While this story and that of "Partial Terry" have the markings of the many exaggerated or fabricated tales that Revolutionaries used in describing the Battle of Wyoming, they both convey important messages about civil war in Pennsylvania. The tropes of fratricide, matricide, and parricide were all intended to underscore the "monstrous" nature of "Toryism." Occasionally, civil war rent families asunder in this manner. More important, however, these tales were meant to suggest that taking up arms against local Revolutionaries was a larger betrayal of the metaphorical family, the dominant imagined community—and thus the nation.[1]

For most Pennsylvanians, civil war was a conflict among various social groups over the constitution of the community. The "family" of European Americans was divided, and at stake was the definition of true American-ness. White men who were liable by law to Revolutionary militia service and loyalty oaths were considered proper patriots until they defiantly proved otherwise. Dissenters became social outsiders whom the Revolutionaries declared "disaffected" (or outright "Tories") if they failed to conform. In other words, those who voluntarily refused to accept new definitions of the community forged during the Revolution were labeled criminal traitors; those who opposed locally dominant Revolutionaries were typically formally disenfranchised and defined as marginal, institutionalizing their previously informally liminal state. Some were allowed to "recant" their unpopular views and reassume membership in the community, often following sustained intimidation. Others who refused to embrace the new order were imprisoned, disenfranchised, and/or deprived of their property. Conversely, when the opportunity presented itself, "Tories" moved to arms by their hostile neighbors often sought to impose the same sorts of sanctions upon their "Whig" opponents. Loyalists also defined their enemies as criminal traitors who were the truly dangerous "outsiders" of the community. Not surprisingly, given the localist motives of Pennsylvania soldiers in general, hostility among combatants in this internecine warfare ran high. All domestic opponents were

1. *Pennsylvania Gazette*, July 30, 1778; Journal of Reverend William Rogers, 265. Williams heard the story from Colonel Butler, who based his tale on the account of a purported witness named Giles Slocum.

subject to plundering, humiliation, arrest, imprisonment, and even execution. Additionally, the presence of free blacks, rebellious slaves, and whites who fought with Indians further complicated the status of domestic opponents by destabilizing a perceived racial hierarchy. The Whig victory in the state's civil war had momentous consequences in shaping the development of the localist white male nation and in defining who could be a full member of that community.[2]

Early War Intimidation of Dissenters

Defining and enforcing new ideals of local citizenship became crucially important as soon as the war began. At the conflict's outset, Pennsylvania Revolutionaries who gained control over local government and militias used those institutions to crush internal dissent. Those who opposed open rebellion in the early phases of the war were, however, not yet seen as a formidable military threat. In 1775, the main British army was hundreds of miles away and unlikely to be able to support an uprising of the disaffected in Pennsylvania. Rather than simply arrest or completely disenfranchise those who disagreed with the actions of local Revolutionaries, the militia—or those subject to service in it by virtue of the "association"—often took up the role of the mob during the constitutional crisis, intimidating their opponents to force them to renounce their previous positions and at least nominally embrace the new order. At this early stage, a program of persuasion and humiliation was typically the preferred course of action. Enforced public orthodoxy created the illusion of a unified community. The targets of mobs and the militia demonstrated that those seen as "Tories" were often members of social groups in disfavor with the Revolutionaries rather than outright "loyalists" to the cause of Britain. In York County, for example, John Adlum remembered that a young Mennonite who refused to join the militia was declared a Tory. Local residents attempted to shame him

2. Robert M. Calhoon, "Civil, Revolutionary, or Partisan: The Loyalists and the Nature of the War for Independence," in *The Loyalist Perception and Other Essays* (Columbia, S.C., 1989), 147–62; Fox, *Sweet Land of Liberty;* William H. Nelson, *The American Tory* (Westport, Conn., 1961), 87–149; and Ousterhout, *A State Divided,* demonstrate how "Toryism" was related to local issues. As Ousterhout notes, casting civil conflict within Pennsylvania in the context of opposition to the Revolution in the state shifts analysis "from England to the colonies themselves" (5). I agree that the term "loyalism" is not always accurate in describing resistance to the Revolution. My use of the terms "disaffected," "Tory," and "Whig" throughout this chapter is an arbitrary convenience for designating contending groups within European American communities and is not meant to convey an adherence to a particular style of Anglo-American politics. My usage of these designations also generally reflects popular Revolutionary-era applications of them.

into doing what was deemed his fair share of military service. Failing to convince him that his religious pacifism essentially equaled treason, the mob commenced public punishment and renunciation of the young man by the traditional act of tarring and feathering.[3]

This formula of invitation to renounce unpopular views and be "reborn" into the community (with the clear threat of humiliation or violence) prevailed throughout the state before the war actually came to the region. James Rankin, for example, was forced to publish a public recantation of his mistakes in state newspapers:

> As I have, in several instances, injured the Committee of York county by sundry public misrepresentations, as well as by personal insults, thereby obstructing the public measures now so necessary for the safety of our country, but being convinced of the bad tendency of my past conduct, and desirous of being restored to a good understanding and friendship with my countrymen, I do thus publicly ask forgiveness of them, and do promise, on the faith and honour of an honest man, that I will in future pay due regard to the rules and regulations of the Honourable Continental Congress, and behave, in all respects, as becomes a good citizen of the United States of America.

Failure to avail oneself of this opportunity for "forgiveness" could result in complete social ostracization—or worse. Those given a chance to redeem themselves were almost always "white" men, the very identity eventually defined as a prerequisite for citizenship. In other words, European American men were assumed "American" until they stubbornly proved otherwise, despite every attempt to include them. Those who remained steadfast in their refusal to renounce their views and take up the Revolution suffered the consequences. James Sheppard found out that standing on dissenting principles was dangerous. According to his loyalist claim, "the rebels wanted him to take the oath in the year 1775 and he refused to do it in consequence of which they tarred and feathered him." William Caldwell, a recent English immigrant shopkeeper, told of his comparable experience when he made the mistake of openly advocating "British Government." As a result, he "was summoned to attend a committee at Reading 14th June 1775, was tried on 15th and sentenced to be

3. Adlum, *Memoirs*, 7–9.

tarred and feathered, which sentence was put in execution. Two hundred men in arms attended in order to see the sentence put in execution." Richard Swanwick, an English-born employee of the royal revenue service, was offered the opportunity to take up office as a Revolutionary official if he renounced his former position. He refused and was imprisoned in the Lancaster jail for drinking to the king's health and the success of British arms. George Harding, an Irish-born Philadelphia carpenter who refused to join the association, "was repeatedly insulted by mobs with continual threats of being tarred and feathered day and night and his property took for the same" in 1775. Less obviously a true loyalist than either Caldwell or Swanwick, Harding was singled out for his refusal to make himself liable for militia service (as his white male Philadelphia neighbors were).[4]

Enforcement of communal orthodoxy was truly a local affair. In Philadelphia, an ardent loyalist, Dr. John Kearsley, threatened a pro-Revolutionary mob in 1775. The Philadelphians offered Kearsley the recourse of reintegration into the community if he openly apologized for his actions. The doctor refused and was beaten, arrested, and jailed. Philadelphia authorities later moved Kearsley to a jail in York County to keep him from inciting other local Tories. Interestingly, far from being reviled in central Pennsylvania, the doctor became quite popular and was called upon to perform medical services. William Pearce avoided the ire of his neighbors by simply relocating rather than publicly renouncing his views. He recalled, "I was summoned to take up arms which I refused to do and was soon after taken up for drinking the King's health and was to be tarred and feathered, but that I escaped from and got for safety into another township where I lived 9 or 10 months there."[5]

For those not willing to leave their homes, disingenuously joining the association or renouncing previous positions were realistic alternatives. Such strategies kept those identified as "disaffected" out of jails and in their neighborhoods at least until the British army began to operate in the region. Thomas Grannon simply stated that he joined the "rebels from fear of imprisonment." Matthias Aspden "thought it best to swim with the stream at the moment and consented to learn the use of arms" when pressed to join the militia, even though

4. Peter C. Messer, "'A Species of Treason and Not the Least Dangerous Kind': The Treason Trials of Abraham Carlisle and John Roberts," *PMHB* 123 (October 1999): 302–32, articulates a secular variant of Great Awakening evangelical thought emphasizing the possibility of individual redemption that permeated Pennsylvanians' ideas about treason and communal forgiveness. *Pennsylvania Gazette,* July 31, 1776; AO12/99/49, AO12/40/235–36, AO12/42/29, AO12/40/9.

5. The treatment of Kearsley is described in Ousterhout, *A State Divided,* 117–19; AO13/90/598.

he disapproved of the Revolution. He noted that he "should have been esteemed either a coward or a traitor" if he had not done so. Samuel Shoemaker revealed how little "loyalism" had to do with Aspden's alienation from the Revolution in his affidavit supporting the latter's loyalist claim. He suggested that Aspden's main "crime" against the Revolution was that "he was a quiet inoffensive man and did not meddle much with politics." As Aspden asserted, neutrality or refusal to take up arms in the militia left one open to the charge of treason. In the world according to the Revolutionaries, neutrality itself threatened the cause.[6]

The subjects of coercion portrayed the Revolutionaries as cynical, self-interested leaders manipulating the gullible and violent masses. William Shepard described how his flight to the British at New Brunswick, New Jersey, resulted in "leaving his family to be maltreated and his property destroyed by an enraged frantic mob." Philadelphia innkeeper Lawrence Fegan noted that he was harassed despite his taking a position as a Revolutionary barracksmaster. He complained that "the mob fired into his house and wounded and robbed his wife . . . and committed every possible depredation on his property and unless [he] had escaped from their bloody search [he] must have fallen an instant victim to their horrid cruelty." Both Shepard and Fegan took care to portray the mob as mindlessly "frantic" or "cruel." They implied that the masses were acting upon direction from others who stood to gain from using the people's emotions. Henry Norris explicitly attributed the actions of the mob to ambitious and scheming Revolutionary leaders who, he believed, directed the "rabble" against him. He explained that certain persons were "determined to expose him to the fury of the mob and to make a public exhibition of him." Similarly, the openly loyalist lawyer Isaac Hunt recounted how he was seized by the mob and paraded in a cart through Philadelphia's streets. He "expected every moment to be torn in pieces by [the] multitude spirited up to frenzy by the artifices of the usurpers." Here was an emerging "Tory" critique of the Revolution that, ironically, was steeped in the Anglo-American Whig tradition. These "loyalists" portrayed the change in internal government as a factional conspiracy of "usurpers" who utilized "artifices" to delude the masses into supporting them with the popular intimidation of dissent.[7]

6. AO12/101/101, AO12/38/248, AO12/38/256–57.
7. AO12/38/183–84, AO12/38/403–4, AO12/38/418, AO12/42/312–13.

Defining Treason

As the war went on, laws superseded informal communal pressures. Pennsylvania Revolutionaries devised measures that essentially criminalized not only active treason but also passive neutrality. A 1776 militia law imposed a fine on "all able bodied effective male white persons, capable of bearing arms, not associators, between the ages of sixteen and fifty years." Those who refused to pay the non-association fine were subject to imprisonment. In 1777, the Pennsylvania Assembly passed a new militia act that imposed a draft and a higher fine while retaining a substitution option. The "test acts" of 1777 and those that followed throughout the war defined the Revolutionary community even more narrowly by "obliging the male white inhabitants of this State to give ASSURANCES of alliance to the same." Thus, the oath came to replace the public recantation of views under threat of tarring and feathering in communities as an open declaration of membership in the new order. Those who refused the oath were subject to the loss of civil and voting rights. Failure to take the "test," therefore, was a forfeiture of citizenship.[8]

Not surprisingly, religious pacifists were heavily persecuted. They were typically labeled "disaffected" or outright Tories because of their refusal to support the military or take oaths of allegiance. Quakers, in particular, were subject to special hostility from Whig militiamen. Soldiers demanded that Friends either serve in the militia, provide substitutes, or pay fines, knowing full well that most Quakers' religious scruples would not allow them to do so. Many southeastern Pennsylvanians who had previously lived in communities dominated by prominent Friends had the satisfaction of seeing them disenfranchised under the new order. When Quakers petitioned that the militia and test laws were unfair to them, a writer in the pro-Revolutionary *Pennsylvania Packet* defended the laws' necessity. The essayist argued, "if you are separated from Great Britain, and have not entered into any other compact, you belong to neither her nor America: You are in a state of nature and have no civil rights." The "principles which you [the Friends] profess must not only cut you off from the claim of the right of citizens of the State, but renders it the duty of the Legislature, as much as possible, to prevent your poisoning the minds of the youth."[9]

---

8. Quotation on the April 1776 militia law in *Pennsylvania Gazette*, February 26, 1777. On the 1777 militia law, see Rosswurm, *Arms, Country, and Class*, 135–38. Quotation from the bill for the 1777 test act in *Pennsylvania Gazette*, June 4, 1777. See Ousterhout, *A State Divided*, 283–84, on the provisions of various test acts.

9. *Pennsylvania Packet*, August 15, 1778.

This powerful message attacking Quaker "principles" in order to justify their marginalization was echoed by soldiers. The Philadelphia militiamen who believed that certain white men were forced to fight while neutrals, such as the Quakers, continued to prosper in their civil pursuits, declared that "the people will no longer submit to see the public burden so unequally borne." The Committee of Privates also declared Quaker pacifism to be illegal and an unfair burden to those who were forced to serve in the militia. They saw the Friends as disaffected people who clung to "the antiquated and absurd doctrine of passive obedience" at the expense of the larger community.[10]

Enlisted men's disdain for their Quaker neighbors was often expressed in harassment and plundering. In February 1776, while recruiting in Chester County, Colonel Anthony Wayne ordered his men that "no insult be offered to any of the inhabitants of this place or to any religious society." He feared that his newly raised troops would abuse the many Quakers in the county who refused to support the war. Destruction of Friends' property also followed Washington's victory over Cornwallis at Yorktown in 1781. Pent-up anger at neutral neighbors exploded during celebrations of the battle. Philadelphia Quakers complained of "outrages and violences committed on the property . . . of our religious society by companies of licentious people parading down the streets, destroying the windows and doors of our houses, breaking into and plundering some of them." Indeed, even when some Quaker families sent members to serve in the military, they still remained subject to persecution by local Revolutionaries. Alexander Graydon noted how Thomas Parvin "was an object of much wanton oppression" and was "nearly broken up by the levies on his property for taxes and militia fines," even though his sons were in the militia.[11]

Members of other pacifist religious sects were similarly marginalized by the Revolutionaries, despite the fact that they, unlike the Quakers, had never been dominant in their communities. In Northampton County, Moravians were deeply distrusted by the local militia. Their avowed neutrality in the war, coupled with their refusal to take up arms, caused Northampton troops to see them as evaders of public service—or worse, closet traitors. Several members of the militia used Moravian pacifism, like that of the Friends, as an excuse to plunder their properties. The troops, according to one observer, "have taken several

10. The statement by Philadelphia militia is in *Pennsylvania Packet,* November 13, 1775; the enlisted men's critique of Quaker pacifism is in "A Representation of the Committee of Privates," ibid.

11. General Orders, February 18, 1776, Wayne Papers, 1:27, HSP; "Representation of the Society of Friends to the President and Executive Council of Pennsylvania," December 6, 1781, Feinstone Collection, DLAR, item 2072; *Alexander Graydon's Memoirs,* 325.

of them [Moravians] from their houses, bound them. They have taken all their most calculable effects under pretense of hiring a substitute." Soldiers also resorted to deception and "persuaded [Moravians] to sign as associators, by means of trickery and lies." When a group of Moravians subsequently petitioned the state government, protesting their treatment, Northampton militiamen were livid. They demanded that "an immediate stop be put to their petitions and petitioning of an unlawful set of disaffected men." The soldiers believed that these men deserved no protection under the law because they refused to help defend the community or even take the oath of allegiance to the Revolutionary Pennsylvania Constitution. Like Quakers, Moravians were simply treated as residents who had no civil rights. Comparable disdain was shown toward other religious pacifists in the state. In Lancaster County, where most Mennonites lived, the local militia declared them to be "Black-Guards, villains who are lazy."[12]

Other groups suffered for their political views. With the implementation of the state constitution, moderate Whigs increasingly came under suspicion for Toryism. Those who were willing to fight in the early phases of the war but were unable to support independence and/or the new radical regime were labeled "disaffected" members of their communities. Many times, class tensions compounded political ones. Moderates who opposed the new state constitution were typically members of the upper sort who disdained rule by what they considered "the rabble" in an unbalanced form of republican government. Once again, the militia exposed and harassed those deemed lukewarm patriots. Moderates, who viewed themselves as prudent Whigs, often found it difficult to fathom why they were characterized as disaffected. Indeed, true "revolutionary" status was becoming ever more narrowly defined. James Allen, for example, was a political moderate who was as dubious of the radical rank-and-file Philadelphia citizen-soldiers as they were of him. He entered the militia in 1775 because, as he explained, "I believe discreet people mixing with them may keep them in order." Allen was no longer able to fit in when Independence was declared. Although he had supported colonial resistance to British imperial policy and the early part of the war, Allen could not bring himself to accept separation from the mother country. He soon had to leave Philadelphia out of

12. William Woodford to George Washington, October 3, 1777, Washington Papers, Library of Congress, 3d ser., reel 44; the quotation regarding trickery used against Moravians is from John Ettwein, quoted in Kenneth Gardiner Hamilton, "John Ettwein and the Moravian Church During the Revolutionary Period" (Ph.D. diss., Columbia University, 1940), 160; Petition of the Field Officers and Others of the Second Battalion Northampton Militia, May 25, 1778, PRG, reel 14, frames 120–21. The militia commentary on Mennonites is quoted in Ousterhout, *A State Divided*, 110.

fear for his own safety as people increasingly identified him as disaffected. Allen noted that the Revolutionaries' use of the term "Tory" "included everyone disinclined to Independence tho' ever so warm a friend to constitutional liberty and the old cause." Unlike Dr. Kearsley, Allen found no respite when he left his community and moved to Northampton County. His wife and daughter were stopped on the streets by the local militia and their carriage was destroyed. Allen lamented that "all power is in the hands of the associators who are under no subordination to their officers." A short time later, Allen noted that he was singled out at his home "on account of my political views" by Northampton militiamen who offered insults and demanded blankets.[13]

Obviously, a significant aspect of Revolutionary militia service was policing the community and repressing dissent. Soldiers also made sure that their own institutions were purged of political moderates who supported the war in general but opposed radical internal revolution. A group of York County men declared their view of such dissent: they had "ever since the beginning of the war been in some measure possessed of a sense of malignancy of the external enemies; and much more of the internal enemies of American independence. . . . In this great struggle, he who is not with us is against us." In other words, any form of neutrality, dissent, or disagreement with those who saw themselves as the representatives of the Revolutionary community was treason. There was no middle ground. Myles Snowden, who was heavily persecuted early in the war, stated as much: "party disputes became so violent that all those who did not take an active part with the rebels in their desperate measures were held forth as enemies to the cause and marked for victims." Recalcitrant political moderates typically received the same treatment as religious pacifists. They were viewed as residents with limited civil rights, and many times their goods were subject to seizure. Again, militiamen were at the forefront of such confiscations from those who refused to swear allegiance to the new constitution. In Philadelphia, troops were allowed to "seize the horse or man [servant or slave?] of every person resident whether [of] this city or districts who does not produce a certificate of having taken the oath." Similarly, in Chester County, the local militia was authorized to impress blankets and other supplies from "person[s] who refuse to bear arms or take an active part in the defense of their bleeding country." At times, the militia facilitated the administration of the oath with

13. See Wood, *Creation of the American Republic*, 232–33, on "gentry" opposition to the radical Pennsylvania frame of government. Entry: October 14[?], 1775, Entry: January 1777[?], and Entry: February 17, 1777, James Allen Diary, HSP.

the threat of force. In Northampton County, Robert Scott and his comrades were deployed to "bring the Tories to justice and punishment and take the oath of allegiance." (Scott's statement suggests that those who were willing to take the test, even under duress, could still reintegrate themselves into the community.[14])

Soldiers increasingly viewed wealthy men who otherwise supported the internal Revolution, but avoided military service, as another internal threat. Philadelphia militiamen, in particular, consistently condemned the affluent who were never in the army as failing to live up to their communal obligations. The militia especially resented merchants and well-off artisans who never served but appeared to prosper from the extra opportunities created by the absence of serving soldiers who were protecting the city. Even Pennsylvania Continental officers became angry with Philadelphia businessmen, whom they condemned as "our internal enemies [who] regardless of either liberty or peace, live at home in lazy security accumulating wealth at our expense." When stricter laws against non-association were passed, the militia in Chester County declared that it was "much elated with the thoughts of establishing civil and military authority among these people who live in ease and in general affluent circumstances and never did anything to the support of the war."[15]

Many poor white men who served now found themselves in a position to criticize formally the politics of their prominent neutral and moderate neighbors, as evidenced in an Pennsylvania newspaper essay that asserted, "the militia of Pennsylvania have many enemies. The Tories all hate them; [as do] the trimming half way men, who have purchased moderation." Soldiers grouped anyone who opposed the radical Revolutionaries in the state under the general rubric of disaffection. Dissent, even apathy, indicated potential treason to the state. Thus, the new government, supported by the militias in local communities, effectively disenfranchised many of their political opponents. Significant numbers who no longer enjoyed full citizenship in Pennsylvania were prominent, propertied men. Fluid definitions of American identity and citizenship were no longer simply based in primarily economic terms, that is, as a prerogative of all propertied men. Rather, being subject to and obeying the test

14. Petition of Inhabitants of the Fourth District, York County, PRG, reel 14, frame 778; AO12/42/301–6; Instructions to the City Battalions of Militia, June 9, 1780, PRG, reel 16, frame 322; Supreme Executive Council to Major General Armstrong, August 31, 1777, prg, reel 12, frame 926; RWPF, file W3305.

15. Petition of Pennsylvania Officers to George Washington, August [?], 1777, Washington Papers, Library of Congress, 4th ser., reel 43; Andrew Boyd to Vice President George Bryan, June 20, 1778, ibid., reel 14, frame 296.

oaths and militia laws were becoming the assumed prerequisites for membership in the Revolutionary community.[16]

Opportunities grew for the "disaffected" to strike back against those who marginalized them. As widespread hostilities commenced within Pennsylvania in 1777, active military resistance to the Revolutionaries became a more feasible alternative for many. Civil war wracked the state. In addition to "true loyalists," other Americans simply alienated from the Revolution took up arms or otherwise assisted the British army or Indian warriors. Military activity in the state, however, led to even more draconian state treason laws meant to deter and punish any aid given to the enemy. In 1777, as the British army began its Philadelphia campaign, the Pennsylvania Council of Safety passed an emergency ordinance authorizing the confiscation of personal property without trial of anyone who joined or assisted the enemy. This measure was later superseded by a confiscation law passed by the assembly in March 1778 authorizing the seizure of entire estates of "traitors." Additionally, those summoned for trial on suspicion of treason who did not appear could be declared guilty without a trial. This attainder for treason carried a death penalty and an automatic loss of property, which would be sold for public use. The confiscation of property was also meant to be a symbolic emasculation of patriarchs who had betrayed the community.[17]

Essentially, the Revolutionaries defined internal dissent as criminal activity. Those who refused to take the test oath or support the militia laws were seen as various sorts of disaffected persons who deserved legal punishment, much like those who assisted or joined enemy forces. The result was that much of the civil war in Pennsylvania was prosecuted by Revolutionaries as police actions. With the exception of Tories who were formally enlisted into British regular or provincial units who served with the main army, anyone found in arms as militia or irregulars against the Revolutionaries or assisting their enemies was subject to civil law and not treated as a prisoner of war. This process was, ironically, supported by British policies and actions in the war. With the early decision to treat the rebel military as, for the most part, any other European army, the British quietly granted the "rebels" credibility as a belligerent power. Loyalists pointed out the ill effects of such a policy in a petition to the king and Parliament, arguing that an active Tory suffered "the immediate forfeiture of all

16. *Freeman's Journal,* January 9, 1780.
17. Ousterhout, *A State Divided,* 171–73, and Henry Young, "Treason and Its Punishment," explain the Pennsylvania treason ordinance of 1777 and treason law of 1778.

his goods and chattels, lands and tenements; and if apprehended, and convicted by the rebels, of having enlisted, or prevailed on any other person to enlist into his Majesty's service, it is considered as treason, and punished with death." They disgustedly pointed out that for a rebel soldier, "no forfeiture is incurred, or penalty annexed, to his entering into the service of Congress; but, on the contrary, his property is secured, and himself rewarded." Thus, the Revolutionaries were able to consolidate their claim to represent entire communities and define their American opponents as traitors. Unlike in the English Civil War, when both Parliamentary supporters and Royalists treated each other as they would any other respectable European opponent (at least in the early phases of the conflict), Tories and Whigs accused each other of being traitors and lawbreakers. As a result, much of the civil war itself was characterized by arrests, intimidation, confiscation of property, and imprisonment rather than much open battle. The stakes, of course, were very high. Whoever won the internal struggle in the state would be in a position to define citizenship. Without full British sanction for their actions, however, loyalists were at a distinct disadvantage in claiming the mantle of the lawful community and dubbing rebels treasonous.[18]

Civil War in the Southeast

When the British occupied Philadelphia in 1777–78, approximately 1,400 Pennsylvanians were enlisted into loyalist units despite the risks to life and property. Many came from the ranks of marginalized members of the community, including Roman Catholics, slaves, and moderate Whigs. Even a few Quakers,

18. Petition of "his Majesty's American Loyalists" quoted in *Pennsylvania Gazette,* June 19, 1782. Barbara Donagan argues in "Atrocity, War Crime, and Treason in the English Civil War," *American Historical Review* 99 (October 1994): 1137–66, that Royalists and supporters of Parliament, for the most part, treated each other as they would a legitimate foreign military enemy. This adherence to conventional European rules of war was meant to prevent the conflict from degenerating into a bloody total war based on revenge (as happened in the civil war in many parts of America during the Revolution). Donagan asserts that the imposition of civil authority over enemy prisoners served to break down limits on violence later in the war. For American Tories and rebels captured by loyalists, the specter of civil justice always loomed over their actions. Henry Young points out in "Treason and Its Punishment" that, despite the fact that the Revolutionaries adamantly prosecuted and issued bills of attainders of treason against Tories, the British government neither prosecuted nor issued acts of attainders against any active Pennsylvania Revolutionaries (288). Although loyalists arrested Whigs and confiscated their property, there was no formal legal apparatus by which to try them in Pennsylvania under imperial authority. Thus, the British attempt to limit the destructive nature of the war ultimately undercut loyalist claims to represent legally constituted authority.

such as George Davis and John Boucher, were so irritated by their treatment from the Revolutionaries that they joined the British army. Richard Henry Lee feared—with good reason—that while Philadelphia was occupied, the British would take advantage of the "weak and divided . . . people of this state [Pennsylvania] . . . from various causes" to recruit active loyalists. Many of the "weak and divided" who had been effectively stripped of their citizenship or civil rights were also at least willing to assist the forces of the Crown with supplies, intelligence, and the taking up of political posts during the occupation.[19]

As a result, Revolutionaries reacted by stepping up their enforcement of their treason laws to deter active assistance to the British. Instances of jailing the disaffected increased. Joel Arpin, a Philadelphia hatter under suspicion by his neighbors on the eve of the enemy occupation, was "taken prisoner before the British took Philadelphia and kept in Gaol five months . . . [and] lost all his property." This was despite the fact that Arpin "took no part either for or against the Americans" even after the British arrived. George Rine, a Lancaster miller, so feared "being confined to the common gaol" that he fled to British lines in 1778. Henry Wakefield explained that the rebels were about to put him in "gaol for refusing their illegal demands." James Smither, who provided the British army with intelligence, "was by order of congress apprehended at his own house in Philadelphia and put in close confinement in the new Gaol." Charles Stedman was jailed in 1777 and "was locked up day and night in a damp room, debarred the use of pen, ink and paper and was obliged sometimes to drink the water he washed his face and hands in." When Stedman became ill, "all medical relief was denied him unless he would take the oaths to the state. Under the circumstances, he thought a temporary compliance was pardonable more especially as he was threatened with public execution on the charge of high treason." John Hales of Philadelphia "suffered close imprisonment, severe trials and rigorous treatment till a short time before the happy arrival of the British troops." John Bittle, another Philadelphian who joined the loyalist troops, was "taken by the rebels and confined in Philadelphia Gaol on the 17th of May for six months and tried for his life for his loyalty for the King."[20]

---

19. See Siebert, *Loyalists of Pennsylvania*, 41–42, on the numbers and composition of Pennsylvanians who enlisted in loyalist units during Howe's occupation of Philadelphia. AO13/24/107–10, AO13/24/49–50; Richard Henry Lee to George Washington, November 20, 1777, Washington Papers, Library of Congress, 4th ser., reel 45.

20. AO12/100/354, AO12/40/94, AO12/42/374–75, AO13/25/454–56, AO12/42/266–71, AO13/24/236, AO13/25/45–46.

As Bittle's account suggests, the specter of execution for high treason always hung over the heads of all imprisoned loyalists. Joseph Galloway, a prominent loyalist who became superintendent of police and essentially in charge of civil government in Philadelphia during the British occupation, feared for his own life. He recalled that he was in "the most imminent danger of being taken and put to death, one of his valuable friends being shot by a party of militia sent in pursuit of your memorialist." A mariner told Joseph Thomas, a Chester County man who helped guide the British fleet in the area, that he "would have been hanged had he not made his escape and was secreted for the space of five months until the British arrived in Philadelphia." William Rankin explained that some members of the secret loyalist association that he tried to form in York County were "put to death by the rebels." In 1777, James Molesworth was the first to be officially executed for treason in Pennsylvania after an army court-martial found him guilty of recruiting pilots for the British army. Following the British evacuation in 1778, the state formally tried and executed two elderly Quakers, John Roberts and Abraham Carlisle, for treason, arguing that they had assisted the enemy by holding official positions and providing intelligence. Again, the message was clear: those defined as internal enemies of the state would be treated as criminals, not as honorable combatants in war. George Harding did not learn the lesson and made the mistake of remaining in Philadelphia after the Revolutionaries retook the city. He was tried for treason, convicted, and sentenced to death. Harding described how he "was led to the place of execution, bound like a Malefactor, and after being forty minutes under the gallows, was reprieved in consequence of Sir Henry Clinton being informed of his situation who demanded him as he has since been told."[21]

Confiscation of goods and land was the other prominent penalty imposed on Tories. Matthew Ormsby, when "taken prisoner in the month of February 1778, was stripped stark naked, dispossessed of every thing he had in the world." Even poorer persons were subject to "dispossession" of their property should they assist the British in any manner. William Henery, an illiterate, recent Irish immigrant to Chester County, miscalculated when he accepted pay for serving as a guide for the British army. The Revolutionaries quickly retaliated by confiscating his meager possessions, reducing him to complete destitution. Caleb

21. See John E. Ferling, *The Loyalist Mind: Joseph Galloway and the American Revolution* (University Park, Pa., 1977), 35–64, on Galloway's role in the occupation. AO12/38/20, AO13/25/477, AO13/71, pt. 2/194; see Ousterhout, *A State Divided*, 154, on the execution of Molesworth, and Messer, "A Species of Treason," on Abraham and Carlisle; AO12/40/10.

Hill, a landless farm laborer, similarly learned the difficult lesson that crossing the Revolutionaries could lead to economic catastrophe. Hill took a position under Superintendent Joseph Galloway during the British occupation and suffered the loss of his only valuable property, "three horses and two cows." Martin Lawlor, a Philadelphia truckman who decided to carry on his trade for the British in 1777–78, also lost his property to the Revolutionaries.[22]

By the time of the British occupation, it was also clear that Revolutionaries saw white women with "Tory" spouses or with their own politically dissenting views as dangers to the body politic. Despite popular assumptions about the inability of women to hold coherent views on politics, the reality of the war made women subject to some of the same informal and legal sanctions as those imposed on male Tories. Charlotte Sorgen, the widow of a prominent Tory who died in 1775, "made herself very obnoxious by receiving loyalists into her house and went into New York about two months after the British troops left Philadelphia," as she could not remain at home because of her politicized actions. Similarly, Elizabeth Webster, whose husband was killed trying to reach British lines, could not keep her political opinions to herself and thus rendered herself a communal outsider. She explained that "on account of her speaking against the measures of the Americans, she found it necessary for her safety to fly from Philadelphia in October 1775 leaving a great deal of property behind her." Margaret Locke went a step further: "during the stay of the Royal Army in Philadelphia, your petitioner by her great assiduity and vigilance discovered a spy within the city, who was thereupon secured." Because of her actions, she "exposed herself to the hatred and revenge of the Rebels, thereby her goods were plundered and taken away out of the tender of the Roebuck Man of War, whereby she was deprived of all that she possessed and reduced to great distress."[23]

The state government typically relied on its soldiers to seize the property of people who assisted the British. Andrew Boyd, sub-lieutenant of the Chester County (Revolutionary) militia, reported that his men "took some Tories and their property." Enlisted man William Clark distinctly remembered that he took "traitor Robert's horses and cattle." Toward the end of the British occupation of Philadelphia, George Washington formally authorized local Pennsylvania militiamen to keep all goods taken from those who were known to have

22. AO13/26/335–37, AO12/43/328–31, AO12/100/65, AO13/26/229.
23. See Kerber, *Women of the Republic*, and Mary Beth Norton, *Liberty's Daughters: The Revolutionary Experience of American Women, 1750–1800* (Ithaca, N.Y., 1996), on the developing perception that women were able to make wartime decisions about political allegiances that could affect their ability to remain in communities. AO12/102/80, AO12/102/64, AO12/38/350.

helped the British. Alexander Long stated with pride that he "was one that assisted in taking four wagon load[s] of flour from the enemy being stored in a Tory's mill." Ebenezer Ferguson was "engaged" near Doylestown, Bucks County, "to surprise the Tories and take the provisions." Some women who tried to protect their families' property from such confiscation portrayed the Revolutionary army's behavior as essentially criminal. Margaret Lister, for example, felt that she was "exposed to the rage and rapine of a villainous and incensed soldiery" because of their hatred for her husband. Others witnessed gruesome atrocities. When Richard Swanwick left his Chester County home to serve as a guide for the British army, he entrusted his wife with the care of a chest full of papers and deeds, which she dutifully buried to protect them from the local militia. When the soldiers came to their house, Swanwick's wife kept the secret, but she must have watched in horror as "the militia tortured the memorialist's Negro man into confession."[24]

Rank-and-file Revolutionary troops were also called upon to arrest those suspected of treason. John Hill, a Bucks County soldier, recalled taking "into custody a man named Doan, a pretended Methodist preacher, we seized him while in the pulpit" and lodging him in the jail at Newtown to await trial. Andrew Keen of Philadelphia proudly participated in the capture of "a band of 72 refugees and Tories" from his city. Keen's use of the popular term "refugees" in conjunction with Tories is telling. It was meant to suggest the disenfranchised, uprooted nature of such persons. Interestingly, however, Tories often used the term in reference to themselves, implying that they were victims of intolerance, unjustly turned out of their homes. In either formulation, the Revolutionary militia typically took responsibility for turning persons into refugees.[25]

As long as the British army was able to protect them, many Pennsylvania "Tories" responded in kind. They, too, defined their internal European American enemies as common lawbreakers, traitors, oppressors, and plunderers, and they reacted by confiscating the property of active Whigs and threatening them with imprisonment. Many simply inverted the Revolutionary formula for community by casting themselves as solid citizens and attempting to marginalize the rebels. The British army reinforced such a worldview, often employing

---

24. Andrew Boyd to President Wharton, October 20, 1777, PRG, reel 12, frame 1311; RWPF, file S3160; George Washington to Brigadier General John Lacey, Jr., February 18, 1778, in *The Writings of George Washington*, ed. Fitzpatrick, 10:478; RWPF, files S22365, S22237; AO13/71/156, AO12/42/29.

25. RWPF, files W5298, S22343.

their loyalist forces in raiding activities and authorizing them to confiscate goods of known rebels to supply the forces of the Crown. Thus, Tories took their revenge upon those who had taken their property. John Johnson, a Philadelphia coach maker who had been persecuted and suffered "confinement" for suspicion of harboring anti-Revolutionary sentiments, served under Galloway during the occupation confiscating the arms of rebels, whom he called "disaffected persons." Anthony Yeldall was employed in the loyalist police to "discover the disaffected inhabitants and take from them all military stores." In another case, a group of loyalists appeared to confiscate, purposefully, only contraband rather than personal property, intending to make their side appear less draconian than the rebels. While hauling supplies to the Continental army on the Philadelphia Road in 1782, Thomas Bedwell was stopped by a group of Tories who declared that they "wanted nothing but public property and would return all private property" despite the fact that "the owners were damned rebels."[26]

Other loyalists sought to capture prominent Whigs. Like their Revolutionary opponents, they saw their military role as a policing one that facilitated justice for traitors. In 1778, a group of loyalists sortied out of Philadelphia "in order to assist some of their friends who had expressed a desire of taking refuge here, to avoid the horrid tyranny and implacable persecution of the rebels." Along the way, they captured a member of a Revolutionary committee and reported with satisfaction that he was "in confinement." In the same year, the loyalist Philadelphia Light Dragoons and Bucks County Volunteers reported that they arrested "a number of militia officers, justices of the peace, and collectors of fines, under the new state and some other disaffected persons," and a Pennsylvania Tory newspaper noted that "William Hamet, an intrepid young man, who had suffered much by the rebel plunderers, and desirous of serving his country by securing its enemies, hearing that there were two rebel officers at Benjamin Vanleer's in Jersey, passed over the Delaware with a design to take them." As suggested in the account of Hamet, when loyalists controlled the press in Philadelphia, their stories of rebel actions and Tory counteractions respectively emphasized crime and punishment. Revolutionaries' confiscations of Tory and neutral goods that were bound for trade in occupied Philadelphia were consistently characterized as simple theft. The *Pennsylvania*

---

26. North Callahan, *Royal Raiders: The Tories of the American Revolution* (New York, 1963), 160–62, discusses the employment of Pennsylvania Tories by the British in raiding and foraging. AO12/42/57–62, AO12/42/45–46; Examination of Thomas Bedwell, July 28, 1782, PRG, reel 19, frame 907.

Evening Post reported in 1778 that "a rebel lighthorseman, loaded with several wallets across his shoulders, and a large basket on his arm full of market truck, of which he had robbed the country people coming to market, was brought in, having been taken a few miles from the lines, at the very time he was plundering." That same year, Pennsylvania loyalists surprised a detachment of Continental troops at a Bucks County mill who were "guarding a considerable quantity of cloth belonging to the poor people of the country, of which they had been robbed by orders from the rebel head-quarters." Thus, rebel soldiers were generalized as lawless oppressors of "the poor people of the country."[27]

Because the British largely chose to treat the enemy as honorable combatants, Tory portrayals of Revolutionary soldiers' criminality were difficult to sell to civilians who often saw the war as one between contending armies. Nevertheless, active Tories did attempt to convince neutrals to accept their version of community during the British occupation. Tories carefully portrayed the rebellion as carried out by a small faction of self-interested leaders who manipulated the masses and mercilessly suppressed all dissent. Loyalist Daniel Batewell simply called them "factious leaders." It was these power-hungry men, who were previously outsiders, Tories argued, who led the community astray by coercion and who would stop at nothing to advance their standing at the expense of an orderly, just society. This formulation suggested that rank-and-file Revolutionaries were not to blame for what had transpired and that they might reenter proper provincial society. The *Post* mourned the tragedy of decent people dying for the rebel cause, lambasting leaders who were "sending into eternity so great a number of souls, to gratify their thirst after wealth and power." Artfully, the essay also suggested that "Tories" or evaders of militia service would not profit off the war at the expense of ordinary people: rather, prominent Revolutionaries would. The result, according to loyalists, was Revolutionary "tyranny" in which the people were burdened unnecessarily by bloodshed, heavy taxes, and levies on their property simply to empower a new group of social leaders. Symbolic absolution from this "tyrannical" regime was offered in the form of Sir William Howe's offer of amnesty for those who pledged allegiance to Britain. Between September 30, 1777, and June 17, 1778, nearly 4,500 persons took the oath, including close to 2,000 rebel soldiers. While many probably took the oath out of expediency in order to protect their families

---

27. *Pennsylvania Evening Post*, February 3, 1778; February 17, 1778; March 18, 1778; April 24, 1778; February 19, 1778.

and property, others had come to feel that Revolutionary communities were truly oppressive.[28]

William Rankin, for example, was a moderate Whig from York County who served in the Revolutionary military. By the time of the British occupation, he had become so alienated from the radical regime that he secretly began to recruit a loyalist association. Rankin noted that the numerous members rejected being "obliged to submit to the tyranny of their rulers, the payment of heavy taxes, and ultimately to remain under a government truly oppressive and which they abhor." Ironically, American anti-tax ideology was a rich source for Tory propaganda. Loyalists argued that the taxes demanded by the Revolutionaries were far more ruinous and unjust than those required under the empire. In an essay in the *Royal Gazette* focusing on taxes in Pennsylvania, a Tory argued that "had Great Britain demanded one thirteenth part" of the current state tax burden, "the meanest Plebeian upon it would have been taught to exclaim, that they were an oppressed, abused and undone people." These were powerful messages criticizing the supposed selfish and shortsighted nature of the Revolutionaries who oppressed ordinary people.[29]

As both Tories and Whigs came to abhor each other as criminal elements within their communities, not surprisingly, combat between them was often extremely violent and revealed intense resentment on both sides. For many, victories over neighbors whom they saw as betrayers of their community were their most salient memories of the war. James Fulton of Chester County suggested that intimidation and fear were important weapons in civil war. When rumors that "the Tories intended to rise and burn" Philadelphia were circulating in late 1776, he recalled, he was part of a party sent "for the purpose of overawing the malcontents." Similarly, George Simmers, a Lancaster militiaman, also implied the use of unconventional warfare as a means of dealing with domestic enemies when he explained how he was engaged in "keeping down the Tories." The methods used to suppress the Tories were brutal at times. A loyalist newspaper reported in early 1778 that the Whig militia dealt severely with those suspected of abetting the British. Militiamen under General John Lacey were purported to be guilty of "inhuman violence" and "republican persecution." The report stated that "David Coombs, being accused of having

28. AO13/72/339; *Pennsylvania Evening Post*, February 12, 1778; *Royal Gazette*, January 24, 1781; Howe's proclamation is reprinted in *Major Andre's Journal*, 38–39. Ousterhout found in *A State Divided* that 4,347 people took the oath of allegiance to the British and that 1,289 were "soldiers" and 603 were militiamen (170).

29. AO12/42/205–6; *Royal Gazette*, October 23, 1779.

brought provisions to the Philadelphia market, the valiant captain Young, of Cumberland, drew his sword and run it through the body of the poor unarmed man." Also, "John McKenny was arrested for the same offence; having tied a rope about his neck, and his hands behind him, they dragged him after a horse in full gallop, until the unhappy man was to all appearance dead." The account suggested to neutrals and Tories that the Revolutionaries engaged in terror campaigns of violence. Indeed, it appeared that Lacey and his men were extremely frustrated with local residents, whom they deeply distrusted. Lacey justified his police actions by explaining to General Washington that "every kind of villainy is carried on by the people near the enemy's lines; and from their general conduct I am induced to believe but few real friends to America are left within ten miles of Philadelphia."[30]

As hostility between Pennsylvanians mounted late in the British occupation, it is clear from a report in the Tory *Pennsylvania Evening Post* that both Hovenden's Pennsylvania Loyalists and the Chester County Dragoons were at least present during the British army's surprise attack on Lacey's troops at Crooked Billet on May 1, 1778. Although the *Post* only reported that several wagons belonging to the rebels and approximately fifty prisoners were taken, the Revolutionaries recorded that the enemy committed atrocities against the militia, burning prisoners alive. The *Pennsylvania Packet* reported that among those singled out for mistreatment was the Philadelphia schoolmaster and ardent Whig Captain John Downey, whose "body was found with one of his hands almost cut off, his head slashed in several places, his skull cut through, his brains coming out at his nose and scattered all around." Although no Tories openly admitted involvement, given the reputation that Lacey was garnering for his actions in the loyalist press, it would not be surprising if some of the atrocities were motivated by vengeance and deemed necessary for "keeping down the Whigs."[31]

As with the case of growing animosity toward the British regular army, southeastern Pennsylvania was spared some of the worst horrors of a cycle of retributive violence by the withdrawal of royal forces in June 1778. When the new British commander, Sir Henry Clinton, decided to evacuate the city, he took his formally constituted loyalist units with the main army. Thousands of other "Tories" who feared Revolutionary reprisals left with the army as well.

30. RWPF, files W5298, S22779, S22511; *Pennsylvania Evening Post*, February 26, 1778; Lacey quoted in Ousterhout, *A State Divided*, 170.
31. *Pennsylvania Evening Post*, May 1, 1778; *Pennsylvania Packet*, May 20, 1778.

Many of them had assisted or engaged in trade with the Crown's forces. Those who held prominent loyalist civil posts under the British were also apt to leave. In a sweeping movement, literally thousands of Pennsylvanians alienated by the Revolution left their communities, usually for good. Those who remained or who would return did so with the hope of attaining "forgiveness" for their past actions from the Revolutionaries, who were now firmly again in control of state and local governments. The brevity of the British occupation, coupled with the significant number of Americans who left with the redcoats, served to dampen the violence and vehemence of civil war, at least in the southeast and south-central parts of the state. And with the British gone, the atmosphere of emergency dissipated. Some Whigs were again willing to at least consider reintegration of the "disaffected" who publicly renounced their former actions and adhered to Revolutionary laws.[32]

Civil War on the Frontier

Pennsylvanians who lived on the frontier were not quite so fortunate in regard to internecine violence. Civil war transpired in the region throughout the war. As in the rest of the state, European American adversaries in the region marginalized their counterparts by declaring and treating them as traitors and civil criminals. Additionally, control over lands by rival groups was also at issue. In the Wyoming Valley, conflicting Pennsylvania and Connecticut claimants used the discourse of criminality to describe each other. As Connecticut created a dominant local government under the rubric of "Westmoreland County," its citizens attempted to marginalize rival Pennsylvanians as traitors to the Revolution (and potentially to confiscate their lands). Adonijah Stanburrough, a well-known Pennamite, and others were sternly summoned to appear before the Westmoreland (Connecticut) Committee of Inspection. They were "suspected of Toryism, and subverting the Constitution, and endeavoring to betray the inhabitants of this town [Westmoreland] into the hands of the enemy." Connecticut authorities in the region skillfully presented their local cause as that of the nation. As they requested military assistance from Congress "as a means of preventing any insults or hostilities from the Indians or tories," they suggested that such matters were "for the good of the Continent in general."

32. On the loyalist withdrawal, see Siebert, *Loyalists of Pennsylvania*, 54.

Pennsylvanians responded by suggesting that the Yankees were the true criminals. Stephen Chambers, a Pennsylvania officer from Northumberland County, called the Connecticut claimants "lawless banditti who are not possessed of either honor or truth."[33]

The Pennamites and Yankees continued the war between them that had already broken out before 1777. Each side sought to destroy the other's ability to continue living and farming in the region. Pennsylvania claimants who became "loyalists" recounted their flight to join Colonel John Butler's Rangers and Indian allies as necessary, due to what they portrayed as lawless Connecticut attacks on their property. William Pickard joined Butler during the "great dispute between Pennsylvania and Connecticut" because "his house and barn were burnt by the rebels." William Vanderlip's family had their land "under Pennsylvania" and "the rebels took the stock, burnt the other things." As a result, William and his father left together to join the loyalist rangers to strike their Yankee enemies' settlements, which they soon did. Butler's troops who were "to act in concert with the Indians" were likewise characterized by Revolutionaries as criminal. The *Pennsylvania Gazette* reported that "strolling parties of Indians and Tories, about 30 and under in a company, made frequent incursions into the settlement, robbing and plundering the inhabitants, of provision, grain and live stock."[34]

During this war over land and resources, appellations of "Whig" and "Tory" were arbitrary and deeply contested. Articles of capitulation at the Battle of Wyoming revealed that Pennsylvanians who fought with Indians against the Connecticut communities believed the "Tory" label to be misleading. They stipulated that "the properties taken from the people called *Torris* [*sic*] up the River be made good." These European Americans openly suggested that the taint of treason was the construction of the Yankees. Sometimes, even those identified as Whigs were leery of taking on the name, as they felt that it might misrepresent their beliefs. In the frontier part of Cumberland County, well south and west of the disputed Wyoming Valley, militiamen refused to join the main American army in the East because they feared that "our women and children will fall a sacrifice to savage cruel barbarity as there was of late a number

33. Committee of Inspection to Adonijah Stanburrough and Others, January 1, 1777, *Susquehannah Company Papers,* ed. Taylor, 7:33; Officials of Westmoreland to Connecticut Delegates in the Continental Congress, August 6, 1776, ibid., 7:20; Stephen Chambers to Edward Hand, June 13, 1779, Hand Papers, 1:98, HSP.

34. AO12/40/319, AO12/40/424; Lieutenant Colonel John Butler to Governor Sir Guy Carleton, June 14, 1777, *Documents of the American Revolution,* ed. Davies, 14:116; *Pennsylvania Gazette,* July 30, 1778.

of wicked Tories joined in a combination and wont to conduct the Indians down to murder the Whigs (as they call us)." Taken in tandem, these two telling moments suggest that, more than loyalty to Britain or adherence to an independent United States, local disputes fueled civil war.[35]

Whenever European Americans fought alongside anti-Revolutionary Indians, however, the issue of race came to the fore. The image of "white savagery" was typically invoked to describe Tories in the region. Such discourse suggested that though these European Americans had turned their backs on their cultural background and allied with Indians, they retained the fundamental prerequisite for inclusion in the Revolutionary community: whiteness. The *Pennsylvania Gazette,* for example, reported on the capture of a young woman by "three Indians and twenty-seven white savages." While one could betray "civilization" and become a "savage," racial status was imagined as intrinsic. Portrayals of frontier Tories were particularly harsh, as they implied that loyalists, unlike "the Indians," were acting on inclination rather than "nature." Characterizations of loyalists as "savages" recurred in Revolutionary accounts of frontier raids. James Dunlop of Cumberland County reported that a number of local Tories "left their habitations and [are] supposed to be joined to the savages." In 1778, the *Pennsylvania Packet* reported that word had arrived from Carlisle that "33 Tories lately formed the horrid design of joining the savages in murdering and scalping their neighbors." Later that year, the paper reported the New York capture of the Tory John Snow, "one of those who had transformed themselves into savages." John Piper of Bedford County characterized Tories in the region as "still more savage" than the Indians. The marker of this greater "savagery" appeared to be their whiteness. According to the Revolutionaries, "Tories," who were subject to all the benefits of American white identity, committed the most monstrous sort of treason: a betrayal of the racial community. With such imagery in mind, the metaphorical use of patricide and fratricide employed in accounts of the Tory and Indian attack on Wyoming is comprehensible. In addition to the horrifying tale of intra-familial violence supposedly perpetrated by "Partial Terry," a report told of "Thomas Hill (whose father was killed by the Indians [in the] last Indian War) with his own hands killed his own mother, his father-in-law, his sisters, and their families." While most of the combatants held rival land claims and had

---

35. Deposition of James Atherton and Son, PRG, reel 12, frame 383; articles of surrender are quoted in Graymont, *Iroquois in the American Revolution,* 171; Petition of Cumberland County Residents, Path Valley, May 18, 1778, PRG, reel 14, frame 47.

no kin ties, the emphasis on savage sons who killed their families indicated anxiety over racial disunion.[36]

Despite and perhaps partly because of these concerns, the ideology of biological race retained its immutable quality in the frontier civil war. One remained "white" no matter how terribly one betrayed "white" society. For all the angry rhetoric, frontier Revolutionaries treated their Tory enemies who fought with Indians as European American civil criminals. Whig militias typically captured and imprisoned frontier Tories who then awaited trial. Abner Mundell and his comrades "caught upwards of 100 Tories and lodged them in the jails." Richard Gunsalus "arrested two of the Tories who w[ere] engaged with the Indians in committing aggressions[?] on the Americans." John Allen suggested that different tactics were necessary when fighting white and non-white enemies, noting that he was "endeavoring to capture Tories and defend the frontier from Indian depredations." Implicitly, capture and imprisonment awaited loyalists, while no such niceties were reserved for "the Indians." This practice essentially metamorphosed into Whig policy. On Sullivan's expedition into Iroquois country, the capture of Tories starkly contrasted with the slaughter of Indians. One observer wrote of a battle in which "eight of their [Indians'] scalps were taken on the spot" and the "two prisoners" captured were "one white man and one negro." The African American was possibly either a runaway slave or a chattel of the Tories who had pecuniary value. Nonetheless, execution for treason remained a threat for such captives. Some militiamen even took the law into their own hands. William Dougherty "took a number of Tories and handcuffed them and confined them. . . . When one White and Isaac Boser[?] were hanged by our party, this declarant cut them down before they were dead and saved their lives." Lynching, although brutal, was not practiced on Indians. That Dougherty's comrades took the time to hang their captives suggests that, rather than kill the Tories on the spot, they performed European vigilante customs to indicate their victims' criminality.[37]

This treatment of frontier Tories as criminals evinces the extent to which a biological view of race was becoming ingrained in the mentalities of common Pennsylvanians. Whites, in the eyes of Revolutionaries, could never lose their

---

36. *Pennsylvania Gazette,* May 19, 1779; James Dunlop to Jonathan Hoge, June 22, 1778, PRG, reel 14, frame 309; *Pennsylvania Packet,* May 6, 1778, and August 13, 1778; Lieutenant John Piper to President Wharton, May 4, 1778, PRG, reel 13, frame 1287; *Pennsylvania Evening Post,* August 18, 1778, 297, and July 30, 1778, 264.

37. RWPF, files S22395, S23246, S22622, S23246; "Extract of a Letter from Sullivan's Expedition," *Pennsylvania Packet,* September 7, 1779; RWPF, file W4182.

inherent whiteness, even if they fought alongside (and like) hostile Indians. They therefore always had recourse to civil law and, by implication, redemption in the community by enduring their punishment. Whigs captured, imprisoned, and tried Tories instead of preemptively slaughtering them. In the worst cases, they lynched them rather than scalping or mutilating them. Conversely, Indians were never seen as deserving treatment given to whites, even if they acted, dressed, lived, and worshiped like Europeans. The Pennsylvania government recognized the pervasiveness of this view and crafted policies accordingly. In 1780, when the state proclaimed a scalp bounty for Indians, it promised "1500 dollars for every Indian or Tory found in arms against us and 1000 dollars for every Indian scalp." There was no provision for Tory scalps. Such treatment also affected the way in which Tories treated their Whig enemies in the region. They, too, treated whites as criminals. For instance, when a group of Bedford County Tories enjoined Richard Weston to become part of their force, they informed him that "if he refused to join said company he would be hung or banished."[38]

Slavery, Freedom, and Race in the Pennsylvania Civil War

In conjunction with the consolidation of racial ideology on the frontier, reactions to slave resistance in Pennsylvania's civil war cemented a Revolutionary American identity based on white supremacy. As is well known, the Commonwealth passed the first gradual emancipation law in the United States in 1780. The traditional explanation for Pennsylvania's leading the way toward abolition in the North was the quiet influence of antislavery Quakers coupled with the logic of natural rights ideology that fueled the American Revolution. Given the status of most Friends within Revolutionary communities during the war, however, it is difficult to believe that their arguments would seem particularly persuasive to the radical government. Furthermore, most Whigs agreed that "natural rights" only applied to white males, the de facto biological prerequisite for citizenship and liability to militia service and test oaths. Behind the shift in attitudes toward chattel bondage was a fear of servile insurrection, a defense of economic interests, and, most important, a desire to preserve the system of racial hierarchy. The slave population in Pennsylvania was large enough to be potentially devastating in the event of rebellion, yet not

---

38. President Joseph Reed to Lieutenant Peter Kachlein, April 11, 1780, PRG, reel 15, frames 1139–40; Examination of Richard Weston, Bedford County, May 22, 1778, PRG, reel 14, frame 93.

absolutely vital to the economy; thus, the eventual emancipation of persons deemed inferior seemed a plausible move.[39]

Even before the war began, white Pennsylvanians were acutely concerned about the possibility that conflict with Britain might lead to a slave uprising. In 1774, a rumor spread through the province that British officials were pondering emancipating slaves and servants in exchange for help in quelling any colonial rebellion. (The rumor was also making the rounds among apprehensive Virginians.) Anxiety increased upon the commencement of hostilities in 1775 and exploded after Dunmore's proclamation. Indeed, it was soon clear that Pennsylvania slaves were thinking that the Virginia governor's policy was the beginning of emancipation through military action. Mark Bird, a Berks County master seeking the return of his "Negroe Man, commonly called CUFF DIX," explained, "as Negroes in general think that Lord Dunmore is contending for their liberty, it is not improbable that said Negroe is on his march to join his Lordship's own black regiment." Given these actions, white Pennsylvanians feared that Dunmore's force might make a foray into their communities and incite slave revolt. Additionally threatening to Pennsylvanians was the fact that Dunmore's force was multiracial, composed of white and black Tories. Quietly lurking behind the Whig anxiety was a concern about racial hierarchy in general.[40]

These issues were clearly expressed in a 1775 *Pennsylvania Evening Post* report that recounted how "a gentlewoman, going along Second Street [in Philadelphia], was insulted by a Negro near Christ Church. And upon her reprimanding him for his rude behavior, the fellow replied, 'stay you d——d white bitch, till Lord Dunmore and his black regiment come and then we will see who is to take the wall.'" This anecdote was publicized for good reasons. It was primarily meant to mobilize the population behind the Revolutionary cause. It suggested that both British policy and African American expectations were an immediate threat to social stability. The aggressive "Negro" did not defer to the class status of the "gentlewoman." Nor did he recognize white supremacy, although he did explicitly call the woman "white." Readers would also find the image of a black man menacing a white woman particularly disturbing. It

---

39. For a historiographical discussion of older scholarship that attributes the gradual emancipation law in Pennsylvania to Quaker activism and natural rights ideology, see Nash and Soderlund, *Freedom by Degrees*, xiv–xv and 74–98. I build upon Nash and Soderlund's argument that the actions of slave runaways, economics, and antislavery activism all contributed to the law.

40. See ibid., 77, and Holton, *Forced Founders*, 140, on the prewar rumors of the British emancipation of slaves; *Pennsylvania Gazette*, July 17, 1776.

suggested that white womanhood would be vulnerable to enraged and empowered black men. Significantly, the account did not specify whether the man was free or a slave. It only duly noted his racial status. The actual incident may or may not have ever occurred. Given African Americans' actions in striving for their freedom through British military service, such an encounter may well have happened. The incident's propaganda utility, however, makes it equally plausible that the confrontation was embellished or perhaps invented. In any case, its dissemination would have sent the same message to Pennsylvania blacks and whites: the war destabilized racial hierarchy, and whites were outraged.[41]

The threat that the British army's policies of expediency posed to white privilege continued to be a significant motif in Whig accounts of the war. With Howe's army in Philadelphia in October 1777, the *Pennsylvania Packet* recorded the treatment of captured American mariners from the frigate *Delaware,* highlighting the supposed height of British barbarism as "a certain Captain Hogshaw not only refused to punish a negro for striking one of our officers, but in direct words said that the negro was as good as any of us." It was of course bad enough that the British employed an African American against the Revolutionaries, but the implication of racial egalitarianism enforced by military power was meant to chill Pennsylvanians. Again, whether the *Delaware* incident actually happened is immaterial. More significant is the narrative's message to readers. When the British resorted to arming slaves, they threatened far more than the institution of chattel bondage.[42]

During the British occupation of Philadelphia in 1777–78, the many Pennsylvania slaves who ran to the royal forces further destabilized white supremacy in the state. George Bryan, later one of the prime forces behind the 1780 gradual emancipation law, commented that "by the invasion of this state, and the possession the enemy gained of this city, and neighborhood, [a] great part of the slaves hereabouts were enticed away by the British army." Gary Nash and Jean Soderlund estimate that at least one hundred slaves from the Philadelphia area attained freedom by running to the British army during the occupation. They also found that the slave runaway rate increased between 1776 and 1780 to one out of every twenty-six slaves in the state per year. Most probably sought their freedom by entering British service. Quite simply, white Pennsylvanians experienced their first significant slave insurrection. That so many free blacks also cast their lot by assisting the Crown's forces suggests, not

41. *Pennsylvania Evening Post,* December 14, 1775, 576.
42. *Pennsylvania Packet,* October 16, 1777.

surprisingly, that African Americans in general took their chances with the hierarchical yet (of necessity) racially inclusive military coalition rather than remain in Revolutionary communities that shared an increasing commitment to a white male basis for citizenship. Despite Sir William Howe's lack of an organized emancipation policy, the presence of the British Black Guides and Pioneers Regiment, consisting of escaped Virginia slaves and officered by Scots, provided a symbol for the liberating possibilities of maintaining one's attachment to the empire.[43]

Indeed, this insurrection in the state extended beyond those slaves who joined the British. Those who remained in Revolutionary communities also expressed their anger and desire for freedom. In Bucks County in 1776, for example, a portion of the local militia did not want to march out of the community because they feared that a slave, Sampson, would make good on his threat to "burn the houses and kill the women and children of the Associators when they marched out." Sampson specifically targeted the Revolutionaries, and the fear of his threats was enough to prevent an entire militia unit from turning out to fight the British. Clearly, the image of slaves rising up during the disorders of war and menacing white women and children was potent—and the soldiers felt that their first duty was imposing civil order and enforcing the racial and class hierarchy at home.[44]

In the wake of these conflicts, Pennsylvanians took up a debate on whether to pass a gradual emancipation bill. How could people who were so acutely concerned about slave insurrection suddenly become willing to consider an end to the institution of perpetual bondage? Many Pennsylvanians were well aware of the reality of their situation. The state's slave population was large enough to present a very real threat of servile rebellion. In 1780, there were almost seven thousand slaves in the Commonwealth. On the other hand, slavery's profitability (vis-à-vis free labor) was decreasing in the region, and the slave population, only about 2 percent of the state's total, was small enough that gradual emancipation was feasible with minimal economic impact. Thus, the wartime actions of slaves themselves in terms of joining the British or (less frequently) the Revolutionaries, simply running away, or even threatening white families of soldiers created an atmosphere of discomfort with the institution of

---

43. George Bryan, quoted in *Race and Revolution*, by Gary B. Nash (Madison, Wis., 1990), 60. See Nash and Soderlund, *Freedom by Degrees*, 95, on the runaway rate, the slaves who joined the British during the occupation of Philadelphia, and the composition of the Black Pioneers.

44. Minutes of the Committee of Safety, Bucks County, July 29, 1776, *PA*, 2d ser., 15:365–68.

perpetual bondage in which immediate discussions about its future took place. In 1778, after the British departed from Philadelphia, the state's Supreme Executive Council—with George Bryan as its president—pressed for the consideration of an abolition bill. The Council argued that the massive flight of slaves seeking freedom with the enemy had already made gradual emancipation more practical, noting that "no period seems more happy for the attempt than the present as the number of [slaves] . . . has been much reduced by the practices and plunder of our late invaders."[45]

Moreover, even with the British departure from the state in 1778, the destabilizing effects of British military policy utilizing emancipated slaves became painfully visible by 1780 in other nearby states. In 1779, Sir Henry Clinton, the new British commander-in-chief, issued a proclamation similar to Dunmore's, offering freedom to slaves of rebel masters willing to assist the British. The *New Jersey Journal* ridiculed the proclamation in verse:

> A proclamation oft of late he sends
> To thieves and rogues, who only are his friends;
> Those he invites; all colours he attacks
> But deference pays to Ethiopian blacks

In the now familiar Northern motif, critics did not simply condemn the British practice of freeing slaves; they also underscored the ill effects in terms of showing "deference" to blacks. This was, from a Revolutionary perspective, a perverse inversion of the social order. Insurrection continued as well. In June 1780, the *Pennsylvania Gazette* reported that in neighboring New Jersey, "Ty, with his party of about 20 blacks and whites, last Friday afternoon took and carried off prisoners, Capt. Barns Smock and Gilbert Vanmater; at the same time spiked up the iron four pounder at Capt. Smock's house, but took no ammunition: Two of the artillery horses, and two of Capt. Smock's horses, were likewise taken off. The above mentioned Ty is a Negroe, who bears the title of Colonel, and commands a motley crew at Sandy Hook." Yet again, the fearful image of slave insurrection was compounded by a threat to the racial hierarchy in which an African American was purportedly granted an officer's commission to preside over the plunder of white Whigs. The British military presence in New

---

45. See Nash and Soderlund, *Freedom by Degrees*, 7 and 83, on the slave population in Pennsylvania in 1780 and the "declining utility of slaves" during the war; see 101 for the quotation from the Supreme Executive Council.

York and New Jersey, too, still provided possible protection and freedom for runaway Pennsylvania slaves until the end of the war.[46]

As the war shifted to the South, slavery clearly proved a major military liability to Revolutionaries in that region. Thousands of slaves were either confiscated or freed in exchange for service to the British army during its occupation of Georgia. In South Carolina, with its black majority population, roughly one out of every four slaves sought freedom by going to royal lines. John Laurens's 1779 plan to arm South Carolina slaves and free them in return for Revolutionary military service was received in that state's legislature "with horror by the planters," and the body discussed instead a proposal to send a flag to the British offering to withdraw the state from the war. Slavery's role in the war was not only destabilizing society but also threatening the alliance of the thirteen states against the British. Pennsylvanians took up the debate about the future of chattel bondage in their state within this larger American context of crisis.[47]

During this exchange, the most vocal proponents of emancipation pointed to the ideological inconsistency of slavery with the new republic's principles of liberty. Their language, however, was steeped in paternalistic humanitarianism and sensibility. In 1778, the Supreme Executive Council presented a draft of a bill for emancipation that argued for gradual emancipation and expressed a condescending view of African Americans: "it is not proposed that the present slaves, most of whom are scarcely competent of freedom, should be meddled with, but all importation must be forbid[den], if the idea be adopted." Another draft of the emancipation bill offered by the assembly to the public in 1779 asserted, "we are enabled this day to add one more step to universal civilization, by removing as much as possible the sorrows of those, who have lived in undeserved bondage." The language of the bill suggests that whites could demonstrate enlightenment and pity by ending slavery. Significantly, however, it makes no reference to political and civil rights for African Americans beyond freedom from thralldom.[48]

46. See Quarles, *Negro in the American Revolution*, 113–14, on Clinton's 1779 "Philipsburg Proclamation" (the *New Jersey Journal* sonnet is quoted on 114); *Pennsylvania Gazette*, June 21, 1780.

47. See Frey, *Water from the Rock*, 81–142, on the number of slaves who ran to the British in South Carolina and Georgia. On the reception of Laurens's plan by the South Carolina legislature, see Quarles, *Negro in the American Revolution*, 62–64; see 63 for the "horror" quotation from Governor John Rutledge to Laurens. Pennsylvanians had earlier been moved by slave insurrection and disorder in other areas to discuss possible abolition. According to Nash and Soderlund in *Freedom by Degrees*, 41–42, William Southby, a prominent Quaker, circulated a petition for general emancipation in 1712 in the provincial assembly, which was willing to consider it partly because of concern with the recent slave uprising in New York.

48. *Pennsylvania Packet*, November 28, 1778; *Pennsylvania Gazette*, December 29, 1779.

A careful solution was being crafted: a gradual freeing of slaves with no clear statement on what their status would be beyond simply free persons. No one mentioned full citizenship, and in a state where militia service and test oaths were only required of white males, few would assume that free blacks would receive the benefits that went along with such obligations. The abolition of slavery and the question of racial equality were distinct issues, and most whites were not much interested in the latter. Even antislavery Quakers forbade free blacks from joining their meetings in the 1770s and 1780s. Furthermore, some language in drafts of the emancipation bill reified racial categories. One version declared, "it is not for us to enquire, why, in the creation of mankind, the inhabitants of the several parts of the earth, were distinguished by a difference of feature or complexion," demonstrating the extent to which popular racial ideologies were increasingly centered around the concept of skin color. While this draft rejected complexion as a rationale for slavery, it did not specify civil equality among racial groups. Ultimately, the only groups that were vocal about the extension of civil equality to all "races" were the slave and free black communities in Pennsylvania. In 1781, when the legislature considered amending the emancipation law and reenslaving some free blacks, "divers Negroes" petitioned to protect their "common rights of mankind."[49]

Among whites, however, the ideology of paternalistic humanitarianism toward slaves was not sufficient to raise enough support for the gradual emancipation bill to become a law. In 1774, on the eve of war with Britain, Pennsylvania's white antislavery activists engaged in a long public campaign to convince provincial residents of the evils of chattel bondage. This appeal to reason and the supposed natural rights of all people not to be held in perpetual bondage did not result in much public support for the principle—let alone legislative recourse. In the end, it was the slaves' seeking liberation in the tumult of war that made most white Pennsylvanians uneasy enough with the presence of a large slave population to take action. (Enslavement was not the most profitable form of labor in the region in any case.) Also, as white male identity was becoming the cornerstone of American political subjectivity, the idea of an African American threat to racial hierarchy in the form of slave

49. See Nash and Soderlund, *Freedom by Degrees*, 29, on the Friends' ban on African American membership at their meetings during this period. They assert that free black membership in meetings became possible only in the 1790s, "after a long internal conflict over the issue." *Pennsylvania Gazette*, December 29, 1779; Nash, *Forging Freedom*, 3–99, addresses the campaign by the African American community in Pennsylvania for an end to slavery and the acquisition of equal rights (the petition is quoted on 64).

insurrection was particularly disquieting. A charge to the assembly from Supreme Executive Council President Joseph Reed indicates the complexities underlying the supposedly magnanimous impulse for gradual abolition. Reed noted, "our anxiety to perpetuate and extend the blessings of freedom, and enlarge the circle of humanity, induce us to remind you of the bill for emancipating the children born of Negro and Mulatto parents." Reed's use of the term "anxiety" is telling. He was, of course, suggesting that he was "anxious" to see the assembly do "justice" and demonstrate "public virtue." Yet he also embedded an appeal to the subconscious "anxiety" about order and racial hierarchy that white Pennsylvanians had felt since the beginning of the war.[50]

The resulting gradual emancipation law was the first and one of the most restrictive passed in the Northern states. It would only free the children of slaves born after the passage of the law (on March 1, 1780) when they reached the age of twenty-eight. The law, therefore, would not free any slaves until well into the nineteenth century and minimized the economic impact on masters. Complete abolition of slavery did not occur in the state until 1847—and the voting rights of free black men had been formally rescinded in 1842. The law made for an easy and lengthy transition from slave state to white supremacist free state. It also helped deflate the potential for further slave insurrection in the present war or any subsequent ones. Current slaves had the knowledge that if they were patient, their progeny would at least be free of perpetual and heritable bondage. Nonetheless, Pennsylvanians continued to follow closely the threatening actions of nearby former slaves who continued to wage war against the Revolutionaries. In February and June, the *Pennsylvania Gazette* reported on two raids carried out against Whigs in New Jersey by parties "consisting of blacks and whites." Slaves in the state also continued to run away as they sought to free themselves immediately. In 1781, for example, Jack ran away from his master in Lancaster County. With occupied New York still within reach, even after most hostilities had ceased, the opportunity to gain freedom by offering his services to the British remained an alternative to gradual emancipation.[51]

50. *Pennsylvania Gazette*, September 15, 1779.
51. Consult Nash and Soderlund, *Freedom by Degrees*, 111, regarding the provisions of Pennsylvania's 1780 Gradual Emancipation Law. See Lois Horton, "From Class to Race in Early America: Northern Post-Emancipation Racial Reconstruction," *Journal of the Early Republic* 19 (Winter 1999): 629–49, on the consolidation of racism in the North in the wake of gradual emancipation and the subsequent 1842 Pennsylvania law (as well as other, earlier state laws) forbidding black suffrage. *Pennsylvania Gazette*, February 13, 1782, June 12, 1782, and March 14, 1781.

Aftermath

The course of civil war in Pennsylvania—especially the angst generated by slave insurrection and the violent challenges to racial hierarchy—helped define the American community even more distinctly. The de facto "family" of politically capable persons, i.e., white men, circumscribed other constructions of being a Revolutionary. In other words, white males were assumed patriots until they proved otherwise. Of course, many such people chose to oppose the Revolutionaries for varied reasons, often related to local conflicts, yet their treatment by their enemies was typically the same. They could not be defined, like "Indians" or "blacks," as biological outsiders; their status was carefully delineated in legal terms. Treason laws and the diverse reasons for which certain persons were accused of breaking them further refined the nation of white men by suggesting an array of locally acceptable behaviors. Tories obviously tried to regain the power to define the community by responding in kind, treating their Whig foes as the real traitors and criminals. Although civil penalties were often harsh, including public humiliation, loss of property, imprisonment, and even execution, their implication was clear: those white Americans who violated the law might again return to the community after doing penance. While many "loyalists" fled the United States during and after the war, others attempted to remain in and be reintegrated into their prewar communities. For white men, this was possible if the community deemed that they had paid a price equal to the level of their treason.[52]

Some had so transgressed the notions of community that they were not permitted to return. Joseph Galloway, perhaps the preeminent Tory in Pennsylvania, was denied his request to come home in 1793. In 1783, a group of Philadelphia light horse and militia officers declared their strident sentiments that "such persons as have joined the enemy . . . ought not be suffered to return or remain among us." In Philadelphia that same year, Henry Welling and Christopher Wilson were lucky enough to have their death sentences for joining the British army commuted. City petitioners, however, called for the banishment of the two men because, if they remained, they would be "a great source of uneasiness to the liege citizens who have risked their lives and fortunes in

---

52. See Wallace Brown, *The Good Americans: The Loyalists in the American Revolution* (New York, 1969), 172–80, and Robert M. Calhoon, "The Reintegration of the Loyalists and the Disaffected," in *The American Revolution: Its Character and Limits,* ed. Jack P. Greene (New York, 1987), on the large numbers of Tories who returned or attempted to return to their prewar American communities.

defense of their dear rights and liberties." Worse, those who took up arms with Indians to fight against the Revolutionaries faced a long road as they tried to convince their neighbors that they would be fit for inclusion in the community. A few continued to live among Indians rather than leave the region or seek to return home. Simon Girty, for example, continued to assist Ohioan Indians as they resisted the expansion of the United States well into the 1790s. Over time, however, the hostility toward European American enemies of the Revolutionaries began to abate. Despite calls for lifetime exile, numbers of Pennsylvania loyalists and disaffected persons resumed life at home as public men.[53]

Many Tories who did return to their prewar communities faced varying receptions that correlated to how serious the nature of their betrayal seemed. Returning loyalists commonly faced continued intimidation from former neighbors. Mob actions resulting in beatings and public humiliation were typical as well. Localist animosity toward "Tories" did temper over time, however. Many nationalist elites called for reconciliation for the sake of a new and stronger United States. Ordinary people meted out their punishments to people they believed had betrayed them and, when they felt that former Tories had fully paid the price, they eventually tolerated the reintegration of Tories into the community. Many loyalists never fully recovered their lost property or estates, but, significantly, they were again allowed to enjoy the benefits of citizenship. With the exigencies of war over, some conservatives sought the abolition of the test laws requiring oaths of allegiance from all white men to the radical Pennsylvania Constitution. In 1786, the test acts were revised to allow all who had not done so during the Revolution "another opportunity" to regain citizenship by declaring allegiance to the state if they had not joined or directly assisted the enemy during the war. By 1789, an oath of allegiance was no longer required; it was recognized that some valuable members of the community who were previously seen as Tories could not abjure allegiance to the king. This paved the way for white men who had resisted the Revolutionaries to return to Pennsylvania as citizens regardless of their wartime views.[54]

53. See Wallace Brown, *Good Americans*, 180, on the rejection of Galloway's request for permission to return to Pennsylvania. *Pennsylvania Evening Post*, May 30, 1783; Petition of Philadelphia Inhabitants, February 19, 1783, prg, reel 20, frame 167. On Girty, see Boatner, *Encyclopedia of the American Revolution*, 435.
54. Robert M. Calhoon, *The Loyalists in Revolutionary America, 1760–1781* (New York, 1973), 500–501, and Calhoon, "The Reintegration of the Loyalists and the Disaffected," discuss the mob actions against returning Tories to punish them and nationalists' pleas for reconciliation. The quotation from the revised test law is in Brunhouse, *Counter-Revolution in Pennsylvania*, 181; see also 180–81 and 197–98.

The contrasting treatment of "nonwhite" Americans in Pennsylvania following the war further underscored how prominently the white male localist nation had emerged from the disorders of armed conflict. While European American Tories might throw themselves either successfully or unsuccessfully upon the mercies of justice and the opinions of their former foes, Indians and African Americans were treated quite differently. With no perceived innate biological qualification for citizenship, they remained outsiders in imagined communities of European Americans. In fact, a pervasive pan–European American "white" identity was constructed by ordinary Revolutionaries in no small part by using "the Indians" as a negative racial reference point, making the latter group unfit by definition for inclusion in their communities. Indian groups, for the most part, had no desire to be incorporated into the new republic's body politic; their desire to protect their independence was viewed as a continued obstacle to "settlement" by most Pennsylvanians. State authorities cynically attempted to invoke the romanticized image of benign Indian-white relations under William Penn by purporting to treat Indians "fairly." They essentially regarded the region's Native inhabitants, however, as conquered people—a result of the authorities' understanding of the Treaty of Paris that ended the war in 1783. Incursions upon Indian lands and consequent armed conflict continued in the greater Pennsylvania frontier into the 1790s.[55]

For African Americans in Pennsylvania—most of whom *did* want full equality and rights as citizens of the United States—the emerging white male national identity boded ill. Ironically, a returning European American Tory who was allowed back into the community might expect more economic opportunities and social prominence than a free black who fought for the Revolutionaries. In the wake of the war, as the free black population grew in tandem with the decline of slavery, white racism became even more pronounced. The dichotomy of perceived skin color—white versus black—superseded the older one of free person (or temporary servant) versus slave. As was the case on the frontier, cultural convergence among African and European Americans made racial ideology necessary in order to rationalize white privilege. Yet the openly white supremacist society that developed in Pennsylvania by the nineteenth century had its roots in the Revolution. Laws that restricted liability to both the militia and the test laws to white men suggested that free black men

55. Daniel K. Richter explains Pennsylvanians' treatment of Indians and Native perceptions following the Revolution in "Onas and the Long Knife: Pennsylvanians and Indians, 1783–1794," in *Native Americans and the Early Republic,* ed. Hoxie, Hoffman, and Albert, 125–61.

were less than full citizens even if they owned significant amounts of property. While Pennsylvanians carefully dismantled slavery, they took no strong measures to ensure full civil, economic, and legal equality. At the very close of the war, Carl Baurmeister (a German fighting for the British) made an entry into his journal that demonstrated the views of many ordinary white Pennsylvanians at the time. In October 1783, he recounted an incident in which a free black family bought two recent Irish immigrants as servants. According to Baurmeister, "this occurrence was very provoking to the old Irish settlers. They threatened to kill the bold negro if he did not immediately free the two Irishmen upon having the purchase price refunded to him and if the governor did not immediately proclaim a law that a freed slave could never hold slaves. The incident stirred Philadelphia for two days." Obviously, the Irish Philadelphians felt that white indentured servitude to even a wealthy free black was demeaning and "unnatural." They asserted that race should trump class and thereby claimed the privileges of whiteness that they hoped the war had secured.[56]

As a whole, the motivations, military identities, and ways in which soldiers treated and viewed various opponents defined the meaning of the Revolution and helped construct an imagined localist white male American nation. With multiple concepts of liberty, manhood, and communities in flux before the conflict, the war forged a new definition of citizenship that at once embraced heterogeneity and competition yet purposefully precluded participation by various outsiders determined through biology or law. Soldiers' contributions to nationhood did not end with the advent of peace, however. Building collective memories of the Revolution would be as vital as the war itself to the genesis of the United States.

---

56. See Nash, *Forging Freedom*, 173–211, on the growth of racism in postwar Philadelphia, especially after about 1800. Carl Leopold Baurmeister, *Revolution in America: Confidential Letters and Journals, 1776–1784, of Adjutant General Major Baurmeister of the Hessian Forces*, trans. and annot. by Bernhard A. Uhlendorf (New Brunswick, N.J., 1957), 593.

7

The Memory of the American Revolution

On July 4, 1814, while the United States was again at war with Great Britain, Nathaniel Britton Boileau had the honor of delivering the Independence Day oration in Montgomery County, Pennsylvania. Boileau, a radical Democratic Republican serving as the state's Secretary of the Commonwealth, devoted most of his speech to rallying patriotic support for the American cause in the War of 1812. Purposefully, Boileau chose to give his address at the site of the Crooked Billet Massacre, where the British had burned captured militiamen during the Revolution. He grew up on the farm where the atrocity occurred, and this memory marked the beginning of his well-known disdain for Britain (which was manifest in his Independence Day speech). As he exhorted the crowd to support the current war, Boileau appealed to Revolutionary veterans to share their experience and motivations with this new generation:

> Ye heroes of the revolution, patriots in the days of trial, although your heads are bleached with years, and the day of vigorous action and exertion be past, your country demands much from you; your experience and your counsel are put in requisition—tell your sons that more than thirty years of experience have taught you, that liberty is an inestimable gem, worth preserving, worth purchasing at the expense of all they have—tell them of the labors, the toils, the dangers, the privations you underwent to procure it—shew them your honorable scars and tell them it was not for yourselves alone that you spent your wealth, your strength and your blood, but to purchase a rich inheritance for them, to whom you commit the invaluable prize for safe-keeping.[1]

While the meaning of the Revolution remained subject to contentious partisan debate, by 1814 certain common elements emerged in the early republic's collective memory of the nation's birth. Boileau's appeal to veterans to share their memories to animate their "sons" was a common enough trope. The former soldiers were portrayed as "hoary headed citizens" who had sacrificed their material well-being and blood for the greater good of the nation. Boileau was also careful to define his terms, noting that "patriotism . . . is the love of our country, a sincere devotion to *its* interests" [emphasis added]. Thus, true patriots were nationalists who put other interests aside for the sake of the United States. Boileau also heavily critiqued the British government for its nineteenth-century policies, connecting them to the "tyranny" against which the colonies had originally rebelled. Not surprisingly, he characterized the War for Independence as a unified struggle against Britain for the establishment and preservation of the new nation. This constructed continuity between the Revolution and the War of 1812 was meant to spur young men to live up to the patriotic deeds of their fathers.[2]

---

1. See Woodward and Craven, *Princetonians*, 335–49, on Boileau's life. Len Travers, *Celebrating the Fourth: Independence Day and the Rites of Nationalism in the Early Republic* (Amherst, Mass., 1997), 24, explains the prominence of oration as the culminating act of celebration on the Fourth of July. "An Oration Delivered by N. B. Boileau on the Fourth of July, 1814," Bucks County Historical Society, Spruance Library, Manuscript 39, Folio 1, 26–27.

2. The most well-known division in interpretations of the Revolution in the early republic was among the supporters and members of the Federalist and Republican parties. Other groups, however, including

At first glance, it appears that Boileau's imagery of the Revolution slighted the localist worldviews that animated former soldiers. Indeed, commemorations of the War for Independence in the early republic were used to help define the nation that fancied itself economically vibrant, increasingly democratic, and united. As a result, the Revolution was remembered as a glorious, selfless, national struggle against Great Britain. So prevalent was this understanding of the past that Peter Keister, who had served as a frontier ranger against "the Indians," felt compelled to state to the court hearing his pension application—or perhaps the court itself interpolated—that "such was the nature of their service that he cannot state any prominent fact which entered into the history of the country." This assertion suggested that his account of the Revolution was superfluous to the "real" narrative of the nation. Veterans' constructions and continuing reconstructions of the localist white male nation, however, were central to the early republic's memory of the Revolution. Upon closer scrutiny, this worldview permeated the politics, society, and memory of the new nation. Peter Keister's account (despite the disclaimer) contained what many people would believe were "prominent facts" in the country's history.[3]

Even Boileau's oration demonstrated the vitality of former soldiers' perspectives on the Revolution to nineteenth-century American identity. Boileau, himself a veteran of the War for Independence, shrewdly made the past relevant to the present. Most obviously, he chose the site of the Crooked Billet action, an atrocity known mostly to Pennsylvanians. In an attempt to garner support for another war against the British, Boileau consciously summoned up past redcoat misdeeds near the audience's homes. In a further appeal to local pride, he made references to specific Pennsylvania militiamen killed in the action, declaring, "I conjure you by the ghosts of the heroes of the revolution, by the ghosts of a Downey, a Pinyard, and Thompson and their comrades, whose bones lie mouldering beneath the clods of yonder valley." He also linked resistance to the War of 1812—and, implicitly, Federalist opposition—with Toryism by equating "our internal enemies in the time of revolution" and "our internal enemies now."

---

marginalized ones (such as white women and free blacks), also used commemorations of the Revolution to remember the war in ways relevant to their present situations. On these points, see Travers, *Celebrating the Fourth,* and especially Simon P. Newman, *Parades and the Politics of the Street: Festive Culture in the Early American Republic* (Philadelphia, 1997). "Hoary headed citizens" quotation from Boileau, "An Oration," 10. See Sarah J. Purcell, "Sealed with Blood: National Identity and Public Memory of the Revolutionary War, 1775–1825" (Ph.D. diss., Brown University, 1997), on the nationalist utilization of a constructed united movement for independence against Britain in the early republic's collective memory of the Revolution.

3. RWPF, file R5819.

Thus, Boileau suggested a continuity of intra-community conflict. He also spoke to racial identity by charging the British with being "insidiously employed in stimulating the savages of the wilderness to harass and murder the defenseless inhabitants of our frontiers." Boileau further buttressed his points by employing an analogy involving African slaves and the treatment of American citizens by the British government. He suggested that both impressed U.S. seamen and slaves were taken from their countries, homes, and families. Boileau argued, however, that "the case of the poor African was enviable compared to that of [the American sailors]." The latter was forced to "raise his arm against his country" or else "suffer the most excruciating tortures." Embedded in this part of the narrative, given that slavery was on the road to extinction in Pennsylvania, was a sentimental deploring of African slavery coupled with the time-honored comparison of submission to British policy to thralldom. The analogy itself reveals a crucial element in the orator's (and the presumably receptive audience's) cosmologies: the African slave was not an "American." Finally, Boileau reaffirmed the male public subject in his statement that white women had an important, albeit subordinate, role in the new nation and its trials. As republican mothers, he implored them to "instill into their souls the principles of virtue, morality and religion.... Teach their infant tongues to lisp the praises of patriots and heroes, and long live the republic."[4]

Ultimately, this speech contained an appeal to American identity and a memory of the Revolution consistent with those of humbler veterans such as Peter Keister. The formal public American nation was white, male, and at once localist and nationalist. Various competing local interests balancing each other out at the national level seemed to be one of the main strands tying diverse Americans together. Additionally, over the course of the late eighteenth and early nineteenth centuries, suffrage was expanded to increasing numbers of white men. The attainment of universal white manhood suffrage by the 1830s, in fact, completed the biological definition of citizenship. This emerging concept was solidified over the course of decades by significant contributions by veterans in terms of their actions and their memories of the past. Politicized by the Revolution, they shaped their recollections to speak to the political and social realities of the postwar period. Former soldiers' memories of the war as one undertaken to defend the local concerns of white males resonated with the dominant culture of the early republic. By the 1810s, 1820s, and 1830s, when the United States paid homage to common Revolutionary veterans with pension

4. Boileau, "An Oration," 31, 30, 10, 11–12, 27–28.

awards, the old soldiers' worldviews persevered, developed, and prevailed. Still, enhanced political roles for white men in the increasingly individualist capitalist republic came at a price.[5]

Postwar Politics and Memory

Immediately after the Revolution, veterans retained a powerful voice in shaping the new nation. One might assume that, given their wartime localism, many former soldiers would oppose the creation of a strong national government and the 1787 constitution. Nevertheless, ordinary veterans (like many other social groups) were divided on the question of a powerful federal union. In Pennsylvania, no trans-regional class alliance emerged in opposition to the constitution. Federalists and anti-Federalists took positions based on complex interstices of perceived class, ethnic, religious, and political interests. This dynamic suggests the continuation of localist worldviews as voting coalitions varied. Historian Owen S. Ireland has found that animosity among various ethnoreligious communities based on their views of the Revolutionary state constitution helps explain Pennsylvania's majority vote to ratify the federal constitution. He argues that groups of people such as Quakers, German sectarians, and Anglicans who were disenfranchised and marginalized under wartime test acts and militia laws voted against their Presbyterian and Reformed Lutheran enemies who supported the radical 1776 constitution and opposed the new national one. Other groups who supported the Revolution but became alienated from the policies of the constitutionalists also tended to support the Federalist position.[6]

Additionally, defenses of the federal constitution were compatible with a localist worldview. The very structure of government recreated the system of dual federal-state sovereignty that Anglo-Americans knew under the British

---

5. Even during the Revolution, property requirements for white male franchise in most states declined. Only Massachusetts actually increased its material qualification for voting. In Pennsylvania, at the urging of the Committee of Privates, franchise was extended to all taxpayers during the war. On property qualifications, see Morgan, *Birth of the American Republic*, 93–94. See Wood, *Radicalism of the American Revolution*, 6–8, 294–95, on how the Revolution set the context for achieving the then radical notion of universal white manhood suffrage by the 1830s.

6. Saul Cornell, *The Other Founders: Anti-Federalism and the Dissenting Tradition in America, 1788–1828* (Chapel Hill, N.C., 1999), demonstrates the diversity of class groups and interests within the national anti-Federalist coalition. In *Religion, Ethnicity, and Politics* and "The Invention of American Democracy: The Pennsylvania Federalists and the New Republic," *Pennsylvania History* 67 (2000): 161–71, Owen S. Ireland explains how Pennsylvania Federalists created similarly diverse coalitions.

Empire. While many Americans believed that the British central government had violated colonial autonomy with arbitrary power, direct representation in the House of Representatives supposedly protected local liberties. Some, however, feared that powerful factions would gain control of the federal government and impose tyranny upon the people. James Madison brilliantly spoke directly to such concerns in Federalist No. 10, in which he argued that a large republic was viable precisely *because* of the number of competing interests. The plurality of factions and groups represented in the republic would be sufficient to make sure that none would have the power to dominate the nation. Various imagined communities were, then, the bedrock of the national republic; Madison's perspective resonated with those of ordinary soldiers who fought in the Revolution. Indeed, Madison was as cognizant of this popular view as he was of elite concerns with classical republican political theory. Veterans were therefore as likely as any other group to disagree on the politics of federalism, because federalism did not necessarily entail the jettisoning of a localism. Furthermore, the entire debate over ratification was permeated by the assumption that the true American national subject was a white male, not the non-white Indians and African Americans who were conquered or denied civil rights. Whiteness increasingly defined the postcolonial order. The new nation envisioned by supporters of the constitution could be portrayed as competitive, diverse communities united under the rubric of white male supremacy. Such nationalism, again, could be read by some veterans as utterly consistent with their wartime aims.[7]

Nonetheless, the discourse of politics remained as contested as ever. As in the past, most Americans believed that a virtuous government could only survive through a judicious balance of liberty and order. What constituted proper order and liberty still remained open to debate. A nation of balanced localisms was, of course, as given to internal conflict as to unity. In the 1790s, two agrarian rebellions against federal taxes—the 1794 Whiskey Rebellion and 1799 Fries Rebellion—demonstrated significant and violent internal disagreement over the extent of federal power. Former Revolutionary soldiers were present in the ranks of those who resisted the whiskey excise and the national direct tax of 1798. They framed their opposition to the federal government in terms similar to those used in the constitutional crisis of the 1760s and 1770s.

7. James Madison, Federalist No. 10, in *The Federalist Papers: Hamilton, Madison, Jay*, ed. Clinton Rossiter (New York, 1961). See D. Nelson, *National Manhood*, 29–60, 77–84, on the conflicts of the new republic being mitigated by the "imagined fraternity" of white males.

Veterans invoked the memory of their participation in the Revolution to justify their continued actions against a supposedly tyrannical government infringing upon their local interests. They presented their actions, then, in the context of the past. Defenders of the government, however, remarked that obedience to laws passed in a representative legislature were valid expressions of the will of the majority of the nation's communities. In the case of the Whiskey Rebellion, the nationalized militia raised to crush the "insurrection" had large numbers of eastern Pennsylvania soldiers. The Washington administration masterfully manipulated the inherent local differences of the nation to its advantage. It also established a precedent for how much dissent would be tolerated from groups believing that the government had violated their communal interests.[8]

Polemical polarization over the meaning of the nation grew as time passed. Veterans, like other Americans in the 1790s, 1800s, and 1810s, found themselves increasingly divided along partisan party lines. Federalists and Democratic Republicans both sought to identify themselves as the true heirs of the American Revolution. Public commemorations of the Revolution became important political battlegrounds in the new republic. Fourth of July celebrations, in which veterans often played significant roles as participants, were particularly contentious. Entirely separate Federalist and Republican festivities on the Fourth were common. The former emphasized the orderliness of the Revolution and the role of George Washington. The latter group tended to laud the concept of liberty, Thomas Jefferson, and Jefferson's authorship of the Declaration of Independence. Over time, the Society of Cincinnati, composed mostly of nationalist former Continental army officers, became the bulwark of Federalist commemorations of independence that celebrated an orderly, strong nation-state. Conversely, Democratic Republicans recalled the Revolution as a struggle to protect local interests and the liberty of the people from a tyrannical national government. Not surprisingly, many rank-and-file veterans felt more comfortable with commemorations that emphasized the political participation of common people.[9]

8. See Slaughter, *Whiskey Rebellion,* on the Whiskey Rebellion and its participants' linking of the crisis with the legacy of the Revolution. On the Fries Rebellion, see Paul Douglas Newman, "Fries' Rebellion and American Political Culture," *PMHB* 119 (1995): 37–73, and Robert H. Churchill, "Popular Nullification, Fries' Rebellion, and the Waning of Radical Republicanism, 1798–1801," *Pennsylvania History* 67 (2000): 105–40.

9. Simon Newman, *Parades,* 83–119; Travers, *Celebrating the Fourth,* 69–106; and G. Kurt Piehler, *Remembering War the American Way* (Washington, D.C., 1995), 10–12, show how emerging partisan differences affected the public memory of the Revolution and the celebration of the Fourth of July.

All official ceremonies, however, recognized the white male as the primary political subject. Celebrations of the Fourth were characterized by direct participation by white men only. White women were relegated to secondary or spectator status, and free blacks and slaves were typically excluded. Interestingly, historian Simon Newman has found that "Democratic Republican celebrations were typically more exclusive than those of their Federalist opponents." The more "democratic" Republicans carefully used the Fourth to perform a republic of politically equal white males. Federalists, perhaps more comfortable in their hierarchical view of society, invited women to take up prominent roles in festivities. In the end, the Republicans' construction of the formal public sphere as consisting of white men proved appealing to veterans. By 1800, the Republicans became politically dominant in Pennsylvania and in much of the nation outside of New England by effectively drawing more popular support. The party successfully assumed the mantle of the localist white male nation in most areas. Not surprisingly, by the early nineteenth century, commemorations of the Revolution celebrated the achievements of ordinary (white male) Americans as well as great heroes.[10]

How Pensioners Remembered

By the late 1810s and through the 1820s and 1830s, unprecedented numbers of such former soldiers told their stories. Following the War of 1812, as the first American party system began to collapse, partisan divisions over the meaning of the Revolution cooled; many thought that the Revolutionary generation was passing. Americans were ready to celebrate and reward the contributions of ordinary soldiers in the form of pensions. As historian John Resch has argued, the image of the "suffering soldier," the veteran who selflessly underwent military service to his own economic disadvantage, gained currency. The sentimental impulse to "help" old soldiers, coupled with a desire to celebrate the founding generation, allowed even illiterate veterans to share their memories of the Revolution. Pension applications yielded a vast number of depositions given by veterans in various courts. In 1818, an act of Congress provided half-pay

10. On official participation by white men only in Independence Day ceremonies, see Simon Newman, *Parades*, 83–86 (quotation from 102). See Purcell, "Sealed With Blood," 145, and Resch, *Suffering Soldiers*, 2–3, on the growing public emphasis on the roles of ordinary people in the Revolution prevalent in the later 1790s and the early nineteenth century.

pensions to all men who had been enlisted in the Continental army for nine months and who were in "reduced circumstances." A subsequent act followed that required applicants to append a personal property schedule to prove their indigence. The pension legislation of 1832 was the most liberal of all and offered a stipend to anyone who had served six months in any military capacity, including the militia, regardless of financial need. These veterans were required to recount dates and places of service, the names of officers, and any engagements fought in their depositions. When the old soldiers told their stories in open courts, their narratives were objects of public interest. Not surprisingly, deponents often recounted stories in detail above and beyond the requirement for a pension in the interest of offering their stories for posterity.[11]

The pension applications and their supporting documents revealed that veterans had carefully preserved their memories of the Revolution within a group context. Former enlisted men developed and perpetuated their recollections through interactions with peers. Thomas Beer's wife, for example, recounted how he and "his fellow soldiers" had many "interviews together at her husband's home after the war." John Cuningham described how he "frequently heard" his father and James Drennan "conversing upon events which had taken place while they were together in the service . . . and also when they met, the father of this deponent *always* accosted the said applicant with the appellation of 'fellow soldier.'"[12]

Participants in the Revolution also developed their memories in conjunction with family members. Wives often appended their own recollections to their husbands' in support of their spouses' applications (or their own applications for widows' pensions). Elizabeth Bisson corroborated her brother's and her husband's depositions, which suggests that she discussed the matter with both. She also inserted her own experiences into the narrative, stating, "I remember these things too well. I know the names of nearly all the men and officers at the time of the war. My husband and brother were both out in the service. My husband was badly wounded at Germantown." Other wives who accompanied their husbands to the army knew their anecdotes firsthand and had their own stories to tell the family. James McEwen's daughter, Mary, recalled how her mother, Barbara, "frequently told her of the battle in which

---

11. Resch, *Suffering Soldiers*, 64–92, succinctly explains the sentimental image of the "suffering soldier"; see 118 for the provisions of the 1818 act and the quotation from it. On the provisions of the various federal pension acts, see Dann, *The Revolution Remembered*, xv–xvii.

12. RWPF, files W3647, W3527.

her husband [was] engaged under Washington. She handed Washington a drink of water out of a tin cup and . . . he persuaded the women to get out of the way." Obviously, sons and daughters also were significant audiences for the perpetuation of veterans' memories. Andrew Bryson's daughter explained that she "often heard her father speak of that war, of the exposure, the privations, and the hardships he had endured until its termination." Jacob Krider's daughter, Margaret, indicated how she, too, had heard her father explain his own experience as a suffering soldier. She stated, "I remember hearing my father speak of the hardships he underwent at Valley Forge and I have always understood that he took part in the Battle of Trenton and at Germantown, where he received a wound in the wrist."[13]

Communities were important forums for the sharing and shaping of former soldiers' recollections as well. Henry Schatz's neighbors testified that they had often heard the Montgomery County tailor speak of his participation in the Battles of Brandywine, Germantown, and Stony Point. Philip Bushrang explained that his acquaintance, Jacob Stahley, "was honored and esteemed as one of the surviving soldiers of the Revolution." Some soldiers' stories were so often repeated that listeners could attest to their notoriety. Neighbors of Henry Lausch stated that "his being a Revolutionary soldier is not only traditional in his immediate neighborhood, but notorious throughout his district or wherever he is known." Similarly, Jacob Booz's neighbors stated that his "services in the Revolutionary War were notorious in the neighborhood and never doubted." Whether it was with family, old comrades, or neighbors, veterans clearly were versed in giving narratives of their service long before the passage of pension legislation.[14]

Nonetheless, the accuracy of veterans' memories eroded over the decades. Only a very few were able to remember with the acuity of Jacob Booz, who stated that although age had deprived him of his sight and left him "generally infirm of body, his memory continues retentive and he has a good recollection." As the images and circumstances of Revolutionary service faded, pensioners typically lost track of details such as chronology or the names of their junior officers. Most, however, still recalled one central story line in their depositions that could still command an audience's attention—even with minor inaccuracies. The memory lapses were probably seen by the veterans as regrettable but ultimately inessential to their fundamental retrospective understanding of their service.

13. RWPF, files S22956, R6700, S40756, W10186.
14. RWPF, files S3866, W3472, S4515, S22131.

Commonly, former soldiers would state that they could not recall dates or even the way they entered the army and then follow those statements with vivid descriptions of particular incidents. John Hughey, for example, noted hazily that he entered the militia "shortly after the troubles broke out between this country and Great Britain" and offered a narrative full of erroneous dates for particular campaigns. Sometimes inaccuracies even obscured fundamental explanations of motives, such as when William McCasland admitted that on one of his militia tours he "was drafted or volunteered (I don't recollect which)." Audiences and the courts could ignore such "minor" mistakes, however, and still grant pensions and credence to the narrators' perspectives. In addition, such errors might well have produced sympathy by underscoring the deponents' pitiable condition in their later lives.[15]

Another concern was that veterans might well refashion their memories of the war to enhance their own images. While such self-serving revision doubtlessly occurred, what is perhaps more striking is that many elderly veterans looked back at what might be seen as embarrassing elements of their service—and told them anyway. Franz Dido, for instance, recalled the Pennsylvania Line mutiny and insisted, "I took no part in the revolt—my time had not yet quite expired." He went on to explain that when Pennsylvania settled the terms of the enlistment dispute with the mutineers, "it was found of the men whose terms had expired were getting their discharges, that I myself had but about two weeks more to serve, and thinking that the two weeks would be of but little service . . . got discharged." Dido communicated his clear sympathy for the mutiny and then openly admitted a fraudulent discharge. John Boon told how he ran during the Battle of Camden, "fleeing through an unknown country." Boon then explained that he arrived at a local ironworks where he worked "for some years." He excused his absence without leave from the army by stating that he could not find the remnants of the defeated Continentals and thus could secure no discharge. Nineteenth-century civilian audiences, expecting to hear of martial heroism, might interpret such accounts as evidence of dishonesty or cowardice. The veterans either did not see it that way or did not care if their audiences did.

15. The decay of memory in age was obviously a problem for many of the veterans. Yet as A. T. Welford points out in *Aging and Human Skill* (Westport, Conn., 1973), 229–30, many older people "remember well events which occurred many years before even though they are forgetful of more recent happenings." In other words, short-term memory failed before long-term memory. Furthermore, pensioners exhibited other common signs of aging in their remembrances, such as forgetting minor details (names and dates) that were not important to their stories. Most veterans were able to tell at least one important anecdote from the Revolution in vivid detail. RWPF, files S22131, S22324, W21790.

Running from combat and taking it upon oneself to determine fair discharges were obviously common soldierly behaviors. Moreover, late in life, the narrators might have wanted to tell all the ugly details of war. In any event, deponents generally were relatively candid as long as they did not believe that it might affect their being awarded a pension.[16]

What Pensioners Remembered

Regardless of the honesty or acuity of these memories, the deposition process revealed a dialectic between the veterans' recollections and the popular culture that shaped the expectations of their audiences. It is in these convergences of narrators' and audience's views of the Revolution that popular national identities were most visible. For instance, veterans' accounts simultaneously conformed to the widely popular image of the suffering soldier and bolstered the trope's credibility. Pension applicants and audiences were interested in physical hardship and bloodshed. Angus McCoy recalled his time in the Washington County militia: "our difficulties of fatigue, hunger, and uneasy sensation of mind is bright to my recollection." John Boon "well recollects that the army suffered much fatigue and hardship." Memories of violence in the war revealed the psychological suffering still endured by veterans. They recalled combat vividly (especially so, given the passing of many decades since the event) and refused to romanticize it. Samuel Solomon Dotter purposefully went into detail when he described the carnage at the Battle of Germantown, recalling that "during the battle, our company marched sixteen deep through a gate and every man in our [unit was killed] except three, of whom he was one." John Heneberger distinctly recollected the same battle: "the battle began about daybreak. Our company only gave one fire. The Hessians fired at us from a cornfield, but they shot too high. The bullets rattled among the trees above our heads. . . . There was one man wounded by a cannon shot within a rod of me." Joseph McDonald was typical of those who continued to be haunted by memories of brutal frontier combat. He gave one particular account in his pension application in which he described how "we were attacked by the Indians. . . . Two of the men in our range, William Rankins and James Willens[?] were killed by the Indians. One was on my right and the other on my left side when shot." Simon Krysher

16. RWPF, files W7017, R1017.

similarly offered a stark picture of a painful moment frozen in time. Almost fifty years later, he told of how his captain "was shot through the ear and one George Carter was killed by the Indians; both shots he distinctly recollects."[17]

These stories suggest that veterans connected their identity as men charged with enduring the horrors of war with the image of the selfless, suffering soldier. Like most combat veterans, they could not forget the human cost of their wartime experience. Many were indeed deeply traumatized by it. Yet they also purposefully dwelled upon it, strengthening their claims to having made a singular sacrifice for the founding of the nation. Pension applicants also centered their narratives on their wounds. Of course, many stood to gain their stipends if they could prove that they had been disabled in the war, but again, this was consistent with the notion of veterans suffering for the greater good. Because the nation was born in an act of violence, those who shed their own blood made that clear to the people whom they believed were in their debt. John Hill's only significant story of the Battle of Trenton was that he "received a slight wound in my right leg below the knee." Thomas McFall declared of his service that "at the capture of the Fort Washington [he] was wounded in the left leg by a musket ball and taken prisoner and after eighteen weeks' captivity, was dismissed on parole. His wound yet remains open and deprives him of support by labor." Such accounts buttressed the popular image of Revolutionary veterans as debilitated and still limited in their financial success primarily because of their patriotism. Their narratives made these former soldiers objects of the nation's sympathy and its beneficence.[18]

Courts also shaped the way in which veterans presented their accounts by suggesting language for use in depositions. Court officials very often described soldiers' service as being on behalf of "the common cause," and its repetition suggests that the term was appealing to the audience and to the narrators. It implied both a unified national cause and a plurality of local motivations. Other variations on the term appeared as well. Lewis Bender "served against the common enemy as a private." Like the "common cause," the "common enemy" was a vague term that linked diverse wars within the Revolution to the creation of the nation. These enemies could be Indians, Tories, runaway slaves, or British soldiers. Old soldiers, court officials, and the general public could then reconcile what appeared to be arcane localist tales to a larger struggle for national independence. Such rhetoric created a necessary context in which

17. Dann, *The Revolution Remembered*, 314; RWPF, files R1017, S22735, S22735, S22824, S23791.
18. RWPF, files W5298, S40145.

soldiers could recount their localist narratives of the Revolution as part of the story of nation building.[19]

Some conflicts in interpretation were unavoidable, no matter how malleable the language used. Contesting notions of the Revolution were apparent in depositions and variously negotiated between narrator and audience. Sometimes the courts did more than impart mere patriotism to the veterans' narratives. Influenced by the nineteenth-century conservative backlash against the supposed "excesses" of the French Revolution, some officials sought to eradicate traces of radicalism from the soldiers' stories. Admitting that certain participants in America's Revolution expected that society might be fundamentally restructured was threatening to the functionaries of the established government. As such, they were not above censoring pensioners' accounts. One of the most glaring cases was the deposition of Jacob Stahley, a veteran who was supporting the claim of his erstwhile comrade Peter Shindel. As we saw at the departure point of this study, Stahley declared that he remembered "Peter Shindel to have been actually engaged as a soldier in the cause of the people during the glorious struggle for independence." The word "people," however, was crossed out in the original and replaced with "liberty." Likely, upon reflection, the court believed the cause of "liberty" to be more acceptable than the perhaps Jacobin ring of "the people." Some pensioners were much more audience-aware than Stahley. They believed (probably quite correctly) that recounting collective resistance against Revolutionary authorities would endanger their chances for stipends. They also appeared to have understood that as some Americans started to value the Revolution (albeit in different regional variations) as an orderly, unified defense of liberty by the people against tyranny, statements that implied social radicalism could be viewed unfavorably. As a result, savvy veterans altered or simply lied about their roles in actions that appeared radical. For example, numbers of old soldiers were reluctant to admit their participation in the revolt of the Pennsylvania Line in 1781. George Wiese swore that he was not involved in the mutiny; on the contrary, he claimed, he disclosed "its intent to his officers." Given the widespread participation of enlisted men in the mutiny and their sense

---

19. The term "common cause" was most systematically utilized in the 1818 depositions, which suggests that it was invoked formulaically by the courts. Although popular narratives of the Revolution in the early nineteenth century revolved around the creation of the new independent nation, regional variations of that story continued to be widespread. Waldstreicher describes how diverse areas employed essentially regional concepts of nationalism to understand the republic in light of their local cultures in *In the Midst of Perpetual Fetes*, 246–94. Also see Travers, *Celebrating the Fourth*, 222–25, for emerging regional differences in the commemoration of Independence Day. RWPF, file S39970.

in 1781 that their actions were principled defenses of the military moral economy, this statement invites a suspension of disbelief. It does suggest that Wiese understood the emergence of a conservative collective memory of the Revolution and used it in support of his own claim for a pension.[20]

Another way in which former soldiers enhanced their credibility was by invoking the nineteenth-century pantheon of Revolutionary heroes. This tactic again connected the localist narratives of veterans with the construction of the nation. Memories of encounters with George Washington were classic manifestations of this process. Rare was the pension deposition that did not mention the Continental army's commander-in-chief. Washington's appearance in the personal recollections of soldiers was not surprising; he was, far and away, the most exalted figure of the Revolution. No Fourth of July festivity was complete without a paean to the general and president. By the 1820s and 1830s, Washington was firmly ensconced in American culture as symbolic of the Revolutionary struggle and national character. Old soldiers consistently conjured up some personal connection to this national icon. Adam Sonday explained in his pension deposition that he "thinks it unnecessary to state that he remembers, and shall while he lives, [seeing] the immortal General George Washington." George Black explained how during a skirmish with the British, "if it had not been for General Washington at Chestnut Ridge, the party of the militia to which I was attached would have been cut off by the Hessians, but, he seeing our situation, sent his aid to us." These pension applicants exploited and helped solidify the nineteenth-century idolization of Washington.[21]

Interestingly, a few former enlisted men remembered being on relatively intimate terms with the genteel Virginian. Rather than viewing him with detached awe, they recalled not only serving under Washington but interacting with him as well. John Allen, a former private, presumed to be "acquainted" with Washington. Some soldiers remembered being especially called upon by the commander. Valentine Shoufler stated that he was "ordered to Long Island

---

20. Michael Kammen, *A Season of Youth: The American Revolution in the Historical Imagination* (Ithaca, N.Y., 1988), 26, suggests that the popular memory of the Revolution as conservative and orderly was reinforced by the writings of early historians. In "From a Revolutionary History to a History of the Revolution: David Ramsay and the American Revolution," *Journal of the Early Republic* 22 (Summer 2002): 205–33, Peter C. Messer argues that the transformation of Ramsay's ideas regarding history—first as a tool of social reform, and later as a justification of current institutions—was emblematic of the increasingly conservative nature of Revolutionary histories in the early republic. RWPF, files S23911, S11711.

21. Barry Schwartz, *George Washington: The Making of an American Symbol* (New York, 1987), 119, explains the development of Washington into a symbol of the Revolution and the nation. RWPF, files W26495, W3211.

by General Washington." Similarly, Nathaniel Burrows asserted that following a battle in which all his officers were killed, he took command of his company which "by especial request of General Washington attached itself to a [Continental] regiment." Burrows then went on to describe how he, in particular, was "employed by General Washington on express and other enterprises deemed to be of importance to the service." Abraham Goss recalled that as a young fifer in the Pennsylvania Line, he "frequently played by the direction of Washington." Samuel Graff's attempt to democratize Washington's memory was perhaps the boldest. The militiaman and his comrades captured a British soldier during the Philadelphia campaign and refused to turn him over to their own officers. Instead, Graff asserted, they "took him to General Washington at White Marsh, who treated them with brandy." It is difficult to imagine Washington acknowledging the mundane service of a group of Pennsylvania militiamen, let alone inviting them to share a drink. Typically, the commander-in-chief carefully cultivated the class pretensions of a gentleman officer, keeping his enlisted men at a respectable social distance.[22]

Aloofness from enlisted men was unremarkable among eighteenth-century European and European American senior officers, who had no desire to inspire their men by demonstrating familiarity with them. What is revealing is how these privates fashioned an image of Washington as a populist military leader. Such accounts reveal at least two important and mutually reinforcing factors about how soldiers remembered the Revolution. First, the attempt to create a Washington who was a friend to privates demonstrated how some of the rank and file were changed by the war. Retrospectively seeing themselves as full citizens of the republic with a special stake in its creation, they could place themselves in the same narrative with the commanding general as comrades in arms. Second, the rapid development of liberal individualism as a dominant cultural form in the early nineteenth century contributed to a revised memory of Washington. Didactic fables involving Washington—such as those created by Mason Weems—cast him as a humble, self-reliant man. In such a context, veterans could not help but remember their commander with an image similar to another, more recent general, Andrew Jackson, who was celebrated as a self-made man of the people leading common men into battle. This democratization of Washington's memory by his troops was a function of the nineteenth-

22. RWPF, files S22622, S22506, S22151, S22799, W7566. Washington "did not inspire enthusiastic affection among the rank and file. . . . It was the officers who admired him most," according to Marcus Cunliffe, *George Washington: Man and Monument* (New York, 1960), 108.

century present projected back onto the eighteenth century. Both audience and narrators at the pension depositions would have found the discussion of George Washington as a man of the people consistent with contemporary culture. In this case, subsequent cultural developments validated the soldiers' previously radical visions. A private viewing himself as a "brother soldier" of a commanding officer was a revolutionary notion during the eighteenth century—but not quite so disquieting in the nineteenth. Veterans could freely express this view of the Revolution without fear of suggesting social radicalism or disrespect, as it seemed consistent with present American values about the brotherhood of white men in arms.[23]

Far and away, the most frequent appearance of Washington in soldiers' pension applications was as a brief sighting. Most veterans neither regarded the general with awe nor attempted to exaggerate their relationship to him. Rather, they merely mentioned him in an attempt to validate their own stories of the war, probably in response to questions about Washington from the court or spectators. The majority of deponents blandly recited their sightings of the commander-in-chief in the midst of detailed anecdotes about the rest of their own wartime experiences. Joseph Bitting, for instance, "frequently saw General Washington." In 1777 near Philadelphia, Andrew Gangiver also "saw General Washington." John McCasland recalled that his service at Valley Forge in 1777–78 "was the first and last time he ever saw General Washington." Also at Valley Forge, Conrad Hipple "often s[aw] General Washington." John Campbell "recollects General Washington near Morristown." John Kuntz "saw General Washington frequently" during the Battle of Brandywine. James Hays remembered "General Washington himself at White Marsh." Ludwig Hoffman recounted how, on a long march, "we met General Washington and his guard." These accounts were all plausible scenarios. Washington was a well-known figure among his troops, who often saw him directing his officers and planning the war. In all the above cases, the sighting of the general played a small part in any details offered beyond the requirements for pensions. The invocation of

23. In *The Shoemaker and the Tea Party,* Alfred Young comes to similar conclusions regarding the memory of George Robert Twelves Hewes, a veteran who recalled standing next to John Hancock at the "Boston Tea Party." Hewes was influenced by the retrospective nineteenth-century lower-sort memory of the Revolution that constructed a non-deferential united struggle against the enemy. In the context of growing universal white manhood suffrage in the United States by the 1830s, the imagined impudence of placing a humble soldier on par with Washington would not have been so widely offensive as it would have been fifty years before. On the liberal refashioning of Washington into a "self-made man" and especially on the influence of Parson Weems's mythology on the matter, see Steven Watts, *The Republic Reborn: War and the Making of Liberal America, 1790–1820* (Baltimore, 1989), 144–45.

the commander's name was intended to sanctify the less familiar tales of the pensioners. After dutifully stating how they sighted Washington, soldiers were free to engage in their own stories that emphasized localist perspectives.[24]

The mention of other heroes and events of the Revolution played the same role in the depositions. They allowed soldiers to place well-known persons and happenings in the context of their own service and thus validate the account by invoking popular icons. The Marquis de Lafayette is the only figure who even comes close to the popularity of the commander-in-chief in the recollections of Pennsylvania veterans. Former enlisted men had help remembering Lafayette's role: it was celebrated during the Marquis's celebrated visit to the United States in the 1820s. Audiences were eager to hear stories of the recent returning hero, and reciting the name of Lafayette to add emphasis to one's own stories was another shrewd narrative strategy. John Campbell, for instance, made sure to mention in his catalogue of skirmishes around Philadelphia that he was "acquainted with" Lafayette. Thomas Rowe, a Philadelphia Light Dragoon, took no chances and framed his story with the declaration that he "saw Generals Washington and Lafayette." Frederick Harp described how he fought at Brandywine and "well recollects Generals Lafayette and Washington during the day of the Battle." Philip Nagel still vividly pictured the Marquis at Yorktown, declaring, "Lafayette was here. He was brave. He ordered his men to attack with the bayonet." Thomas Elton was similarly graphic in his description of the officer at Brandywine, declaring assuredly that "Lafayette was wounded in this battle and I think I can show the very spot where this accident occurred." Andrew Wallace took his account of the same battle a step further. He described how he "bore from the field General Lafayette who was . . . wounded."[25]

Pensioners mentioned other famous Revolutionary leaders as well. John Douglas proudly recalled that his "commission was signed by John Hancock." Henry Boyer remembered Baron von Steuben to have been present while he fought a skirmish in New Jersey in 1778. Thomas Rowe spoke of his encounter with Anthony Wayne, the famous Pennsylvania Continental general. Rowe, a blacksmith by trade, recalled that he "shod General Wayne's horse, the General holding the horse himself." Philip Duck stated that he "recollects seeing General Lee near Boston—also General Sullivan—and he remembers Benedict

---

24. RWPF, files S2072, S4197, S9155, S2713, S23681, W2801, S13746.
25. See Dann, *The Revolution Remembered*, xvi, and Purcell, "Sealed With Blood," 254–309, regarding Lafayette and the enthusiastic U.S. popular response. RWPF, files W9772, W2862, W7624, S41912, S22228, S3466.

Arnold being there at that time." In fact, Benedict Arnold, a figure whose treason ignited popular interest throughout the nineteenth century, merited many a mention by soldiers. James Guest recalled "Arnold's being [in] command of the fleet on [Lake] Champlain and his desiring the declarant [Guest] to take command of four guns of a . . . galley" in 1776. Duck and Guest recollected Arnold in neutral terms, withholding judgment on the man for his treason. In contrast, John Joseph Henry could not contain his revisionism in his nineteenth-century retrospective journal. Of Arnold's conduct at the Battle of Quebec, Henry declared, "if Montgomery had originally been our commander, matters might have been more civilly conducted."[26]

Even more interesting to those who listened to the veterans were accounts of Arnold's actual defection. Pennsylvania troops stationed in New York in 1780 could claim some sort of personal experience with the great act of treason. Andrew Ream recalled clearly Arnold's escape from American authorities in an effort to prove that he was indeed attached to the army at that time. George Keller placed himself at the famous hanging of Arnold's British contact, explaining, "in 1780, I joined General Washington in New Jersey and was present at the execution of Major Andre, Adjutant General of the British army, who was hanged as a spy." The ubiquitous Samuel Graff proclaimed that he and his comrades were repairing a road "at the time Arnold passed down the river in a small boat to join the British. That he was seen by all [the] men, but it was not known at the time that it was Arnold." Graff's tale might well have been as exaggerated as his mention of being given a drink by Washington, but one can only imagine the rapt attention of the court, with all present listening to how the disguised traitor slipped away under these soldiers' very noses.[27]

Probably the most important event that helped frame veterans' narratives was the Declaration of Independence. The signing of the document was, of course, the occasion for the great holiday honoring the Revolution—the Fourth of July. The Declaration symbolized the common cause against Britain, and former enlisted men often appended their memories of it to their stories. Such statements also bolstered the hearers' opinions of the soldiers' patriotic motives and certainly did not hurt bids for pensions. For example, Griffith Smith stated that "immediately after the Declaration of Independence," he joined the militia. Jacob Stahley also informed the court that his enlistment coincided with that most famous of dates in American history. He explained, "I resided

26. RWPF, files S2180, S22129, W2862, S12806, S3431; Henry, "Journal," 115.
27. RWPF, files S4067, W3090, W7566.

at Philadelphia in the year 1776 and on the 4th day of July that year, being the day of the Declaration of American Independence, I entered into the service." In truth, few heard of Congress's approval of the Declaration until days afterward. The veterans' tendency to date their service to the Fourth of July represents a shorthand way in which they spoke to some of the expectations of the audience, who, of course, associated the date with the document. Still, the reading of the Declaration was an important event in Revolutionary communities and particularly in Pennsylvania, where it coincided with the rise of the radicals. Additionally, as Pauline Maier has argued, it was an articulation of popular attitudes during the Revolution. Its subsequent "rediscovery" after the War of 1812 as a virtually "sacred" text of the American founding allowed soldiers to meld their memories of the document with popular nineteenth-century patriotism.[28]

The narrative strategy of invoking personal memories of heroes and great events, such as the first "Independence Day," gave veterans a chance to join their own detailed stories to the popular national one surrounding the nation's birth. Thus, veterans could unabashedly assert their localist perspectives on the Revolution as part of the founding. In a culture characterized by persisting regionalism, such accounts appeared consistent with present notions of the heterogeneous nation. That soldiers were so forthright in describing their community-focused motives suggests that they met with some level of audience acceptance. For example, those who lived in the southeastern portion of the Commonwealth during the war stated bluntly that they enlisted primarily to defend their families and the Philadelphia area from the advances of the British army and local Tories. James Wilkens made no apologies for the fact that he left the Continental army when "the British left Philadelphia in June 1778" and did not reenlist. Neither did William Fling, who remembered "after the British evacuated Philadelphia . . . he left the company and returned home, there being no further cause for his services." Pension applicants who served from the secure central parts of Pennsylvania revealed their apathy toward volunteering in the war. Samuel Quigley, John Torrence, and Jacob Long all admitted that they served their tours of duty in the War for Independence as draftees.

28. RWPF, files W3467, W3472. Pauline Maier, *American Scripture: Making the Declaration of Independence* (New York, 1998), 154–60, explains the time frame when most Americans learned of the Declaration of Independence. The Declaration was read publicly to the Continental army on July 9, 1776, and civilians were introduced to the document around the same time. See 3–96 and 155–208 for Maier's discussion of how the Declaration's rhetoric resonated with popular views of the war during both the Revolution and the nineteenth century.

John Weller and Conrad Myers, both of Lancaster County, told stories about their volunteer tours early in the war and left it patently obvious that they had no more fervor for military service as the conflict continued. Veterans who fought on the frontier were perhaps the most adamant about pressing their regional version of the Revolution. As popular memory became more focused on the struggle for independence from Britain, those who had served from the western counties wished to remind their listeners that there was a significant frontier facet to the war. John Craig stated that all his voluntary tours were for "guarding the country from Indian depredations." Daniel Livingston recalled that he fought "for the purpose of protecting the inhabitants of the frontier counties of Pennsylvania against the attacks of the Indians." John Gore explained that he became a patriot only when he was "driven by the Indians and the Tories" from his home.[29]

These varying narratives of the Revolution had the potential to create anxiety among listeners as well. Old soldiers who moved to different regions after the war may well have brought perspectives that varied in substance with those that were regionally hegemonic. While astute audiences might have accepted different local perspectives as evincing the heterogeneity of the union, racial identities could provide other common ground. It was, of course, in the depositions of frontier veterans that whiteness was touted as a central characteristic of the Revolutionary cause. Their tendency to describe frontier war in terms of conflict between "whites" and "the Indians" had far-reaching consequences for the evolving consciousness of national identity. John Dougherty was typical: he described "the Indians . . . committing depredations against the whites" as the central characteristic of the conflict. In the war's wake, veterans continued to assert their "whiteness" rather than any perceived skin color of Indians. Given the widespread popularity among European Americans of the term "red" to describe Indian skin color, it appears that veterans were stubbornly reasserting their self-identity as "white"—and thus as "true Americans." This concept of whiteness (asserted in opposition to "the Indians") figured prominently in the veterans' retrospective accounts of the American Revolution for important reasons. As Gordon Wood has argued, the American Revolution paved the way for the then radical notion of universal white manhood suffrage in the early nineteenth century. Veterans connected their sacrifices—as white men liable to military service—to the founding of the Republic and believed that their enfranchisement was only just. During the period from the end of the

29. RWPF, files S40701, S3364, S4746, S6257, W3434, S22572, W2962, S8253, S22361, S22793.

Revolution to the 1830s, the profound shift from a gendered economic basis of citizenship to a completely biological one occurred. By the time of the pension applications, white manhood had largely replaced male property-holding as the basic prerequisite for voting. Not surprisingly, then, veterans gave depositions that proudly recounted their claims to political inclusion by emphasizing the "white race" in contrast to "the Indians." These references to race were superfluous to the requirements of the pension but obviously important to the deponents. The critical issue that made sense to audiences (in the absence of discussion of the war against the British) was the fundamental importance of whiteness to citizenship. Listeners could conceive of the Revolution as a defense of the white race. Deponents had the satisfaction of recounting how they came to see themselves as Americans, and the biological roots of citizenship were publicly reaffirmed.[30]

The veterans' descriptions of the seeming double standard of combat behavior on the frontier was consciously designed to strike a responsive chord among listeners as well. Those hearing the pension applications would concur with the veterans that one thing that made Americans distinct from Europeans was adaptation to the American environment. The frontiersman who mixed elements of Indian and European cultures, especially methods of warfare, was a staple of literature and popular culture in the early republic. While audiences in the courts might have wished for stories of George Washington, they certainly would have recognized a truly American element in the frontier war. Like the veterans, they would have been untroubled by the contradiction of lauding patriot military culture while characterizing similar Indian actions as "savagery." The Indianized white was archetypal of the new national identity: biologically superior to Indians, culturally superior to Europeans.[31]

By implication, the statements by frontier veterans regarding racial national identity also spoke to the marginalization of African Americans in the early republic. Given popular practices and emerging federal and state laws,

---

30. RWPF, S12779; Wood, "Equality and Social Conflict," 703–16, and *Radicalism of the American Revolution,* 6–8, 294–95. See Joyce Appleby, *Inheriting the Revolution: The First Generation of Americans* (Cambridge, Mass., 2000), 28–29, on the movement toward universal white manhood suffrage beginning in the Jeffersonian era and continuing through the 1830s and 1840s. The pension applications were made in the 1820s and 1830s, a period when—according to Vaughan in "From White Man to Redskin"—the term "red" was used to describe Indians. Veterans continued to prefer to describe Indians as nonwhite rather than as any specific color.

31. Slotkin, *Regeneration Through Violence,* 313–516, asserts the pervasiveness of the Indianized white as an emblem of American-ness in literature and popular culture in the early nineteenth century. Also see Susan Scheckel, *The Insistence of the Indian: Race and Nationalism in Nineteenth-Century American Culture* (Princeton, N.J., 1998), on the nation's attempts to define itself in terms of its relations with Indians.

free black men were increasingly (and explicitly) denied the rights of full citizenship. By the end of the 1830s, the decade in which the most descriptive pension applications were made, most states, including Northern ones, denied the right to vote to African American men. Additionally, the federal government passed laws in the early nineteenth century that restricted naturalization and liability to militia service to whites only. The U.S. government thus continued some of the measures carried out by the Revolutionaries that denied African American rights in certain areas of citizenship. The process of defining the white male political subject happened at an informal level as well. Northern popular racism exploded into violence: Boston, Providence, Cincinnati, and Hartford all experienced anti-black riots in the 1820s and 1830s. Philadelphia saw three such incidents in 1829, 1834, and 1835. In this context of racial tensions, veterans who told seemingly ancient tales of Revolution as a vast war to defend the "white" community would have found receptive audiences in Northern cities among white men who assumed that they were the true citizens of the republic. Thus, the eighteenth century's crucible of white identity formation—frontier warfare—could be applied to the nineteenth century's expanding definition of white privilege in opposition to African American inferiority.[32]

In a sense, then, the pension applications, regardless of whether they explicitly addressed the issue of racial identity, celebrated the antebellum American political subject. White male veterans were invited to share their recollections partly because they were considered valued citizens of the republic who made important contributions to the Revolution and the nation. When the courts and the veterans themselves began to probe the former soldiers' postwar economic situation, however, a less egalitarian narrative clearly emerged. The majority of common soldiers in the war came from the lowest orders of society, and the pension applications reveal that most of them remained impoverished or at least on a tenuous financial footing. Although many were clearly bitter about their situation, their narratives spoke again to the sentimental popular image of the former soldiers suffering for their patriotism. The government offered pensions as recompense for service—not because it viewed poverty as an ill that should be remedied by the state.

32. See Appleby, *Inheriting the Revolution,* 47, on the denial of voting rights for black men by most American states and the federal laws limiting naturalization to whites and militia enrollment to white men. She points out that only Massachusetts, Vermont, and New Hampshire had "'color-blind' constitutions" and that New York allowed only propertied black men the vote, while all white men were enfranchised. See 219 for a discussion of "anti-black riots" in the Northern cities.

Nonetheless, veterans' concerns with postwar economic issues permeated most of the depositions. Former soldiers measured their nostalgic memories of Revolutionary communal and familial solidarity against nineteenth-century society. Narratives commonly indicated a perceived decline of mutualistic values. Conveniently forgetting their own youthful mobility and individualism, some elderly pensioners chided their children for not remaining and helping them. Others chastised their communities in general for not supporting them or respecting their sacrifices. William Dougherty compared his own generation's commitment to community unfavorably to that of the successive generation. Dougherty, being a dutiful son, "was discharged [from Revolutionary service] on account of [his] mother having been left a widow in a helpless condition." By the nineteenth century, the veteran was forced to apply for a pension to survive: "I am old and infirm as well [as] is my wife who now is in the 63rd year of her age and by whom I have had eleven children, nine of whom are living (or were living last time I heard from them)." Dougherty implied that, unlike him, his children showed little respect for the family. William Iddings was similarly disillusioned with the post-Revolutionary generation. The Flying Camp veteran who risked his life to fight the main British army and "received little or no compensation for his services" found himself in a destitute state after the war. Iddings "raised a family of children, but they . . . all left him to do for himself." Iddings was bitter toward authorities who never paid him for his services and children who were unwilling to make sacrifices for him. He fought off danger in the 1770s, but he now believed that neither family nor community cared about him. His petitioning the federal government for support was a painful last resort. Andrew Wallace sought to shame younger people into recognizing his sacrifices and granting him a stipend. He stated, "for twenty-nine years he was a sentinel and defender of the liberty of his country and now, being old and poor, solicits that the present generation will protect him from want and soothe his declining years." Such appeals were, again, entirely consistent with the popular culture of the early republic. Many were deeply concerned with living up to the supposedly selfless accomplishments of the "founding generation." The metaphor of ungrateful children was a powerful one that spoke to the sentimental desire to offer paternalistic assistance to veterans as recompense.[33]

33. Resch, *Suffering Soldiers*, 93–118, suggests that most Americans viewed veterans as being impoverished by their selfless service and deserving of generous federal pensions as a reward for their sacrifices. RWPF, files S42674, S22849, S3466.

More commonly, veterans recalled frustrated individual material goals. The 1818 and 1821 pension acts demanded such responses; a statement of poverty was necessary to be awarded payments. Rather than explaining their status in class or other group terms, veterans needed to speak to these requirements, which demanded personal stories told in isolation from larger social trends. The depositions nonetheless collectively revealed that life remained as difficult for the poor in the early-nineteenth-century United States as it had been in colonial America. Applicants typically placed economic grievances related to their military service at the root of their current poverty. This formulation resonated with popular assumptions about the selflessness of Revolutionary soldiers— and, in many cases, it was at least partly true. Veterans commonly asserted that they spent time as soldiers during a period of their lives when they could have established themselves in civilian employment. When promised rewards for service never materialized, their descent into poverty was accelerated. Many enlisted men who received land on the frontier were defrauded of their land warrants or were forced to sell them to speculators for ready cash in order to survive after the war. John Akeley was typical of those reduced to poverty after he "sold his donation land to a certain John Watson, esq." Robert Gordon lamented that he "by fraud, has been deprived of the land allowance allowed him by Congress [and] that three years of his pay is yet due."[34]

Resentment over the continuing denial of fair pay also persisted into the nineteenth century. Memories of lost pay and monetary bounties among the deponents were amazingly precise and indicate that the loss was not easy to bear. In 1832, Joseph Mendenhall was still ruing the loss of forty dollars' worth of pay. James Wilkens declared in 1818 that he "enlisted for one year and served two years and five months—that he never received but three five-shilling continental notes for his services." John Struthers complained of the lot of frontier rangers who did not get "either pay or rations and not even clothing for part of the time, with the trifling exception of a little flour obtained now and then at the posts or stations, and furnishing their own ammunition." William Wallace, who enlisted into the Cumberland County militia, was pressed into the Continental army. He declared at his pension application that he had never been paid for his time spent attached to the regular army. Philip Duck, formerly of the Fifth Pennsylvania Battalion, deplored the fact that he "never drew or received . . . any articles of clothing or any pay." Samuel Scott was disillusioned that he was

34. RG-2, reel 154, frame 13, and reel 155, frames 222–23.

"discharged without a written certificate, which certificate was promised to him when he returned to Pennsylvania, to receive his pay. But neither was complied with notwithstanding one of the officers of said company received the money." Michael Aily's pension application sounded bitter. He explained that "after having spent the better part of his life in the service of his country, he remains to this day without receiving any recompense for his services." William Wolfe, veteran frontier ranger, noted, "my whole services during these three years amounted to at least eighteen months, for which, although I was promised a liberal compensation, I never received a single cent." Ebenezer Ferguson "was promised captain's pay, but, as yet, he has not been so fortunate to receive any."[35]

Others lamented the worthlessness of the recompense that they did receive during the war. John Hill sarcastically recalled how he "cheerfully stepped forward" for a militia tour "for which Colonel Kelly paid me sixteen dollars and 50 cents in Continental paper, worth then to me one dollar and 20 cents." Zachariah Clossen also remembered Revolutionary-era inflation well enough to put his wages in a material context. He explained how he was paid "a hundred dollars extra" for a militia tour in winter 1778, "but it was almost good for nothing. He remembers paying twenty dollars for one pound of sugar." Alexander Logan complained that the certificate he received in lieu of wages was similarly worthless. He explained, "There were considerable arrearages of my pay due. After the conclusion of the war, I moved to Allegheny County, Pennsylvania. In the year 1789, I had to travel to Chester County to where my old captain lived to get a settlement and a certificate of what was due me and then went to Philadelphia, but no money was to be had and had to sell my claim to a broker for one fifth of the amount, which about paid my expenses back and forth."[36]

Truly, many of those who served in the ranks were in terrible financial condition late in life. John Rybecker, for example, "walked from York County above 150 miles (without a cent in his pocket) to procure his pension and is obliged to crave alms for subsistence during his stay in the city [Philadelphia]." In fact, in the increasingly individualistic culture of the early republic, poverty came to be seen more as a character flaw than a condition of nature, and a few old soldiers felt that they had to apologize for their material situation. Thomas Elton, reduced to utter poverty and abandoned by his family, sought a pension

35. RWPF, files S23803, S40701; Dann, *The Revolution Remembered*, 258; RWPF, files S3470, W3230, S41139; RG-2, reel 154, frame 23; RWPF, files S24020, S22237.
36. RWPF, files W5298, S22173, W2821.

to survive. He prefaced his application with the statement that he had "endeavored in an honest way to keep himself from becoming a charge to the commonwealth," but was unable to avoid it. Abel Evans applied with "considerable reluctance, having seen better days." William Faulkner offered in 1820 to return to the military for his keep in his old age by asserting: "I could be serviceable in the recruiting services and inspection of recruits." Mordecai Dougherty also felt compelled to tell his court that he "would never have" applied for a pension "if he had continued able to labor for his support." Yet Dougherty also applied for the pension based upon "a consciousness of the rectitude and justice of his claim." The old soldier maintained his pride. Poverty had overtaken him in old age, but he still had a sense that he had served his community and that the nation owed him recognition.[37]

This discourse was, of course, all broadly compatible with the sentimental view of Revolutionary veterans. Former soldiers' dissatisfaction with their material status would not be seen as a radically class-conscious plea for economic assistance. As the statements of the pensioners themselves demonstrated, their stories centered on tales of individual disappointment—not that of an entire social group. The only collective identity consistently articulated among them was of selfless soldiers who sacrificed their financial well-being for the good of the nation. These self-presentations were, in part, shrewd narrative strategies that exploited the popular culture of the time to benefit the veterans themselves and to strengthen their pension claims. Nonetheless, their very use of the image of the poor soldier impoverished by a personal choice to serve manifested negative elements of an increasingly dominant culture of liberal individualism. Within the confines of the pension depositions, veterans did not develop a vocabulary to attack class inequality. This is not to say, however, that veterans did not participate in the construction of class-specific views of the Revolution. Their very adherence to describing their service in localist terms and defining communities they believed that they had protected evinced a memory of the conflict specific to common people. Moreover, as Alfred Young found in nineteenth-century Boston, genteel and working-class memories of the Revolution were increasingly at odds. By the 1830s, the former celebrated the orderliness and leadership of the early American patriot movement, while the latter hailed the

---

37. RWPF, file S4179. On the changing conception of poverty in the early republic—from the eighteenth-century vision of a social order ordained by God to a liberal view that saw the individual as culpable but able to be reformed through discipline—see David J. Rothman, *The Discovery of the Asylum: Social Order and Disorder in the New Republic* (Boston, 1970). RWPF, files S22228, S41521, S42720, R3039.

contributions of ordinary members of mobs and the army. Increasingly, the nascent trade unionist movements articulated a "labor republican" view of the ideology of the Revolution that stressed a labor theory of value in opposition to capitalist accumulation. Such urban class-based "memories" of the War for Independence were prevalent in large Northern cities, and Philadelphia was no exception. Many urban veterans who found their postwar prospects limited by the growth of centralized wealth and manufacturing found these ideas appealing. Those who experienced serving in the Philadelphia militia while it regulated the wartime moral economy of the city must have been disillusioned to see their role restricted to that of voting citizens in the early republic. Others who held radical hopes as soldiers that the Revolution might effect equality of economic opportunity did not see those dreams materialize.[38]

Even as vast disparities of wealth between the poorest and richest Americans continued to grow, however, the political equality among white men blunted the disappointment of white working men. The very localist white male nation that the veterans had helped create limited the development of class activism and politics in the United States. Obviously, the localist and exclusive nature of imagined communities made it difficult to coordinate collective working-class action among laborers in different cities and rural areas. Many white working men, too, rationalized their permanent wage-earning status as preferable to racial slavery. White freedom was only meaningful when contrasted with African American "fitness" for slavery due to perceived racial characteristics. Thus, free black workers were not included in the community of free white workers and citizens. Indeed, capitulation to the language of the white male political subject made larger class alliances with African American and women workers difficult, if not impossible. The major parties represented the interests of the "people" in Jacksonian America—that is to say, the voting public. As a result, poor white men saw common interests with wealthy and middle-class white males in terms of perpetuating a system of racial and gender privilege.[39]

38. Alfred Young, *The Shoemaker and the Tea Party*, 143–79. Bruce Laurie, *Working People of Philadelphia, 1800–1850* (Philadelphia, 1980), and Ronald Schultz, *The Republic of Labor: Philadelphia Artisans and the Politics of Class, 1720–1830* (New York, 1993), show the development of labor republicanism in Philadelphia; Sean Wilentz, *Chants Democratic: New York City and the Rise of the American Working Class, 1788–1850* (New York, 1984), chronicles its emergence in New York.

39. Roediger, *Wages of Whiteness*, suggests that white working-class identity was forged in opposition to African Americans. Harry L. Watson, *Liberty and Power: The Politics of Jacksonian America* (New York, 1990), 42–72, asserts the centrality of white male citizenship to politics in Jacksonian America.

Concepts of American identity that veterans forged in the Revolution and continued to build with their memories were dominant by the end of their lifetimes. Although many had never attained the economic security that they had hoped for, they were now active, voting citizens, despite their social class. The government recognized their contributions to the construction of the nation with pension stipends—not because of class injustice but because of the soldiers' loyal service. Like George Washington, the great general so many distinctly recalled, poor white men helped create the world in which they now were citizens. The plurality of communities with which veterans identified sustained American political subjectivity and American culture. In a diverse, individualistic, capitalist republic, a variety of interests would be seen as not only inevitable but desirable as well. Whiteness and male privilege provided the common ground that would render factionalism benign.[40]

"Other" Memories

In contrast to this vision were several counter-hegemonic memories of the American Revolution. African American, Indian, and loyalist veterans all cultivated distinct recollections of the conflict's meaning that contradicted many of the assumptions upon which the United States was based. African Americans were affected by the fact that they rarely shared in the benefits wrought by the Revolution. Slaves certainly recalled the scale of resistance in which they had engaged during the war. Tens of thousands had attempted to free themselves in the conflict and war among afforded the opportunity. This lesson was not lost on slaves of the American Civil War generation who fled in significant numbers to Union lines both before and after the Emancipation Proclamation. Like Revolutionary-era slaves, they made their military potential manifest and forced the hand of the government. These slaves, a few generations removed from the massive eighteenth-century flight to British lines, had certainly heard the stories of kin doing similar things less than a century before. In Northern states, such as Pennsylvania, post-Revolutionary emancipation led to an increase in the free black population and the simultaneous growth of formalized discrimination justified by racism. With the withering of slavery, the fundamental divide of free/slave became one of white/black. African Americans' cultural similarity to European Americans led "whites" to attribute increased significance to perceived

40. D. Nelson, *National Manhood*.

biological differences as a rationale for denying full citizenship to free blacks. Pennsylvania did not deny African Americans the right to vote until 1842, but discrimination and violence against free blacks were widespread in the state during the era in which pension depositions were given. It was in this context that African American veterans of the Revolution who remained in the United States remembered their military service.[41]

Not surprisingly, their pension narratives varied widely from those of poor white men. African American veterans commonly linked the Revolution to freedom from slavery and entitlement to civil rights. Radical readings of Revolutionary ideology permeated their accounts, especially in New England. Rhode Islander Jehu Grant, for instance, was denied his pension because he served after running away from his Tory master. Grant justified his actions by suggesting his loyalty to the United States and its supposed cause of freedom. He invoked part of the new formula of citizenship—maleness and soldiering—by noting that he served when in "full manhood." He further cautiously (yet explicitly) stated that his own understanding of Revolutionary principles guided him. He recalled that he ran away and enlisted "when I saw liberty poles and the people all engaged for the support of freedom, I could not but like and be pleased with such a thing."[42]

In the lower North, where racism was often more vehement, African American pensioners had to be more careful in making their cases for stipends. Typically, their accounts emphasized their faithfulness to duty and country during the war. This was a rhetorical strategy to assuage white fears of African American radical egalitarianism. Oliver Cromwell of New Jersey noted that he attached his discharge "signed by General Washington" and in an enclosed newspaper article was quoted as stating that he "by reasons of his honorable services [was entitled] to wear the badges of honor." Jacob Francis, who lived near the Delaware River in Amwell, New Jersey, also remarked in detail on how he voluntarily enlisted after attaining his freedom and faithfully served his time in the Continental army. Like Cromwell, Francis was painfully aware that his economic future hung in the balance of the court's decision as to whether he was

---

41. See Horton, "From Class to Race," 645, on the denial of franchise to free blacks in Pennsylvania in 1842. Thomas P. Slaughter, *Bloody Dawn: The Christiana Riot and Racial Violence in the Antebellum North* (New York, 1991), and Emma Jones Lapsansky, "'Since They Got Those Separate Churches': Afro-Americans and Racism in Jacksonian Philadelphia," in *African Americans in Pennsylvania*, ed. Trotter and Smith, 93–120, show the informal discrimination and violence experienced by African Americans in early-nineteenth-century Pennsylvania.

42. Dann, *The Revolution Remembered*, 27–28.

entitled to a pension. In one anecdote, he remarked that while stationed at Cambridge, Massachusetts, digging entrenchments,

> General Putnam came riding along in uniform as an officer to look at the work. They had dug up a pretty large stone which lay on the side of the ditch. The general spoke to the corporal who was standing looking at the men at work and said to him, "My lad, throw that stone up on the middle of the breastwork." The corporal touching his hat with his hand, said to the general, "Sir, I am a corporal." "Oh," said the general, "I ask your pardon sir," and immediately got off his horse and took up the stone and threw it up on the breastwork himself.

Like the white pensioners who carefully made reference to major heroes of the war to validate their own stories, Francis was simply locating his own tale in the nation's popular meta-narrative. Francis himself does nothing potentially radical in the story, but curiously, it is one of his clearest memories. Nevertheless, the anecdote, like the Revolutionary War itself, while permeated by the conventions of social deference, suggests challenges to the hierarchy. Even as Francis ridicules the corporal's pretensions to rank and smiles at Putnam's humiliation of the enlisted man, he savors the image of the war in which, at a certain level, rank and status did not matter. The veteran remembered the Revolution as somewhat leveling, grounded foremost in human equality.[43]

The motif of African Americans doing their duty for the United States was apparent in Pennsylvania as well. With the fear of slave insurrection instigated by the British still fresh in the memories of many white residents of the state, it was reassuring to hear of African American patriotism. James Forten, one of the foremost free black Revolutionary veterans in Philadelphia, was described by the early nineteenth-century African American historian William C. Nell as a staunch supporter of the Revolution. Nell explained that Forten, who served as a privateer, was captured by the British and promised material reward and residence in Britain. Forten purportedly replied, "I am here a prisoner for the liberties of my country; I never, NEVER shall prove a traitor to her interests." Nonetheless, accounts of devoted service to the nation were meant to imply reciprocal obligations to African Americans. Forten himself was clear about his radical understandings of Revolutionary ideology. In fact, he proved an outspoken

---

43. RWPF, file S34613; Dann, *The Revolution Remembered*, 392–93.

advocate of racial equality and civil rights. When opposing a proposed Pennsylvania law in 1813 limiting black migration and instituting discrimination, Forten wrote,

> We hold this truth to be self-evident, that God created all men equal, and is one of the most prominent features in the Declaration of Independence, and in that glorious fabrick of collected wisdom, our noble Constitution. This idea embraces the Indian and the European, the Savage and the Saint, the Peruvian and the Lapplander, the white Man and the African, and whatever measures are adopted subversive of this inestimable privilege, are in direct violation of our Constitution.

Forten went further in his case for civil rights for African Americans by highlighting the fallacious nature of the concept of race. He asked, rhetorically, "why are we not to be considered men. Has the GOD who made the white man and the black, left any record declaring us a different species." Forten clearly saw the racist nation as antithetical to the Revolution's principles, which could still be employed to attack injustice.[44]

Indeed, slaves and free blacks usually kept the radical egalitarian implications of the Revolution alive when most whites believed that they had settled the issue by creating a society of politically equal white men. While free blacks in the North became some of the most radical antislavery activists in the early nineteenth century, slaves and free blacks in the South used Revolutionary ideals to resist and at times revolt against slavery. In nearby Virginia, for example, the insurrectionists in "Gabriel's Conspiracy" of 1800 were influenced by radical understandings of natural rights philosophy; Gabriel planned to use a flag with the motto "Death or Liberty." Such a memory of the Revolutionary tradition would prove an important tool for slaves and free blacks to use against both the institution of slavery and institutionalized racism.[45]

Indians, another group necessarily defined as outsiders in the United States, also communicated distinctive memories of the American Revolution in the early nineteenth century. Those who fought against the Revolutionaries

44. Nell on Forten, quoted in *Forging Freedom*, by Nash, 52; James Forten, *Letters from a Man of Colour on a Late Bill Before the Senate of Pennsylvania* (Philadelphia, 1813), in *Race and Revolution*, by Nash, 190 and 192.

45. James Sidbury, *Ploughshares into Swords: Race, Rebellion, and Identity in Gabriel's Virginia, 1730–1810* (New York, 1997), 87, suggests the influence of radical understandings of Revolutionary and natural rights ideology on Gabriel's Conspiracy.

remembered the war as a disaster. Many believed that their British allies presumptively granted their lands to the United States, despite the success of Indians who fought well to protect their independence. As a result, without further British support, they could either attempt to negotiate with the new federal or state governments, resist, or flee the region. For some, such as the Mohawks, the Revolution marked the beginning of the end of their power and independence. In 1789, Joseph Brant wrote:

> It is a critical times [*sic*] for us here I mean we the Indians. I felt very unhappy oftentimes of late. The most difficult part for me is of having a [*sic*] many children which concerns me about them very much. Particularly when our Indian affairs and situation stands so unsettled the civilized cruelties I mean the Yankeys [*sic*] are taking advantage all the while and our friends the English seems [*sic*] getting tired of us. If I have not got so many children I would soon do some thing to drown my unhappiness. . . . If no accident happens I mean to go down to Canada.

Even those who left for British America occasionally found themselves in conflict with their onetime allies, Anglo-American loyalists. As both groups competed for access to lands, they found themselves at odds. Some Indians suggested that perhaps all Europeans or "whites" might be of the same ilk. In 1800 John Deserontyou, a Mohawk leader who settled with his people away from Brant and the rest of the Mohawk nation in Canada, argued that the latter group was "so near the Americans [loyalists], and I told him [Daniel Claus] I could not live in peace so near those people and made the choice of this place as being at a greater distance from them. The Americans are like a worm that cuts off corn as soon as it appears."[46]

For Indians who remained in the trans-Allegheny west to confront the expansionist United States, faith in alliance with the British withered. Although the Crown's forces kept posts in the region that supplied Indians well after the Revolution, Indians found that the British were unreliable allies at best. Ohioan Indians who lost the Battle of Fallen Timbers in 1794 found themselves turned

---

46. See Calloway, *American Revolution in Indian Country*, 272–91, on Indians fighting well in the Revolution and then feeling betrayed by the British negotiated settlement with the United States that ceded Indian lands up to the Mississippi River to the new republic. Joseph Brant to Major Robert Matthews, September 3, 1789, in *The Price of Loyalty*, ed. Crary, 410–11 (and see the John Deserontyou quotation on 426).

away from the British garrison at Fort Miami. This action demonstrated to many Northern Indians that the coalition that had lost the American Revolution could not be depended upon in the postwar era either. Nonetheless, Indian military resistance against the United States continued in the region well into the nineteenth century. Certainly, the memory of pan-Indian unity in the earlier period animated subsequent nativist and accommodationist alliances to resist U.S. expansion through the War of 1812. The American Revolution could be seen by many eastern Native peoples as a high point of the unification of diverse peoples to resist land-hungry Anglo-Americans. It was also the genesis of a new expansionist nation, however—one far more hostile to independent Indian nations in multicultural borderlands than competing European imperial regimes were. The birth of the United States was not a celebrated memory for most Indian peoples who lived in close proximity to its claimed national borders.[47]

Indeed, given the hegemonic memory of the Revolution and popular views of American nationhood, the postwar world would be particularly bleak for Native peoples who attempted to cooperate with the United States. The attitudes of ex-soldiers who came largely from the lower and middling ranks of society help explain the support of many ordinary Americans for actions such as Cherokee Removal. Those Cherokees who had republican government, Christianity, farming, livestock, European gender roles, and a written language could no more be entitled to the rights of whites than the Moravian Delawares at Gnadenhutten. Accommodation to the imperialist United States was not an effective strategy, as its citizens could justify expansion in racial terms. Therefore, not surprisingly, even Indian peoples who attempted to coexist with the new republic would retrospectively see the Revolution as a depressing turning point in the North American balance of power.[48]

Still another group of American outsiders—loyalists—had a distinctly negative memory of the Revolution. For those who remained in the United States

---

47. See Dowd, *Spirited Resistance*, 113 and 123–90, on the defeat of the Ohioan alliance at Fallen Timbers and the persistence of Indian unity through the War of 1812. Jeremy Adelman and Stephen Aron, "From Borderlands to Borders: Empires, Nation-States, and the Peoples in Between in North American History," *American Historical Review* 104 (June 1999): 814–41, argue that the United States was far more hostile and aggressive toward multicultural borderlands than earlier European empires were.

48. Anthony F. C. Wallace, *The Long, Bitter Trail: Andrew Jackson and the Indians* (New York, 1993), and Theda Perdue and Michael D. Green, eds., *The Cherokee Removal: A Brief History with Documents* (Boston, 1995). On the use of racism and exclusion as a rationale for continuing conquest and removal in the early republic, see John Mack Faragher, "More Motley than Mackinaw: From Ethnic Mixing to Ethnic Cleansing on the Frontier of the Lower Missouri, 1783–1833," in *Contact Points*, ed. Cayton and Teute, 304–26.

and attempted to reintegrate themselves, collective memories of the war were left unspoken. Tories who left their communities for the protection of the British Crown, however, articulated their recollections of an unmitigated debacle. Loyalist historians held differing views of the causes of the American Revolution, but most agreed that a small group of self-interested usurpers used the tumult of war to attack an orderly government illegitimately. Many also asserted the centrality of the New England Puritan tradition to republican conspiracies against constitutional government. These historians idealized life before the Revolution and sometimes criticized the weakness of the centralized British government in dealing with colonial dissent. From this perspective, the Revolution was the ultimate breakdown of authority and order.[49]

Rank-and-file Tories were influenced by these tales, but (like their Revolutionary counterparts) they constructed their own distinctive accounts of the war. Not surprisingly, they viewed the Revolution as the destruction of order in their communities as local rebels stripped them of their political rights. David Jones, for example, decried the "American tyranny and oppression" that he experienced at the hands of Revolutionaries in Philadelphia. From the Tory perspective, the rebels had abandoned a satisfactory status quo that mutually benefited all for a "tyrannical" regime that benefited the few. Turning the Whig formula on its head, they asserted that the rebels, not the British government, were engaged in a sinister conspiracy against the liberties of the people. Tories also recalled the Revolution as economically devastating to themselves and their families. Given the Revolutionary confiscation of loyalist estates and properties, most loyalist claims given after the war focused closely on cataloging material losses. While such a recurring motif clearly speaks to the goal of the claim—governmental reimbursement—it also suggests a common Tory memory of the war that focused on economic loss. Joel Arpin, for example, lamented that he "lost all his property" simply because "he took no part either for or against the Americans." Similarly, William Shepard recalled that his decision to seek protection from the British army in New Jersey led to his "leaving his family to be maltreated and his property destroyed by an enraged frantic mob." Henry Wakefield expressed the common Tory view of rebels as lawless as he discussed his own economic losses, noting that "the rebels robbed him of all his property and [were] going to put him to . . . gaol for refusing their illegal demands." Unlike Revolutionaries, who

49. For loyalist historians' views of the Revolution, consult Lawrence H. Leider, ed., *The Colonial Legacy: Loyalist Historians* (New York, 1971); W. Nelson, *American Tory;* and Peter C. Messer, "Stories of Independence: Eighteenth-Century Narratives" (Ph.D. diss., Rutgers University, 1997).

could recall the war as a largely successful defense of their homes and communities, Tories typically lost theirs. The latter group remained considerably bitter in their recollections of their losses and their enemies.[50]

Tories also commonly invoked the trope of serving "government" and a greater cause. While they often recalled taking up arms in response to their specific local situations, they went to great pains to discuss the war in terms of the empire. Again, while the provisions of loyalist claims invited such declarations of ideological commitment to "British government," the regularity of the term's appearance in loyalist accounts suggests that many came to remember their service beyond their own local interests. Jasper Harding was typical of those who stated that they served due to their "attachment to British government." George Sinclair recalled that he was "employed in many secret and dangerous services for government." Significantly, they placed their own particular stories within the rubric of "service for government," something that Revolutionary veterans almost never did. The loyalist memory of the war affirmed centralization and eschewed local autonomy as the basis for the empire.[51]

Indeed, such a view of the Revolution reflected a popular postwar British view of the empire, whose composition changed radically over the course of the eighteenth century. By the eve of the constitutional crisis, constituent parts of the British Empire in North America included French Catholic Quebec and independent Indian nation allies, as well the mainland and West Indies colonies. The exigencies of the war forced the British to utilize every resource available, including Indian allies and freed slaves, to defeat the rebels. With the loss of thirteen North American colonies by 1783, the multiethnic components of the empire grew in importance. Indians and Canadians were bulwarks against U.S. expansion. Freed slaves who settled in Sierra Leone represented the empire in Africa. Moreover, with the loss of the particularly obstreperous colonies that demanded the full rights of British subjects, some of the most vocal opponents of the centralized nature of the empire were gone. London now would be able to rule its holdings with the interests of Britain held foremost even more easily. Vast and disparate people in the empire were held together not by competing local self-interest, as was the case in the United States, but by centralized government.[52]

50. AO13/71/122, AO12/100/354, AO12/38/183–84, AO12/42/374–75.
51. AO13/96/367, AO13/22/261.
52. Edward Countryman, "Indians, the Colonial Order, and the Social Significance of the American Revolution," *WMQ* 53 (April 1996): 342–63, argues that the British viewed Indians as constituent parts of their hierarchical empire. See Eliga H. Gould, *The Persistence of Empire: British Political Culture in the Age of the American Revolution* (Chapel Hill, N.C., 2000), 181–214, on the post-Revolutionary British view of

While loyalists recognized this new view of empire in their memories of the Revolution, they were not always happy with the way it functioned in practice. Granting the rectitude of the British government's leadership, many Tories bitterly recalled its failures against the rebels and its undervaluing of its American allies. Prominent loyalists such as Joseph Galloway testified that the British military mismanaged both the war effort and its friends in America. Significantly, however, Galloway never questioned the principle of British supremacy in the war coalition. He merely suggested that they had been imperfectly utilized and led by Sir William Howe in his 1777–78 Pennsylvania campaign. At another level, enlisted men recalled that for all its centralization and power, the British government was at times little more able to supply and pay its allies than the rebels were. Abraham Pastorius, who served as a guide to the British army in Pennsylvania (and, as a result, lost his property), bitterly recalled that he "never received a shilling" for his service. John Knight, who also guided the king's forces, complained in his loyalist claim that he too "never received any pay." Isaac Taylor, veteran of the Bucks County Volunteers, stated clearly in his recollection that he "served without either money, pay, or clothing."[53]

Other loyalists also encountered difficulties after their Revolutionary War service. Again, they asserted their service to government as the justification for benefits that they felt were unfairly denied them. Veterans of the Black Pioneers in Nova Scotia, for example, soon found that their promised land bounties were either nonexistent or in heavily forested areas unsuited for farming. Others were forced to settle in segregated towns. Thomas Peters, one of the veterans, petitioned the royal government on his own behalf and that of his comrades, complaining of the governor's broken promises of land and the fraudulent confiscations of allotted lands. Peters complained of the "unprovided and destitute condition" of the black loyalists and their families, and he reminded the British that "your Memorialist and other said Black Pioneers . . . served in North America . . . for the space of seven years and upwards." In the language of submission to paternalistic authority, Peters pleaded with the empire to live up to its obligations to its subjects. He further asserted the veterans' commitment to the greater good of the empire by noting that some of his neighbors were "ready

---

the empire as a "looser consortium defined by cultural differences and the paternal obligations that a civilized people owed their less enlightened cousins." Gould asserts that "the second British Empire was at once more diverse and authoritarian than the one George III inherited twenty years before" (210).

53. See Calhoon, *The Loyalists in Revolutionary America*, 481–82, on Galloway's 1779 testimony in Parliament against Sir William Howe; AO12/42/21, AO12/42/65, AO13/70, pt. 1/373.

and willing to go wherever the wisdom of Government may think proper to provide for them as free subjects of the British Empire."[54]

In short, many Tories recalled the Revolution as the beginning of an unpleasant, forced transformation of their lives. As John Loofbourrow recalled, he "was obliged to save his life, to abandon his family and property." With almost nothing left of their earlier lives, men such as Loofbourrow had little to embrace aside from the greater cause of government. When the British lost the war, loyalists knew that returning home would prove difficult (if not impossible). The empire had failed to protect their property and ideas of community. As exiles, they recalled the hardship of building a new life. In 1798, Reverend John Stuart described his feelings in the postwar period: he had "thought it a great hardship to be banished into the wilderness" of Ontario. Yet he learned to accept his situation and tried to place the catastrophe of the Revolution behind him. Stuart acted as a missionary to members of the Mohawk nation in Canada and imagined his old community transplanted to his new one. He noted that "now the best wish we can form for our friends is to have them removed to us." As a result of the American Revolution, the loyalists were building their own new nation as well.[55]

Collectively, loyalist, African American, and Indian memories of the Revolution remained outside the mainstream view in the United States. Loyalists who attempted to reintegrate themselves into their old communities may well have retained their old views on the war, but prudence dictated that they keep such perspectives to themselves. While Indians continued to draw upon memories of resistance and unity during the Revolution in the postwar era, their view of the Revolution as an unjust war of conquest was certainly not shared by most U.S. citizens. Independent and even dependent Indian nations struggled to maintain some level of cultural autonomy, and their recollection of the war was not influential within the American nation. African Americans who remained in the United States most persistently employed their radical memories of the Revolution and its ideals to argue against slavery and for greater civil rights. Within the hegemonic culture of the nation, this was an extremely radical position on the nation's founding, one that appeared utterly inconsistent with that held by white male veterans. Yet they would not let their vision of the Revolution's potential die.

54. Petition of Thomas Peters in *The Price of Loyalty*, ed. Crary, 429–30.
55. AO13/71/175; John Stuart to William White, November 26, 1798, in *The Price of Loyalty*, ed. Crary, 452.

In the end, however, white male former soldiers' narratives of the American Revolution revealed the dominant perception of national subjectivity. Unlike loyalists, most former Revolutionaries suggested that citizens of the United States saw themselves as united not by a commitment to a strong central government but rather by a plethora of different interests. They were intensely competitive and localist, and they held membership in a variety of imagined communities even within specific regions. Indeed, such heterogeneity was viewed as not only benign but even central to the new American nation. Continued localism remained one of the few commonalities among Americans. The potential for serious conflict among citizens was further tempered by white male supremacy. Those defined as biologically unable to be political subjects of the republic—Indians, African Americans, and women—were formally excluded, and class conflict among white men was muted by their shared allegiance to the idea of white male privilege. The localist white male nation reached its zenith by the 1830s, a decade in which many of the pension narratives were given and universal white male suffrage had largely been attained. Despite its apotheosis in the early nineteenth century, the roots of this construct reached to the American Revolution. These beliefs, born in the conflict that created the United States, were consolidated afterwards as veterans remembered their service in ways that buttressed their claims to citizenship.[56]

---

56. Joan R. Gundersen, *To Be Useful to the World: Women in Revolutionary America, 1740–1790* (New York, 1997), 167–84, suggests that during the Revolutionary period, white women were increasingly viewed as unsuited for participation in the public sphere because of their "nature."

CONCLUSION

As the Revolutionary generation passed into history, the idea of the localist white male nation was indeed dominant. While some historians recognize the movement toward universal white manhood suffrage as a turning point in American identity, they typically analyze this process in the context of the early nineteenth century. This concept of citizenship was deeply ingrained in ordinary people's experiences in the Revolution, but it took a variety of forms in the colonial period. The War for Independence consolidated provincial assumptions regarding the centrality of localism and white male political subjectivity, linking them with national identity. The crisis of empire opened the term "American" to redefinition—and the Revolution settled much of the question. The war against imperial authority could never have been won without the significant support of ordinary men who served as soldiers. Once they became agents in the founding of the nation, their worldviews shaped the nature of the republic. Revolutionary leaders typically emphasized unified interests beyond locale and were deeply suspicious of granting more political powers to propertyless white men, but their alliance with enlisted men demanded that they take the interests of the latter group seriously.[1]

Thus, the historical development of the United States cannot be fully understood without an account of how mainstream national identity was forged among ordinary people in the American Revolution. The views of community fostered in the conflict were vital in defining who could and could not be an American. The war also helped transform the Anglo-American provincial valuation of local autonomy into a national ethos. The experience of Pennsylvanians

1. Scholarship locating the construction of the white male nation primarily after the American Revolution includes D. Nelson, *National Manhood;* Roediger, *Wages of Whiteness;* and Saxton, *Rise and Fall.*

was exceptional in many ways but also suggests broader patterns of popular nationalism. Communities were imagined as complex interstices of specific local, class, ethnic, racial, and gendered boundaries. Even within the state, the variety of local situations is dizzying. When viewed from the perspective of ordinary soldiers, however, a pattern of trans-regional adherence to localism emerges. This outlook created strong commitments to what these men defined as their neighborhoods. Rather than advocating a simplistic, narrow-minded provincialism, soldiers understood their primary goal of defending their town, township, or county as consistent with the "American" cause. Even those who had lived in an area only a relatively short time demonstrated and remembered the war as a defense of that particular locale. Such perspectives are comprehensible given the culture, society, and technology of early America. People in a narrowly circumscribed vicinity depended on each other for goods, access to trade, services, and military defense. Moreover, the slowness of travel made what we see as short distances great ones. For a farmer on the far western Pennsylvania frontier, Carlisle was a hazardous week's journey away. Philadelphia could seem almost as distant as London. The epicenter of poorer eighteenth-century Americans' existence was within several miles of their homes, where they lived and made their livings. Most of the people they knew and relied upon for their daily existence lived within those immediate environs. Thus, despite widespread internal immigration within North America, common people quickly became parts of communities in order to survive and socialize.

This is not to evoke an idealized, premodern communal utopia. Revolutionary-era American culture, permeated by market exchange, consumer culture, and connections to a broad Atlantic trade world, fostered an ethic of individualism as well. Helping neighbors was practical: it created mutual obligations that would ultimately improve personal well-being. Constructing new ideas of community that defined oneself and one's family as social "insiders" (in opposition to others) served individual as well as group interests. Indeed, the soldiers' localism accommodated rather than negated their competitive individualism. Communities themselves were fluid and dynamic in this period, too. As pension applications indicate, veterans were significantly mobile. Most Pennsylvania soldiers had left the communities they fought for in the Revolution by the time they sought pensions. Some were as far away as Iowa and Indiana when they offered their reflections on their wartime service. Obviously, former soldiers may have romanticized their attachment to their wartime homes over the years. The Revolution, however, was clearly one of the most crucial events in these men's lives, and their views of community at that time were probably etched in their memories because the war defined their sense of self and nation. Localism was also easily transferable across regions as former soldiers acclimated themselves to the concerns of their new neighborhoods. In other words, while particular views of community evolved over time and among groups, the larger localist perspective circumscribed specific variations.

This general pattern renders the vast variety of regional experiences in the American Revolution more comprehensible. The particular experiences of average Pennsylvanians were obviously not equivalent to those in other regions of the early United States. But while common people elsewhere had different specific motivations and views of enemies from those of Pennsylvanians, their war was based in their views of communities. New England, for instance, offers one pointed contrast to the Revolution in Pennsylvania. Those living around and in the city of Boston, the center of much of the opposition to imperial colonial policy, were particularly concerned with the actions of the central British government. Ordinary Bostonians lived among a sizable occupying royal army in the years leading up to the war. Economic competition with soldiers for scarce jobs, coupled with the unpopular Quartering Act, led many city inhabitants to resent the regulars long before the Revolution began. The 1770 Boston "Massacre" involving violence between British troops and a mob generated further rancor. It would not be surprising to find that soldiers from this region showed far greater ire toward the redcoats in the Revolution than their Pennsylvania counterparts did. Indeed, most volunteers from the Boston area and its environs came into service specifically to counter the martial encroachments upon their liberties by the forces of the Crown. Unlike many Pennsylvanians, these residents of Massachusetts had an extended and unpleasant history of interaction with British regulars and were anxious to fight them. For many soldiers coming from the Boston vicinity, this hatred of the regulars was undoubtedly the central strand in their story of the Revolutionary War. Such motivations, while related to the larger constitutional crisis, were clearly local in nature. It was painfully evident to the regional population that it was situated at the seat of hostilities when the war broke out at Lexington and Concord. That nearby militias poured in to assist the siege of the retreating royal forces in Boston testifies to the immediacy of the threat. As in southeastern Pennsylvania, however, common people's zeal for volunteering in the war faded soon after the main British army left. When the enemy began to operate in the middle colonies, never to return to the Boston area, it became progressively more difficult to raise troops. And again, as in Pennsylvania, high bounties and the draft became the most useful recruiting tools.²

Perhaps the experiences of enlisted men in New York and New Jersey were most similar to those of their neighbors in Pennsylvania. All three states shared a long history of ethnic and religious pluralism. Simmering resentment among these groups fed the fires of civil war throughout the mid-Atlantic area. Furthermore, New York and Pennsylvania shared a similar cultural geography. Both had three distinct regions: a large city, a European American–dominated agrarian region, and an extensive frontier with a large Native American population. One would expect to find distinct urban, countryside, and frontier outlooks among common people in New York broadly comparable to those in Pennsylvania. Nonetheless, even within this single region of early America, there were sharp contrasts. Both New York and New Jersey endured a sustained British presence throughout the war. This helped fuel the fires of bitter civil war within the states: long-term assistance was offered to those opposed to local Revolutionary groups. As a result, the immediate environs of British-occupied New York remained a battleground of violence and counter-violence among Tories, Revolutionaries, and the British between 1776 and 1783. Also, varying social structures accounted for animosity that exploded into war. New York's history of a distinct tenant farming system strongly shaped the war in rural areas of that state. Landlord and tenant disputes often determined who took up which side, and they were at the heart of the Revolution in the New York countryside.³

---

2. David Hackett Fischer, *Paul Revere's Ride* (New York, 1994); Shy, *Toward Lexington*, 267–320; and Hiller B. Zobel, *The Boston Massacre* (New York, 1970), all discuss pre-Revolutionary hostility toward the British army in Boston. See Gross, *Minutemen*, 109–32 and 146–53, for a discussion of the early military resistance to the British threat followed by the town's declining enthusiasm and resort to conscription and bounties.

3. I do not wish to suggest that New Jersey, Pennsylvania, and New York shared the same Revolutionary experiences. Indeed, their colonial pasts were quite disparate; the states were, in many ways, similar only in their shared heterogenous population, culture, social structures, and political institutions. On the coherence of the mid-Atlantic region primarily as a collection of dissimilar, pluralist colonies, see Bodle, "Themes and Directions." On the ethnic dimensions of civil war in this area, see, for example, Adrian C. Leiby, *The Revolutionary War in the Hackensack Valley: The Jersey Dutch and the Neutral Ground* (New Brunswick, N.J., 1962). See Countryman, *People in Revolution*, on New York, and David Fowler, "Egregious Villains, Wood Rangers, and London Rangers: The Pine Robber Phenomenon in New Jersey During the Revolutionary War" (Ph.D. diss., Rutgers University, 1987), on New Jersey. On the effects of landlord-tenant relations on the Revolution in New York, see Edward Countryman, "'Out of Bounds of the Law': Northern Land Rioters in the Eighteenth Century," in *Beyond the American Revolution*, ed. Young, 35–69. For a different interpretation that plays down the importance of class tensions between landlords and tenants, see Sung Bok Kim, "The Limits of Politicization in the American Revolution: The Experience of Westchester County, New York," *Journal of American History* 80 (December 1993): 868–89.

The South displayed other distinct social dynamics during the Revolutionary War. In Virginia, the material concerns generated by the tobacco economy molded the ways in which small farmers and planters understood imperial taxation policies. Class tensions between yeomen and planters as well as land speculators, Indians, and squatters additionally contributed to the way in which ordinary Virginians and elites imagined their Revolutionary communities. The institution of slavery, too, while important throughout early America, was vital to the southern colonies' economies and culture. Keeping the region's large slave population submissive during the war was a paramount concern among white Revolutionaries. Virginia Royal Governor Lord Dunmore's proclamation announcing freedom for all slaves serving rebel masters who joined him against the Revolutionaries—and the subsequent promises of emancipation offered by the British in their late-war southern campaign—certainly energized slaveholders and poorer whites who had a stake in the continued subjugation of African Americans on the basis of race. Fighting the British in the South often signaled a defense of human property and of the racial hierarchy that justified enslaving African Americans. The slave and planter economy also created tensions among Revolutionaries as well. Poor men liable for militia service stood against laws that they believed were inequitable and excused large slaveholders from duty. Although they wished to maintain the status quo at home, ordinary enlisted men resented the plantation owners' privileges. These cases all suggest the centrality of regional variants of class conflict, slavery, and racism toward African Americans to the Revolutionary military experience in the South.[4]

Ordinary southerners were also drawn into the war on account of the actions of the British army around their homes. Royal military policy in the American South in the 1780s involved pacification and intimidation. Expecting widespread Tory support, the British demanded loyalty oaths and dealt harshly with suspected rebels. As a result, those previously neutral were pushed into the Revolutionaries' ranks. Such British actions also sparked some of the most sustained and savagely violent civil war among Americans in the Revolution. Again,

4. See Holton, *Forced Founders,* and Michael A. McDonnell, "Popular Mobilization and Political Culture in Revolutionary Virginia: The Failure of the Minutemen and the Revolution from Below," *Journal of American History* 85 (1998): 946–81, on Virginia. Consult Frey, *Water from the Rock,* 45–142, on British policy regarding emancipation and the white American reaction. Jerome Nadelhaft, *The Disorders of War: The Revolution in South Carolina* (Orono, Me., 1981), discusses the particular anxiety of Revolutionaries regarding slaves in South Carolina, a state with a black majority (5). On the class tensions resulting from militia exclusions that benefited large slaveholders, see Allan Kulikoff, "The Political Economy of Military Service in Revolutionary Virginia," in *The Agrarian Origins of American Capitalism* (Charlottesville, Va., 1992), 152–80, and McDonnell, "Popular Mobilization."

disputes among local groups were exacerbated by the intrusion of armed hostilities. A cycle of revenge for killings and destruction or theft of property was set into motion among factions that eventually became identified as Tories or Whigs. This brutal violence continued over the course of several years, which likely made civil war one of the most important facets of common southerners' experience of the Revolution.[5]

This brief comparative discussion is meant to suggest the ways in which localisms varied across Revolutionary America. It appears that the conflict was ostensibly composed of many different (perhaps even unrelated) wars. Indeed, the unity of the thirteen diverse American colonies seems baffling at first. From a "bottom up" perspective, however, these local variations are the overarching commonality of the Revolution. Most participants in the war actively pursued the conflict when it directly infringed upon their own communities, families, and livelihoods. In general, American opponents were the most detested of all the rank-and-file Revolutionaries' enemies, and the civil war was bitter. Descended, in many cases, from local prewar social and cultural antagonisms, domestic conflict among Americans was a powerful motivator for military activity among the lower and middling sorts in the Revolution. War with Indians was central as well. Revolutionaries were moved to fight various Native American groups out of a desire for land coupled with a developing racialized identity. The British antagonized common residents of the former colonies usually only when the British army operated in the vicinity of the Americans' homes and became part of an area's local conflicts. During these periods of invasion, the royal army alienated locals with its actions and the physical threat it presented. Significantly, it appears that the war against the British was only one (and in many cases, a secondary) part of the average early American's experience of war between 1775 and 1783. Creating, defining, and defending communities were paramount.[6]

---

5. See Shy, "Military Conflict," 229–42, and Ronald Hoffman, "The 'Disaffected' in the Revolutionary South," in *Beyond the American Revolution*, ed. Young, 275–316, on British policy in the South and its effective politicization of those who were previously neutral. On the brutality of civil war in the South sparked by the British invasion, see Nadelhaft, *Disorders of War*, 64; Edwin J. Cashin, *The King's Ranger: Thomas Brown and the American Revolution* (Athens, Ga., 1989); John S. Pancake, *This Destructive War: The British Campaign in the Carolinas* (Tuscaloosa, Ala., 1985); and Hugh F. Rankin, *The North Carolina Continentals* (Chapel Hill, N.C., 1971).

6. Calhoon, "Civil, Revolutionary, or Partisan," 147–62, suggests that civil war exacerbated prewar local conflicts. White, *Middle Ground*, 366–412, remarks upon Revolutionaries' racial hostility toward Indians and desire for their land but shows it developing on a local, village level. Shy, "Military Conflict," explains rancor among Americans toward the British army as contingent upon the army's location and actions in particular regions.

The popular vision of the nation produced by the Revolution persisted well into subsequent centuries. In the early republic, competition, faction, different views of community, and white male prerogative were codified as the foundations of American politics. American politics and society could be pluralistic and conflict-prone as long as a majority agreed on the best interests of white men. What eventually tore the nation apart in the Civil War was the emergence of two sectional worldviews in the 1840s and 1850s that both purported to best protect the interests of white men to the exclusion of the other. Proslavery advocates in the South believed that only the existence and expansion of slavery made white male independence possible. They criticized "wage slavery" in the emerging manufacturing system in the North that forced white men to do the most demeaning manual labor and made them utterly dependent on the whims of the market. Conversely, free labor proponents in the North aimed their criticisms against slavery in terms of how it demeaned the dignity of free white male labor. They argued that only the preservation of the free labor system and its expansion via "free soil" in the West would preserve white male independence. The coming of the Civil War, therefore, can be seen as a crisis of the localist white male nation defined in the Revolution. While competing articulations of community could coexist in the republic, mutually exclusive ones—ones that hoped to preserve racial and gender privilege—could not.[7]

Most historians agree that the Civil War created a stronger, centralized federal government and a sense of a unified nation-state. Still, localism did not fade into oblivion. To an extent, the Union victory in the war heralded the triumph of one sectional vision of the localist white male nation based on the free labor model. Slavery ended, but competitive localisms, dual state and federal sovereignty, and racism persisted. Movements emerging in late-twentieth- and early-twenty-first-century America to return to localist traditions further underscore the degree to which the world forged in the American Revolution is with us still. In an era when communities in the United States remain informally segregated by race and class, attempts to keep tax revenue and power "within the community" take on ominous overtones. In many cases, appeals for local self-determination and control are euphemisms for racial and class politics.

7. Eugene D. Genovese, *The World the Slaveholders Made: Two Essays in Interpretation* (Middletown, Conn., 1988), explains the emergence of the "proslavery" worldview that argued that racial slavery made white yeoman independence possible in the South and critiqued Northern capitalism as demeaning to white men. Conversely, Eric Foner, *Free Soil, Free Labor, Free Men: The Ideology of the Republican Party Before the Civil War* (New York, 1995), suggests that the "free labor" view saw preventing the growth of slavery as necessary to the protection of free white men's dignity and economic independence.

Typically, wealthy communities enjoy far better schools, social services, and infrastructure than poorer ones. Upper-class white privilege is often maintained in the domain of local politics. And many Americans continue to struggle with the problem of imagining common interests with people outside their locale and their own particular social groups.[8]

The second (and related) component of early U.S. national identity—white male supremacy—was limiting in many ways as well. It is difficult to argue that the movement toward greater franchise for white men was not radical in the context of the late eighteenth and early nineteenth centuries. The great bulk of soldiers secured the right to formal manhood and citizenship. The rejection of British notions of balanced government based on institutions that represented social groups was also a significant departure from the European past. Constituent parts of federal, state, and local governments were directly or indirectly representative of voters. Nonetheless, as numerous historians have noted, there was no radical redistribution of wealth in the wake of the American Revolution. While poorer white men may have been gaining enhanced political standing in the republic, their social and economic status did not grow concomitantly. Indeed, as the pension applications make clear, most poor Revolutionary soldiers remained impoverished veterans into the nineteenth century. The ethos of liberal individualism rationalized such material inequity by suggesting that all white men had an equal chance to succeed—and that those who did not were not working hard enough.[9]

Of course, many working-class and poor white men rejected this explanation. Some developed forms of class consciousness that descended from their understandings of Revolutionary ideologies and coalesced as early forms of labor solidarity. Those who imagined a community of virtuous, independent producers criticized a social order in which wealth was accumulated in speculation,

---

8. See, for example, James M. McPherson, *Battle Cry of Freedom: The Civil War Era* (New York, 1988), on the growth of federal power and the unified nation-state during the American Civil War. Eric Foner, *A Short History of Reconstruction* (New York, 1990), examines the persistence of racism and the reemergence of distinctive Northern and Southern variants of capitalism following the end of Reconstruction.

9. Wood, *Radicalism of the American Revolution*, argues that greater freedom for white men and the rejection of monarchy were clearly radical at the time. Wood correctly emphasizes in this work (and in "Equality and Social Conflict") that these elements of the Revolution were major changes in the late eighteenth and early nineteenth centuries. But even the rejection of balanced government based on social hierarchy—although radical by British standards—was at least somewhat consistent with the American colonial past, in which there was no indigenous provincial aristocracy. Resch, *Suffering Soldiers*, shows the continued poverty of many Revolutionary War veterans. Appleby, *Inheriting the Revolution*, and Foner, *Free Labor*, trace the development of liberal individualist culture that attributed class status to individual accomplishment.

mercantile pursuits, and, increasingly, ownership of the means of mass manufacturing. The idea of the localist white male nation, however, inhibited the full development of lower-class consciousness in the early republic and beyond. Northern workers had difficulty imagining common interests with rural laborers in the South. White men always had recourse to formal politics, while women and racial outsiders did not. Formal and informal racism and sexism created divisions among oppressed peoples. Thus, for example, common interests among white men, free black men, and women—all working-class—were obfuscated by the exclusive definition of citizenship. As many historians have demonstrated, the efficacy and unity of labor movements in the United States have been consistently hamstrung by regional, racial, and gender divisions.[10]

The legacy of including white males as political subjects was, in part, the necessary exclusion of those defined as Others. As definitions of citizenship came to hinge on assumptions rooted in beliefs about biological difference, those seen as outsiders could not change their status until the entire nature of national identity was redefined. While some historians have argued that the Revolution paved the way for an enhanced political role for women that eventually led to activism and enfranchisement, "republican women" were still vital negative reference points in early definitions of citizenship. The legacy of the Revolution changed notions about male authority. Traditional views of patriarchal authority vested solely in propertied men gave way to the radical notion that all white men were capable of formal public manhood. Thus, male political privilege was no longer rooted in class status but in biology. Conversely, then, women's inability to be citizens was not necessarily related to the fact that few of them owned significant property. Female exclusion could be entirely explained by their sex. Additionally, as cultural assumptions about gender identity were essentialized, dominant upper- and middle-class ideologies of domesticity further marginalized all women by asserting that they had no role in the "public sphere."[11]

---

10. See Foner, *Tom Paine*, and Rosswurm, *Arms, Country, and Class*, on class consciousness in Revolutionary Philadelphia. Wilentz, *Chants Democratic*, and Ronald Schultz, *The Republic of Labor*, discuss the development of working-class consciousness, racism, and "labor republicanism" that framed much early labor activism. On gender tensions, see, for example, Mary H. Blewett, *Men, Women, and Work: Class, Gender, and Protest in the New England Shoe Industry* (Urbana, Ill., 1988), who shows distinctly different male and female approaches to work and labor activism.

11. On the inferior and informal political role of post-Revolutionary women, see Kerber, *Women of the Republic*; Rosemarie Zagarri, "Morals, Manners, and the Republican Mother," *American Quarterly* 44 (June 1992): 192–215; and Jan Lewis, "The Republican Wife: Virtue and Seduction in the Early Republic," *WMQ*, 3d ser., 44 (October 1987): 689–721. Also see Smith-Rosenberg, "Dis-Covering the Subject," on male political subjectivity being defined in opposition to women as non-citizens.

African American men and women were, of course, excluded from formal membership in the new nation as well. Free black men shouldered some of the obligations of citizenship, such as paying taxes, but enjoyed few of its benefits. In addition to losing the vote in most antebellum states, free black men were also typically banned from liability to militia service and jury duty. Even though African American activists almost always linked antislavery positions with civil rights for blacks, white Americans (including many abolitionists) overwhelmingly saw the two issues as entirely separate. Indeed, the localist white nation needed African American men as negative reference points as much as it required women to fulfill the same purpose. In Pennsylvania, slavery began to give way in the Revolution precisely because many white residents believed that emancipation was the best way to maintain racial hierarchy. If anything, popular white Pennsylvania racism became more vehement in the early republic and antebellum period: racial violence flared in Philadelphia and rural areas. It is not surprising, then, that the end of slavery brought about by the American Civil War did not end racism in the United States. Its persistence in law, practice, and informal community actions through the twentieth century attests to the continuing importance of white male supremacy to many Americans' views of the nation.[12]

The level of hostility that the early feminist, abolitionist, and civil rights movements provoked further testifies to the centrality of the biological concept of citizenship rooted in the American Revolution. Anyone who called for gender or racial equality in the nineteenth century was seen as a dangerous radical. Such persons were typically ostracized by their communities. Others risked their lives if they were too vocal about their views. Such reactions represented more than mere attempts to preserve current power relations. They manifested deep anxieties over threats to the very basis of American nationalism. Many feared that without the shared commitment to white male supremacy, the competing localisms of the United States might overwhelm the nation and lead to chaos. So ingrained were concepts of white and male supremacy that even some radical

12. Vincent Harding, *There Is a River: The Black Struggle for Freedom in America* (New York, 1993), makes clear the consistent equation between civil rights and antislavery made by African American activists in the eighteenth and nineteenth centuries. Foner, *Short History*, asserts the ultimate failure of even radical Reconstruction and the Fourteenth and Fifteenth Amendments to change not only racial power relations in the South but also most whites' views on race. Nancy Isenberg, *Sex and Citizenship in Antebellum America* (Chapel Hill, N.C., 1998), 8, shows that African Americans were denied liability for militia service and jury duty in 1830s Pennsylvania. On race riots in Philadelphia, see Appleby, *Inheriting the Revolution*, 219. On racial violence in rural Pennsylvania, see Slaughter, *Bloody Dawn*.

activists seized upon elements of it to buttress their cause. A few early feminists, for example, attempted to capitalize on their whiteness as an avenue to enhanced political rights, arguing that white women were fit for citizenship, perhaps more so than black men. Conversely, some civil rights activists focused on maleness as a way for blacks to find inclusion in a nation based on gendered power. Such schisms among radicals not only demonstrated the complexity of early American identity but also showed how the internalized idea of the localist white male nation consistently created divisions among oppressed peoples.[13]

Although the overwhelming majority of American Indians had no desire to become full U.S. citizens and give up their cultural (and in some cases their perceived racial) identities, views of Native Americans had sweeping consequences for constructing national identity as well. The frontier Revolution helped consolidate white national identity, and continued interactions with Indians further strengthened that identity. "Indians" were imagined as a singular group by most nineteenth-century whites, a number of whom exploited this racialized image in order to justify conquest and removal. The subsequent glorification of the nation's "Manifest Destiny" expressed the inevitability of an aggressively growing empire of white men. Obviously, one of this book's key arguments revolves around the importance of Othering Indians in popular nationalism. While an impressive array of scholarship has demonstrated the roles of women and African Americans in providing contrasts for defining white male privilege, the centrality of Native Americans to this process is undeniable. Frontier war and its attendant cultural exchange provided a crucible in which racial identity was forged and linked to the new nation. While African American racial Otherness was closely linked to chattel slavery, racialist views of Native Americans were related to warfare. Negative references to Indians and African Americans were, of course, connected; they both contributed to European Americans' common view of themselves as "white." The specific imagination of whiteness, however, depended on locale, as various negative reference points carried different weights across regions of North America. American concepts of race were (and are) fluid and dynamic, varying by region and social group and over time.

13. On popular opposition to the early feminist and abolitionist movements, see Isenberg, *Sex and Citizenship*; Gerda Lerner, *The Grimke Sisters from South Carolina: Rebels Against Slavery* (Boston, 1967); Mary R. Ryan, *Women in Public: Between Banners and Ballots, 1825–1880* (Baltimore, 1990); David Grimstead, *American Mobbing, 1828–1861* (New York, 1998); Henry Mayer, *All on Fire: William Lloyd Garrison and the Abolition of Slavery* (New York, 1998); and Slaughter, *Bloody Dawn*. Debra Gold Hansen, *Strained Sisterhood: Gender and Class Within the Boston Female Anti-Slavery Society* (Amherst, Mass., 1993), treats divisions within reform movements.

Still, the American Revolution was a pivotal moment in the nation's construction of racist nationalism.[14]

More than twenty-five years ago, Edmund S. Morgan posited the entire concept of American liberty as a paradox. He argued that freedom in colonial Virginia was inextricably intertwined with (and, indeed, dependent upon) African slavery. Morgan suggested that black bondage made white freedom meaningful and that this understanding pervaded concepts of individual liberty developing in the early United States. Only the Civil War and its legacy brought the symbiotic relation of American freedom and slavery to a complete end. I would like to build upon Morgan's interpretation to offer a view of the Revolution that asserts a model of American freedom/American exclusion. The enhanced liberty attained by poor and lower-middle-class European American men could not have occurred without explicit reference to those who could not share in the benefits of full citizenship. A shift in political subjectivity from a gendered and economic basis to a purely biological definition placed all but "white men" outside the formal public sphere. The construction of white male national identity and political privilege bridged the competitive communities that were the bedrock of colonial North America. This process allowed for different imagined communities of white men that could conflict and yet coexist.[15]

14. Recent examples of scholarship that posits the importance of women as vital negative reference points in defining male citizenship and privilege include Kathleen Brown, *Good Wives;* Smith-Rosenberg, "Dis-Covering the Subject"; and Kann, *Republic of Men*. A fascinating (and burgeoning) array of scholarship on what has been called "whiteness studies" focuses primarily upon the articulation of whiteness vis-à-vis "blackness." See, for example, Roediger, *Wages of Whiteness;* Saxton, *Rise and Fall;* and Theodore W. Allen, *The Invention of the White Race, Vol. 2: The Origin of Racial Oppression in Anglo-America* (New York, 1997). Allen does discuss the role of Indians in concepts of race. Also see David Roediger, "The Pursuit of Whiteness: Property, Terror, and Expansion," *Journal of the Early Republic* 19 (Winter 1999): 579–600, a historiographical essay on this body of work. Most recent scholarship that centers on the Indian presence in the construction of American identity concentrates on the American appropriation of elements of Native culture (in contrast with European). See, for example, Deloria, *Playing Indian,* and Scheckel, *The Insistence of the Indian*. On the historical development of views of Indians, see Richter, "'Believing That Many of the Red People Suffer Much.'" For essays that take account of racial identity in terms of interactions with African and Native Americans, see Vaughan, *Roots of American Racism*. Ronald Takaki posits the importance of exchanges with Indians, African Americans, and Asian Americans for the construction of whiteness over the course of the nineteenth century. See his *Iron Cages: Race and Culture in Nineteenth-Century America* (New York, 2000). Such myriad loci for the cultural construction of race and racism in America suggest that scholars need to consider locale in the making and refining of such ideologies.

15. Morgan, *American Freedom, American Slavery*. Here, I am also building upon the work of other historians who have suggested that the enhanced freedom for white men that framed early American national identity was predicated on the exclusion of women and racial Others. See, for example, D. Nelson, *National Manhood,* and Clark Smith, "The Adequate Revolution."

While the Civil War and the Thirteenth Amendment brought to an official end the vexed and close relation between American freedom and slavery, I would argue that concepts of the localist white male nation have yet to be disentangled from U.S. national identity. Localist politics continue to obfuscate connections among various oppressed groups of people and limit views of an entire state or the nation as a larger community of Americans. Arguments over how to deal with the legacy and persistence of racism and sexism remain fierce in U.S. politics and society. Race and gender continue to be significant categories through which power is exercised. Furthermore, despite a plethora of scholarship that has demonstrated the subjective nature of "race" as a cultural and historical construct, many (perhaps most) Americans still believe that it is an objective reality. The federal census of 2000, for example, still differentiated "race" and "ethnicity." It is difficult to disengage from the discourse of race when racism remains a pervasive form of social power. The problem, however, clearly derives from our Revolutionary heritage and earlier exclusionary definitions of citizenship. Recognizing this is an important step in truly redefining American identity.[16]

Understanding and dismantling the localist white male nation also requires a more prominent position for the concept of social class. While poor and working-class white men benefited *somewhat* from their inclusion in the public political sphere, their material conditions changed very little. I would argue that the greatest beneficiaries of the new republic's definition of the polity were upper-class white men. Regardless of whether they were conscious of the process, powerful, wealthy white men benefited (and still benefit) from the divisions that biological definitions of citizenship created among underclass and working-class communities. In other words, racism and sexism helped conceal class conflict, a salient aspect of American society. While class politics reared its head intermittently in mainstream U.S. politics throughout the nation's history, widespread assumptions of white male supremacy consistently limited lower-class solidarity. Ultimately, the legacy of the localist white male nation has constrained the lives of underclass and working-class white men as well as women and those seen as members of different races.

Purely celebratory understandings of the American Revolution, then, are not only inaccurate but dangerous as well. Imagining a set of disembodied

---

16. See Fields, "Slavery, Race, and Ideology," and Dana D. Nelson, "Consolidating National Masculinity: Scientific Discourse and Race in the Post-Revolutionary United States," in *Possible Pasts: Becoming Colonial in Early America,* ed. Robert Blair St. George (Ithaca, N.Y., 2000), 201–15, on the problems inherent in views of society and national politics that are trapped in a terrain of racialist discourse.

"American" ideals produced by the conflict that eventually righted all social wrongs in America is intensely misleading. As I have argued, these ideologies were precisely responsible for many problems in the new nation. Founders and ordinary people together created a new national subjectivity in the Revolution that shaped and limited American history for centuries after their deaths. Rather than seeing their racial ideologies, variants of patriarchy, and exclusionary localism as anomalies, we need to understand them as the very fabric of the American nation. It is not my intention to blame ordinary soldiers for all the republic's woes, however. Despite my profoundly critical perspective, careful readers will sense that I also have immense empathy for my historical subjects. Revolutionary War soldiers were, like us, fallible human beings profoundly shaped by the culture in which they lived. While American national identity was—and remains—exclusivist, historical moments of contingency and perhaps even elements of eighteenth-century worldviews may help us now see beyond the assumptions and ideologies rooted in the Revolution.

ESSAY ON SOURCES AND METHODOLOGY

This study is a cultural history of early modern lower orders in America. It was written with the intent of uncovering its subjects' worldviews. Although a few scholars have accomplished this goal, it is no easy task. On the most concrete level, it is difficult because numerous poor people of two hundred years ago could not write. Those who did, more often than not, could not preserve the bulk of their written documents. Letters, printed forms, and journals were lost in the tumult of work, moving, war, and life. Ordinary people and their families simply did not save their papers for posterity as frequently as elites did. I was lucky enough to encounter a surprisingly underutilized resource in which the lower and middling sorts were invited to give oral accounts in open court sessions of what they did in the Revolution. The Revolutionary War Pension and Bounty-Land-Warrant Application Files offer more than eighty thousand firsthand accounts of the war by enlisted men, mariners, spies, and even women of the army. I also used another set of retrospective accounts—the Loyalist Claims—that were given by enemies of the Revolutionaries. These documents, like the pension depositions, offered firsthand accounts of the war, mediated by the commissions hearing the claims. Like many Revolutionaries, loyalists who did not write or leave many documents did leave a record of their service. These sources, combined with the less numerous written records generated by common soldiers in the Revolutionary period, allowed me to begin to probe how average people viewed the events of 1775–83.

Like any kind of historical evidence, the pension applications and loyalist claims are both useful and problematic sources. They are enlightening because they give a voice to veterans. The large number of applicants who signed their depositions with an "X" demonstrates that the files are a written record left by many who were unable to write. Nonetheless, they present researchers with serious difficulties. I have attempted to interpret these sources carefully. The Revolutionary War Pension Applications are certainly as much documents of the nineteenth century as they are of the late eighteenth. Therefore, in the chapters that discuss what actually happened during the War for Independence, I have corroborated my conclusions with supporting evidence from Revolutionary-era sources whenever possible. The most important of these late-eighteenth-century documents include the Records of Pennsylvania's Revolutionary Governments, newspapers, diaries of soldiers and officers, and numerous units' orderly books. My argument about the centrality of localism to Revolutionary soldiers is based as much on troops' behavior during the war, the wartime records they left, and the commentaries of officers and other leaders as on the pension applications. In the first parts of the book, I used deponents' stories that seemed least colored by a nineteenth-century memory of the war. Conversely, in discussing soldiers' memories, I relied on those stories that were least consistent with the actual wartime behavior of enlisted men and analyzed them in the context of early-nineteenth-century culture.[1]

Other difficulties are inherent in these retrospective accounts. The most salient problem is the possibility of fading or embellished memories being presented in the later period that do not accurately reflect the culture of the 1770s and 1780s. In this respect, the accounts of Tories are less problematic than those of the Revolutionaries. The loyalist claims were given far closer to the actual war than the U.S. service pension depositions were. In July 1783, Parliament passed a compensation act for those Americans who lost property in royal service. Various commissioners heard loyalist claims up to 1789. Thus, most former "Tories" were fortunate enough to have the chance to describe their service from the previous few years. While some forgetfulness and exaggeration occurred, widespread memory loss due to aging was not a major issue. Additionally, the culture of the mid-to-late 1780s was not nearly as removed from the Revolutionary era as the 1820s and 1830s, when U.S. veterans gave their accounts. Most loyalists were still smarting from their losses of property, security, and

---

1. Michael Kammen and Michael Schudson explain the relationship of "collective memory" (or how various cultures tend to remember their pasts in ways that are relevant to their present) to individual memories. See Kammen, "Some Patterns and Meanings of Memory Distortion in American History," and Schudson, "Dynamics of Distortion in Collective Memory," both in *Memory Distortion: How Minds, Brains, and Societies Reconstruct the Past*, ed. Daniel Schacter (Cambridge, Mass., 1995), 329–45 and 346–64, respectively.

sense of community when they gave their claims. They remembered the events very well and rarely confessed that they could not recall names or events.[2]

In contrast, former Revolutionary soldiers sought pensions between forty and fifty years after their service. I recognize that the memories of men in their sixties, seventies, and eighties were often faulty in some respects. Overwhelming evidence has demonstrated that memory skills erode with aging. Yet, as scholars of the process of memory point out, older people can clearly remember events from much earlier in their lives. Moreover, memories tend to focus on the formative events from the beginning of adulthood. Psychologist Daniel Schacter asserts that elderly persons recall "fewer personal experiences from the more distant past, with one curious exception: the gradual decline in memories over time shows temporary reversal around late adolescence and early adulthood. The elderly recall more experiences from these years than those immediately following." Most pensioners were discussing experiences from precisely this period of their lives. Additionally, older people tend to look back on their experiences, recall them, and evaluate them in a "life review." In this context, the opportunity to share stories of soldiering in court must have been viewed as an ideal time to place their life experiences within a larger narrative of American history. This process allowed veterans to assess, over the passage of time, what aspects of their service were most important. Typically, as a result, pension depositions featured clear and purposeful stories. Even when veterans' memories of certain details deteriorated, their recollections of larger general frameworks of events remained largely intact. Many applicants did indeed forget the more mundane details of their service, such as the date they enlisted or the first names of their junior officers. Still, their descriptions of particular experiences are often remarkably vivid. Many times a single anecdote is recalled in amazingly minute detail, which suggests that it was the soldier's most significant memory. Carefully analyzed, these narratives can reveal what the veterans saw as the central meaning of their Revolution.[3]

---

2. Wallace Brown, *Good Americans*, 181, describes the 1783 compensation act of the loyalist claims. People tend to recall events surrounded by emotional trauma clearly. On this point, see Daniel Schacter, *Searching for Memory: The Brain, the Mind, and the Past* (New York, 1996), 192–217. Certainly the recent experiences of loyalists were wrenching ones that left strong impressions in their recollections of the past.

3. The quotation about older people remembering events in the past more clearly than recent happenings is in Welford, *Aging and Human Skill*, 229–30. The quotation from Schacter is in *Searching For Memory*, 297; see the same work on the process of life review and the cultural role of elderly people as society's expert "storytellers" (280–308).

Nevertheless, veterans still refashioned memories over time (consciously or subconsciously) to eliminate unpleasant aspects or embellish their importance. The likelihood of revision was increased by the presence of the court and the audience hearing the deposition. Undoubtedly, this sort of "editing" happened. Generally, it is also easy to identify. For example, Samuel Graff's story of his taking an enemy prisoner directly to Washington—and the commander-in-chief being so pleased to be distracted from his work by the tedious service of a few militia privates that he "treated them with brandy"—rings false. (Such exaggerations are analytically interesting in their own right: they indicate the ways in which veterans *wanted* to remember the war and are thereby still suggestive of the narrator's sense of the meaning of the conflict.) Many, however, were relatively honest in weighing their actions. Elderly persons engaged in life review, according to historian Paul Thompson, have an intense "desire to remember" that entails "a special candor which goes with a feeling that life is over, achievement is complete." Veterans were looking back on one of the most important parts of their lives: their contributions to the founding of the nation. A number of them recount embarrassing experiences. Others were willing to share detailed stories that were unnecessary for their applications. In general, deponents were reasonably honest about their service so long as they felt it did not endanger their chances for being granted material reward. Sometimes, the less savvy did not even realize that their excessive truthfulness might undermine their applications. Thomas Badge, for instance, was blissfully unaware that the loyalist claim commission that heard his case was looking for evidence of committed ideological adherence to British government before it would offer recompense for losses. According to the commission, Badge explained that his "motive for joining the British was because he thought the British army would conquer."[4]

This issue of the courts mediating the narratives presents another analytical problem and source of intervention in the text. In the case of the Revolutionary pension applications, the depositions were given in open court. The public would often gather to hear the stories of aging veterans of the War for American Independence. Veterans were, of course, speaking to the expectations of both the court and the public. In contrast, the loyalist claims were held in private, with the claimant, under oath and alone, speaking with the commission. Because compensation for loyalists was meant more as an economic reward

4. RWPF, file W7566; the quotation about candidness in life review is in Paul Thompson, *The Voice of the Past: Oral History* (New York, 1978), 112–16; AO12/38/139.

for service than a celebration of the war and its veterans, discussions centered on the former soldiers' motivations and property. Deponents with more political sense than Thomas Badge asserted their claims with the aim of speaking directly to the expectations of the commissioners. In both the loyalist claims and pension depositions, the court's intervention in the documents is often painfully clear. In some cases, the deponent is referred to in the third person—perhaps indicating paraphrased summary rather than verbatim testimony. Other clerks retained the applicants' voices more clearly and employed first-person references, thereby suggesting that they were acting as amanuenses for the applicants. Such narratives, however, offer the historian little more certainty that they are more accurate reflections of what deponents said than those applications in which the speaker is identified as "he." Careful textual analysis and the implementation of supporting evidence play a crucial role in building interpretations of the deponents' uses of key terms and phrases.[5]

The official requirements for recompense shaped responses as well. In the loyalist claims, any loss of property, salary for public office, or income due to the deponents' loyalty was an acceptable claim. Tories focused their narratives to establish their reasons for fighting in defense of the British Empire, and they related how their actions led to material losses. Detailed discussions beyond these requirements might help their claims but were not necessary. Consistently, loyalists went out of their way to describe the sorts of oppression that they experienced at the hands of Revolutionaries in their communities. While such accounts certainly did not hurt their claims, they demonstrated a consistent Tory memory that emphasized the exclusive, oppressive nature of the American communities they were forced to flee. Also, not all the claimants were wealthy. While propertyless people could not apply, many small propertyholders did. If their material losses may not have looked as significant as those of more prominent Tories, such claimants may have concentrated instead on their suffering and dutiful service.[6]

In the U.S. pension laws, the veterans' poverty and service were the initial reasons for recompense. In the 1818 pension acts, all former Continental soldiers, sailors, and marines who asserted their financial distress qualified. Following widespread outcry in response to fraud (and the perception of fraud), a subsequent 1820 act required all deponents, including those already awarded

---

5. The celebratory and public nature of the pension claims is described in Resch, *Suffering Soldiers*, 119–21. See Wallace Brown, *Good Americans*, 183, on the nature of the loyalist claims.

6. See Wallace Brown, *Good Americans*, 181, on the eligibility for recompense.

pensions under the 1818 act, to apply and submit a property schedule to prove their indigence. Not surprisingly, these pension requirements made the 1818 and 1820 depositions typically unrevealing statements of time and type of service followed by statements of poverty. Also, those in Continental service were more likely to have written records of their service than militiamen and thus often did not have to give detailed descriptions of their wartime experiences to prove their status as veterans. The more liberal 1832 act provided pensions for anyone who could demonstrate that he had served at least six months in any military capacity—including service in the militia, rangers, and so on. The applicants needed only to produce documentation of service or to state their unit, officers, how, where, and when they entered the military, and to name any battles in which they participated. The 1832 pension applicants, however, were far less likely to have written records of enlistment or discharge. Poor records for state service and the passage of time insured that many of these applicants would have to explain their service a bit more completely than earlier deponents who had the requisite documents. Additionally, by the 1830s, when the last pensions were awarded to veterans, there was an even stronger sense that the generation was passing and that the depositions offered an important moment for national storytelling about the past. The 1832 pensions typically contained the most qualitative accounts of the Revolution. The many stories offered by veterans above and beyond the required elements were apparently important memories of the Revolution that they felt compelled to share. Unfortunately, of all the deponents, these applicants are the furthest removed chronologically from the war.[7]

Another issue regarding the pension applications needs to be addressed. The study's evidentiary base has an age bias. Those who typically gave the most descriptive accounts under the 1832 act were very young in the Revolution; most had been born no earlier than the 1750s. This may well account for why they did not discuss in much detail the constitutional crisis with Britain and its role in the Revolution. These pensioners were, after all, children during the era of the Stamp Act, and many were barely teenagers when the war began in 1775. Most simply did not yet have an adult stake in the colonial-Parliamentary arguments nor the cognitive skills to understand them fully. The deponents' age probably also partially explains why they employed regional and class-based variants of Whig discourse on the political situation in Pennsylvania in the

7. Resch, *Suffering Soldiers*, 119–45, discusses the 1818 and 1820 pensions. See Dann, *The Revolution Remembered*, xv–xvii, on the requirements for the granting of 1818, 1820, and 1832 pensions.

1770s and 1780s rather than addressing it from an imperial perspective. I am comfortable with this age bias, however. Historians of the Revolution agree that the vast preponderance of common soldiers were not only poor but were also young men ranging from their late teens to their mid-twenties. If my sample is skewed toward the majority, it is less a problem than a boon. In other words, I am privileging accounts given by those who were disproportionately represented in the ranks.[8]

Finally, a few words about methodology are in order. Some readers might be uncomfortable with terms used in this study, such as "many," "most," and "numbers," that are not backed up with statistical data. My focus, however, is qualitative, not quantitative. In order to uncover the cosmologies of ordinary participants in the Revolution, I examined most closely what they said. Unfortunately, a limited number of Pennsylvania soldiers left descriptive accounts regarding what they thought about the Revolution. Even among the pension applications, many of the accounts are perfunctory recitations of dates of enlistment and officers that yield little insight into the deponents' worldviews. I made the most of those detailed sources that did provide a window into the perspectives of my subjects. The concept of "representativeness" justifies this methodology. For example, when I encountered perhaps fifty soldiers who enlisted at the same period of time in the same area, and ten of them detailed why they entered the service, I felt that I could assume somewhat comparable motives among the others. Additionally, a perusal of the different men and units whose voices are cited as evidence in this study demonstrates a relatively large number of qualitative sources. The book does not hinge on a single journal or ten pensions and loyalist claims. Rather, it is based on a wide array of vivid firsthand contemporary and retrospective accounts, views of soldiers by military and political leaders, and other accounts of troops' wartime behavior.

My early attempts to count the soldiers who acted in certain ways for particular reasons were soon frustrated as I realized how little numbers meant in the context of the sort of history I hoped to write. One of my goals was to be sensitive to complexity among my subjects, and I soon discovered a vast range of motivations and experiences among enlisted men. Patterns appeared, but no single one could be called quantitatively dominant. To dismiss significant but

8. Trussell finds in his sample of Pennsylvania regulars that the average age of the soldiers was twenty-five, with very few older than thirty: see his *Pennsylvania Line*, 244–47. On the agreement among scholars of the Revolution from various interpretive perspectives on the youth (late teens to early twenties) of the great bulk of enlisted men, see Gross, *Minutemen*, 148; Martin and Lender, *Respectable Army*, 90; Neimeyer, *America Goes to War*, 15–24; and Royster, *Revolutionary People*, 373.

rare evidence of soldiers' perceptions based on their comparison with more common accounts did not make sense. In fact, to do so would have hidden from view what turned out to be my thesis. The plurality of soldiers' experiences ultimately revealed the importance of their localist outlooks, which, of course, varied by region and were shaped by particular situations. An attempt to enumerate, for example, how many men joined out of anger toward British actions near their homes might reveal forty out of sample of a hundred who mentioned discomfort over redcoats' deeds. Perhaps ten of those forty explicitly stated that they enlisted to seek revenge against the king's forces. Ten is hardly a convincing number in a statistical appendix. Textual analysis of enlisted men's descriptions of why they served proved far more effective. Recall, for example, the story of Charles Wallace, who gave a vivid account of how his father was killed by a British raiding party. The younger Wallace reenlisted out of "a spirit of revenge for the death of his father." With widespread British raiding and intimidation of citizens in the environs of Philadelphia in 1777–78, it seems safe to assume that Wallace's motivations were both important in their own right and comparable to those of at least some of his neighbors. Presented in conjunction with other detailed accounts that decried British deeds, Wallace's story becomes a particularly powerful one for understanding the Revolution among people of his social group and region.[9]

Furthermore, quantitative evidence can sometimes be more obfuscating than enlightening. The practice of substitution among Pennsylvania Revolutionary troops provides an example of how statistics might produce misleading conclusions. The ubiquity of substitution suggests that it allowed well-off colonists to avoid service by hiring out poorer men who needed the bounty. This is true to an extent, but reading the accounts of the substitutes themselves shows that a large number went in place of fathers and older brothers. Economic concerns were certainly part of these men's motives—but not exclusively on an individual level. Relieving older relatives from service demonstrated a commitment to the integrity of family farms and businesses. An analysis based on a reading of a muster roll that identified soldiers only as substitutes without mentioning for whom they went misses this familial dynamic. It is difficult, therefore, to infer qualitative motives and worldviews from only quantitative sources. Still, I do not mean to denigrate quantitative history. Indeed, some of the most important assumptions that undergird this book are based on the findings of such historians of the Revolution.

9. RWPF, file W2286.

At the heart of the issue of how scholars should approach their subjects is a curious dichotomy of methodological assumptions among social and cultural historians. Particularly in regard to work in the early modern era, it seems to be a general convention that "bottom up" studies utilize quantitative perspectives while "top down" work is qualitative. This tendency derives largely from the nature of sources: literate elites generated many descriptive accounts, while lower sorts produced few. Obviously, there is a place for both interpretive tools in analyses of elites and common people, and historians are beginning to recognize as much. Scholars of ordinary people are finding new sources and creative ways of analyzing other, more familiar ones. Close examination of journals, commonplace books, court records, and petitions can reveal heretofore unknown aspects of the fabric of common people's lives and their role in actively shaping the history of early America. This book is meant as a contribution to that endeavor.

INDEX

abolitionist sentiment, 19, 20
Acker, Christian, 161
Adams, John, 31
Adlum, John, 27–28, 50, 127, 133, 148, 197–98
African Americans. *See also* free blacks; slavery
  in British army, xx, 108–9
  in Continental army, xx, 85–86
  expectations of as threat to social stability, 221–22
  marginalization of in early republic, 254–55
  memories of veterans, 261–64, 270
  national identity and, 282
  in Pennsylvania, 11–13
  racial identity and, 19–20
  white male identity and, 230–31
Aily, Michael, 258
Akeley, John, 257
Alison, Benjamin, 69
Allen, James, 203–4
Allen, John, 68, 219, 247
Alworth, James, 81
Amburn, Samuel, 140
American identity. *See also* national identity
  on frontier, 185–86
  localism and, 271
  veterans and, 235, 261
  white manhood suffrage and, 273
Anderson, Isaac, 148
Andre, John, 135, 150–51, 152
Andrews, Arthur, 150
Anger, Frederick, 66
Anglicans, 8, 237
Anglo-American military culture
  anti-army history and, 125–26
  attitudes of rank and file toward British, 126–29
  burial of enemy dead, 134–35
  captives, treatment of, 131–34
  cease-fires, 135
  frontier tactics and, 135–37
  limited war, ideology of, 130–31, 138
  truce, flag of, 135
  violence and, 138–41
anti-black riots, 255
apprentices, 15, 47–48, 75
Armstrong, James, 96
Armstrong, John, 142
Arnold, Abraham, 70
Arnold, Benedict, 250–51
Arpin, Joel, 208, 267
Aspden, Matthias, 199–200
Associated Loyalists, 106, 112
Association, 37. *See also* militia (Penna.)
Atlee, Samuel, 131, 133, 143
Awl, Jacob, 62
Axe, Frederick, 73

Badger, John, 47
Baird, Francis, 42
Barnitz, Jacob, 148
Barton, William, 188
Batewell, Daniel, 213
battle. *See also specific battles*
  experience of, 138–46
  human toll of, 123–25, 244–45
Baurmeister, Carl, 231

Beatty, Erkuries, 175, 188
Bechtel, Borick, 142
Bedford County, 180–81
Bedford County militia, 70
Bedwell, Thomas, 212
Beer, Robert, 136
Bender, Lewis, 245
Bender, Philip, 66
Berks County militia, 80
Berlin, Ira, 11
Bird, Mark, 221
Bisson, Elizabeth, 241
Bitting, Joseph, 249
Bittle, John, 208
Black, George, 70, 247
Black, Thomas, 178
"Black Boys," 25
"black code," 20
Black Company of Pioneers, 106, 269
Blacksnake, 169
Blyth, Benjamin, 52
Boileau, Nathaniel, 153, 233–36
Boon, John, 243, 244
Booz, Jacob, 242
border claims. *See* land disputes
Boston, 27, 39, 275–76
Boston "Massacre," 275
Boston Tea Party, 249 n. 23
Boucher, John, 207–8
Boudinot, Elias, 142
bounties offered for military service, 45
Boyd, Andrew, 210
Boyd, Thomas, 132, 171
Boyd, William, 140
Boyer, Henry, 46, 250
Brady, Samuel, 164, 167
Brandywine, Battle of, 119–25, 141
Brant, Joseph, 109–10, 112, 165, 265
Brant, Molly, 114
British
    army of, compared to Continental army, 116–18
    attitudes of colonial rank and file toward, 124–25, 126–29
    colonials joining forces with, 53–54, 57–58
    confiscation of property by, 149–50, 152–53, 211–12
    discipline in army, 113, 116
    frontier and, 112, 114
    hostility toward, 148–53, 275

    Indians and, 25–26, 109–11, 265–66
    invasion of middle colonies by, 42–44, 148–49
    narratives of misdeeds of, 44, 149, 151–52
    postwar view of empire, 268–69
    racial identity, manipulation of by, 60–61
    resentment toward actions of, 56–57
    rewards for service offered by, 59
    slaves joining forces with, xx, 41–42, 61–63, 108–9, 221–23, 224–25
British Black Guides and Pioneers Regiment, 223
British Indian Department, 110–11
British Legion, 108
Brodhead, Daniel
    Delawares and, 180
    description of actions of, 174–75
    on enemy army, 126
    at Fort Pitt, 89–90
    on Indians, 190, 191
    occupation of Indian land and, 65
    scalping and, 167
Brown, John, 45
Brown, Thomas, 95
Bryan, George, 222, 224
Buck, Philip, 110
Bucks County, 223
Bucks County Dragoons, 106
Bucks County militia, 81
Bucks County Volunteers, 212
burial of enemy dead, 134–35
Burkhart, Jacob, 133
Burns, Levi, 88
Burrows, Nathaniel, 73, 248
Bush, Solomon, 140
Bushrang, Philip, 242
Butler, John, 40, 66, 169. *See also* Butler's Rangers
Butler, Richard, 99
Butler, William, 95
Butler, Zebulon, 195–96
Butler's Rangers, 106, 109, 217
Byrne, John, 140

Cadwalader, John, 138
Cald, John, 62
Caldwell, William, 198–99
Campbell, John, 249, 250
Campbell, William, 165
captives, treatment of
    on frontier, 167–70, 219
    in Revolutionary war, 131–34, 145, 152–53

INDEX

Carlisle, Abraham, 209
Carothers, John, 72
Carrol, Dennis, 102
"cause of the people," xi
cease-fires, 135
central counties and war weariness, 71–72
Chambers, Stephen, 217
Chaplin, Joyce, 16
Cherokee Removal, 266
Cherry Valley, 169–70
Chester County, 73, 204, 205
Chester County Dragoons, 215
Chester County militia, 79, 81
Chew, Benjamin, 47
children, ungrateful, metaphor of, 256
Christie, Edward, 62
Christy, James, 135
citizenship. *See also* franchise
  biological definition of, 236, 253–54, 281–85
  definitions of, 205–6, 231
  free blacks and, 254–55
  manhood and, 22
  white manhood and, 63
Civil War, 279–80, 285
civil war
  community and, 196–97
  on frontier, 216–20
  as military resistance to Revolutionaries, 206–7
  reactions to slave resistance in, 220–25
  Revolutionaries in, 208–11
  in southeast region, 207–16
  Tories in, 211–14
  violence between Whigs and Tories in, 214–16
Clark, Elizabeth, 113
Clark, Esther, 62–63
Clark, William, 210
class identity. *See also* lower sort; middling sort; upper sort
  constitutional crisis and, 29
  Continental army and, xxi, xxii, 86–89, 94–96
  labor solidarity and, 280–81
  memories of Revolution and, 259–60
  militia service and, xxi, 38–39
  of officers in army, xxii, 92–94
  officers' views of Indians and, 189–92
  patriotism and, 203–4, 205
  in Pennsylvania, 13–16
  Revolution and, 285
Clinton, Henry, 107, 153, 209, 215–16, 224

Clossen, Zachariah, 258
Coen, Edward, 136
Coleman, James, 94
Coleman, Sukey, 62–63
Committee of Privates
  commissioning of officers and, 50–51
  fair militia law and, 38–39
  formation of, 37
  influence of, 80
  Provincial Assembly and, 49
  Quakers and, 38, 202
"common cause," service on behalf of, 245–46
community. *See also* localism
  being "reborn" into, 198, 228
  civil war and, 196–97
  definition of, 34
  enforcement of orthodoxy of, 199
  free blacks and, 260
  ostracism from, 228–29
  racial identity and, 228–31
  views of, xiii–xiv, 273–75, 279–80
Connecticut, provincials from, in Pennsylvania, 6, 65–66. *See also* Wyoming Valley
constitution, federal, 237–38
constitutional crisis
  Adlum on, 27–28
  essays about, 28–29
  in frontier region, 25–26
  interpretations of, 24
  in Philadelphia, 26–27, 29
  politics of, 34
  in rural region, 27
Continental army
  attitudes of rank and file in, toward British, 124–25, 126–29
  British army compared to, 116–18
  desertion from, 99–100
  discipline in, 94–97
  economic motivations for enlisting in, 36 n. 1
  frontier tactics used in, 135–37
  localism and, 84–85
  mutiny in, 100–104
  occupation of Indian land and, 65
  officers of, xxii, 92–94
  overview of, xix
  Pennsylvania battalion of, 39–40
  petitions by enlisted men in, 98–99
  rank hierarchy in, xxi, 86–89
  recruitment for, 39, 45, 70–71

Continental army (cont'd)
   subcommunity identity of soldiery within, 97–104
   white men and, 85–86
   women in camp of, 90–92
Continental Congress. *See* Continental army; Flying Camp
Continental Western Department, 191
conventions of war. *See also* limited war, ideology of
   strains on, 145–54
   total war, ideology of, 158, 163, 187
Cook, William, 99
Coombs, David, 214–15
Coontz, Theobald, 161
Cornstalk, 64, 179
Cornwallis, Lord, 120, 121
Council of Safety, 44
courts-martial, 96–97
Craig, Isaac, 93
Craig, John, 253
Craven, John, 132
Crawford, William, 171–72
criminals
   dissenters as, 206–7
   Revolutionaries as, 212–13
   Tories as, 209, 219–20
Crofts, Benjamin, 47
Cromwell, Oliver, 262
Crooked Billet, 152–53, 154, 215, 233
Crosby, David, 42
cultural identity, 7–8
Cumberland County, 71, 72, 217–18
Cumberland County Committee of Privates, 51, 52
Cumberland County militia, 72, 80–81
Cunningham, John, 241
Cunningham, Thomas, 94
Curry, Roger, 94
Custard, Conrad, 73

Darlington, William, 132
Davis, George, 207–8
Davis, John, xx
Davis, Thomas, 145
Deall, Daniel, 88
Dean, John, 178
death by execution, 94–95
Declaration of Independence, 50, 251–52. *See also* Independence Day celebrations
Deem, Jacob, 70

deference, ethos of, 13–14, 51
Delaware Indians. *See also* Gnadenhütten Massacre
   allegiances of, 64
   at Kittanning, 17
   in Ohio country, neutrality of, 69
   as targets for revenge, 179, 180
   torture of Crawford by, 171–72
   violence of, 182
Democratic Republicans, 239, 240
Denison, Nathan, 66, 169
Denniston, William, 58–59
Depue, John, 111
Deserontyou, John, 265
desertion from army, xviii n. 9, 99–100
Dickerson, Henry, 186
Dickey, Thomas, 151
Dickinson, Philip, 63
Dido, Franz, 102, 103, 243
Dill, Matthew, 80
Dinney, Alexander, 94
disaffection, 205
discipline
   in British army, 113, 116
   in Continental army, 94–97
   European-style battles and, 138–39
   in militia, 82
dissenters
   as criminals, 206–7
   intimidation of, 197–200
   policing and repression of, 204–6
   women as, 210
Döhla, Johann Conrad, 126
Dorland, Lambert, 132
Dotter, Samuel, 47, 244
Dougherty, Andrew, 178
Dougherty, John, 68, 161, 174, 253
Dougherty, Mordecai, 259
Dougherty, William, 219, 256
Douglas, John, 250
Dowd, Gregory Evans, 176, 185
Downey, John, 215
Doyley, Daniel, xx
Draper, Lyman, 169
Drennan, James, 241
Drummond, George, 57
Duane, James, 68
Duck, Philip, 133, 250–51, 257
Dunlop, James, 218
Dunmore, Lord, proclamation of, 41–42, 221, 277

Dunmore's War, 10
Dunn, Thomas, 47

Edge Hill, battle at, 142
Edwards, Samuel, 62
Eighth Pennsylvania Regiment, 70–71, 180
Elder, John, 186
elite. *See also* officers; upper sort
  anti-army sentiment and, 125–26
  frontier military culture and, 192
  as officers, xxii, 37, 86
Elliot, Matthew, 67, 110–11
Elliott, William, 178
Elton, Thomas, 42, 55, 250, 258–59
emancipation
  gradual emancipation law, 220–25
  in Northern states, 261
  proponents of, 225–26
  support for, 226–27
empire, British postwar view of, 268–69
English Civil War, 207
enslavement, white use of trope of, 32, 236
equality, 29, 52, 260
Equiano, Olaudah, 20
Erwin, Bacchus, 62
Eschelman, Abraham, 148, 165
ethnic status. *See also* racial identity
  enlistment and, 75
  identification with British counterparts and, 127–28
  liberty, concept of, and, 30
  "white" identity and, 175–76
Evans, Abel, 259
Eyler, Jacob, 133

Fallen Timbers, Battle of, 265–66
Farmer, Lewis, 101
Faulkner, William, 259
federalism, politics of, 237–38
Federalists, 239
Fegan, Lawrence, 200
Fergus, James, 135
Ferguson, Ebenezer, 211, 258
Fiscus, Abraham, 79
Fling, William, 73, 252
flogging, 94
Flying Camp, xix–xx, 42–43, 45
Flying Crow, 40
Forten, James, 263–64

Fort Miami, 265–66
Fort Niagara, 110, 114
Fort Pitt, 89–90, 179, 191
Fort Washington, 129, 145
Fort Wilson Riot, 84, 104
Foster, John, 174
Founders, views of, xi
founding generation, 256
Fourth of July. *See* Independence Day celebrations
Fourth Pennsylvania Battalion, 85, 93
Fox, Joseph, xx–xxi
Frailey, John, 55, 73, 151
franchise. *See also* citizenship
  American identity and, 273
  manhood and, 23
  political activism for, 30–31
  property and, 15–16, 237 n. 5
Francis, Jacob, 262–63
Franklin, Benjamin, 8, 21
Franklin, William, 60–61
fraternization between troops, 127–29
free blacks. *See also* African Americans
  community and, 260
  in Pennsylvania, 12–13
  voting rights of, 227
Freemoyer, David, 171, 174
French and Indian War, 5, 10, 25
Friends. *See* Quakers
Fries Rebellion, 238–39
frontier. *See also* frontier military culture
  American identity and, 185–86
  British and, 112, 114
  civil war on, 216–20
  definition of, xvii–xviii
  early Revolutionary period on, 40–41
  fighting in eastern theater and men from, 69–71
  frustration with Britain on, 25–26
  regional support for war on, 72, 74
  vengeance and war on, 165–66, 182–86
  warfare on, 63–71
frontier military culture
  adaptation to, 188
  ambush and, 165–66
  captives, treatment of, 167–70
  civilization and, 188–89
  eastern Pennsylvanians and, 187–88
  elites and, 192
  European military culture and, 186–87
  Gnadenhütten Massacre and, 185

frontier military culture (*cont'd*)
  language of, 161–63
  overview of, 159–60
  preconceptions about Indians and, 160–61
  process of development of, 172–73
  scalping and, 166–67
  torture and, 170–72
  total war aims of, 163–65
frontier rangers, xix
Fulton, James, 214
Fulton, Jesse, 140

Gabriel's Conspiracy, 264
Galloway, Joseph, 209, 210, 228, 269
Gandee, Urich, 145
Gangiver, Andrew, 249
gender identity. *See also* masculinity
  appeals to, 44–45
  cultural construction of, xv–xvi, 281
  in Pennsylvania, 21–23
Georgia, 225
German Pennsylvanians
  concept of liberty and, 30
  factions within, 8
  federal constitution and, 237
  localism and, 3–4
  in Pennsylvania Line, 128
  regions settled by, 7–8
Germantown, Battle of, 141, 152
Gibson, John, 179, 185
Gilchrist, Adam, 96
Gilman, Samuel, 140
Girty, George and James, 111
Girty, Simon, 67, 111, 229
Gnadenhütten Massacre, 155–57, 172, 182–86, 266
Gordon, Robert, 257
Gore, John, 253
Goss, Abraham, 91, 248
gradual emancipation law, 220–25, 226–27
Graff, Samuel, 128, 147, 248, 251
Graham, Michael, 129
Grannon, Thomas, 199
Grant, Jehu, 262
Gray, Isaac, 58
Gray, John, 178
Gray, Robert, 81
Graydon, Alexander
  on frontier tactics, 136–37

  on motivations to enlist, 35–36, 39
  on Negroes in army, 86
  on Thomas Parvin, 202
  reaction to draft, 93
  recruiting party of, 48
  on surrender of Fort Washington, 129, 145
  on war booty, 147
Greene, Nathanael, 104, 120
Greninger, Henry, 81
Griffith, Evan, 58
guards, picking off, 146
Guest, James, 251
Gunsalus, Richard, 219
Gushert, Isaac, 78

Haldimand, Frederick, 112, 114
Hales, John, 208
Halttunen, Karen, 162
Hamet, William, 212
Hancock, John, 250
Hand, Edward, 164–65, 179, 190, 192
Hand's Rifle Regiment, 90, 144
Harding, George, 199, 209
Harding, Jasper, 105, 111, 268
Harp, Frederick, 250
Harrison, James, 23
Hartley, Thomas, 186–87, 188
Hawkins, John, 91, 142, 151
Hays, George, 142
Hays, James, 73, 249
Heckewelder, John, 183–84, 185
Hefflebrower, Jacob, 139
Hendry, John, 134
Heneberger, John, 141, 244
Henery, William, 209
Henry, John Joseph, 40, 129, 134, 135–36, 251
Henry, Samuel, 152–53
Hesser, Frederick, 140
Hewes, George Robert Twelves, memory of, 249 n. 23
Hill, Caleb, 209–10
Hill, John, 58, 211, 245, 258
Hipple, Conrad, 249
Hipple, John, 138
Hoffman, Ludwig, 249
Holben, Lorentz, 161, 178
Holmes, Charles, 106
Hood, Thomas, 53
Hooper, William, 54

Hovenden's Pennsylvania Loyalists, 215
Howe, William
  amnesty offer of, 213–14
  Brandywine, Battle of, and, 119–20, 121
  Galloway on, 269
  landing in New York, 42
  on limited war, 130–31
  on occupation of Philadelphia, 55, 57
  orders on plunder, 150
  on soldiers, 115
  on treatment of prisoners, 134, 147
Howell, David, 182
Howell, John, 58
Hubley, Adam, 82
Huffnagle, Michael, 190
Hughey, John, 243
human toll of battle, memories of, 123–25, 244–45
Hunt, Isaac, 200
Hunter, Samuel, 70
hunter/warrior ideal, 89–90
Huston, James, 174
Hutson, John, 165
"huzzah," 129

Iddings, William, 189, 256
Independence Day celebrations, 233–36, 239–40
Indianized warrior identity, 40, 136, 173, 177–78, 183, 186
Indians. *See also* pan-Indian unity; *specific tribes*
  as alienated from Revolutionaries, 172–73, 180–82
  British and, 25–26, 109–11, 265–66
  differentiation among, 110
  frontier warfare and, 63–65
  land and, 65, 159–60, 163
  localism and, 4
  memories of, 264–66, 270
  motivations to fight among, 69
  national identity and, 283–84
  as negative reference point, 162, 178, 193, 230
  neutrality of, 40–41, 69, 156, 179, 180, 191
  officers' views of, 189–92
  Othering of, 283
  in Pennsylvania, 8–11
  in Pennsylvania Line, 86
  preconceptions about, 160–61
  racial identity of, 17–19, 176–77
  revenge taken against allied or neutral, 68
  treatment of, in frontier civil war, 219–20
  as warriors, xx
  individualism, 274. *See also* liberal individualism
"Intolerable" or Coercive Acts, 27
Ireland, Owen S., 237
Irish Catholics, 60–61
Iroquois Indians, 64, 166, 169, 182. *See also* Sullivan, John
Irvine, William
  capture of, 131, 142
  Delawares and, 191
  on desertion, 99
  on Indians, 182
  on militiamen, 65
  on war booty, 147
  on women in camp, 91–92
Irwin, Nathaniel, 151

Jackson, Andrew, 248
Jackson, John, 59
Jackson, Judith, 113
Johnson, John, 212
Johnson, William, 166
Johnston, Francis, 89, 99, 101
Jolly, Luke, 96
Jones, David, 60, 267
Jones, William, 160
Juncken, Henry, 52
Juniata Valley, 5, 15
Justice, Jacob, 95

Kachlein, Andrew, 42
Kayashuta, 166
Kearsley, John, 199
Keefer, Joseph, 163–64
Keen, Andrew, 55, 211
Keister, Peter, 67–68, 235
Keller, George, 251
Kelly, William, 140
Kennedy, David, 99, 132
Kentner, George, 66
Kerber, Linda, 22
Kessler, Peter, 46
Kiashuta, 40
Killbuck, 180, 185
Knight, John, 269
Knyphausen, Wilhelm, 120, 121
Konkle, Lawrence, 162
Kreider, Jacob, 43, 55

Krider, Jacob, 140, 242
Krider, Margaret, 242
Kroesen, Garret, 133
Krumbine, Peter, 46
Krysher, Simon, 244–45
Kuntz, John, 249

labor solidarity, 280–81
Lacey, John, 152, 214–15
Lafayette, Marquis de, 120, 250
Lancaster County, 72, 203
Lancaster County militia, 71
land disputes
  between Indians and loyalists, 265
  Indians as obstacles in, 159–60, 163
  between Pennsylvania and Virginia, 6–7, 65–67
  squatter-speculator conflict, 15
land grants, 45
land hunger in frontier, 65
Lardner, John, 93
Laurens, John, 225
Lausch, Henry, 242
Lawlor, Martin, 210
Laycock, John, xxi, 59
Lee, Richard Henry, 40, 208
Lenox, Margaret, 105
Leonard, George, xx
Lewis, Benjamin, 161, 178
Lewis, Ezekiel, 167
liberal individualism, 248–49, 258, 259, 280
liberty, 29–32, 284
limited war, ideology of, 124, 130–31, 138, 144–45, 153–54
Lindsay, Samuel, 108–9
liquor, 88–89, 139
Lister, Margaret, 211
Livingston, Daniel, 79, 253
localism. *See also* community
  American identity and, 271
  Civil War and, 279–80
  Continental army and, 84–85
  federal constitution and, 237–38
  frontier warfare and, 68–69
  German Pennsylvanians and, 3–4
  Indians and, 4
  limitations of, xxiii
  military service and, 43–44, 56
  nationalism and, xiv
  overview of, xiii–xiv, 2–3
  in Pennsylvania, 32–33
  regional experiences of Revolution and, 275–78
  trans-regional adherence to, 273–75
Lochry, Archibald, 163
Locke, Margaret, 210
Lockman, Mathias, xx
Logan, Alexander, 138, 258
Long, Alexander, 211
Long, Andrew, 147
Long, Jacob, 55, 146, 252
long hunters, 10
Long Island, Battle of, 143, 144
Loofbourrow, John, 105–6, 270
Loudon, Archibald, 160
lower sort
  bodily punishment for, 94–95
  in Continental army, 86–88
  as enlisted men, xxi, 255–56
  masculinity and, 22–23
  in Pennsylvania, 13
  support for Revolutionary ideology among, 49–52
  women in army camp, 91–92
loyalists. *See also* Tories
  narratives of veteran, 266–70
  occupation of Pennsylvania and, 58–61
  ranks of, 53

Maclay, William, 162
Madison, James, 238
Magaw, Robert, 133
Maier, Pauline, 252
Majoribank, Thomas, 53
manhood. *See* masculinity
Marler, Samuel, 89
Marshall, Patrick, 140
Martin, Joseph, 175
masculinity. *See also* Indianized warrior identity
  Continental army and, 88–90
  enlisted men's notions of, xiv
  entitlement to natural rights, whiteness, and, 31
  guards, picking off, and, 146
  identification with British counterparts and, 128–29
  loyalist soldiers and, 114–15
  martial prowess and, 39–40, 55–56
  in Pennsylvania, 21–23
  political activism for franchise and, 30–31
  material gain, enlistment for, 36, 46

INDEX

McCalester, Richard, 71
McCalister, James, 89
McCarty, John, 97
McCasland, John, 137, 249
McCasland, William, 243
McCaslin, John, 70, 164
McClean, Alexander, 66
McCormick, James, 79
McCoy, Angus, 46, 68, 244
McDonald, Alexander, 57
McDonald, Joseph, 244
McElnay, John, 45–46, 148
McEwen, Mary, 241–42
McFall, Thomas, 245
McGonnagel, Neal, 97
McKay, Neal, 135, 141
McKee, Alexander, 67, 111
McKenny, John, 215
McKinley, John, 81
McMaster, James, 136
McMichael, James, 142–43
McNeil, Hector, 96
McNeil, Hugh, 105
McVaugh, John and Jacob, 48
Megaw, John, 68–69, 178
Mendenhall, Joseph, 257
Mennonites, 203
Meredith, John, 54
Miami Indians, 182
Middlekauff, Robert, 120
middling sort
    bounties offered for military service to, 45
    constitutional crisis and, 28–29
    in Pennsylvania, 13
    support for Revolutionary ideology among, 49
Miles, Jacob, 62
Miles, Sally, 63
Miles, Samuel, 131, 144
Miles's Rifle Regiment, 45
military culture, 17. *See also* Anglo-American military culture; frontier military culture
military service
    apathy for, 71–76
    benefits of, xiii
    bounties offered for, 45
    invasion of Philadelphia and, 55–57
    localism and, 43–44, 56
    motivations for, 278
    national identity and, xv, 78

    political activism and, 49–52
    rank order in, xxi–xxii
    recruitment and, 35–36, 44–45, 48, 55–56
    refusal to serve in eastern theater, 69–71
    regions and, 5
    substitute for, xxi, 46
    types of, xviii–xxi
militia, xix, 78, 84. *See also* militia (Penna.)
militia act, 201
militia (Penna.). *See also* Committee of Privates;
    specific county militias
    bonds among men in, 80
    discipline in, 82
    discord and disputes in, 79
    dissenters, treatment of by, 197–200, 204–6
    draft system, 46, 73
    election of officers in, 80–81
    motivations to serve in, 38–39
    name of, 37
    overview of, xix
    politicization of, 83–84
    relations between officers and enlisted men in, 82
    role of, 38
    tours of duty, 78–79
    white men and, 83
Miller, Henry, 146
Miller, John, 140
Mingo Indians, 40, 74, 182
Mitford, John, 47
Mohawk Indians, 166, 265. *See also* Brant, Joseph
Molesworth, James, 209
Montgomery, Richard, 134–35
Montgomery County, 233. *See also* Crooked Billet
Moody, James, 111
Moore, Abbey, 63
Moore, William, xxi, 146, 161, 178
Moravian Indians, 156–57, 172, 183, 266
Moravians, 202–3
Moreland, Moses, 48, 140
Morgan, Edmund S., 284
Morgan, George, 64, 179
Morris, Daniel, 74–76
Morris, John, 125–26
Morris, Samuel, 135
Morrison, James, 70
Moser, Christian, 102
motivations. *See also* vengeance as motivating factor
    to enlist, 35–36, 46
    given by veterans, 252–53

motivations (cont'd)
  for Indians to fight, 69
  for military service, 38–39, 278
Muhlenberg, Henry, xv n. 6, 61, 63
Mullen, John, 94
Mundell, Abner, 219
Munsee Indians, 155–57
Murphy, Samuel, 165
Murray, Jeremiah, 102
Muse, Fauntley, 186
mutiny, 100–104, 116, 243, 246–47
Myers, Andrew, 162, 174
Myers, Conrad, 253

Nagel, Philip, 250
Nailing, John, 23
Nash, Gary, 222
Nason, Thomas, 62
Nathan, James, 46
national identity. *See also* American identity;
  localism
  development of, xvi, 273–75
  freedom/exclusion model of, 284–86
  white male supremacy and, 280–85
nationalism, xiv, 78
Native Americans. *See* Indians
naturalization, 16
Nell, William C., 263
neutrality
  of Indians, 40–41, 69, 156, 179, 180, 191
  as treason, 200
Neville, John, 64
New Jersey
  British invasion of, 42
  experience of Revolution in, 276
  narratives of British misdeeds in, 44
  runaway slaves and, 224–25
Newman, Simon, 240
New York
  experience of Revolution in, xviii n. 9, 276
  Pennsylvania troops serving in, 43
  runaway slaves and, 224–25
New York City, Howe landing in, 42
Nice, John, 131, 134
Nichola, Lewis, 73, 94
Nicholas, George, 42
Nisbet, Alexander, 148
Norris, Henry, 200
Northampton County, 202–3, 206

Northampton County Associators, 51–52, 70, 178
Northumberland County militia, 157

oath of alliance, 201, 204–5, 277
officers
  battle, view of, 142–44
  discipline of, 95–96
  election of, 50–51, 80–81
  elite as, xxii, 37, 86
  enlisted men and, 82, 96–97
  frontier war and, 164–65
  Indians, view of, 189–92
  martial honor and, 144
  rank/class consciousness of, 92–94
Ohioan Indians, 64, 265–66
Oliver, Stephen, 178
Oneida Indians, 64, 176
Ormsby, Matthew, 209
Orner, Martin, 186
outsiders
  blacks classified as, 63
  opposition to Revolutionary ideology as
    defining, 52–53

Page, Bernard, 59–60, 66
pan-Indian unity
  colonial wars and, 11
  notions of community and, 69
  racial identity and, 19, 181
  Revolution and, 266
Paoli Massacre, 151
Parke, Theopolis, 96
parole, granting of, 133, 169
Parr, James, 73
Partier, Peter, 58, 106
Parvin, Thomas, 202
Pastorius, Abraham, 269
patriot position, 32–34
Patterson, Alexander, 167
Paxton Boys, 17–18, 136
Paxton Township, 4–5
Pearce, William, 199
Peebles, John, 109, 121–22, 127, 135, 151
Penn, William, 8
Pennamites, 6, 65–66, 216–17
Pennsylvania
  class identity in, 13–16
  common ground in, 32–34
  cultural heterogeneity of, 7–13

Dunmore's proclamation and, 41–42
early map of, xix
gender identity in, 21–23
localism in, 32–33
overview of, 1–2
political culture of, 24–32
regions of, xvii–xviii, 5–7, 32
slavery in, 11–12, 31–32
as subject of work, xvi–xvii
Pennsylvania Constitution of 1776, 49–52, 83
Pennsylvania Continental Artificers, 99
Pennsylvania Council of Safety, 206
Pennsylvania Line
  ethnic composition of, 128
  mutiny of, 101–3, 243, 246–47
  petition by privates of, 98
  racial composition of, 86
Pensell, John and Henry, 195–96
pension legislation, 240–41
Peters, George, xxi, 62, 108
Peters, John, 115, 116
Peters, Thomas, 269–70
Philadelphia. *See also* Philadelphia militia;
    Committee of Privates
  anti-black riots in, 255
  apathy for military service in, 72–74
  civil war in, 207–8
  class identity in, 14
  constitutional crisis in, 26–27, 29
  Continental army and, 39
  enforcement of treason laws in, 208–11
  evacuation of, 107
  imperial taxes and, 26–27
  occupation of, 42, 55–57, 207–8, 222–23
Philadelphia Light Dragoons, 106, 212
Philadelphia militia, 83–84. *See also* Committee of
    Privates
Pickard, William, 66, 217
Pickering, Timothy, 192
Piper, John, 181, 218
Pipes, Joseph, 167
Plunkett, Thomas, 29
political culture of Pennsylvania, 24–32
political organization
  federalism and, 237–39
  localism and, 3
  taverns and, 22–23, 48, 89, 114
  virtual representation, 30, 32–33
Pontiac's War, 5, 10, 17, 19, 25

Porter, Andrew, 92
Potter, James, 163
poverty, views of, 255, 257, 258
Presbyterians, 237
Princeton, Battle of, 141
Proclamation of 1763, 25
Proctor, John, 72
property
  British raids on and confiscation of, 149–50,
    152–53, 211–12
  confiscation law, 206
  confiscation of by Revolutionaries, 209–11,
    267–68
  franchise and, 15–16
  militia confiscation of, 204
  white male franchise and, 237 n. 5
Pyott, Ebenezer, 133–34

Quakers
  abolitionist members of, 20
  federal constitution and, 237
  free blacks and, 226
  Indians and, 9
  military and, 5
  militia and, 38
  persecution of, 201–2
  regions settled by, 7
  slavery and, 31
Quartering Act, 275
Queen's Rangers, 106, 108, 110, 112, 120, 152
Quigley, Samuel, 46, 252

racial hierarchy, concerns about, 221–23, 226–27
racial identity. *See also* ethnic status; pan-Indian
    unity; "white" identity
  African Americans and, 19–20
  Boileau on, 236
  British manipulation of, 60–61
  brutalization of warfare and, 179–81
  community and, 228–31
  concepts of, as fluid and dynamic, 283–84
  cultural construction of, xv–xvi
  current beliefs about, 285
  double standard of military actions and, 177–78
  Forten on, 264
  on frontier, 218–20
  Gnadenhütten Massacre and, 182–86
  identification with British counterparts and, 128
  of Indians, 17–19, 176–77

racial identity (cont'd)
  as justification for frontier war, 173–74
  narratives of veterans and, 253–55
  overview of, 16–17
  in Pennsylvania, 16–21
  whiteness and, 18, 21
racism
  after Civil War, 282
  brutalization of warfare and, 179–81, 182
  in Pennsylvania, 19–20, 261–62, 282
Rankin, James, 198
Rankin, William, 209, 214
Ream, Andrew, 251
Ream, Henry, 46
Reed, James, 132
Reed, Joseph, 83, 102, 180, 227
Reem, George, 164
Rees, Thomas, 157, 162
Reformed Lutherans, 237
refugees, 211
regional experiences of Revolution
  Boston, 275–76
  New York and New Jersey, 276
  South, 277–78
Reily, James, 89
religious pacifists, persecution of, 201–3
Resch, John, 240
retreat, 141–42
Revolution, celebratory understandings of, 285–86
revolution, understanding of, 33–34
Revolutionaries, as criminals, 212–13
Revolutionary ideology
  enlisted men and, 36–37
  opposition to, 52–54, 59–60, 67
  persecution of Tories and, 208–11
  support for, 49–52
  "whiteness" and, 63
Rice, James Jeremiah, 59
Riddle, David, 63
rifles, 135
Rine, George, 208
Ritter, Jacob, 122–23, 124
Rivington, James, 109–10
Roberts, John, 209
Roberts, Nathan, 57
Roberts, Owen, 106
Robertson, Alexander, 67
Roeber, A. G., 3–4
Rogers, Thomas, 62

Rogers, William, 169, 190, 195
Roush, George, 164, 176
Rowe, Thomas, xxi, 250
Rudolf, Jacob, 164, 178
rural region
  constitutional crisis and, 27
  definition of, xvii
  politicization process in, 51–52
Rybecker, John, 258

Sanders, William, 150
"savagery"
  double standard of, 157, 177–78
  Indianized warrior identity and, 173
  Indians and, 17, 161
  loyalists and, 218–19
  in narratives of veterans, 254
  scalping and, 166–67
Sayenqueraghta, 163, 169
scalping, 17, 166–67, 170, 188
Schatz, Henry, 242
Schenderachta, 112
Schuyler, Philip, 43
Scots-Irish Presbyterians, 7
Scott, Robert, 50, 70, 160, 206
Scott, Samuel, 257–58
Scowden, Theodorus, 43, 185–86
Second Pennsylvania Regiment, 94
Secord, Solomon, 111
Seneca Indians, 40, 112, 163, 166, 169
servants, enlistment of, 47–48
71st Highland Regiment, 120
Shabosh, Joseph, 156
Shaefer, Adam, 81
Shaffer, Jacob, 46, 134
sharpshooters, 135
Shawnee Indians. See Cornstalk
Shepard, William, 200, 267
Sheppard, James, 198
Shields, David and John, 78
Shikellamy, 176
Shindel, Peter, xi, 246
Shoemaker, Nancy, 176
Shoemaker, Samuel, 200
Shoufler, Valentine, 247–48
Showers, Michael, 66
Shrawder, Philip, 70
Sierra Leone, 268
Simcoe, John, 110, 113, 114, 115

Simmers, George, 58, 214
Simpson, Andrew, 64
Simpson, Michael, 148
Sinclair, George, 111–12, 268
slavery
 comparison of submission to British policy to, 32, 236
 fighting for British and, xx, 41–42, 108–9, 221–23, 224–25
 gradual emancipation law and, 220–25
 military service and, 61–73
 in Pennsylvania, 11–12, 31–32
 runaways from, 222–23, 227, 261
 in South, 225, 277
Smith, Abraham, 62
Smith, Griffith, 50, 251
Smith, Lucy, 62–63
Smith, Matthew, 170
Smither, James, 115, 208
Smock, Barns, 224
Snow, John, 218
Snowden, Myles, 204
Society of Cincinnati, 239
Society of Friends. *See* Quakers
Soderlund, Jean, 222
soldier, definition of and types of service, xviii–xxii
Sonday, Adam, 247
Sorgen, Charlotte, 210
South, 225, 277–78. *See also* Virginia
South Carolina, 225
Sparre, Jacob, 55
Specht, Christian, 46
Spencer, Isaac, 62
squatter-speculator conflict, 15
Squaw Campaign, 164–65
St. Clair, Arthur, 99–100
Stahley, Jacob, xi, 50, 242, 246, 251–52
Stamp Act, 30
Stanburrough, Adonijah, 216
Stedman, Charles, 208
Stericher, Justus, 48
Steuben, Baron von, 250
Stewart, George, 187
Stewart, Walter, 102
Stiles, Joseph, 92
Stockbridge Indians, 86
Strembeck, Jacob, 140
Struthers, John, 159, 161, 174, 186, 257
Stuart, John, 179, 270

Stump, Frederick, 18
substitute for military service, xxi, 46
"suffering soldier" image, 240, 244, 259
suffrage. *See* franchise
Sullivan, John
 at Brandywine, 120
 expedition against Iroquois of, 164, 169, 171, 175, 187, 190, 219
Susquehannah Company, 6
Swagers, George, 178
Swanwick, Richard, 199, 211
Swisshelm, John, 165

Taplin, Jane, 91
tarring and feathering of dissenters, 198, 199, 201
taunting, 129
tavern culture, 22–23, 48, 89, 114
taxes, imperial, 26–27
Taylor, Isaac, 269
Temmington, Thomas, 97
test acts, 201, 229
Teter, Michael, 88
Thomas, Asa, 141
Thomas, Joseph, 209
Thomas, Joshua, 53
Thompson, George, 147
Thompson, James, 167–68
Thompson, Moses, 62
Thompson, Peter, 89
Thompson's Rifle Battalion
 discharge of weapons and, 90
 fraternization with British, 127
 Indianized warrior identity and, 40
 infighting and, 85
 mutiny in, 100–101
 recruitment appeals, 44
 siege of Boston and, 39
Thornton, Harmenius, 139–40
Thornton, Robert, 47
tomahawks, 135–36
Tomson, David, 59
Tories. *See also* Tory ideology; Tory military life
 community and, 105, 228–29
 as criminals, 209, 219–20
 evacuation of Philadelphia by, 215–16
 Pennamites labeled as, 65–66
 as refugees, 211
 retaliation against Revolutionaries by, 211–14

Tories (cont'd)
   as savages, 218–19
   service to government and, 268
   as soldiers, xx
   violence between Whigs and, 214–16
Torrence, John, 252
torture, 170–72
Tory ideology
   civil war and, 207
   critique of Revolution, 200
   imperial outlook and, 33
   narratives of, 196
   Revolutionary ideology and, 52–53, 59–60, 200, 214
Tory military life
   African Americans and, 108–9
   collective action and, 115–16
   discipline and, 113, 116
   ethnicity, nationality, and, 107–8
   Indians and, 109–11
   masculinity and, 114–15
   Revolutionary military life compared to, 116–18
   service to government and, 111–12, 114–15
   tours of duty, 105–7
   women and, 113–14
total war, ideology of, 158, 163, 187
treason
   arrest of persons suspected of, 211
   definitions of, 200, 201–7
   enforcement of laws regarding, in Philadelphia, 208–11
   penalty for, 206, 209, 219
treason act, 58
Treaty of Paris, 182, 230
Trenton, Battle of, 141
Tritt, Peter, 129
tropes
   children, ungrateful, 256
   enslavement, white use of, 32, 236
   patricide and fratricide, 196, 218–19
   "suffering soldier," 240, 244, 259
   "Toryism," 196
truce, flag of, 135, 146–47
Trussell, John, 86
Turner, Edward, 110
Tuscarora Indians, 64

Unami Indians, 155–57
upper sort. *See also* elite; officers

   as avoiding militia service, 38–39
   opposition to Britain and, 35–36
   in Pennsylvania, 13
   women in army camp, 90–91

Van Artsalen, Jacob, 58
Vanderlip, William, 66, 217
Vandyke, John, 70, 178
Vanmater, Gilbert, 224
Vanzant, George, 161–62
vengeance as motivating factor
   in frontier war, 165–66, 182–86
   in hostilities, 148–53
   in military service, 58–59, 67–69
Vernon, Gideon, 54
veterans
   accuracy of memories of, 242–43
   African American, narratives of, 261–64
   appeal to share memories to, 234
   constructions of nation and, 235
   development of memories of, 241–42
   embarrassing events, retelling of by, 243–44
   heroes, narratives about, 247–51
   language of, 245–46
   loyalist, narratives of, 266–70
   mobility of, 274
   motives given by, 252–53
   pension legislation, 240–41
   postwar economic situation of, 255–59
   racial identity of, 253–55
   radicalism in narratives of, 246–47
   recollections of, 236–37
   sentimental view of, 259
violence. *See also* "savagery"
   European-style battles and, 138–41
   memories of, and psychological suffering, 244–45
   mythology of Indian, 155–56
   racist brutalization of warfare, 179–81, 182
   between Tories and Whigs, 214–16
Virginia. *See also* Dunmore, Lord, proclamation of
   experience of Revolution in, 277
   Gabriel's Conspiracy, 264
   land disputes between Pennsylvania and, 6–7, 66–67
virtual representation, 30, 32–33
Volunteers of Ireland, 106, 107, 108, 109, 112

Wakefield, Henry, 208, 267
Walker, Justice, 108

Wallace, Andrew, 151, 250, 256
Wallace, Charles, 56–57
Wallace, William, 257
war booty, 147–48
War for Independence, 234–35, 247 n. 20, 285–86
War of 1812, 233, 235
Washington, George
　Brandywine, Battle of, and, 119, 120–21
　confiscation of property and, 210–11
　narratives of veterans about, 247–50
　in Philadelphia, 39
　Whiskey Rebellion and, 239
Washington County, 66–67
Washington County militia, 183
Watts, Frederick, 152–53
Wayne, Anthony
　atrocities toward British and, 152
　on British actions in New Jersey, 145
　on desertion, 99
　on liquor, 99
　mutiny and, 104
　on own men, 126
　Paoli Massacre and, 151
　on Pennsylvania Line mutiny, 102, 103
　Quakers and, 202
　Rowe and, 250
　at Ticonderoga, 43
weapons, unauthorized firing of, 90
Webster, Elizabeth, 210
Weems, Mason, 248
Welch, James, 97
Weller, John, 42, 253
Welling, Henry, 228–29
Wertz, George, 68, 178
Westmoreland County, 65, 180
Westmoreland County militia, 162, 164–65, 178
Weston, Richard, 181
Wharton, Thomas, 56
Whig discourse
　civil war and, 207
　Committee of Privates and, 80
　community definition and, 52–54
　on liberty, order, and virtue, 24
　moderate, as Toryism, 203–4
　motivation to serve in militia and, 38
　Tory cooptation of, 59–60, 200, 214
　worldview and, 33, 34

Whigs
　anti-army history of, 125–26
　loyalist capture of, 212–13
　violence between Tories and, 214–16
Whiskey Rebellion, 238–39
White, David, 163
White, John, 91
White Eyes, 69, 179, 180
"white" identity
　African Americans and, 230–31
　as binding, 192–93
　entitlement to natural rights, manhood, and, 31
　European ancestry and, 18, 21, 175, 177
　in narratives of veterans, 253–55
　pan-Indian unity and, 181
　patriotism and, 228
　political equality and, 260
　popular understandings of, 177
　published references to, 174–75
　return to community and, 228–30
　white male supremacy, xiv–xv, 280–85
"whiteness," definitions of, 175–76. *See also* "white" identity
White Plains, Battle of, 142–43
Wiese, George, 246–47
Wiggins, Thomas, 146–47
Wileman, Thomas, 134
Wilkens, James, 73, 252, 257
Williams, Ennion, 92
Williams, Venus, 63
Williamson, David, 172, 183, 186
Wilson, Christopher, 228–29
Wilson, George, 71
Wilson, James, 84
Wolf, Peter, 161
Wolfe, Adam, 174
Wolfe, William, 258
women
　in British army camp, 113–14
　captivity of, 168
　confiscation of property and, 211
　in Continental army camp, 90–92
　as dissenters, 210
　enslaved, as fleeing to British army, 62–63
　as negative reference point, 281
Wood, Gordon, 253
Woodley, Philip, 62
Woods, Henry, 185

Wormington, John, 111
wounds
  battle described in terms of, 139–40
  pension narratives centered on, 245
Wyandot Indians, 182
Wyngenund, 172
Wyoming Massacre, 167, 168–69, 195–96, 217–19
Wyoming Valley, 65–66, 175, 178, 188, 216–17

Yeager, Henry, 55
Yeldall, Anthony, 212
York, Thomas, 62
York County, 71, 72
York County militia, 80, 81
Yorke, Thomas, 53
Young, Alfred, 249 n. 23, 259

Zeisberger, David, 183
Zumbro, Jacob, 139

www.ingramcontent.com/pod-product-compliance
Lightning Source LLC
Chambersburg PA
CBHW021353290426
44108CB00010B/226